Images of the outcast

MANCHESTER
UNIVERSITY PRESS

Images of the outcast

The urban poor in the Cries of London

SEAN SHESGREEN

Manchester University Press

Published by Manchester University Press
Oxford Road, Manchester M13 9NR, UK
www.manchesteruniversitypress.co.uk

British Library Cataloguing-in-Publication Data
A catalogue record for this book is available from the British Library

ISBN 0 7190 6292 6 *hardback*
0 7190 6293 4 *paperback*

First published 2002

10 09 08 07 06 05 04 03 02 10 9 8 7 6 5 4 3 2 1

Designed in Adobe Caslon and Meta fonts
by Max Nettleton FCSD

Typeset by Graphicraft Limited, Hong Kong

Printed in Great Britain
by the Alden Press, Oxford

Contents

List of illustrations

Plates

the plates are placed between pp. 132 and 133

Figures

Acknowledgements

Institutions, colleagues, friends and family have helped me write this book; by way of thanks, I name them here. I am particularly grateful to the institutions and persons allowing me to reproduce prints and drawings without fee: Jonathan Gestetner; his Grace, the Duke of Marlborough; the Boston Museum of Fine Arts, Boston; the British Museum, London, and Sheila O'Connell; Cotsen Library, Princeton University, Princeton, and Andrea Immel; the Firestone Library, Princeton University, Princeton; the Folger Shakespeare Library, Washington DC; the Guildhall Library, London, and Jeremy Smith; the Houghton Library, Harvard University, Cambridge; the Lewis Walpole Library, Farmington, and Joan Sussler; the Newberry Library, Chicago; Northwestern University Library, Evanston, Illinois; Nottingham Castle, Nottingham; the Pepysian Library, Magdalene College, Cambridge; the Yale Center for British Art, New Haven and Scott Wilcox. Half of the images in this book come from the Lilly Library, Indiana University, Bloomington; Joel Silver is responsible for bringing about the Lilly's generous co-operation.

Five institutions awarded me fellowships to study in their archives: The Huntington in San Marino, the Yale Centre for British Art in New Haven, the Houghton Library at Harvard University in Cambridge, the Lilly Library in Bloomington and the Lewis Walpole Library in Farmington, where Joan Sussler guided me through the extraordinary collection of prints she curates. The British Academy awarded me a grant to travel to England, where Sheila O'Connell, Ralph Hyde, and Jonathan Gestetner made my trip pleasant and productive. I am particularly thankful to those scholars who have written letters in support of these fellowships: Richard Wendorf, Stephen Behrendt, Carole Fabricant, Heather Hardy, Bernadette Fort, Joan Thirsk, and Ralph Hyde.

For time to sit down and begin writing this book, the NEH awarded me a summer fellowship in 1989, and my academic home, Northern Illinois University, gave me two research leaves to carry the work forward. The Newberry Library, Chicago, awarded me a senior NEH to finish the book in 1998–99; James Grossman and Adam Stewart made the Newberry a utopia in which to work. The illustration of this book was made possible by a subvention from Jerrold Zar and Frederick Kitterle of Northern Illinois University; without these deans' generosity the book could not have appeared in its present form. Parts of this book previously appeared in *Word and Image*, *Princeton University Library Chronicle* and *Hogarth: Representing Nature's Machines* (Manchester University Press), which have allowed me to republish them here.

Paula McDowell read portions of the manuscript and offered thoughtful suggestions. Andrea Immel, Linda David, Erin Blake, Samuel Kinser, Sarah Maza and David Bywaters read the entire manuscript and helped shape it. I am deeply indebted to Sarah Maza and David Bywaters for repeated guidance, the first on content and the second on style.

This book is affectionately dedicated to Juliette Maza Shesgreen, Deirdre R. Shesgreen and Sarah Crawford Maza.

Sean Shesgreen
Dekalb, Illinois

1

Picturing the London outcast

PRESENT-DAY shoppers combing boutiques for luxuries as different as afternoon tea in decorative caddies, Lily of the Valley cologne, triple-milled soap from Yardley and painted china from Royal Doulton can find all of them adorned with sentimental likenesses of the poorest of the urban poor: milkmaids, primrose sellers and ballad hawkers from London's past. These picturesque figures, pressed into service in order to evoke 'a delightful return to the quality discerning Londoners enjoyed in times past' and borrowed from a set of images described as the most enduringly popular of all English prints ever published, are the ghosts of a rich iconographic tradition depicting city characters of many stripes.[1] Their portrayal began with likenesses of street hawkers published in France about 1500 and spread all over Europe in the sixteenth century, flourishing even in the era of industrialization. Representations of the denizens of city streets were particularly important in England where they inspired such well-known artists as William Hogarth, Thomas Rowlandson, and Theodore Gericault, sojourning in London when his *Raft of 'The Medusa'* floundered in Paris.

This study is a social history of such images published in England from the time of Elizabeth I to the age of Victoria. It explores the designs themselves as well as the conditions under which they were created, produced, copied, pirated, sold and interpreted. It asks who bought images of urban outcasts and why. For why indeed would rich people or connoisseurs buy likenesses of the men and women whom they banished from their houses or relegated to their back doors because they bartered kitchen grease with servants, harvested rags and bones, killed rats or prostituted themselves in public to make ends meet? Did these pictures represent a dark, elusive reality interesting to 'the better sort'? Did they aestheticize, regulate and order on paper the collective lives of city streets with their burgeoning commerce and carnivalesque turmoil? Did they purvey escapist fantasies or gratify historical curiosities by illuminating the mysterious lives of the inhuman beings who trawled the streets and gutters of London for a living?

This book is the history of a popular tradition that, eschewing satire and comedy initially, did all of these things and more, making London's anchorless people the subject of art long before they became the object of sociology. It argues that the images making up the London Cries, as the tradition is called, represent a unique means of understanding England's social world, but especially its notoriously obscure 'lower orders'. Hawkers, pictured standing at doors or loitering upon thresholds, were literally as well as symbolically liminal. Like other marginal figures, they speak about norms and values that are central to their culture; their depiction offers windows into how England's social world was imagined and represented from premodern to modern times.

Pictures of hawkers, animated by poetry or prose recording their shouts or naming their trades, are called 'Cries'.[2] Spelled with a capital 'C' to distinguish vendors' likenesses from their yells, the metaphorical term 'Cries' identifies storied images that represent sounds silently, sounds and voices that, in life, were common, vulgar, transgressive, even threatening, socially and politically. The very first set, the Cries of Paris, appeared on wood, cut by an anonymous artist working about 1500. This early ensemble marked the beginning of a tradition of images depicting peddlers, not as clowns or louts, but as dignified city labourers.[3] That tradition lasted without a break but with infinite variety to the twentieth century. The Cries of Paris spawned the Cries of Nuremberg, Vienna and London, to be followed later by Boston, Philadelphia and New York.[4] Established as a genre by 1550, Cries pictured what was local about this or that city, just when those places looked ever more alike to nostalgic beholders. They sold to urban buyers interested not only in the human landscape of the city, but also in how society organized itself and represented that organization in art.[5]
A special category of common life akin to 'beasts, birds, flowers, fruits, flies and wormes', the Cries originated in books of trades and illustrated annals of costumery – called 'Habits' – that expressed a new curiosity about people whom authors and artists branded 'the Lower Orders', or, more sympathetically, 'the humblest classes'.[6]

London Cries ranged in price from a halfpenny for a common sheet aimed at the shop window of a country bookseller to a half guinea for a set of seventy-four 'Fine Prints proper to Collect in the Cabinet of the Curious'. They survive in three main formats, each physically distinct from the other.[7] I describe the formats in the chronological order in which they surfaced, even though after they declined, all three enjoyed sporadic currency.[8] In the earliest format, from the 1590s and later, hawkers appear communally, gridded in parallel on single-leaf prints bearing a generic title or no name at all. Created by faceless continental and English engravers, these sheets, issued separately and measuring twenty by thirty centimetres, employ a miniature scale to crowd together as many as thirty-six figures in visual lists of look-alike ciphers. Such fly sheets were displayed, not alone, but with maps and also with allegories of the continents, elements, or seasons. Robert Walton's advertisements, Samuel Pepys's way of preservation, John Evelyn's chalcographical theorizings and John Overton's broadside Cries, discussed in chapter 2, show that these programmatic prints were gathered together as a single artifact and viewed as a visual encyclopedia of the world bringing new social, economic and ethnographic knowledge into view.

In the late 1600s, broadside Cries were dethroned by ensembles of prints in which vendors appear in individual portraits, each assigned to its own leaf with leaves arranged in special sequences. Casting hawkers as single characters, these ensembles underscored but also promoted, after Cromwell, the new visibility of commoners and, below them, 'necessary people', the somebodies – or, in the case of Cries, the nobodies – in the portrait. Introduced into England by Dutch and Italian artists, ensembles offered as few as two or as many as a hundred genre portraits, the former to be framed and hung, the latter to be bound and shelved. The more integrated suites gathered uniform images together using a device borrowed from books, the engraved title page, which bestows unity on many different designs.[9] As well as bearing one general title, ensembles carry, on individual leaves, particular captions that encouraged dismemberment for framing or reselling.

About 1750, Cries appeared in a third format, the illustrated book. This format is native to England, flourishes in the nineteenth century, and falls into two classes. In early books, Cries are organized like diptychs, the left sheet carrying the hawker and the right bearing the long text. In later books, Cries appear as scattered illustrations to continuous texts. Of course, even broadsides and ensembles carry some letterpress: a title, a ditty, a paragraph of prose. Only the English picture book of hawkers balances illustrations with texts so elaborate as to be independent of the designs they serve.

By the end of the Victorian period, when the prototypical English worker was urban, hawkers in all formats were so popular that Walter Besant, a prodigious writer of books about the capital, claimed 'everybody who studies London possesses, among his collection, pictures of the street cries'.[10] Like philately and numismatics, collecting Cries was a popular Victorian hobby, particularly among men cultivating anthropology and politics with nationalistic overtones. In the course of the twentieth century, however, these thriving images vanished. While French and German historians created a literature on Cries, English scholars belittled them as antiquarian or ignored them as popular and ephemeral.[11] Today they are only known to a few art historians and partisans of mass culture like Dwight Miller, Tessa Watt, Karen Beall, Keith Moxey and Celina Fox.[12] For that reason, they call for illustration.

The single-leaf sheet, defined as any print issued independently and not belonging to a series or illustrating a book, is exemplified here by a late sixteenth-century woodcut.[13] This cut (**1.1**) comes from the print collection of Samuel Pepys (1633–1703), who catalogued it as 'A very

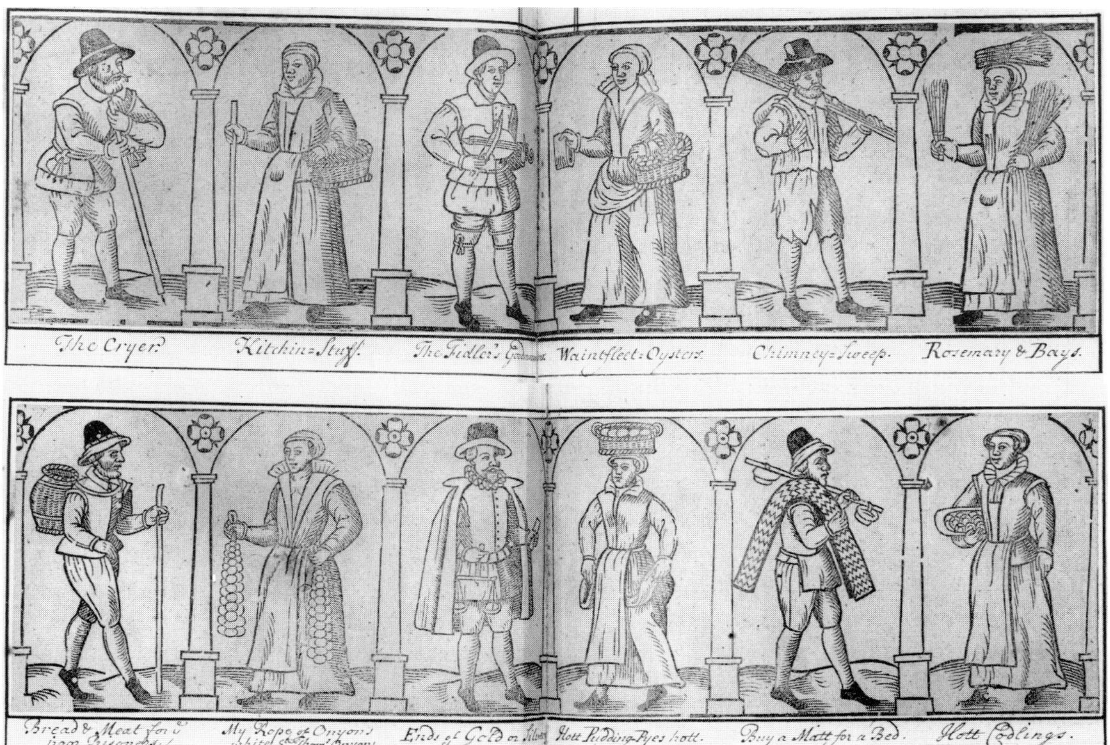

1.1 Anonymous, 'The Cryer', late sixteenth century

antient Sett there of [Cries]; in Wood; with the words then used by the Cryers'.[14] It was made by an anonymous English craftsman–designer in a style evoking the cheap devotional prints of early 'Jesus makers'. For convenience, I call it 'The Cryer' (**1.1**) after its lead figure who read proclamations and announced whatever was lost or found, for example, children.[15]

This woodcut shows, in addition to the crier, a basket woman selling 'Hott Pudding Pyes', a man peddling straw mats to sleep on, and nine other vendors. In it, men alternate with women to illustrate male and female trades, the former specializing in hardware or holding public offices, the latter dealing in victuals and articles of domestic life. All saunter along an arcade, a formulary setting popular in early sheets. The twelve peddlers are identified by either trades or shouts, inked into Pepys's elephant folio where the sheet was mounted (with a second part) after its printed captions had been cropped and thrown away.

Fly sheets like this from Pepys's library collectivize vendors, picturing them in a single panorama to emphasize their identity as typical of the urban masses. Ensembles, a later, more popular and longer-lived format, anatomize hawkers and particularize them. Depicting figures frontally, such ensembles spotlight peddlers' distinctiveness, historical identities, and topical links. This prototypical format, which I also call the series or cycle, is illustrated by a design belonging to the Dutch artist Marcellus Laroon (1653–1702) and four prints by the English satirist Thomas Rowlandson (1756–1827). Laroon's 'Six pence a pound fair Cherryes' (**1.2**), a glamorous figure, comes from *The Cryes of London drawne after the Life* (1687), the first images of hawkers issued as an ensemble. A comparison of Laroon's ensemble with Rowlandson's four little-known images suggests the format's range of possibilities. 'Here's your Potatoes

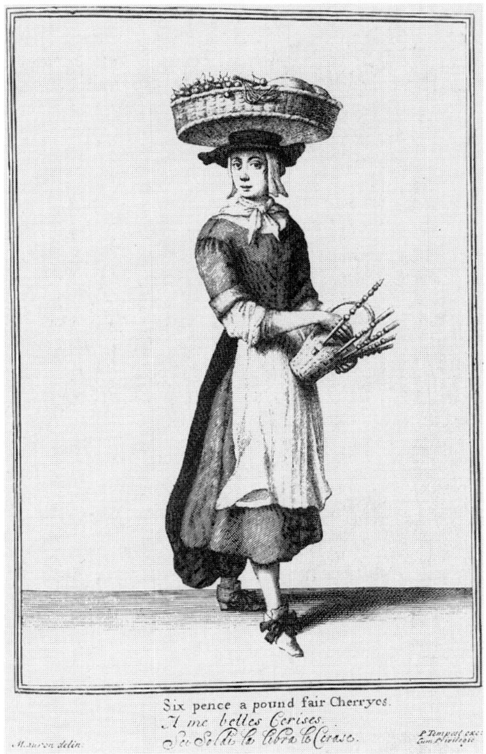

1.2 Marcellus Laroon, 'Six pence a pound fair Cherryes', 1687

four full Pound for two pence' (**1.3**); 'Buy my Moss Roses or dainty sweet briar' (**1.4**); 'Light your Honor, Coach unhired' (**1.5**); and 'Pray remember the blind' (**1.6**) were published in 1811 without a title page to draw them together in a bookish way. These images, among the least literary of Cries, get their unity from their common shape and comic subjects. Laroon's static portrait of a single figure contrasts with Rowlandson's dynamic social pageants, swarming with rogues. The moods of the two artists' prints also differ. Laroon's image shows an obliging hawker with serious, portrait-like naturalism; Rowlandson's employ a spectrum of moods: ethnic caricature in the first (the potato woman is Irish); erotic satire in the second and third, where the young 'ladies' are whores and the link boy a pimp; and pathos

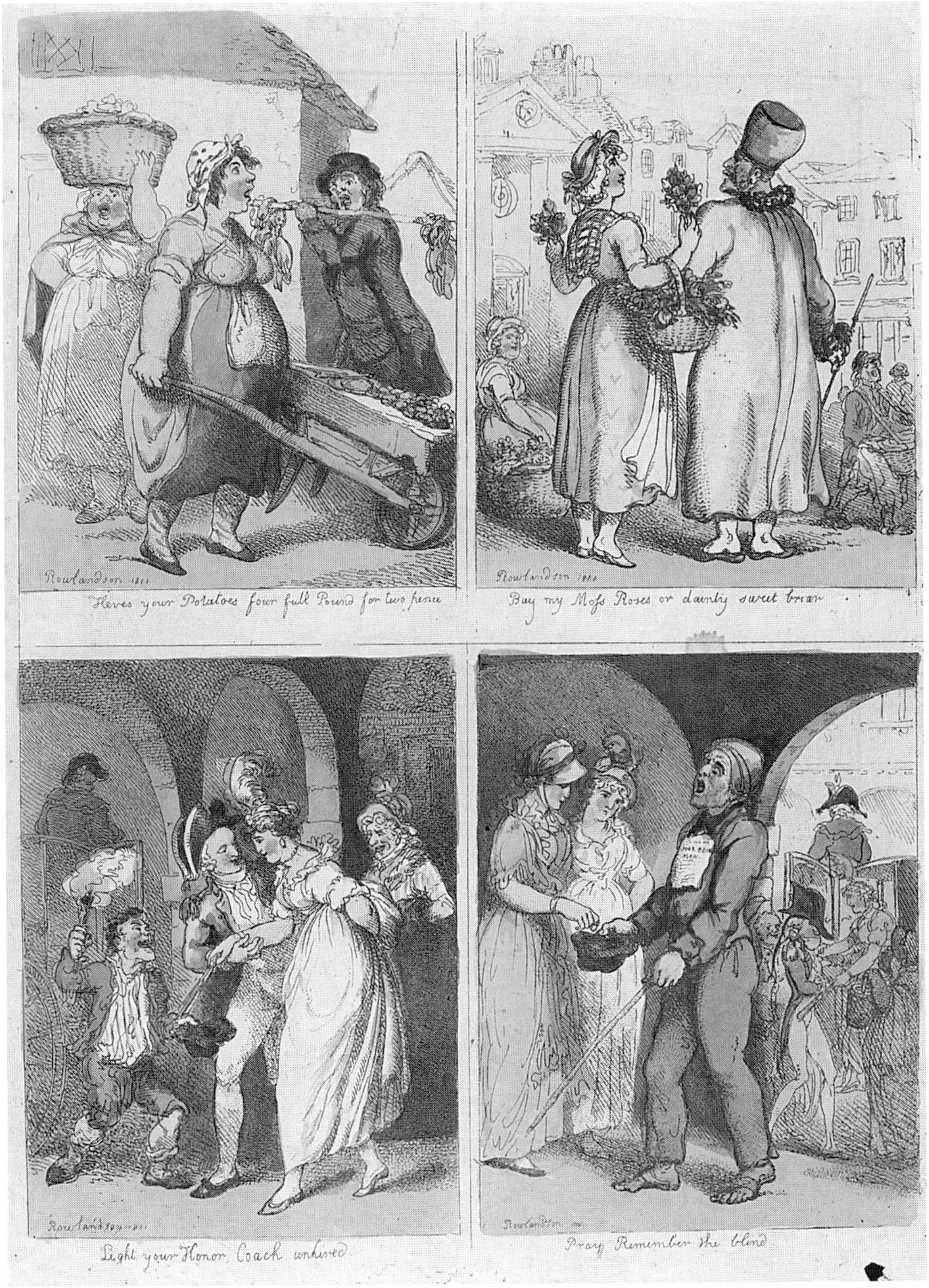

1.3–6 Thomas Rowlandson, 'Here's your Potatoes four full Pound for two pence', 'Buy my Moss Roses or dainty sweet briar', 'Light your Honor, Coach unhired' and 'Pray Remember the blind', 1811

in the last – though the blind man may be a fraud.[16] The world of Cries resembles the reversible world of carnival, where the trickster/impersonator's spirit rules festive celebrations.

Of all the formats that Cries take, by far the most prolific is the illustrated book, published chiefly in the nineteenth century in popular and polite versions. Created as a miniature volume for children in the eighteenth century, the Cries in book form is England's 'word-centred' contribution to the genre. It is illustrated here by the title page to *The Cryes of London Engraved and Sold by I. Kirk, in St Paul's Church Yard* (**1.7**), published in 1754, a date placing it among the earliest illustrated children's books to appear in Britain.[17] Books of Cries later surfaced as illustrated volumes created in a high Victorian style for the gentleman's library table, the antiquarian's study and the collector's shelf, for which Thomas Busby's colored *Costume of the Lower Orders of London* (*c.* 1819) was intended. Balancing historical portraits with biographical texts, Busby's quasi-anthropological volume claims to draw its characters 'from known individuals, [because] it is presumed they will be found unusually interesting'. In fact, Busby's book is not about

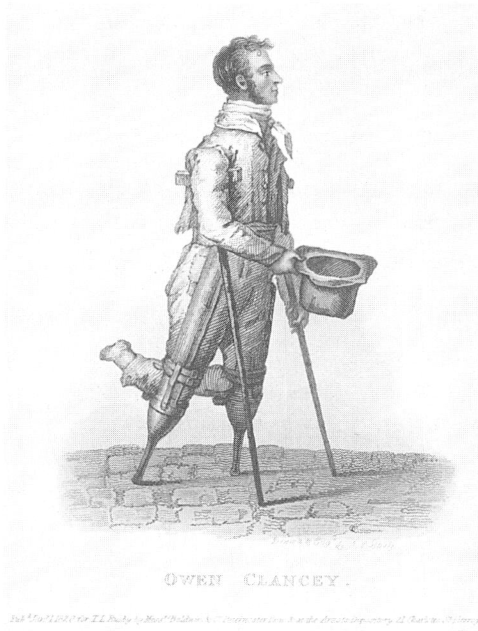

1.8 Thomas Busby, 'Owen Clancey', from *Costume of the Lower Orders*, *c.* 1819

the costumes of the 'meaner sort' or their identities, but about these individuals' mental pathologies and physical mutilations, illustrated by Owen Clancey (**1.8**), the 'unfortunate mariner' whose 'legs were fatally frost-bitten by being shipwrecked on an island in North America', requiring the proud sailor to support himself with two crutches and two wooden legs.[18] This paraplegic, with Busby's other human oddities like the 'Mechanical Fiddler' (**7.8**) and a 'rhapsodic' or lunatic bellringer, illustrate the 'progress' of the London Cries; it begins in broadsides picturing hawkers as representative and typical, but it ends in books showing vendors as bizarre, deformed, freakish and mad.

The popularity of Cries in broadsides, ensembles and books inevitably meant that hawkers surfaced on single prints that play off the genre. These separately issued designs featuring one or two figures are rare and not true Cries; they will be analysed as they

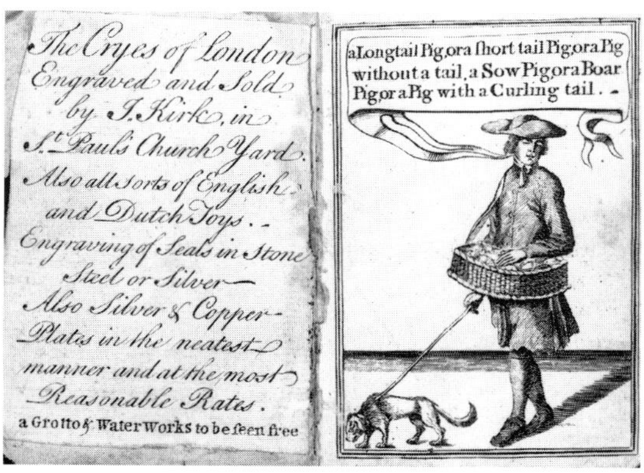

1.7 Title page to *The Cryes of London Engraved and Sold by I. Kirk, in St Paul's Church Yard*, 1754

illuminate the genre, as will a handful of panoramas, playing cards and jigsaw puzzles picturing street vendors.[19]

As the Cries metamorphosed from broadside to ensemble to book, it enlarged its scope, becoming increasingly inclusive before turning promiscuous in the callings, ranks and identities of those it portrayed. The sample of Cries just examined includes figures that range from Laroon's spic-and-span cherry seller to Rowlandson's genteel 'lady' with the feather head-dress, led by a parasitic link boy and followed by a grandmotherly crone, her pander. What was the status and identity of those who peopled London's mean trades or vile occupations, whose name is legion: mountebanks, rag pickers, porters, costermongers, shoe-blacks, milkwives, mercuries, dust men, *lazzaroni*, mechanic preachers, ranters, Merry Andrews, fiddlers and beggars?[20] Skeptical historians reading this book in draft have raised the question insistently. Queries about the standing of such marginal figures, whether in society or in art, are difficult to answer.[21]

To the jaundiced eyes of legislators and magistrates worrying about good order, those who performed 'the most servile, the most sordid, and the most ignoble offices in the community' looked homogenous and untrustworthy.[22] England's Vagrancy Act of 1572, reiterated in 1592, lumped hawkers and peddlers with vagabonds, tricksters, sojourners, masterless men and sturdy beggars.[23] It collapsed distinctions among people living on the edges of society, mandating that all the mobile, insubordinate and frugal be punished as the 'devil's poor'.[24] For these people, the Act decreed sentences written in blood and executed with civil pageantry calculated for its power to grip the imagination and fix the memory: flogging them 'grievously' until their backs were bloody, setting them in the stocks, and burning them 'through the gristle of the right Eare with a hot Iron of the compasse of an Inch about, manifestinge his or her rogyshe kinde of Life'.[25]

In a nation of shopkeepers, the legal status of itinerant peddlers was never high. As early as 1623, hawkers inspired grievances authored by 'honest' merchants. One such complaint, set down in the Wardmote records of Cornhill, griped about the 'the great abuse and annoyance at the South Gate of the Royall Exchange (**2.5**), by the standing there of Ratcatchers and such as sell birds, plants, trees, doggs, and other things, to the great annoyance and trouble of Merchants, Gentlemen, Ladies, and others going to the Exchange and Upper Pawne there'.[26] Peddlers annoying ladies and gentlemen, seldom divided into honest or dishonest, were pigeonholed as a single class.[27] They dwelt between town and country, an interstitial space where the bailiffs and tip-staffs of officialdom seldom trespassed.[28] In this no-man's-land that these go-betweens half invented and half discovered, they lived their floating, catch-as-catch-can lives 'without calling, without magistracie, without ministry, without God in the World'.[29] Types to be wary of, they stood in relation to shopkeepers and guildsmen as quacks and mountebanks did to doctors and apothecaries. Marked people pursuing 'Employment[s] few sober men do meddle with', they survived far from the comforts of middle-class life, beyond honour, beyond respect, beyond law.[30]

The repute of those figures whom artists selected for inclusion in the Cries is a separate question from the status of the marginal in society, though the two are linked. At one end of the spectrum, the Cries feature respectable vendors, many of them valued, even rich in their own orb; coopers and milkmaids, vital to city life, were not outcasts – note the location of the milk seller in George Cruikshank's 'British Bee Hive' (**1.10**); but even their status was paradoxical. At the other end, Cries feature undesirables and criminals: mountebanks, gamblers, procurers with strumpets, and sturdy beggars.[31] Between these two classes, the genre hosts a range of other 'mixed' characters: entertainers like bearwards; costermongers who doubled as gamblers; women who sold apples in the morning and turned midwives in the evening; flower girls who sold sex; and people trading in filth like chimney sweeps, rag-and-bone merchants, dustmen and buyers of 'kitchen stuffe', grease got by barter to be sold to soap or candle makers. Such traders represent only the most glaring of distinctions. Other layerings, together with the notion of an 'aristocracy of rags', emerge in Laroon's *Cryes*.[32] This suite of images raises questions for the study about the inclusive or exclusive character of the genre: which outcasts are represented and which are not? Who qualifies for inclusion or exclusion and why?

Beyond the highly politicized question of social representation, there is a compounding complication. The repute in which street vendors stood, though usually low, was not fixed, but shifted over time, both in art and society. During the sixteenth and seventeenth centuries, when hawkers served rich and poor alike, it was highest. William King, in his *Journey to London* (1698), claimed that even though a friend volunteered 'to shew me the Princes of the Blood, the Prime Minster of State, the Lord Mayor, and other Officers belonging to a *City of so immense a greatness as that of London*, yet I refus'd the Civility, and told him *that I took more pleasure* to see honest John Sharp of Hackney, in a *White Frock*, crying *Turneps ho! four bunches a penny*, than Sir *Charles Cottrel*, *making room for* an Embassadour'.[33]

By the Victorian age, when Andrew Tuer, writing in *Old London Street Cries* (1885), pointed out that vendors had become 'benefactor to the poorer portion of humanity', the status of hawkers had plunged.[34] The turning point in the social decline of hawkers began shortly after King's *Journey to London* of 1698, but the sharpest drop dated to the nineteenth century. The earliest example of this drop appears in a bizarre punishment Joseph Lancaster recommended in his pedagogical treatise, *Improvements in Education as it Respects the Industrious Classes of the Community* (1805). If a boy sings when he reads, ridicule him, Lancaster exhorts: 'Decorate the offender with matches, ballads; (dying speeches, if needful:) and, in this garb send him round the school, with some boys before him, crying matches, &c. exactly imitating the dismal tones with which such things are hawked about the streets in London . . .'. Such treatment, Lancaster pledges, 'is sure to turn the laugh of the whole school upon the delinquent'.[35] Lancaster's oriental punishment is all the more striking for being both descriptive and proscriptive: not only does it illustrate the low regard in which street hawkers were held, it also teaches and spreads the attitude it dramatizes.

By the middle of the nineteenth century, the social position of street sellers sank to its nadir, where it remained. The new outcast status of hawkers, indeed their utter lack of human standing (even in the eyes of the common people), appears in an incident from 1850 and its more chilling aftermath. That event, in contrast to the Lancaster tale, is told in blood, not mirth. In January of that year, a quarrel broke out between a ginger-bread seller and his Stalybridge customers. The ginger-bread man, 'a big, good humoured fellow' going by the name of Sheppard, was seen expostulating with a crowd. Suddenly Sheppard was on the ground and under the feet of the crowd, who formed a ring around him, kicking him with iron-tipped clogs as if he were a stuffed sack. They left him pulp, according to an eye-witness, 'Lord' George Sanger, himself a costermonger–showman–circus star:

> 'Kicked to pulp' is by no means too strong an expression, for that is literally what happened to the poor ginger-bread seller. When the crowd with the kickers suddenly melted away, there lay the body – I can see it now – a ghastly, shapeless thing in the clear sunlight, with the dust of the roadway blotched here and there about it with purple stains. It was one of those things that a man once seeing carries for every after as a shuddering recollection . . . Some time after the brutal deed had been done one or two constables made a leisurely appearance, looked at the body as though such sights were common to their ordinary day's work, and the corpse was removed.[36]

In the course of the Victorian age, the fortunes of street vendors had plummeted so low that new subcategories were invented at the bottom of the scale to contain them. Promoted by socio-economic impulses aimed at charting but also easing urban poverty, the last volume of Henry Mayhew's *London Labour and the London Poor* (1862), which describes itself as 'a photograph of life as actually spent by the lower classes of the Metropolis', divides street traders into a hierarchy among 'Those that *will* work, those that *cannot* work, and those that *will not* work'. It subdivides these three classes into eleven smaller groups, ranked in descending order of status from 'Enrichers' to 'Prostitutes'. Each of these eleven groups is again split into four more subdivisions, which, in outline alone, consume ten pages of tiny print.[37] So prostitutes are 'Professional' or 'Clandestine', and 'Professional Prostitutes' are 'Seclusives' who live in private houses, 'Park Women', 'Thieves' Women', and so on, down the ladder of Victorian infamy.

In popular art, this shift from low caste to outcast is mirrored in one print from 1649 and another from 1840. These two engravings, offering bird's-eye views of occupations in England, contextualize the London Cries' traders, who play small roles in both images. The first design is Randle Holme's (1627–99) 'Manifold Degrees and Callings as to Temporal Imployments' (**1.9**).[38] A 'world picture' or cosmography, it features the king, his court and the nobility in the top row, and, in the bottom tier, musicians (61, 62), a peddler carrying his pack (63), a tinker (64), a beggar (68) and three Merry Andrews (69), among others. George Cruikshank's 'British Bee Hive' (**1.10**), a humorous remake of Holme's 'Manifold Degrees', appears when England is urban and class is a thorny fact.[39] It shows the queen bee herself on the top of the social heap, and, at the teeming bottom, shoe-blacks, coalheavers, costermongers, dustmen, and sweeps.[40] Both tableaus reveal where street hawkers stand on England's social pyramid, but the images are different, especially in tone.[41] In Holme's rectangle, a geometry borrowed from the natural sciences, constructs a system of taxonomy and authorizes a hierarchy of honor. As in a cabinet of curiosities, each classifying box in 'Manifold Degrees' is as important as the sum of all combined. In Cruikshank's 'Bee Hive', executed when England was more class-conscious than in the days of the Stuarts, an animal allegory naturalizes a social pyramid, and the individual scene is less important than the total form. In the seventeenth-century image, England's hierarchy of money and rank is schematized by means of a denotative idiom – horizontal and vertical lines creating an abstract effect having vaguely scientific allusions. But the same hierarchy is represented under the category of the organic and much more connotative idiom – the beehive – in 1840, when England, ruled by a hated Queen Victoria, was beleaguered by

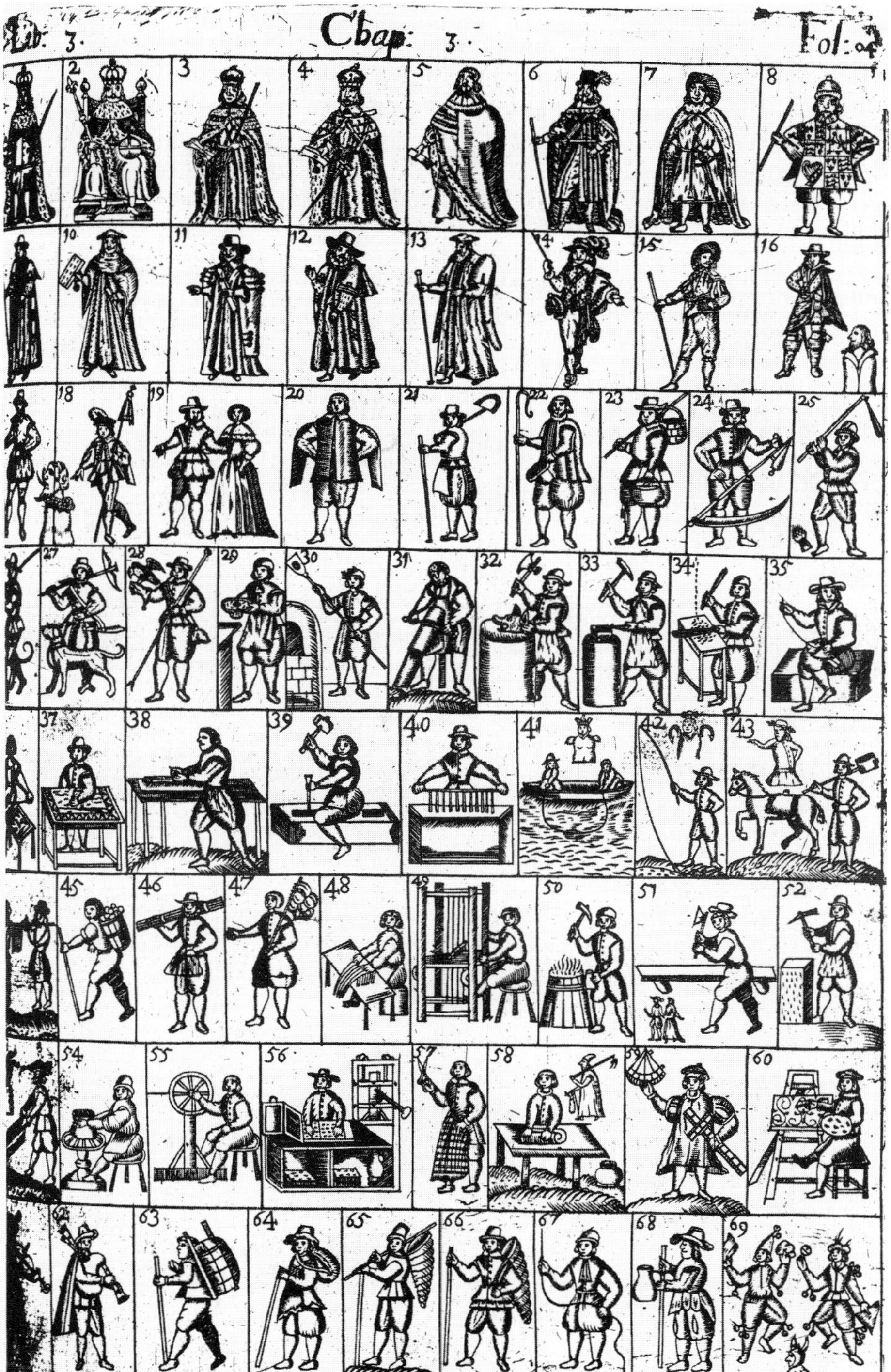

1.9 Randle Holme, 'Untitled Table of Manifold Degrees, Habits, and Callings as to Temporal Employments', from *The Academy of Armory* (1688), a cosmography translating the creatures of the world into the forms of heraldry

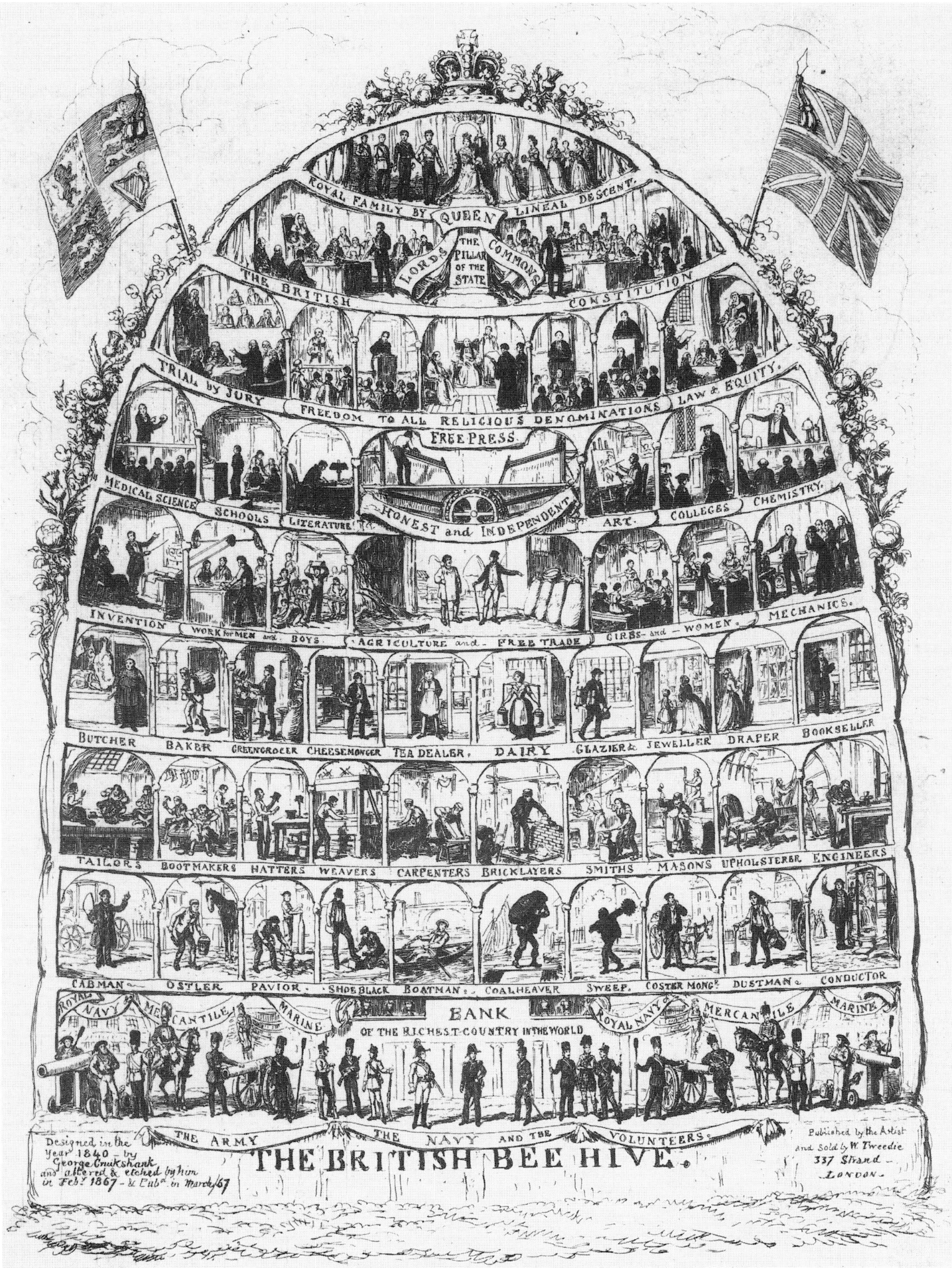

1.10 George Cruikshank, 'The British Bee Hive', 1840

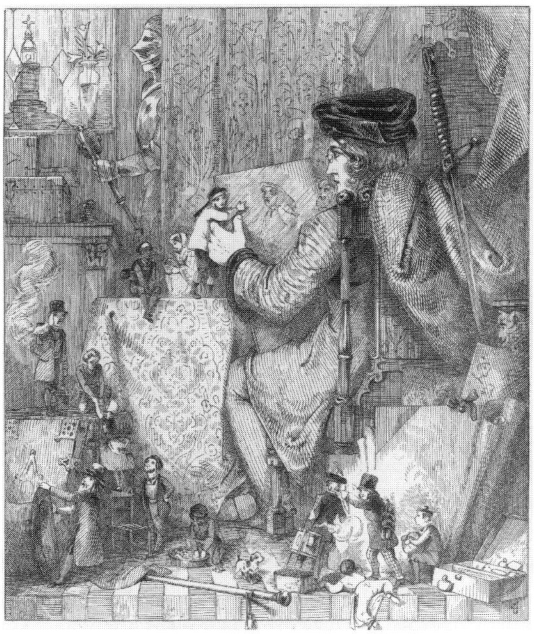

1.11 John Leighton, Frontispiece to *London Cries & Public Edifices from Sketches on the Spot*, *c.* 1847

flux, riven by classes, obsessed by work and consumed by social fears, all of which are reflected but also denied in the London Cries, devoted equally to mirroring life and modelling it.[42]

Art is often said to strip life of fact and clothe it in myth. This commonplace about art's transformative powers, manifest in the case of royal portraits and noble allegories, paradoxically applies to aestheticized low life. Hawkers, in their journey from the streets of London to the engraver's copperplate, endure a metamorphosis at the hands of lying artists and deforming publishers – the latter arguably the most important figures in printmaking because they designed or selected images, wrote captions and financed publication.[43] Even in Cries that are intensely social or documentary (as many are), vendors undergo a reverse incarnation that alters them from living human beings to representations, stereotypes and ciphers.

The transmutation of vendors from historical men and women to figments of the imagination is visualized by John Leighton in *London Cries & Public Edifices from Sketches on the Spot* (*c.* 1847), one of the last illustrated books of hawkers to appear in English art. In the frontispiece to that volume, Leighton portrays himself in the act of taking likenesses of his subjects (**1.11**). Shut off from the world and from the City (the window of his studio frames the lantern of St Paul's), the bespeckled artist labours, not 'on the Spot', as his publisher's title claims, but in confinement and solitude, conditions for creativity after romanticism. In this room of his own, he is sequestered from what Henry James calls 'the Real Thing', the historical actualities that inhibit the portraitist who requires fakery to create art and falsehoods to render an illusion of truth.[44] What Leighton does see are his craft's props: a suit of armour, a medieval sword, old books, swags of drapery and a giant top hat – the standard lumber in the ateliers of Victorian artist-antiquarians.[45] Leighton also sees a cast of Lilliputian street vendors, creatures of his imagination clambering over his props, as they snake their way to the drawing table; the old clothes man, in wending his way along, stumbles upon the top hat and, venting a proclivity for thievery, filches it. On Leighton's table, three of these fairy folk wait their turn to be sketched; a dustman, whose appearance is, to his own amazement, monumentalized into a pathos-filled portrait, betrays the gap between 'fact' and fiction.

Do images of hawkers, as Leighton's print seems to argue, stand apart from history, an autonomous and hermetical genre? Do pictures of peddlers tell more about the tastes of artists, publishers, and their customers than they reveal about the streets of London? History exists inside as well as outside of pictures, which tell us about art and life. Musing on the historicity of popular prints, Henry Angelo (1780–1852) described Samuel W. Fores's collection of 'twenty-five folio volumes of the most choice caricatures of the last and present century' as 'an invaluable *recueil*, showing not only what we were, but the age we live in'.[46] Art transcribes and clarifies history, but it also enhances it.[47] And history offers beacons to art. It illuminates the paths its narratives can credibly follow, even as it allows for some departures from these routes. Such discrepancies between social reality and its plausible depiction in art or literature are now called 'slippages'.[48] Art's transcriptions of history and history's cues to art are powerful forces in social prints, which are memorial and commemorative as well as imaginative and mythic. Cries, which have class, status and money among their themes, are the quintessence of social art. They are structurally committed to social description; they belong to the art of estates and speak eloquently about those who earn their bread on the streets of England's capital.

By way of clarification, let me say that it is wrong to claim, as so many semiologists do, that all art is woven from threads drawn from other artistic texts and lives in a web of intertexuality. Rather, all vital art is woven from two different but complementary threads, one drawn from artistic texts and the other from life. Likewise, great art enjoys a double existence, the first in other art, the second in history.

Pictures of vendors resemble vendors in history, depending upon this artist's aesthetic principles and that publisher's business practices. Take Marcellus Laroon, for example. Hired by his powerful bookseller-patron, Pierce Tempest, he sketched hawkers under a rubric that mixed naturalism and aestheticism. His *Cryes* offered portraits like the chair mender (**1.12**), which is socially instructive (especially in picturing costume) and formally attractive (especially in inventing attitude). It was popular enough to induce another artist to pirate it; but the pirate, known only as 'JM', critiqued the original image (**1.13**) by adding a background (though he was blind to crucial properties of dress, like the chairman's coat vent and low, buttoned pocket). That background featured a building and a sniffing dog; the architecture gives scale to the hawker while the suspicious cur highlights the fellow's alien status – and his stench. Later on, Paul Sandby, annoyed perhaps by the idealizing styles of JM and Laroon, whose street vendors could pass as gentlemen, corrected them with his chair mender (**plate 1**), a feral brute. After Sandby, vulnerable to the criticism that he pictured life with too much social realism, Francis Wheatley moved in the opposite direction. Under the 'industrializing' influence of Colnaghi & Company, the auction house employing him, Wheatley feminized chair mending (**1.14**). He replaced selling with buying and men with women, many looking sexually possessable.[49] In addition, he made caning seats into a rural trade carried on before a cottage door located, by the sorcery of romantic art, in the precincts of St Paul's Cathedral. In Cries, myth-making like Wheatley's seldom goes unchallenged, though responses to it can be equally operatic in how they exaggerate what is vexing, squalid or criminal about the hawking life. Thomas Rowlandson's watercolor 'Old Chairs to mend' (**1.15**), answering Wheatley's soothing design, is less mordant than Sandby's fierce retort to Laroon. Still it is a gleeful, satiric riposte, especially telling in its gin-shop setting and its action, which defines the partnership between a portly woman and a mutilated man as founded on a common addiction to liquor.

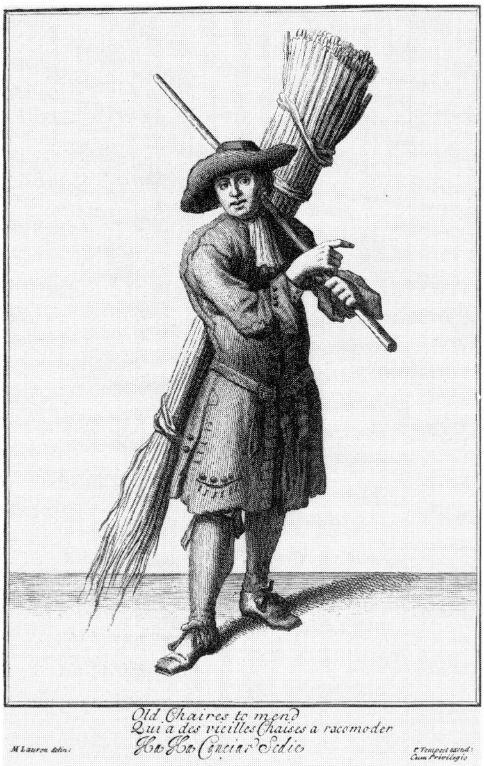

1.12 Marcellus Laroon, 'Old Chaires to mend', 1687

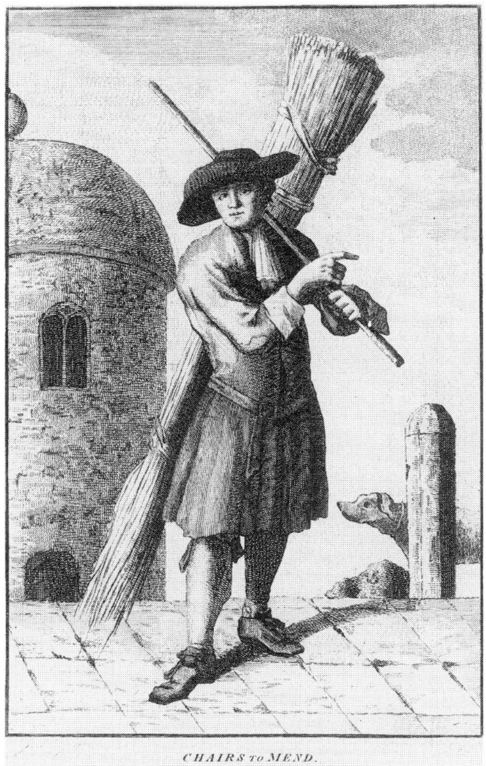

1.13 JM, 'Chairs to Mend', late seventeenth century

So one draftsman, usually a native Englishman, sketches peddlers for the social revelations they offer. He battles the aestheticism of a forerunner, perhaps a Frenchman or an Italian, only to be attacked by other artists sketching peddlers from other agendas based upon patronage, money, ideology, party zeal or sectarian preference. Even as one artist dethrones another, all come together to create an aesthetic chain reaction by which the Cries reinvents and enshrines itself, taking on an historical life of its own. Rather than applying higher and higher standards of naturalism to Cries, printmakers plunge into or recoil from the world about them or from each other's pictures, constructing images that oscillate between social and aesthetic poles.[50] These pictures, the artists who created them, the publishers who bankrolled them, the buyers who purchased them, and the hawkers who sell in them, are this book's pageant.

Though I gloss the London Cries in the context of history and its texts, I do not chronicle hawkers as they really were. Rather, I present an account of hawkers as they appear in art and an analysis of the art in which they appear, though such art cannot be understood apart from the factual world of the Vagrancy Act (1592), the French Revolution, the Seditious Meetings Bill (1795) and the Napoleonic Wars. This account rests on the history of living hawkers from the 1500s, when they minister to rich and poor in indispensable ways, to the 1800s, when they 'accommodate the less affluent with the necessaries of life in the smallest quantities', according to George

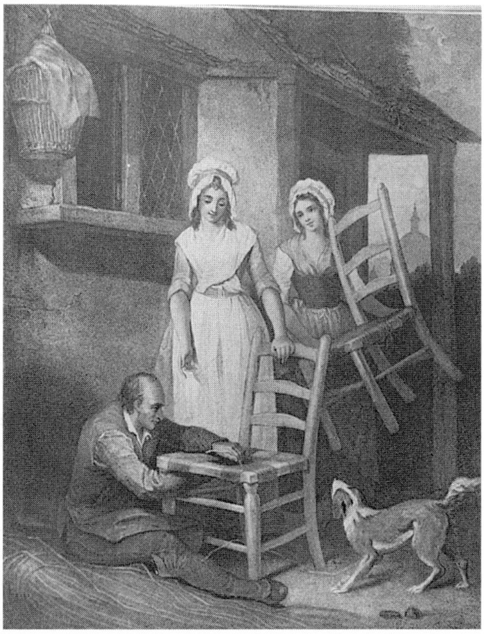

1.14 Francis Wheatley, 'Old Chairs to mend', 1795

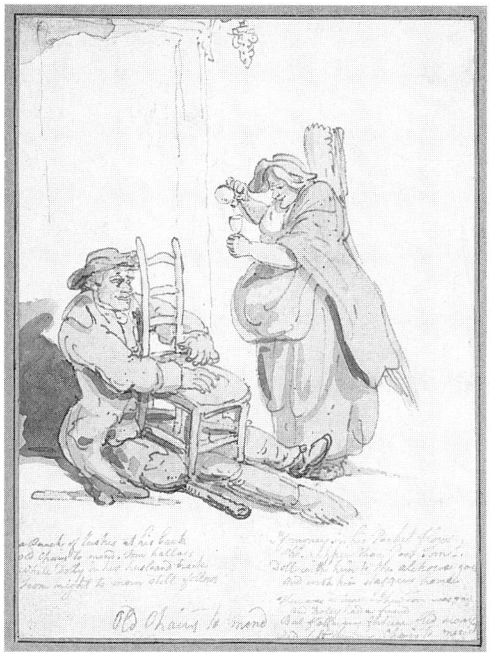

1.15 Thomas Rowlandson, 'Old Chairs to mend', 1820

Cruikshank's *Cries of London*.[51] My aim is not to document the declining fortunes of peddlers by which they became 'squalid with want'; nor is it to measure, in any positivistic way, the gap between material facts and artistic formulations. I mean instead to scrutinize how social representations are created and to examine the role that the artistic stereotyping of hawkers plays in aestheticizing people who followed what Edmund Burke disdained as 'servile employments'.[52] I view Cries not as the passive recipients of ideological bulletins, but rather as active instruments molding values or reinforcing beliefs. As well as documents, they are catechisms that stipulate how hawkers should behave; they are also apologies that justify why the lower orders are lower and must remain so.[53]

The Cries of London, a kaleidoscope of forms and themes, not only crosses disciplines, it subverts them. Its 240 or more works of art divide into thousands of individual images realized in different media, created by a miscellaneous assembly of craftsmen, published across four centuries, devoted to a subject matter ranging from the domestic hawker of mops to the exotic Turkish vendor of medicinal rhubarb from Tibet. The protean genre was shaped by monied book dealers, some chasing 'best sellers' based on personal knowledge of wealthy buyers who came to their clubbish shops to talk, practice connoisseurship or bargain, others aiming at men, women and children from the most populous stations in English society.[54] To lessen the deforming effects produced by the 'fearful symmetries' of chronology, history of ideas, stylistics, and other common paradigms of scholarship, I have fashioned this study as a set of essays that survey, by theme and period, the three chief formats of the Cries.[55] In looking at Cries by format, I am following a mechanical principle stemming from seventeenth-century practice, by which prints were arranged in cabinets of engravings, catalogued in elephant folios, and itemized in sale or probate inventories according to the formal logic of their presentation.[56] The focus on format, as well as enjoying the sanction of history, permits the combination of two approaches commonly separated: the survey of diffuse genres of popular prints and the analysis of particular themes and subjects.[57]

Allowing for varying degrees of overlap, the three formats of the Cries conveniently succeed one another in a chronology stretching from the 1590s to the 1860s and after. The broadsheet was popular from the late 1500s to the late 1600s, when the ensemble eclipsed it. The ensemble was fashionable to the late 1700s, when the illustrated book, which made its debut in the 1750s, began to overshadow all other formats. In charting the rise and fall of the three formats according to this chronology, the survey aims to show the characteristics, sweep, dynamism and evolution of the Cries, incompletely documented, never before mapped, and known in name only. This is a book of recovery and interpretation, of analysis and close reading. As a way of revealing meaning, it employs the methods of ecphrasis, defined in 1715 as 'a plain declaration or interpretation of a thing'; it offers a set of close phenomenological interpretations that bring to light relationships within works and among them.[58] Rooted in the excitement of looking, it shows how pictorial detail and theme are linked. Aiming to explore the pleasures of Cries and their literary texts, the study arranges, deciphers and analyses the designs sympathetically and historically, seeking to discover how they were created, sold, bought and enjoyed, as well as how they look to the modern viewer. It links Cries to each other in ways their artists, publishers and audiences linked them, endeavouring to catch what their first purchasers saw in them when they hung them on their walls or added them to their cabinets of curiosities.

I begin my account of the Cries in chapter 2 with an inquiry into the first broadsides imported by foreign artists into England, where native craftsmen quickly pirated them. This piracy inaugurated a rivalry, in the production of Cries, between English and Continental artists; I trace this increasingly fierce competition across the history of British printmaking, to which this book is a contribution. Focusing in chapter 2 on sheets published between 1590 and 1688, I look at the social origins of Cries in England, their early audiences, their role in expressing as well as shaping London's consumer revolution, and their ties to other popular art, like Wenceslaus Hollar's *The Severall Habits of English Women from the Nobilitie to the Country Woman, as They Are in These Times* (1640).

I widen my focus in chapter 3, where I shift from broadside to ensemble and move inside the genre to examine the dynamic between two ensembles by continental artists. The first of these ensembles is *The Cryes of the City of London drawne after the Life*, published in 1687 and based on sketches by Marcellus Laroon, who came to England from the Netherlands around 1660; the second suite is 'Golden Pippins', 'Shoe-Black', 'Lamp-Lighter', and 'Chimney Sweeper', scraped in 1739 after designs by Jacob Amigoni, a Venetian painter working in England. He created his oils in reaction to Laroon's, still selling well at mid-century, when it had achieved the status of a classic. Though these two continental artists are separated by more than a generation, their ensembles of hawkers are united, not just by how they break with one format and espouse another, but also by how they elevate the status of Cries on the strength of an increased formal complexity appealing to rich collectors.

One value in studying an extracanonical genre is that, in addition to exhuming unjustly neglected images, this enterprise sometimes overturns long-received views of canonical works of art, re-establishing first meanings, even challenging distinctions between such connoisseurial categories. Laroon's and Amigoni's Cries caught the eye of one foreign craftsman and three native artists practising at mid-century. The little-known J. S. Müller, the well-known William Hogarth and the unknown G. Child all reacted either with flattery or anger to the Cries created by these two foreigners. The images that embody the three men's reactions, published about 1740, surrounded the depiction of hawkers in art with a new and intense excitement, to which I devote chapter 4. Using Laroon's and Amigoni's Cries as innovative lenses to analyse Müller's highly plotted Cries, Child's 'Golden Pippins' and 'Chimney-Sweeper's Boy', and Hogarth's 'Enraged Musician', I demonstrate how deeply these men were entangled in what Mark Hallett calls 'a collective, historically determined framework of satiric practice' that had, at its centre, the London Cries.[59]

The ensemble, introduced into England between 1687 and 1739 by Laroon and Amigoni, was commandeered after 1760 by native artists in a revolution begun by Paul Sandby, but kept alive by Francis Wheatley and Thomas Rowlandson, whose Cries I link in chapter 5. Waxing in importance during the eighteenth century, the suite waned after 1800, when it was supplanted by the illustrated book, treated in chapter 6. Viewing nineteenth-century Cries in book format as the outcome of a struggle in which words cannibalize images, chapter 6 focuses on miniature children's volumes dating back to 1754 as well as on elegantly illustrated tomes for wealthy men originating in 1804. I conclude my study in chapter 7, where I seek the genre's overarching purposes and central themes, not only its increasing espousal of the picturesque and its exclusion of the outcast, but also its anti-picturesque reaction to this espousal.

Across all seven chapters, I weave three levels of analysis: aesthetic, cultural and social. In opposition to those art historians who dismiss such popular prints as beneath consideration, I argue for their inclusion, on the grounds of their power and effect, in a broadened canon of English art. But this study is also a contribution to the cultural and social history of early modern England. It approaches Cries as commodities that, like the very goods and services they picture, were bought and sold. Available in large paper editions, run off in red, 'antique' brown or other special colours, and even sold as signed proofs printed on satin for rich collectors, they were themselves objects of a range of practices I recount in documenting how, beginning in the seventeenth century, the response to prints was coloured by their standing as wares to be bought and sold. Finally I argue that Cries are documents about urban life as it was lived from the sixteenth century to the nineteenth. They are not, let me repeat, transparent reflections of historical reality; indeed the book's thesis is that while these images oscillate between social and aesthetic poles, they inexorably evolve in the direction, not of increasing realism, but of increasing idealism. Whatever the actualized techniques and subjects of this or that Cries, the genre's larger movement is away from the frank depiction of social life toward mawkishness and prettification, even as accounts of hawkers in prose (for example, Mayhew's in *London Labour*) move in the opposite direction, becoming increasingly sociological and anthropological. But Cries also become ensnared in debates and caught up in internecine wars about visual methods or ideologies as these attacked or defended the 'meaner sort'; such debates are illustrated by the warring aesthetics of Laroon's picturesque 'Old Chaires to mend' (**1.12**) and Sandby's satirical retort (**plate 1**). So pictures of hawkers turn self-referential: at first they steal from and flatter one another, as JM's 'Chairs to Mend' (**1.13**) steals from Laroon's 'Old Chaires to mend' (**1.12**); later they cite and malign each other, as Rowlandson's 'Old Chairs to mend' (**1.15**) maligns Wheatley's 'Old Chairs to mend' (**1.14**). Their growing self-referentiality is compounded by their increasing fame: the more Cries gained in popularity, the more their production intensified, the more they borrowed. They took most from Marcellus Laroon, whose *Cryes of the City of London* had a formative, pervasive, and ultimately baneful influence on Cries, molding them as a category of picturesque art. Only in the late 1860s did such overborrowing help ensure the bankruptcy of the vanishing Cries. In the contest between history and iconography for the right to depict hawkers, art triumphs over life in popular English prints.

2

Broadsheet Cries and British commerce

CONTINENTAL engravers visiting in England at the end of the sixteenth century cut the first London Cries and printed them as broadsides (**2.1**).[1] Native craftsmen made copycat Cries (**2.2** and **2.3**) to rival these prints.[2] Who would have wanted these copper scratchers' busy, cluttered cuts?[3] Cobbled together from commonplace figures in templates repeated from one sheet to the next, they put no value on originality and have little in common with fine prints by old masters like Goltzius, Bosse or Wenceslaus Hollar, the first great engraver to work in England. They were part of print sellers' standard inventories, a motley class of images that Robert Walton, in his 'Advertisement of *Several things that are made and sold by* Rob. Walton *at the Globe and Compasses*' (1655), describes half-dismissively as 'many several sorts of small sheets, and of half sheets, I know not how many hundred; but in a little time I purpose to give you a fuller and more particular account'.[4]

When scholars moralize stylistic differences between elite and popular art, they brand these sheets simple, coarse, vulgar and mechanical, worthy of the attention only of children.[5] The distinguished literary historian, Frank Percy Wilson, goes out of his way to warn readers against these boring pictures cut by clumsy English craftsmen whom John Evelyn, their contemporary, stamped 'lamentable fellows'.[6] Wilson, cataloguing English prints that illustrate social life in the time of Shakespeare, promises that the scholar searching for early Cries 'will be disappointed at the crudity of most of the representations, especially if he comes to them with memories of such notable craftsmen as Paul Sandby, Francis Wheatley and Thomas Rowlandson'.[7]

Some of the prints Wilson mentions (**2.1** and **2.2**) were tossed off without so much as a title or a publication line to tell who cut them, where they were sold, or what they cost.[8] No London shops advertised or sold prints in the 1590s; no law protected their artists, who acted as designers, engravers, printers, and even hawkers of these fugitive sheets.[9] And no censors required artists to display the imprimatur that French prints bore.[10] For convenience, I name the earliest surviving example 'The Bellman of London' (**2.1**) after the character (centre alcove) carrying lantern and bell through the streets 'to prevent the daunger arising by fier and other hurtes etc. throughe the wholle Towne'.[11]

Dating such cuts and attributing them to an artist or school are vexing, speculative ventures. The fabrications of nameless craftsmen working before the advent of publishers, they appeared in styles so alike that they are difficult to link to any individual or anchor to any epoch.[12] Celina Fox dates the earliest sheet, 'The Bellman of London' (**2.1**), to 'about 1600'.[13] Sixteen hundred seems right, but perhaps it appeared in the early 1590s?[14] Executed in a classical idiom casting hawkers as figures of senatorial dignity, it has stylistic ties to the workshop of

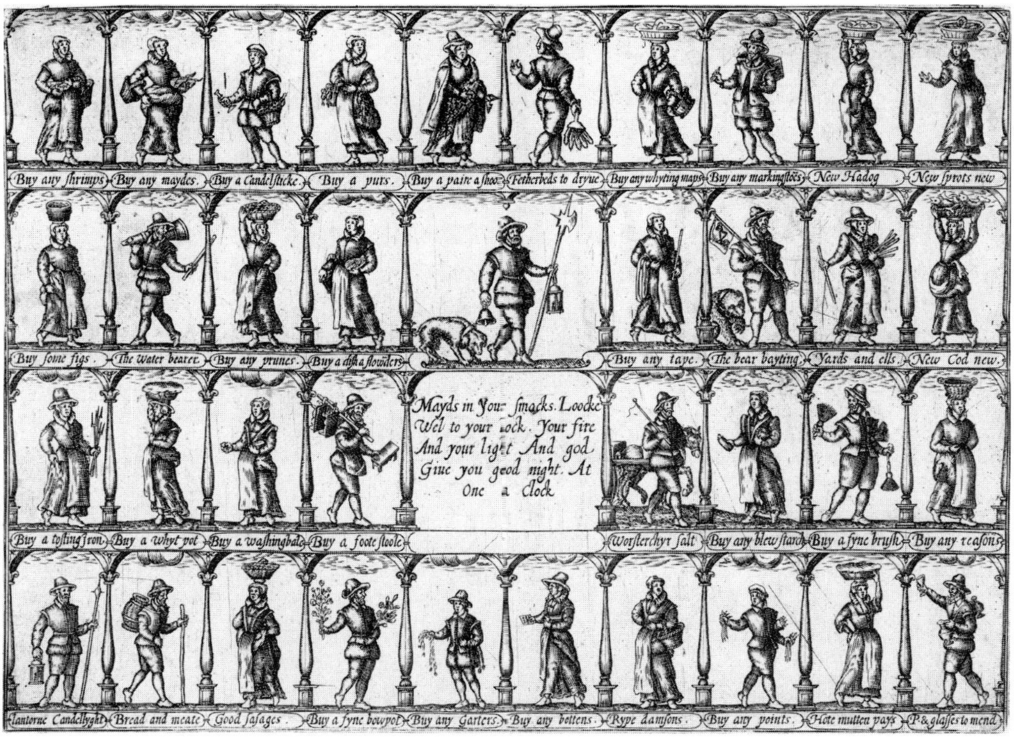

2.1 Anonymous, 'The Bellman of London', *c*. 1590s

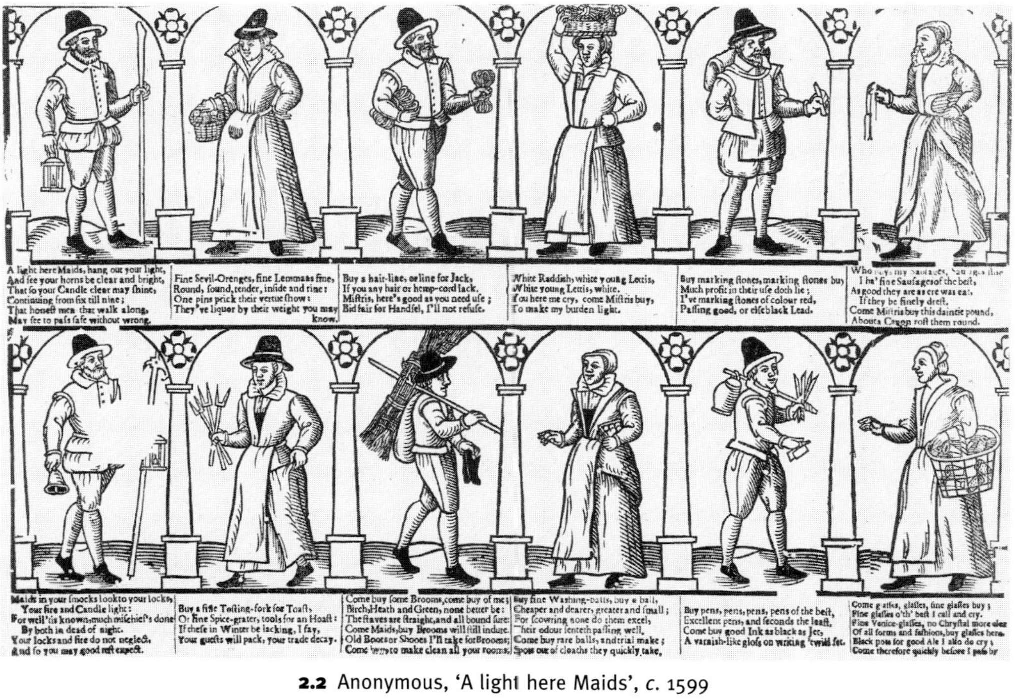

2.2 Anonymous, 'A light here Maids', *c*. 1599

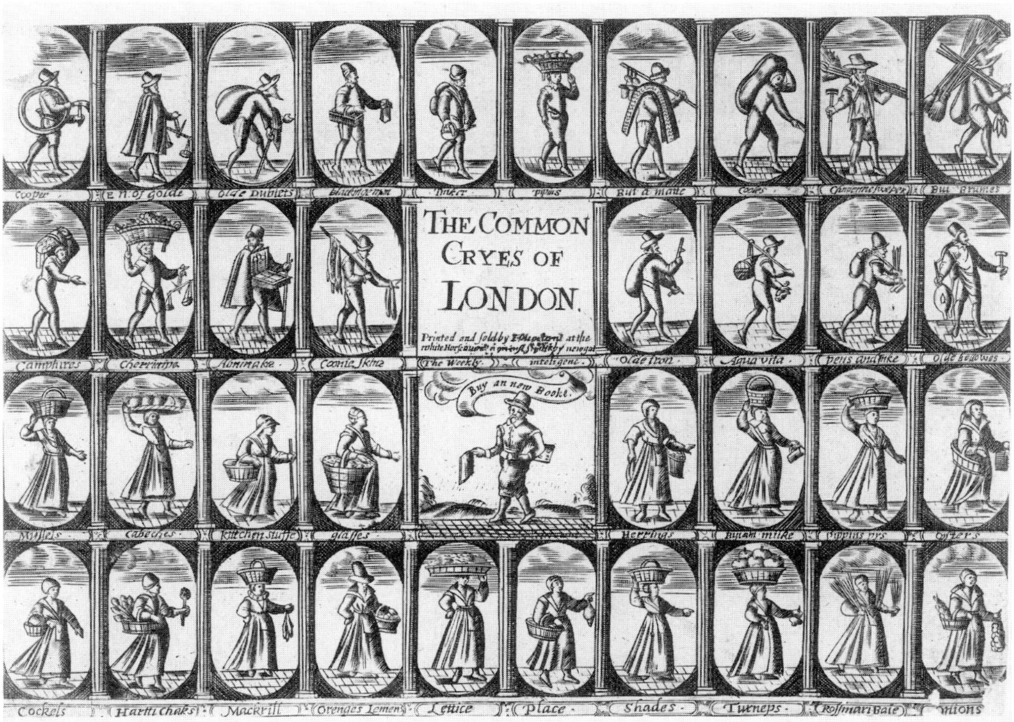

2.3 John Overton, 'The Common Cryes of London', second state, after 1667

Remegius and Franz Hogenberg, who drew maps for Christopher Saxon's *Atlas of England and Wales* (1579) and did town plans of Bristol, Norwich, York and London for *Cities of the World* (1572–94), a universal atlas. The Hogenberg brothers worked in London and thereabout from 1568 to 1587, when Franz returned to the continent to scrape the Cries of Cologne.[15] 'The Bellman' shares, with Franz's Royal Exchange (**2.4**) of 1569, a balance between graceful figurines and neat architecture, the latter enlivened by a menagerie of animals – dogs, bears, and horses. By contrast, Hollar's 'Royall Exchange' (**2.5**) mutes the architecture but amplifies the number and especially the costume of the figures blanketing the interior court of the bourse.

The continental artist's 'Bellman' was answered by two native prints, a woodcut and an engraving done by English craftsmen. The woodcut is an untitled print from the British Museum that I call 'A light here Maids' (**2.2**). It appeared in 1599 and is executed in that peculiarly English style Roy Strong describes as archaic, isolated and mannered.[16] The engraving is titled 'The Common Cryes of London' (**2.3**) and is the earliest example of the genre to bear a canonical title. Because it carries the name of John Overton (1640–1713) and the address of his print shop at the White Horse 'over against St. pulkers by newgat', this impression of 'The Common Cryes' appeared after 1667, the year he moved to that address. But a variant impression of the same design exists, distinguished by a rat-catcher who appears in its central panel; it may be as early as 1610 or 1620.[17]

The debut of these broadsheets reflected and energized the growth of visual culture in England. Such sheets offered new possibilities for the assimilation and treatment of old

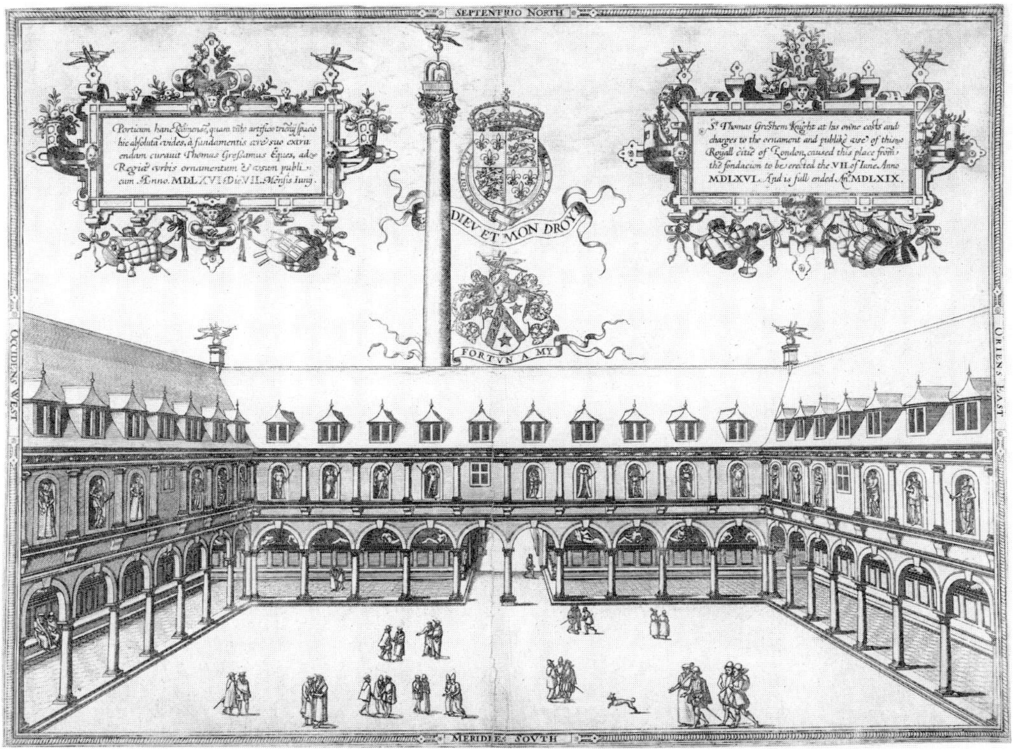

2.4 Franz Hogenberg, *The Interior Court of the Royal Exchange*, 1569

literary themes about the origin and dazzling new material bounty of cities with their distinctive social orders.[18] In images and words, they celebrate all sorts of goods and services as well as those who vend them. Some of these items are familiar, even banal: 'a paire of shoos', 'Good Sasages', and 'Garters'. But others are rare or exotic by any standards, present or past: drying feather beds, damsons, and 'maydes', a fish of the skate family. The ever-varying contents of these broadsides provide a glimpse of the getting and spending changing the face of London at the end of the seventeenth century. Their unvarying honeycombed form, networks of disciplinary knowledge and power, offer a fresh way of analysing London and its economic exploits, which they render as a spectacle. But these sheets are not simple reflections of buying and selling; they are implicated in that commerce in two different ways. First, they are themselves consumer goods; as items bought and sold, they are part of the very operation they record. Second, they procreate, bringing into existence other kinds of broadsheets and other types of commerce. After 1640, early sheets aimed at consumers from the middling and artisan classes generate more elaborate, larger and more costly designs – fashionable and highly specialized luxury goods of a new order aimed at the wealthiest class of buyers. These were the first Cries to be collected.[19]

The earliest broadsheets, whose similarity appears in their ill-cloaked iconographic debts to each other, have never been the subject of serious study.[20] Though they are the mass media of their own age, they have

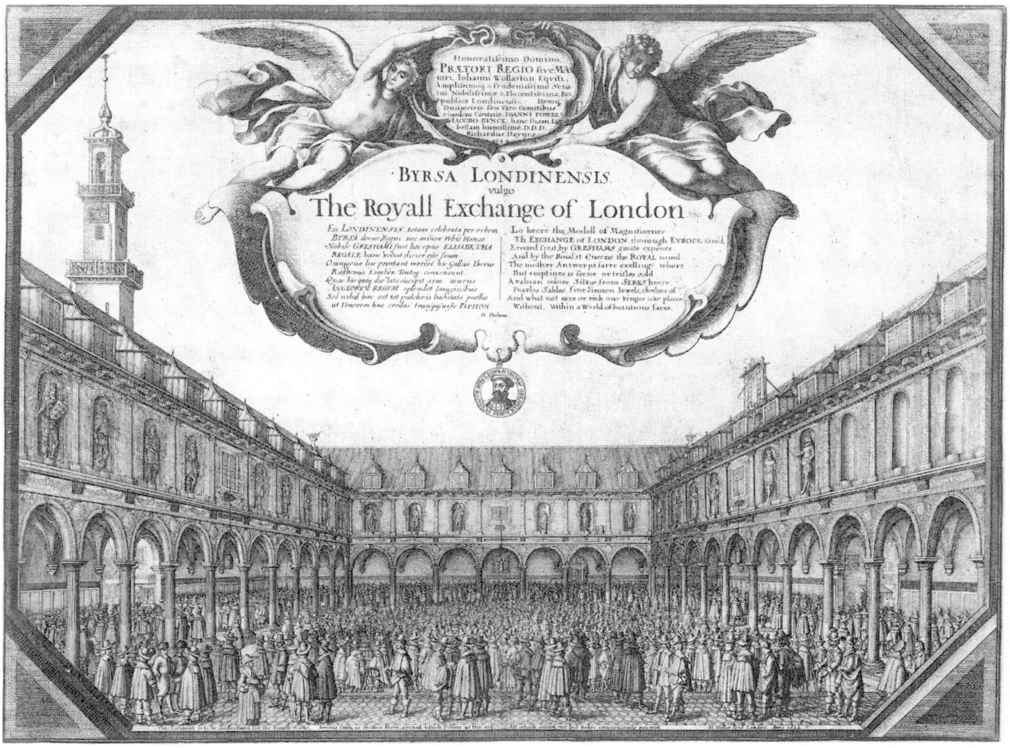

2.5 Wenceslaus Hollar, 'The Royall Exchange of London', 1644

been shunned by scholars in all disciplines.[21] They have escaped the maws of the most source-hungry of all academic writers, social historians. They have even been ignored by students of the very material culture they portray and fuel.[22] Is the cause of this neglect the prints' formal banality? The hawkers in the Cries are repetitive and so tiny that their faces are impossible to decipher. The puzzling merchandise they hawk, magnified to the point of distortion, is still hard to name. Vendors' accoutrements are only clear from their cryptic legends, which, like the images they accompany, have a literalness that thwarts the esoteric, allegorical or privileged readings beloved of literary scholars.

What social changes brought these sheets to birth in England in the late 1500s? Who acquired them when they first appeared and what did buyers see in them? The poor did not buy them. Though they were among the cheapest images on the market, their texts, necessary to decipher their rough images, would have baffled the unlettered. Of course, one schooled buyer could have read or an 'ale knight' might have sung or cried the words while unalphabeted listeners looked over the performer's shoulder. But with barely enough money to put bread in their mouths, few needy people could have afforded to buy them for themselves.

Unlike ballads going for a halfpenny or a penny, these prints cost sixpence – more if they came from copper plates, less if from wood, as does 'A light here Maids' (**2.2**).[23] Classified as 'great sheets' or 'pot' sheets by print sellers like Peter Stent (active 1642–65), they measure eighteen by twenty-six centimeters and cost two-thirds of a day's wages for a labourer in the building trades.[24] Construction workers made eight pence daily between 1580 and 1626, more between 1626 and 1639, when earnings ranged as high as ten pence a day.[25] Such labourers, if they could read, were more likely to buy a broadside promising them 'all the Newes in England, of Murders, Flouds, Witches, Fires, Tempests and what not' for a copper, the price of a pot of ale or admission to the Globe theatre's pit.[26]

Bureaucrats, lawyers, doctors, clerics, and those just below them bought the first Cries of London.[27] These middling sorts of city buyers, ranging from merchants to academics, flourished in England from the time of Chaucer's Wife of Bath.[28] In the seventeenth century, when London mushroomed into Europe's largest city, nine times as populous and twenty-five times as wealthy as its closest provincial rival Norwich, professional types, thriving tradesmen and civil servants multiplied, absolutely and proportionately.[29] By the end of the seventeenth century, London supported a thousand apothecaries, for example.[30] Provincial visitors carrying heavy purses, in town to go to law, let blood, take a purge or shop, also bought these cuts as souvenirs of sojourns in the nation's urban lodestone.[31] Below this class of people, small shopkeepers, clerks, journeymen, innkeepers and even farmers living in the capital or in big provincial towns (but not in the countryside) acquired these fly-sheets as decorations. So did people seeking 'pleasant Phantasies for Gentle-womens work' as well as 'goldsmiths, chafers, gravers, painters, carvers, embroiderers, drawers, needle-women, and all handicrafts [workers]', who bought them as patterns to copy or prompts to inspire them in their labours.[32] When the first Cries appeared, the English art market was not yet divided into elite and popular; instead, many social classes and callings patronized a few print sellers who catered to customers with overlapping demands. Connoisseurs whose interests shaped academic art composed a small share of the market for Cries.[33] Nevertheless, the middling sorts and those a little less prosperous bought most of these sheets, which explains why few have survived.

Sold initially in the ateliers of engravers, Cries were increasingly offered in print shops, enchanting new retail stores bearing names like 'The Golden Lion' and 'The Globe and Compass'.[34] Unlike the old-fashioned 'bespoke' businesses in which craftsmen, under the control of guilds, made goods to order for rich connoisseurs, these shops allowed opportunistic publishers and engravers to produce prints for cheap, anonymous, mass sale unregulated by the London Stationers or any other Company.[35] A curiosity in the realm of retail specialties, these art marts first appeared in London under the leadership of the Dutchman Hans Woutneel, who dabbled in prints a few years before he died in 1603.[36] They surged into general view after 1620, when they grew to include the 'emporium' of Peter Stent at 'the sign of the Crowne' in Giltspur Street, Master Thomas Jenner's premises 'going up the stairs of the Royal Exchange in Cornhill', and the print shop of John Overton at the sign of the White Horse without Newgate.[37] Here, well-to-do artisans, commercial people, rich Londoners and tourists bought pictures of their dazzling new world, in which prints were novel, coveted wares.[38]

Such buyers did not collect prints, they used them. They passed these engravings from hand to hand, studying their characters and noting their details or stories. Or they hung them up as cheap murals, a genre popularized all over northern Europe by Maximilian I's monumental woodcuts.[39] They glued these sheets to hanging canvases and nailed them to bare walls in order to cheer up the offices, garrets, and drab shops of scriveners, artists, poets, hack writers and others following trades that shut them in.[40] Robert Walton recommended his London Cries, which he sold with maps and allegories, as 'a most commodious ornament for every man's house, and therefore you may either have it in paper coloured or not, or else on cloth, with or without rollers and ledges . . .'.[41] Keepers of coffee shops and ale houses were especially fond of decking their walls with illustrated sheets that might draw in customers: in Arundell Street's eateries and drinkeries, John Gay records, 'Now hangs the Bell-Man's song, and pasted, here, / The Colour'd Prints of Overton appear'.[42] Public house decoration has a long history: Sir John Falstaff, assuming the role of interior decorator, advised Mistress Quickly to spruce up her bagnio with broadsheets and woodcuts, not hanging cloths: 'And for thy walls, a pretty slight drollery, or the story of the Prodigal, or the German hunting in waterwork, is worth a thousand of these bed-hangers and fly-bitten tapestries.'[43] The custom of sticking prints to the walls of taverns was fueled by the fact that, before the first public exhibition held in the great room of the Society of Arts in 1760, engravings of all sorts were sold there.[44] Moreover, artists' clubs, like the Rose and Crown or the Society of Virtuosi of St Luke, gathered at the Half Moon, the Turks' Head, the Rose Tavern and other ale houses, whose owners sometimes doubled as stationers.[45] George Humble, the first Englishman specializing in the sale of prints, owned a brewhouse in Westminster.[46] In addition, these stationers' engravings, selling plain or 'coloured on cloth', often featured – and flattered – 'baggage people such as rogues, tinkers, peddlars and such like' who haunted tippling houses.[47]

In these 'penny universities', as alehouses were called, hard use destroyed the fragile sheets, which were only rarely framed, glazed, mounted or bound as things of value before 1640.[48] Or they fell victim to one of the yearly 'spring cleanings', when old almanacs, ballads, and prints – smudged, tattered, and oppressively familiar – were torn down so that new ones might be put up in their place.[49] One melancholy bit of evidence, itself a print, suggests that Cries ended their life in privies: 'Sawney in the Boghouse' (*c.* 1745), a scatological satire, shows a Scot vainly attempting to use an up-to-the-moment English outhouse, the walls of which are plastered with engravings. The largest of these is a Cries of London resembling (deliberately, perhaps to satirize?) Laroon's 'Twelve Pence a Peck Oysters', which also features a barrow hawker.[50]

Like their role as casual decorations, their layout promoted their ruin: the columns and alcoves into which they are organized invited cutting up, followed by certain destruction; this razoring is illustrated in Pepys's reformatting *The Manner of Crying Things in London* (**2.22–2.37**), originally configured as two tall sheets.[51] The disfigured state of the few surviving sheets dramatizes how narrowly they escaped annihilation (though Pepys's reformatting made them into something new that suited his needs and guaranteed their preservation).[52] Their survival rate was one in ten thousand, Tessa Watt estimates.[53] The commonest prints always become the scarcest.[54]

Bureaucrats and professional men of the middling sort like Pepys rescued these sheets from oblivion, preserving them in their cabinets, from which one or, very rarely, two mutilated copies have come to us today. When these images first appeared in England, they provided Pepys and other buyers with entertainment joined to instruction. Touting discoveries, inventions, 'chimaeras', and news in the style of ballads, early modern prints satisfied a need to see the world in lifelike pictures. While academic paintings elevated the past, using inherited traditions and aesthetic laws, popular prints reported the present, based on a draftsman's view of the ocular truth of things.[55] The knowledge they strove to impart was documentary and factual. Appealing to the curious, they were empirical; they used styles that were plain and transparent.

Such prints displayed the extraordinary in culture or nature, everything from giant 7½ lb radishes and exotic seashells, to the 'mysteries' of glassblowers and printmakers, to the kidney stones, two-headed children, and 'scientific' contraptions of the Royal Society, whose president was Samuel Pepys.[56] One typical print promised 'The true descripcion of this marveilous straunge fishe which was taken on thursday . . . the. xvi. day of June, this present month, in the yeare of our Lord God. M.D.L.X.IX'.[57] Such prints gratified the curiosity of dilettantes like John Evelyn (1620–1706), who, in his *Sculptura: or the History and Art of Chalcography and Engraving in Copper* (1662), advocated using images to expound 'all the *Sciences* [i.e., knowledge] by them [prints] alone, and that with as much certitude, and infinitely more expedition, than by the most accurate method that was ever produced'.[58] According to Evelyn, an enthusiastic collector himself, prints were manifestly 'superiour to all those *Abstracted termes*, and *secondary intentions* wherewith *Masters* commonly torment and weary [the] tender and weak Capacities' of the very young. In his view, everybody from children and adolescents to princes and nobles 'might receive incredible advantages, preparatory to their entrance into the *Schoole Intellectual*, by an Universal, and choice Collection of *prints* and *cuts* well design'd, engraven and dispos'd, much after the manner and method of the above nam'd *Villeloin* [the writer Michel de Marolles, Abbe de Villeloin (1600–81)], which should contain, as it were, a kind of *Encyclopaedia* of all intelligible, and memorable things that either are, or have ever been, *in rerum Natura*'.[59]

Collectors like Evelyn and his friend Pepys also tied engravings to maps created by the new cartographers who belonged to the same guilds as graphic artists. Like atlases with elaborate pictorial margins, prints united people, nature and the social order; but they also divided humanity up by gender, calling and race. As reports observing and analysing the theatre of the world, they helped fix national identities, and they memorialized the history of Europe, especially the history of cities.[60] So Pepys arranged the ten thousand engravings in his collection, not by artists with special visions or styles, but by topics composing the 'science' of cosmography, that 'universal comprehension of *Naturall* and *Civill* Story' in which the world and its peoples pass in review.[61] One of his elephant folios held 'My Collection of Prints relating in general to France, but more particularly to Paris & its Environs', acquired (on a trip to that capital) at the urging of Evelyn, who told him: 'They will greatly refresh you in your study and by ye fire side, when you are many years return'd.'[62] A sister atlas featured Pepys's 'Prints & Drawings (as farr as extant and recoverable) relating to the Citys of London & Westminstr'. He broke this volume into 'chapters' variously titled, 'Mapps &c introductive', 'Buildings & Monuments', 'Thames & its Views', 'Vulgaria', 'Habits', and its companion, 'Crys', prefaced by this title: 'Cryes consisting of Severall Setts thereof, Antient & Moderne: With the differ. Stiles us'd therein by the Cryers.'

Pepys was fond of Cries and Habits; the two are allied and sometimes synonymous, though the latter focus more on costumes. As well as three English sets, he owned two sets of Carracci's *Trades of Bologna* (1646 and 1660), Vaccario's *Cries of Rome* (1612), and Bonnart's *Cris de Paris* (1675), probably bought for him by his cousin, John Jackson, who went on the Grand Tour at his uncle's expense in 1699.[63] Writing to Jackson sojourning on the continent, Pepys implored him to buy more of three categories of images, which the young man had failed to acquire in sufficient quantities: 'I wish you had met with a great number of frontispieces, and can only recommend the making of them more, as also of religious prints and in particular of Habits, in your passage through Spain and Portugal.'[64] Pepys wanted more Habits because they granted him 'as speedy and as profitable a discovery as the times will enable, of the whole world, and the most observable things therein', as he learned from his own copy of Peter Heylyn's *Cosmographie* (1677), a cultural geography for armchair voyagers.[65] In creating this atlas, Pepys, like John Stow before him and Tom Brown after him, was exploring 'with a Travellers Eye, all the Remarkable Things of this Mighty City', in which there are 'more New Countries, and surprising Singularities than in all the Universe besides'.[66]

But what 'Remarkable Things' about London did Samuel Pepys and other middling buyers see in the 'Crys' they pasted into their folios, lingered over on tavern walls, displayed in their libraries or hung in their closets, those bowers where both sexes manifested and validated their private selves?[67] From the sheets' honeycombed forms, viewers mastered a fresh way of looking at London. In their contents – the broadside's surprising merchandise – viewers saw a new frenzy of consumption that would bring disaster to London or raise it up to a utopia 'bigger than Heaven', depending on their viewpoint.[68]

From a formal perspective, these early sheets are constructed as figures in arcades. Why this monotonous geometry, so cold to human values like face and expression? Such gridirons renounce Wenceslaus Hollar's way of picturing hawkers who sell their 'temptations' amidst throngs of city-goers in his 'Royall Exchange of London' (**2.5**). They treat hawkers not naturalistically and expressively by massing them into a crowd, but scientifically, following the methods of natural history. Separating them from each other, from their social superiors and from their environments, they immobilize this perambulating community and break it down into its constituent members. They treat their subjects as specimens classified by means of appearances under various headings like 'The Water Bearer' or 'Bread and meate', after the methods of early zoologists and especially botanists, whose herbals decontextualize nature's parts, sort them by species and genera, and organize them by lists, so prominent a feature of these sheets that it is hard to write about them without falling into list-making. Focusing on static taxonomy more than narrative, they abstract their subjects and universalize them, picturing them against a white background. Hawkers are sketched diagrammatically, as plants are; they carry their wares in their arms or hands, as flora are shown to bear blossoms or fruit.[69] They materialize in a space that is striated, out of life's torrent. Instead of surfacing in their own surroundings or appearing in their (often vexed) links to other hawkers and customers, they are denatured, 'classicized' by an architecture of public order. By means of a mannerist conceit, a few vendors problematize their isolation: the water carrier in 'The Crier' (**2.1**) thrusts his baton into the alcove of his neighbour the prune seller, as if to protest to his sequestration or challenge it.[70]

In capturing hawkers under so many bell jars, the sheets make sense of urban anarchy carried on by the lower orders. 'The Bellman' (**2.1**) and 'The Common Cryes' (**2.3**) demystify London and its rude mechanics; they condense this vast population and abridge it. Both trade on the dazzle of systematic thought, with its power to order the unorganizable. By means of cubicles that diminish the tiny hawkers, the sheets code, classify, rationalize and quantify a metropolitan shopping scene growing so turbulent it threatened to exceed the capacity of human consciousness to understand or control it. Their counting, coding and classifying, all forms of quantification, represent early analogues to statistics gathered by economists, politicians and policemen in the interests of the knowledge that spawns control.

From the sheets' frames, viewers learn about a different way of observing London; from their content, they discover a new wave of buying and selling. Early Cries identify the merchandise for sale in London, but they also expose a remarkable new technique being used to sell it. The new art of selling surfaces in the fanfare hawkers use to display their wares. Every article, from sausages to marking-stones, is exhibited by a showy, insistent gesture. This speech of the limbs and especially of the hands, integral to the artisanal culture of peddlers, invited intervention. Unlike the contained, self-referential manners of 'the Quality', it was active, productive, and aimed at others.[71]

Hawkers' theatrical gestures, enticing buyers by means of the eye, were new strategy in the late 1500s.[72] Designed to overshoot the intellect and strike the gaze, this intoxicating technique was concocted by peddlers to sell, but also to assert their collective opposition to authoritarian cultures of the printed word, the text and the contract.[73] John Stow, London's first historian, denounces the 'meretriciousness' of hawkers' and shopkeepers' appeal to the gluttony of the eye in his tale about the anarchic burgeoning of cheap luxuries, trinkets, articles of grace, knickknacks and exotic gear coming to England from the four corners of Europe.[74] Pointing to objects identical or similar to those in 'The Bellman of London' and 'A light here Maids', Stow grumbles about the 'very gay Shew' put on by merchants who set up shop 'about the Year 1580, from the city of Westminster along to London':

> Some of the wares sold by those Shop-keepers were, Gloves made in *France* or *Spain*, Kersies of *Flanders* Dye, *French* cloth or Frizado, Owches, Brooches, Agglets made in *Venice* or *Milan*, Daggers, Swords, Knives, Girdles of the *Spanish* Make, Spurs made at *Milan*, *French* or *Milan* caps, Glasses, painted Cruses, Dials, Tables, Cards, Balls, Puppets, Penners, Inkhorns, Toothpicks, Silk-Bottoms and Silver-Bottoms, fine earthen Pots, Pins and Points, Hawks-Bells, Saltcellars, Spoons, Dishes of Tin. Which made such a Shew in the Passengers Eyes, that they could not but gaze on them, and buy some of these knicknacks, though to no Purpose necessary.[75]

In this new selling by spectacle, the glass mender from 'The Bellman' is the sheet's most energetic monger: he flourishes his goblet above his head with a ceremony that mimics religious ritual. This sacramental view of commodities also surfaces in the way hawkers' chattels are magnified out of proportion to the niches' scale in the same sheet. Toasting irons look like harpoons, while, in 'The Common Cryes' (**2.3**), turnips look like prize pumpkins. And captions draw the eye more to the merchandise than to the hawkers. With a few exceptions, the legends of 'The Bellman' (**2.1**) deflect the gaze away from the vendors to what they sell: 'Good sasages' (not 'the butcher') and 'Buy a Candelsticke' (not 'the candlestick maker'). In the same way, 'A light here Maids' (**2.2**) highlights heterogenous merchandise rather than homogenous merchandiser, while 'White Radishes', 'Pens', 'Brooms' and the like excite by how they add up to a full field of goods.

As well as picturing how hawkers sell, the first Cries show what they sold and celebrate it. In the colonnades of 'The Bellman' (**2.1**), audiences discover – or rediscover – the 'Worsterchyr' salt and washingballs making England's capital into Europe's latest consumer dream world, 'a perpetual *Mart*', as the pseudonymous N. H. called it, 'where any sort of Goods may be purchased at a convenient and reasonable Rate'.[76] Indeed, revelations about the wares traded in London are the souls of these sheets. Their foodstuffs and little appurtenances are exotic and luxurious by Renaissance yardsticks. When the hand-to-mouth fare of a labourer was a hard, pinching, and monotonous diet of ale, bread and cheese, with an odd morsel of cheap flesh such as tripe, offal, plucks or sheepsheads, the 'Oysters', 'Cockels', 'pippins pys' and 'Harttichaks' hawked in 'The Common Cryes' (**2.3**) were carnivalesque treats. When the worldly goods and chattels of Francis Wade (*d.* 22 April 1623), a labourer, were a bond of money worth £22 and one platter of pewter, when people of all ranks thought of what they could grow in their gardens or make at home (because what they could buy was little in quantity and humdrum in quality), then the brooms and 'Venice-glasses, no Crystal more clear' hawked in 'A light here Maids' (**2.2**) stirred people's imaginations.[77] Even the crockery sold by the 'whyt pot' vendor would have excited Londoners viewing 'The Bellman' (**2.1**) in the early modern period. So would the forks offered by the 'toasting iron' hawker; cutlery of any kind was extremely rare before 1725.[78]

Behind the first Cries' fascination with consumer goods lie four linked changes in the social life of English men and women: a shift from agriculture to commerce;[79] the trickle down of conspicuous consumption from 'his Grace to his grocer', but especially to the aping middling class; a hunger for ostentation as a form of self-expression; and a thirst for material culture as a fountain of hedonistic delight.[80] These changes revolutionized the practice, but more importantly, the morality of buying and selling. They replaced hoarding, meant to strengthen social bonds (illustrated by Francis Wade's bond of £22 held by Nicholas Wade, probably a kinsman), with producing aimed at profit and consuming aimed at show.[81] They transformed London from a town of petty fairs and xenophobic, local markets (bedeviled by scarcities) to a stirring city of consumer extravaganzas appealing to visitors coming to do the year's business and have fun.

Before Elizabeth I, consuming and owning were different matters. Ordinary people consumed a narrow range of foodstuffs, which they grew, raised or bought. By contrast, the handful of durable goods they owned were of their own manufacturing or came by bequest. When common people bought, they did so for their families, not for themselves, as we do. And they bargained with peasants and artisans, not hated middlemen, 'caterpillars who come between bark and tree', in the words of a phrase popular during the seventeenth century.[82] Peasants hawked, bartered or exchanged the raw materials of the countryside in regional economies where hard cash played a small role, going for leases or rents paid quarterly in coin and amounting to hemorrhages of money. As late as the eighteenth century, city people laboured at home, just as rural folk tilled the land, not simply to produce income, but to avoid squandering cash, their 'Hearts' Blood'.[83] Except among the high, who used showy expenditure to affirm rank by intimating bottomless wealth, buying was a catastrophe to be avoided at any cost, an attitude the reverse of our own.[84]

The death of marketing and the birth of shopping has prompted Margaret Spufford to call the seventeenth-century 'a period given over, with the exception of the Commonwealth, to [the] monstrously frivolous'.[85] Such frivolity surfaces in two ways in these sheets, which divulge changing patterns of consumption (in reality, a mounting emphasis on food) and which also identify new categories of goods consumed (especially luxuries). In telling detail, 'The Common Cryes of London' (**2.3**) mirrors shifting patterns of expenditure, especially among the well-to-do gentry and nobility. Increasingly these classes spent less on showy funerals with hundreds of paid mourners or on big retinues of menials; Sir Walter Raleigh, when he rose in favour with Queen Elizabeth, kept 500 servants.[86] Instead, elites indulged in what Stubbes called 'belly cheer'.[87] Their epicurean tastes soon trickled down through the ranks of English society; Lupold von Wedel, travelling in England in 1584, observed: 'I have seen peasants presenting themselves statelier in manner, and keeping a more sumptuous table than some noblemen do in Germany'.[88] Such cheer, from imported sweetmeats to pantry staples, was the costliest article in seventeenth-century homes. Sarah Fell, to run her comfortable Quaker household in the 1670s, spent fifty percent of her yearly outgoings on food.[89] Among the army of peddlers trading in victuals, fishmongers in 'The Common Cryes' (**2.3**) hawk mussels, herring, oysters, cockles, mackerel, plaice and shad, an array that conjures up a Rabelaisian imperialism of the belly.[90] Even if it is exaggerated, such an assortment of salt-water fish, copious by any standard, highlights the matter of choice, a perplexing and novel dilemma in Stuart England compounding people's ambivalent feelings about buying.

In the seventeenth century and beyond, vegetables and especially fruits were scarce, dear, bitter, stunted and 'brought only to the tables of the Great, and of a small number among them'; but in the sheets, they seem articles of everyday diet.[91] Hawkers in 'The Common Cryes' (**2.3**) offer lettuce, artichokes, turnips, and onions. Those with their 'pipins', oranges, 'pippins pys', and 'cherrierripe' heralded yet another gastronomic fad tied to the retail revolution: snacking.[92] No wonder foreigners envied Britons' diet for its plenty. 'Other Nations esteeme us gluttons', Fynes Moryson thundered in 1617; he prayed an ardent, new prayer, 'God deliver mee from meates, that invite to eate beyond hunger'.[93]

When shopping turned from an ordeal into a pleasure, men and women read these pot sheets as little encyclopedias of England, Turkey, France and Spain's 'chiefest treasures'.[94] Here were early 'shop-at-home' catalogues picturing an entrepôt world in which everything was for sale – the London Donald Lupton mocks as 'a gally-mophrey of all sciences, Arts & Trades'.[95] Such catalogues, in which objects were fortuitously jutaxposed to suggest enigmatic ties, appealed to the reader-as-buyer and the reader-as-window-shopper. In this they resembled English fairs, which operated as educational spectacles, relays for the diffusion of the exotic commodities of elites and the cosmopolitan values of the capital, said to be 'a great world' because 'there are so many little worlds in her'.[96] The sheets instructed viewers about goods only heard of and never before seen. Or they reminded viewers of provisions recently encountered for the first time in stalls, shops and peddlers' packs. In words and pictures, these panoramas enhance the reach of the human eye and take the measure of a commerce that, according to John Denham, wrapped England's capital in

a thicker cloude
Of busines than of smoake, where Men
lyke Ants,
Toyle, to prevent imaginarie wants,
Yett all in vayne, increasinge with their store
Their vast desires, butt make their wants the
more.[97]

In addition to disclosing fashions in food, broadside Cries identify new categories of goods, especially commodities to satisfy the procreating 'wants' of Denham's 'Cooper's Hill' (1642). As London's markets, once local and regional, became national and international after the triumphs of Elizabeth's Merchant Adventurers and East India Company, notions like 'necessity' and 'luxury' shifted meaning.[98] By seventeenth-century standards, nothing in 'The Bellman', 'A light here Maids', or 'The Common Cryes' is a necessity. Shoes, if old, are an exception. Luxuries – the goods Stow singles out for condemnation as 'to no purpose necessary' – abound.[99]

Some of these indulgences are dear, some cheap; their range is wide: footstools, mats, gold and silver jewellery, and that supreme indulgence, flowers. Gentlemen and the middling sort of better-offs seldom resisted the call to buy a fine 'bowpot', a variant of 'bough-pot', meaning pots or bouquets of flowers.[100] A few of these extravagances 'smell of beyond the seas'. The most striking examples come again from the realm of food: Spanish figs for Lent, prunes, tempting raisins and lemons, also indispensable to 'take away the spots or red Pimples of the Face' or in 'sweet bagges to lay amongst Linnen'.[101] Raisins were devoured 'in all places, and with all Persons in England' so that Fynes Moryson wrote, 'The very Greekes that sell them, wonder what we should doe with such great quantities thereof, and know not how we should spend them, except we use them for dyeing or to feede Hogges'.[102]

'The Common Cryes' (**2.3**) overflows with a new category in the housekeeping of Tudor and Stuart people: decencies. Sometimes called 'conveniences', these were the things that, in the words of the pseudonymous N. H., 'not only keep them [people] from Want and Poverty, but render them pleasant and sociable'.[103] They include the bellows and almanacs peddled in 'The Common Cryes'. Glasses or crystal, hawked in both 'The Common Cryes' and 'A light here Maids' (**2.2**) were an especially swank convenience. They were suddenly cheap after 1630, when they were imported from Italy or blown by Jean Carre, the Antwerp glassmaker who worked in the old hall of the Crutched Friar near the Tower.[104] They are cried up by rich and poor alike earlier, as when Falstaff sings, 'Glasses, glasses, is the only drinking'.[105]

In picturing London as a horn of plenty spilling out decencies and luxuries gathered from all over Britain and Europe, broadside Cries show England's capital enlarging life's boundaries, pushing back its frontiers, and becoming the gateway to a larger world. The city of these tableaux is an artful utopia whose dynamism has harvested, perhaps created, splendours that might never have come to pass in the small world of the English village.

Of course, these images are more than products of a naive impulse to mirror the consumer revolution and other so-called 'trends of the time'. As well as reflections of shopping, they are also its agents. Like other forms of art, they are engines of desire and catalysts of social life, not just their passive reflections. In the act of picturing candlesticks, washing balls, fine brushes and Waintfleet oysters, the sheets whet people's appetites for these things. Manipulating taste and fuelling consumption, they serve as primers of the good life. They tell people how to furnish their houses, spend their leisure, eat their dinner and adorn their bodies. In an epoch when that eager young merchant Marmaduke Rawdon (1610–69) is counselled by his uncle 'to winn gold and weare gold', these sheets draw the eye to accessories of dress, fashion, and personal adornment.[106] They play up things needful to proclaim, in a flash, a stranger's status to other strangers. In the realm of the ostentatious, gold jewellery stands out in 'The Crier'. And in 'The Bellman', so do garters, points (loose strips of linen or soft leather used to fasten garments), buttons, purses, gold jewellery again and 'blew starch' – in such hot demand the crown worried about how much wheat or corn it consumed, and Stubbes, a professional fulminator against vices, branded it 'the devils liquore'.[107]

The first Cries go beyond singing 'Buy, buy, buy', the siren song repeated twenty-three times in the captions to 'The Bellman of London'. In a preening, self-conscious way, they implicate themselves in the buying and selling they trumpet. The hawker occupying the big central panel, the viewer's entry into 'The Common Cryes' and the heart of the sheet, is a chapman. Magnified to catch our eye, he also snares our attention by strolling left where everyone else parades right.[108] While most vendors' patter is one or two words ('cooles', 'olde dublets'), his cry appears as an imperative sentence: 'Buy an new Booke'. And while other hawkers' shouts appear in a small italic hand inside a cartouche placed below the figures, the chapman's cry appears in big lettering within a banderole floating over his head. In the panel above the chapman, the name, shop, and street address of John Overton appear. By soliciting the viewer to 'Buy an new Booke', naming the bookseller, telling the way to his shop 'without newgat', and offering a nominal portrait of Overton, the tableau is one of the earliest examples of printed advertising in England. Though primitive and unfocused beside today's target marketing, the sheet purveys a genuine nugget of publicity, provoking the voguish selling and buying of the luxuries it pictures.[109]

The publication line of 'The Common Cryes' proclaims that the broadsheet itself is 'Printed and sold at the White Horse', where it and similar goods may be had. In a more focused way than 'Buy an new Booke', these words solicit the reader to purchase the engraving he or she is in the act of enjoying from John Overton's printshop at the sign of the White Horse. An advertisement within the broadsheet promoting its sale, these words highlight the dual status of 'The Common Cryes'. It is both a picture and a consumer good, one of a growing storehouse of popular prints with instructional value and decorative appeal. The newest form of popular culture, these exotic images demonstrate taste and style. They quench a thirst for trendy engravings, woodcuts, illustrated books and paintings, and they inculcate consumerism in the middle echelons of English society, just as that society shifts from an oral to a print culture.[110]

From this perspective, the 'Cryes' is itself a commodity drawing attention to its salable status. A luxury article to adorn dwellings, it competes with the purses, brushes, footstools and flowers that vendors ply in its own niches.[111] Boosted by the aesthetic movement cultivated by Henry Peacham's and Richard Haydocke's writing on art, it was prized for its prestige as well as its intellectual utility.[112] It confers rank or status on the owner who uses it to decorate a parlour, study, and especially a closet, which Samuel Johnson defined in his *Dictionary* (1755) as either 'a small room of privacy and retirement' or 'a private repository of curiosities and valuable things', two related meanings that illuminate the link between print collecting, connoisseurship and these cabinets. So it reflects, records, and even participates in the rage for things that first surfaced in England in the seventeenth century. This is the rage that consumed other rages a century and a half before the Industrial Revolution replaced crafts from workshops with artifacts from factories producing the ultimate in standardized, mass-produced and machine-made goods.[113]

As well as bestowing prestige on their owners, perhaps these images also operated on a level that was not aesthetic, but quasi-religious or magical; perhaps they conferred physical and spiritual boons upon those who nailed them up in homes or alehouses. The nature of these blessings is suggested by the fact that the lead figures enshrined in the big double alcoves of the earliest sheets all belong to a higher order than mere hawkers roused by small gains. Figures of protection, these archetypes are the town crier, the bellman, the nightwatch. The noblest and most venerable of all street characters, these civic authorities, whose historic roles overlapped, protected the city from the catastrophes it feared most. The town crier shouted out proclamations concerning the safety of lives and property. The watch kept good order in the street; he looked for riot, debauchery and suspicious behaviour. The bellman 'walk[ed] with a bell in the night tyme, viz from the hower of xj until iiij of the clocke in the morning and every night, as much as lyeth in him, to prevent the daunger arising by fier and other hurtes etc throughe the whole Towne'.[114] The odd-man-out among these figures of sanctuary seems to be the mundane bookseller, but he is a later addition, a self-portrait inserted by the self-promoting John Overton after 1667. The original inhabitant of that shrine was the rat-catcher and his apprentice whose apocalyptic malediction appeared beneath them: 'Hee that will have neither / Ratte nor Mousse / Lett him plucke of the tilles / And sett fier of his hows'. Their task was to rid London of the most terrifying and characteristically urban of all vermin, whose evil glamour rendered it at once the subject of taboo and worship. So they too are icons of protection.[115] To a city fearful of spectres ranging from plague to fire, the patron saints in these sheets were portentous figures; their ties to the sacred appear in their benediction. Even when this benediction was comic, it concluded by invoking the deity in the words, 'And Gods Blessinge' or 'And god / Give you good night', recorded in a watch's caption from two early London Cries.[116]

If what is represented on an image is actually present in it, as many people believed, and if images partake in the life they depict, perhaps these sheets possessed a lure going deeper than their formal charms, which are scant.[117] Perhaps the owners of these prints sought in them those special benefits that religious people expected when they hung up pictures of saints or erected statues in the belief that a specific force, like the ability to bring rain or keep safe on journeys, was present in them? Among the superstitious, perhaps the images had prophylactic force and acted as talismans or sources of solace, like the amulet of a hare's foot that Pepys wore about his neck and called 'my preservative against wind, for I never had a fit of the collique since I wore it'?[118] Possessed of shielding vigour, they may have preserved houses from fire, or people from robbers and murderers, in their owners' view. No evidence exists to prove that early Cries were cult objects or worked 'picture magic'. However, the power of images speculated about here, suggesting that these Cries also operated on a level that was more than aesthetic, would explain their existence by an appeal that goes deeper than mere artistic attraction.[119]

That literary art depicting watchmen and criers performed in this way at this time is suggested by Robert Herrick's (1591–1674) 'The Bell-man'. This short poem reveals that the presiding figures of early Cries were empowered in the realms of religion and the supernatural, which allowed them to safeguard Londoners against enchanted creatures like goblins, in people's imaginations.

From noise of Scare-fires rest ye free,
From Murders Benedicitie.
From all mischances, that may fright
Your pleasing slumbers in the night:
Mercie secure ye all, and keep
The Goblin from ye, while ye sleep.[120]

Herrick's poem is a litany of the Bellman's secular and sacred powers; but its prayer-like formula indicates that its recitation invokes the benedictions it enumerates, in the way that perhaps the sheets did as well.

If the watchmen in the first Cries possessed a priestly character, their common peddlers enjoyed no such sacerdotal standing. Indeed, their order and regimentation in the sheets may have startled those who knew them by sight or reputation, for they were widely regarded as a class of people 'base by byrthe, meane by estate, & servyle by calling'.[121] Peddlers had been around since the Middle Ages.[122] In the time of Chaucer, they are the first people to accost the anonymous Kentish poet of 'London Lickpenny' as he leaves Westminster and enters the City of London. They introduce the poet to the city as a world that, filled with hustle and noise, is different from the country, filled with quiet. The penniless ploughman's stumbling verses offer one of the earliest references to the city's hawkers in English literature:[123]

In to London I gan me hie,
Of all the land, it beareth the prize;
Hot peascods one gan to cry,
Strawberry ripe and *cherries in the rise*:
One bade me come near and buy some spice,
Pepar and saffron, they gan me bede:
But for lack of money I might not speed.[124]

Unlike the jostling hawkers of ribs and Paris thread who animate this poem, the peddlers in the first Cries are methodical, decorous figures. They are distanced from the eye, a technique that imparts dignity. But they are also miniaturized, making them into an array of weakly differentiated figures designed to showcase their various goods at the expense of their identities. Few offensive or flattering details about them stand out. They have no expression and little character beyond their gender, age, calling and estate. The sole exception is the Jew in 'The Bellman of London', who has a religion and tribe. Except for him, figures' individuality is submerged in their labours, which follow universal forms.

Hawkers in all three broadsides keep their nondescript dress neat and becoming; they seem to cultivate a fondness for appearances unlikely among peddlers bearing roots and fish. Their costumes are not just trim and presentable, they are uniform: doublets and breeches for men, skirts and bodices for women. This sartorial uniformity offers a static iconography of urban dress and fixes hawkers' identities in their trades; it also highlights their collective nature and obliterates any differences in wealth, honour, or respect among them. No rich and poor divide this flourishing estate. All enjoy a measure of prosperity that suggests no class system among city labourers. They belong to one economic degree, 'the Working Trades, who labour hard, but feel no Want', from Daniel Defoe's (1660–1731) famous seven-step ladder of ranks and riches, describing the 'Conditions of all the People' published in his

Review of 25 June 1709.[125] The exception are the two chimney sweeps (**1.1** and **2.3**) whose torn pants show they belong to Defoe's 'Poor, that fare hard'; departures from the Platonic type, they offer the individual specimen with its imperfections and accidental deficiencies.

All others are uniformly prosperous because they follow callings that are decent and useful. No hawker deals in gewgaws or baubles, despite the moralistic frowning of Stow about such people's trade in 'painted Cruses, Dials, Tables, Cards, Balls, Puppets, [and] Penners'. Vendors offer substantial wares or essential services: cleaning chimneys, bartering new brooms for old shoes, carrying water to people's houses. No scoundrels lurk among these honest traders – no bawdy baskets, whipjacks, morts, nips, jugglers, or clapper-dudgeons from the underworld of the late Renaissance.[126]

Hawkers' respectable callings are matched by respectable conduct. These are law-abiding and peaceable types having a spirit and discipline that make them look more like soldiers and officers than 'needy and mean' street hawkers 'stirred with small profits'.[127] They are also purposeful and busy; they do not divide up into indolent and industrious, hostile and accommodating, compliant or dangerous. In the pursuit of their trade, vendors balance ardour with civility and eagerness with deference.

But who do they defer to? Their customers are nowhere to be seen. The gridiron sheets, interesting for what they leave out, deracinate hawkers, lifting them from their everyday surroundings, often agitated by strife. In their new circumstances, they enjoy a sovereignty untarnished by overtones of servitude, such as might be created by images of labourers producing commodities or elites consuming them. Moving through arches and classical columns, they inhabit an idealized space that avows their status as unfettered figures; here they seem timeless icons with no troubling ties to trade or toil. They have no worries about money, no oppressive overlord, no ticking clock. Free men and women, they are master and mistress of their fates.

Like the architecture they inhabit, these hieroglyphs enjoy an identity that is public and collective, composed of what Chaucer called 'estate', 'condicion', and 'degree'. Peddlers have a name in their occupations. They personify hawking, expressing in their rank and callings a notion of the city and its urbanity. What they do is who they are: they derive their social, professional, and economic identity from the objects they sell or the tools they carry. Just as the king at the top is identified with the state ('L'etat, c'est moi'), so the cooper at the bottom is identified with his particular calling ('My coopering trade, it is me').[128]

This powerful link between hawkers and their callings rides on the assumption that they create the wares they sell or are closely tied (by blood, for example) to the people who do. The broadsheets show only the bond between seller and product or service, never that between commodity and buyer or between seller and buyer. So the axiom of the sheets is the medieval one of 'we are what we produce and sell', not the modern one of 'we are what we buy and consume', even though that premise by which people view themselves in the likeness of things was already powering the tie between popular prints and their purchasers.

The diligence of the hawkers and their orderliness is the same from 'The Bellman' to 'A light here Maids' to 'The Common Cryes'. The regularity of the three typical sheets combines with their look-alike frames and the shared iconography of their figures to give an impression of artistic uniformity. In fact, the three sheets are executed in two different idioms. In contrast to the English style of 'A light here Maids' and 'The Common Cries', the continental manner of

'The Bellman of London' is more artful and intricate. Its hawkers look sculptural; their dignity, proportion, and beauty is stereotyped; it has a provenance stretching back centuries. Such stately, harmonious poses are stiffened by self-control; they are commonly linked to social superiority and have little of the strain or awkwardness of hard-handed people who perform labours certain to deform. The hawkers' athletic contrappostos, intellectual and imaginary rather than plausible, speak of the mind's superiority to the body. They lack the submission that goes hand-in-hand with lifting and toting; their carriage derives from precepts of corporeal discipline in classical art. Indeed the theatrical airs, refinement, and pretentious gestures of these hawkers recall the same features in saints from Italian Renaissance paintings or gods and goddesses from the statuary of Rome or Greece. Posing to evoke the cherished antique, mongers pantomime in ways that speak of public virtue, Olympian assurance and propriety in a superior degree.

'A light here Maids' and 'The Common Cryes of London' offer more actualized, less artful figures; they are not idealized, aristocratic, and Greco-Roman, but English, provincial and bourgeois. Though based on sculpture-like models, they are flat, two-dimensional and understated. Especially in 'The Common Cryes', where the copying is diluted, the hawkers are not solemn and high serious, like the glass seller in 'The Bellman of London', but naive, awkward and occasionally comic, like the buffoonish Jew buying old clothes with stoop and agitated reach. Their gestures have an awkward naturalism rather than a dance-like ritualism; their poses are filled with movement and haste, enemies of bodily elegance and marks of plebeian breeding.[129] In a pell-mell ballet that catches the urgency of real street trading, the men scoot between columns mimicking the load-bearing work they do, while the women chase down cobblestone streets so swiftly that their skirts billow out behind them. What they lack in grace, they make up in energy, conveying an impression of urban life as tumultuous and hurried.[130]

Despite the wider social range of 'The Common Cryes', hawkers in all these sheets are celebrations of prosperity and concord, reflecting the ideals of civil life rather than the realities of street vending. They are medieval guildsmen from a unified and godly city. In this utopia of orders and not of classes, peddlers come together in a cityscape where differences in calling appear paltry. The goldsmith, the most prestigious member of the great Twelve London Livery Companies and sometimes (like William Kip) an artist–engraver, is bedfellow with the oyster woman, historically the foe of the Company of Fishmongers who were anxious to drive her sort out of business.[131] And a Jew freely walks the streets of London, even though there were no Jews in England in this period.[132] An image of cohesion so deep could only delight the eyes of rich urban print buyers like Pepys, whose privilege it justified in the realms of culture and politics.

Of sheets published between the 1590s, when the broadside first appeared, and 1687, when the ensemble made its debut, thirteen examples survive.[133] This handful of images divides up into two categories based on whether they appeared before or after 1640. The eight published before 1640 are strikingly alike in style and layout; five are variants of just three prototypes, exemplified by 'The Bellman of London' (**2.1**), 'A light here Maids' (**2.2**), and 'The Common Cryes' (**2.3**). Laid out horizontally in ornate colonnades, these sheets differ in small ways; all repeat or modify mechanically the simple figures and complex frames of the three paradigmatic plates, themselves interrelated by borrowing.

Triply anonymous, they lack artists, publishers and, in some case, titles. Such Cries were not valued as expressions of the talent, vision, sensibility or originality of any craftsman; they were created to be bought, enjoyed and jettisoned.

Prints in the second category, published after 1640 but before 1687, are more experimental, elaborate and diverse. Their novel forms and variations reflect buyers seeking greater formal intricacy and makers in contact with continental art and artists like Hollar, who returned to London in 1652 when the Interregnum eased England's isolation from the rest of Europe.[134] All five of these inventive sheets shift from horizontal to vertical layouts that direct the eye away from the frames, drastically simplified, to the figures, drastically complicated, a strategy that reverses the style of earlier, less elaborate sheets. These intricate Cries bear titles, dates, booksellers' names and print shops' addresses, but not artists, probably English engravers whose roles were still unacknowledged, to say nothing of distinguished from each other. None the less, the number and scope of prints published in London was increasing at this time. So was their status as art and their popularity, recorded in a drawing (sketched for Laroon's *Cryes*) that shows an itinerant London print seller hawking small, cheap sheets from his pocket and big engravings from his shoulder.[135]

Objects of enjoyment, aesthetic curiosity and practical interest, these Cries appealed to a small circle of amateurs and connoisseurs, as well as to that group buying images of hawkers before 1640. They also attracted a new clique forming within this circle, collectors. These men, though they did not expect genius, demanded formal resourcefulness. As well as being keen about the products of printmaking, they were interested in its processes and techniques, so they paid a premium for proofs, unique printings and early impressions rich in the lustrous contrasts and delicate effects that mark the bound copy of *The Manner of Crying Things in London* preserved in the Huntington. In the short history of broadsheet Cries, these engravings represent a little flowering just before the format is eclipsed by the ensemble. After 1688, they vanish for fifty-three years until William Hogarth's 'Enraged Musician' (1741) revives the depiction of many hawkers on one sheet.

Late seventeenth-century sheets, reacting against the thumb-nail scale and uniformity of earlier sheets, are notable for their readability and diversity. They differ not just from the Cries that precede them, but also from each other, as two examples show. *The Manner of Crying Things in London* (**2.6–2.37**), published in 1642, was formatted as sixteen designs cut on two tall coppers; only a single impression from one of these two copperplates has survived in this tall format (**2.6–2.26**). At a time when the print sellers Peter Stent and John Overton confined Hollar 'to hard Labour, and small Pay', to wit, twelve pence for sixty minutes measured 'by the Hour-glass', Stent sold *The Manner of Crying Things* for twice that amount – about two shillings – to buyers of the middling sort and rich collectors; Samuel Pepys and the second Earl of Ellesmere owned copies.[136]

The second example, another vertical sheet, survives as an untitled fragment bearing six hawkers (**2.38**). It was published about 1655 by Robert Walton (1618–88), who called himself 'the oldest in *London* of this way', meaning print selling.[137] In an advertisement entitled 'The names of severall Maps and Prints, that are Printed, Coloured, and sold by the said Robert Walton', he offered it as a surround for a map in words that link images of hawkers with cartography as complementary aspects of the same 'Ornament': 'This Map [*A Curious New and Plaine Mapp of England, Ireland, Scotland and*

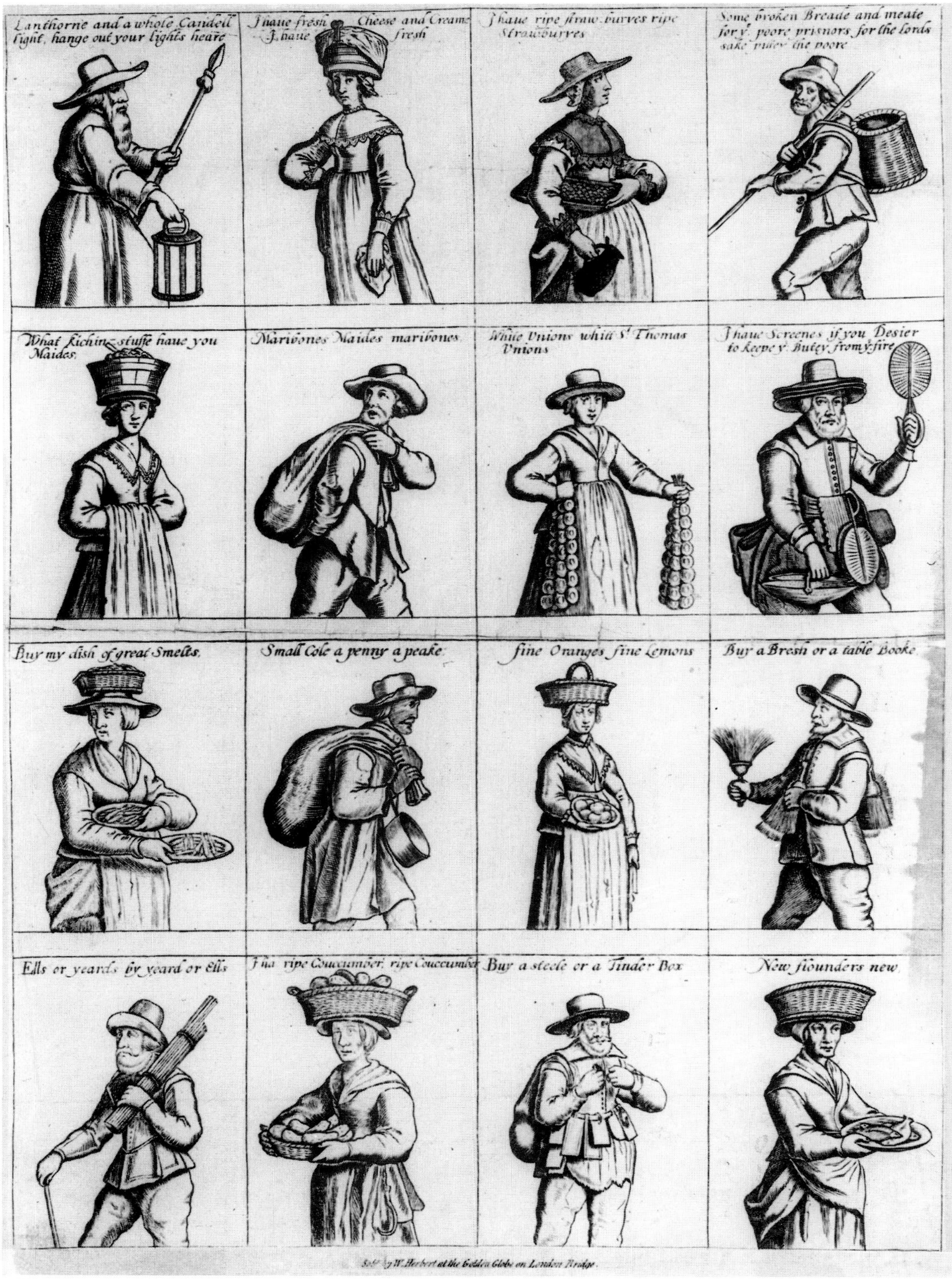

2.6–2.21 Anonymous, *The Manner of Crying Things in London*, c. 1644

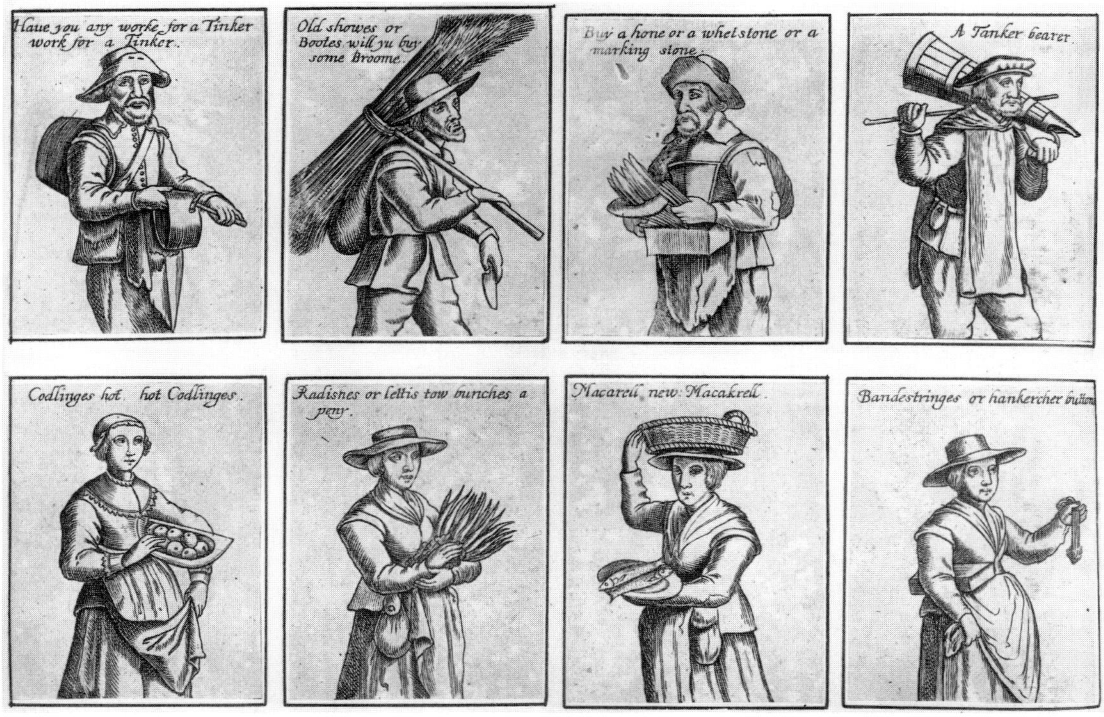

2.22–2.29 Anonymous, *The Manner of Crying Things in London*, c. 1644

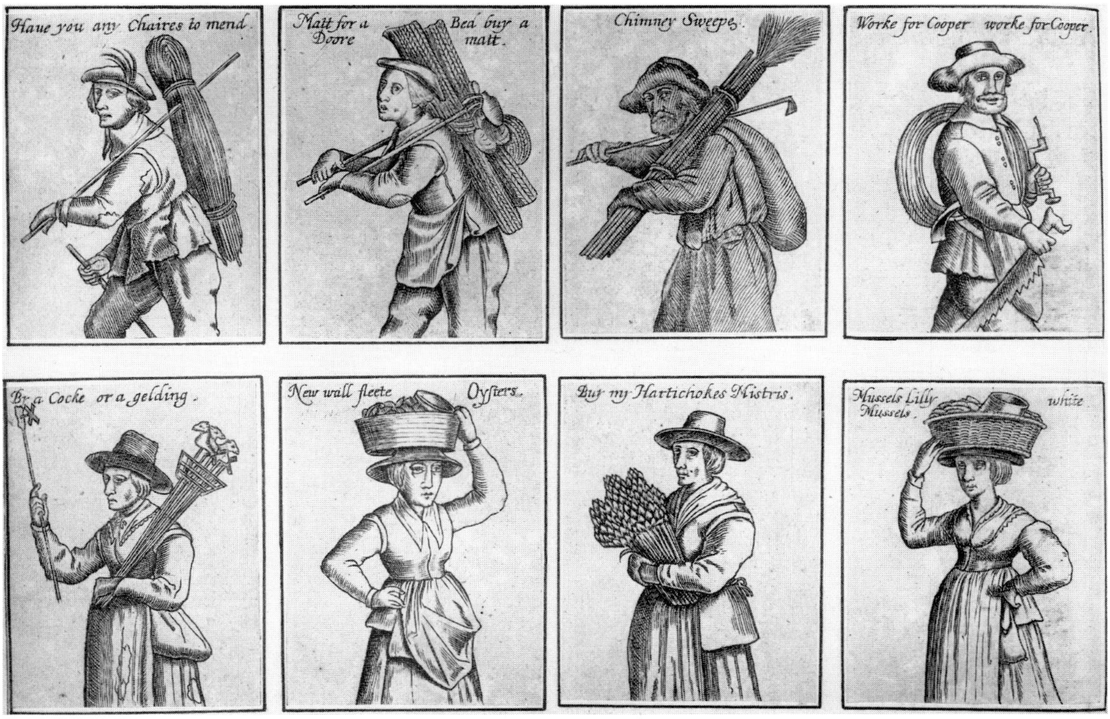

2.30–2.37 Anonymous, *The Manner of Crying Things in London*, c. 1644

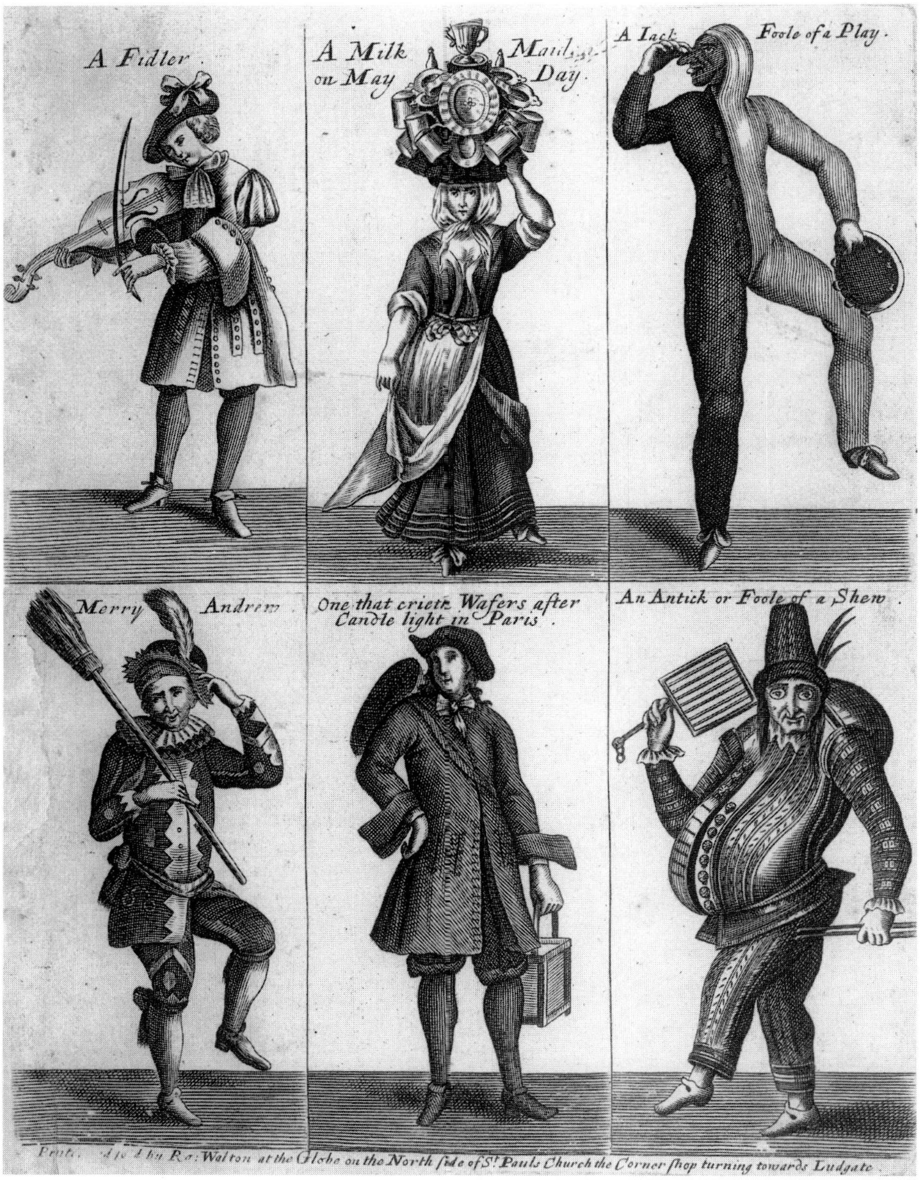

2.38 Robert Walton, *Cries of London*, *c.* 1655

Wales cut by Hollar], with a Description and a briefe Chronology of all the remarkable passages and actions that have happened ever since the long Parliament began 1640 to this present yeare; and this is a most commodious Ornament for every mans house, and therefore you may either have it in paper coloured or not, or else on Cloth, with or without Rollers and Ledges, or you may have it inlarged with severall Pictures, as the 5 Senses, the 4 Seasons, the 4 Elements, and the Cries of London and the like'.[138]

Stent's and Walton's sheets of Cries resemble and indeed dovetail with certain seventeenth-century Habits, most notably Hollar's *Severall Habits of English Women*

(1643) and its continuation in *Aula Veneris* (1644), translatable as *The Court of Venus*. All four titles are costume prints and reveal the link between Cries and Habits. Whether they are called Theatres, Cries, or Habits, all respond to as well as fuel a revolution in male and female dress. That revolution, inspired by France rather than Spain, took place when women, banished from the court of James I, returned to Whitehall shortly after Charles I ascended the throne.[139] Hollar's *Court of Venus*, esteemed a textbook in wielding the engraver's needle and so 'not to be judged without a magnifying-glasse', was marketed as 'Foreign Dresses' or the 'Habits of foreign women'. Hollar's *Habits of English Women*, *Court of Venus* and *The Manner of Crying Things in London* were sold by Stent, who charged four shillings each for the two Hollars. Specifically, Stent's and Walton's Cries complete and perfect Hollar's *The Severall Habits of English Women from the Nobilitie to the Country Woman, as They Are in These Times* (1640), which, except for one peasant, limits itself to British ladies of wealth and sartorial elegance.[140] Of the twenty-six portraits in *Habits of English Women*, sixteen show ladies of fashion wearing the grandest clothes that costumiers labouring for the Caroline court could tailor; one of these figures (**2.39**) is Queen Henrietta Maria (1609–69), the 'à-la-mode' French wife of Charles I.[141] Nine of Hollar's portraits show citizens who wear smart, stylish outfits; in this class, the woman with the scissors at her side (**2.40**) is a successful seamstress of the kind who sewed the elegant garments of the ladies begowned in the highest fashions. Only one figure in the book belongs to the lower orders; an afterthought, the last of the twenty-six figures is a dressy peasant – notice the pattens on her feet – hawking roots from a basket (**2.41**).[142]

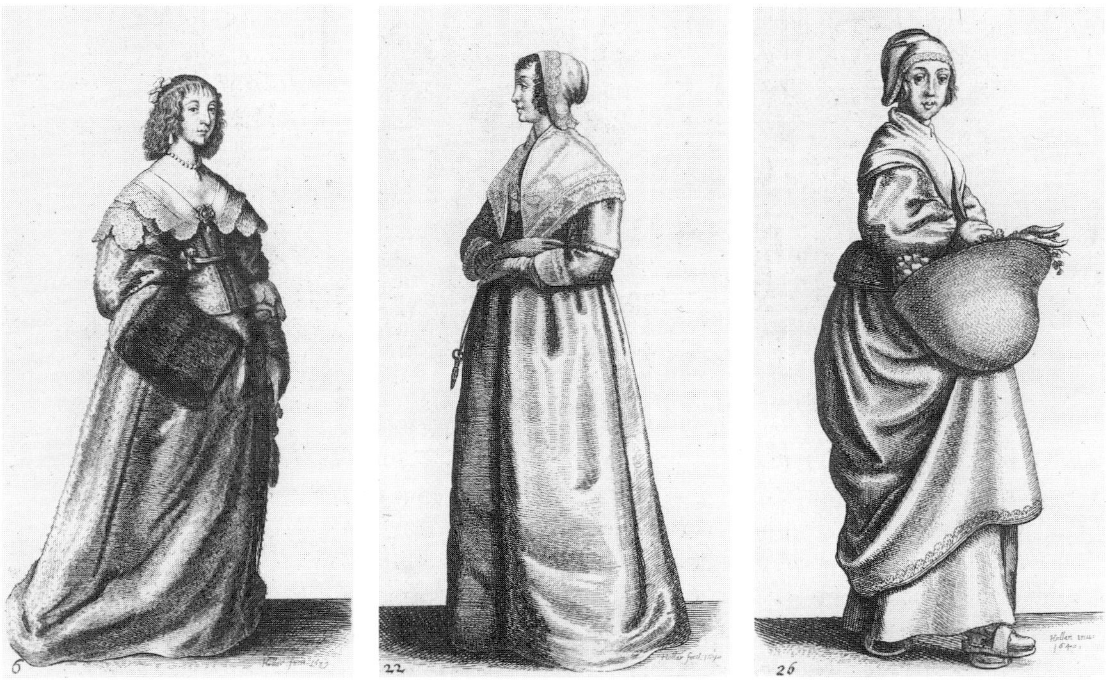

2.39–41 Wenceslaus Hollar, *Severall Habits of English Women*, plates 6, 22 and 26, 1640

The two post-1640 broadside Cries sold by Stent and Walton augment Hollar's narrow account of the costume of the rich by an equally narrow account of the costume of the London poor executed in vernacular styles. Taking up where the portrait of Hollar's rural vendor of roots stops (**2.41**), the sheets present urban hawkers' dress from different slants to enlarge the sartorial mapping of those urban classes slighted by artists working in Habits.

The broadside closest to Hollar's *English Women* is *The Manner of Crying Things in London*. Unlike Hollar's *English Women*, however, it defines costume as the occupational dress of the urban underclass, the garb that distinguishes street hawkers from other commoners but also from each other, by summoning up the special marks of their trades. Vendors, depending on what they sell, wear odd work garments, uniforms shaped by ritual, or stylish dress mandated by the unspoken wishes of the rich people they serve. The garb of some is protective, designed to shield their underclothing or bodies; the dress of others is contrived to ease drudgery. The tankard bearer (**2.25**), to repel water splashing from his cone, plies his trade in a narrow tabard of leather. Or is it baize? The codling seller (**2.26**) uses a short, broad apron to cradle apples. And the knife sharpener (**2.24**) arms himself in a breastplate of stiff leather to stop his abrasives from striking his chest and eating up his tunic. The raspy stones have already cut his apron down to a tiny, ragged triangle, an emblem of the over-production and under-consumption typical of all such wretches.[143]

Like *The Manner of Crying Things*, Walton's untitled London Cries is a conventional example of Habits, like Hollar's. Every figure, male and female, wears a distinctive, showy, or exotic outfit, except for the 'Foole of a Play'; and every one of these outfits is pictured with a dressmaker's precision. The Antick's coat of many colours is especially gaudy; the milkmaid's 'hat' or pyre is an eye-catching extravaganza of architecture and opulence. But the fiddler is the most intricately tailored of all, as appears in his stylish cockade, huge bow tie, gathered cuffs of pleated silk, and coat showered with buttons, tokens of money in the seventeenth century when they first appeared in England.[144]

Though Walton's sheet apes Hollar's *English Women*, its six figures have a smaller reach and cover a different territory. Five of its figures, tied to London's reviving theatrical and artistic life after 1660, perform rather than pose or sell; even its most conventional hawker, the dancing milkmaid (escorted by her 'fiddle', who supplies her music), entertains rather than toils. All five actors, strutting their parts in histrionic styles, use exaggerated gestures and wild, theatrical motions. Merry Andrew scratches his head in a deliberately quizzical way, while the other figures jump, dance and leap off their stages in a spectacular manner. The artful ebullience and high-spirited movement of this sheet's performers are as much a reaction to earlier broadsides like Stent's *Manner of Crying Things*, whose inert street vendors seem paralysed, as it is a reflection – and an enthusiastic embodiment – of what scholars call 'the commercialization of leisure', a movement hawking new urban entertainments organized for spectators rather than participants.[145]

Walton's thespians also reshape the London Cries, ushering in new figures who crowd out street sellers proper. Featuring dramatizations of frolic instead of ceremonial exhibitions of labour, the sheet broadens the scope of the Cries, shifting it away from mechanic trades toward witty, celebrative character books.[146] Such 'Theophrastan' treatises by Thomas Overbury, Joseph Hall, John Earle and Samuel Butler were at their zenith between 1608 and 1642, when they include in their repertory the Frenchman, the Fool, the Buffoon or Merry Andrew, the Fiddler who loves a new song, '& hates naturally the Puritan, as an enemy to this mirth', and the 'fayre and happy Milke-mayd' who is never alone, 'for she is still accompanied by *old songs*, *honest thoughts* and *prayers*'.[147]

By the time of Walton's death in 1688, broadsheet Cries were plummeting in popularity. Exhausting their creativity by over-borrowing, they were rendered obsolete and unfashionable by the appeal of the ensemble. Among ensembles, Laroon's from 1687 was the most influential. With its superior intricacy, illusionism, and especially its portraiture, it shifted Cries away from popular art toward 'high' culture.[148] The rise of the ensemble and fall of the broadsheet is heralded in the peculiar printing history of *The Manner of Crying Things in London*, which scholars have ranked 'the most sophisticated of the early *Cries of London*'.[149] Run off from a pair of large coppers, this work came from the press as two tall sheets, each measuring 42 × 31.5 cm and each bearing sixteen designs for a total of thirty-two. But the same plates were also used to run off thirty-two individual leaves in states that seem to be proofs. These thirty-two leaves were printed by means of a torturous strategy employing masks, one of which slipped when 'Have you any worke for a Tinker' was being impressed; the blunder (**2.42**) reproduced both 'A Tinker' and the bottom third of the abutting design, 'A Tanker bearer', accidentally 'unmasked' in the process.[150] After printing, the thirty-two individual leaves, each measuring 9.5 × 8 cm, were then bound together and sold as an ensemble. A single copy survives from the library of the second Earl of Ellesmere, who called it 'The Manner of Crying Things in London', a title of his own devising inscribed in his hand

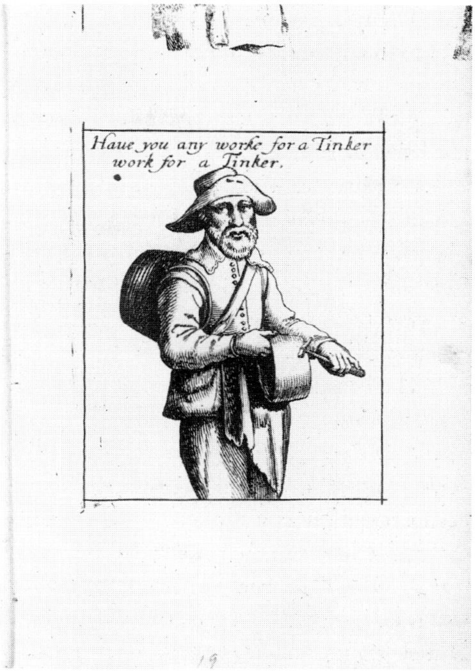

2.42 Anonymous, 'Have you any worke for a Tinker', from *The Manner of Crying Things in London*, c. 1644

about 1642.[151] A transitional work in chronology as well as in format, *The Manner of Crying Things* dramatizes, by its printing as a sheet and as an ensemble, the birth of that new paradigm.

In the late seventeenth century, when the fortunes of real hawkers began to tumble, print buyers and artists neglected broadsheet Cries, except for *The Manner of Crying Things in London*, plagiarized repeatedly and still in print in 1740.[152] No doubt iconic images depicting hawkers as stiffly industrious figures performing useful labours in an orderly way were novel and arresting when they first appeared. But these celebrations of the grandeur of the metropolis gradually lost what freshness and authority they first enjoyed, especially in the face of louder and more frequent complaints about real-life orange women, strumpets, foists, and bear-baiters loitering about the Royal Exchange who, in the tales of their neighbours from the respectable world, engaged in 'cursing and swearing to the great annoyance and grief of the inhabitants and passersby'.[153] As a seventeenth-century aesthetic of imitation was eclipsed by an eighteenth-century one of originality, these sheets, particularly the early examples with their standardized arcades and look-alike figures repeated from one sheet to the next with little development in approach, fell out of style. To English buyers with tastes increasingly tutored by fashionable prints from dealers like Arthur Tooker, who offered 'Italian, German and Low Countrey Prints', or John Garrett, who promised 'all sorts of large and small Maps and pictures, coloured and uncoloured, choice of all sorts of Foreign prints in Mitzo tinso, Dutch Prints, Drawing Books, and Coloured Pictures for Gentlewomens Works', even the most adventurous of these sheets looked coarse, mechanical and crude, much as they seem today to literary historians like Frank Percy Wilson and connoisseurs like Richard Godfrey who, in *Printmaking in Britain* (1978), relegates them a class of image represented by 'the crude woodcut purchased from a street-hawker's basket', which, Godfrey thinks, are 'best passed over in discrete silence'.[154]

After the Restoration, when French engravings came into vogue, English print buyers remained keenly interested in Cries. But in the course of the Georgian period, they sought the genre in engravings that were less naive, more stylish and up to date; in a word, more continental: more Dutch, more French, more Italian. Alongside these ordinary buyers, a smaller but wealthier class of patrons entered the print market, pulling it in an unexplored direction. These virtuosi demanded hawkers in designs that were still more naturalistic but also more contrived than those in the archaic broadsheets churned out to delight their less urbane fathers and grandfathers.[155] To satisfy such collectors, a coterie of foreign artists created innovative London Cries. However, they published them not as broadsheets, but as ensembles created by means of an entirely new technique, a novel style from the continent that Henry Peachem drew attention to in 'Of Drawing, Limning, and Painting' from *The Compleat Gentleman* (1636), where he described it as 'cut to the life, a thing practised but of later yeares'.[156]

3

Tailoring the poor: the ensembles of Laroon and Amigoni

THE LAST broadsheet Cries of the seventeenth century, Walton's untitled engraving, appeared between 1673 and 1688. The first suite, Marcellus Laroon's *Cryes*, made its debut in 1687, so the decline of the single-leaf dovetails neatly with the rise of the ensemble. Laroon's pioneering Cries, recently acknowledged 'the most interesting series of prints of this period', was continuously republished until 1739, when Jacob Amigoni challenged it with a rival suite.[1] These two artists' suites are the subject of the present chapter. Though Laroon (1653–1702) and Amigoni (*c.* 1685–1752) are of different generations, both men came to England from the continent, both cultivated English connoisseurs from the elite classes, and both shared a knowledge of the aesthetic traditions of France and Italy that shaped their depiction of hawkers. The chronological distance between their designs is further abridged by the popularity of Laroon's *Cryes* in the 1730s, when, republished twice, it moulded Amigoni's ensemble, also devoted to individual human figures. Both works establish the new suite's formal boundaries and stage its main debates, which shift from economic themes like the world of consumer goods to social stereotyping and aesthetics, issues internal to the genre.[2] Together the two suites propagate a current of innovative naturalism that runs from the end of the seventeenth century to the end of the Victorian age.

The engraved versions of both suites are the work of copper-scratchers cutting the 'inventions' of artists labouring for booksellers and print publishers. These artists, building reputations and claiming high rank, worked in an epoch when the rich middling sort, as well as connoisseurs and *virtuosi* among the aristocracy, first valued prints as art, estimated them for their originality, cherished them as capital investments and collected them as fashionable luxury goods. Marcellus Laroon invented *The Cryes of the City of London drawne after the Life* as an ensemble of forty individual sketches; but, in response to hot demand, he quickly expanded it to seventy-four designs. These were engraved, issued and reissued by various booksellers until 1821. To vie with Laroon's *Cryes*, in 1739 Jacob Amigoni painted a portfolio of four designs which are more cohesive than the Dutch artist's diffuse suite.

Like the craftsmen who cut the first Cries, Laroon and Amigoni were both foreigners; as late as 1702, when Anne became queen, London had no native artists of repute.[3] 'In London about 1700', George Vertue wrote as an eye-witness, 'the state of print engraving on copper was at a low ebb. Indeed Mr R. White was still living . . . but was declining much. & I think besides him could not be found any Master, as one may call so, in London'.[4] So Cries remained in the hands of continental artists who shaped it using French, Italian and Dutch conventions. Still, these two artists' careers differ from those of earlier immigrants like the Hogenbergs. The Hogenbergs came to England at the call of great patrons, whose households they joined and whose artistic agendas they executed.

By contrast, Laroon and Amigoni came to England without invitations. Moving to London for long periods of time or settling there permanently, they threw themselves on an open market that originated in 1660, when the Restoration promised artists patronage and prosperity.[5] That market peaked in the 1760s, when London dislodged Paris as the art capital of Europe, a national triumph Hogarth recorded and – ever the braggard – claimed credit for.[6] Laroon and Amigoni worked for themselves and for whatever public or private parties paid them. The Italian lived in England for ten years, leaving in 1739 with a fortune of £5,000 in his pocket; the Dutch artist emigrated there, dying of tuberculosis at Richmond in Surrey on 11 March 1702.[7]

More important, while the Hogenbergs were mere engravers, Laroon and Amigoni were artists: they drew sketches, executed commissions in oil and painted portraits, aristocratic as well as royal. Neither of them engraved, though some of their continental colleagues did, for example, Bernard Baron (1696–1762). Laroon's and Amigoni's ensembles, reflecting their creators' training and practices, differ from broadside Cries in scope, content and style. The costume images of Laroon's *Cryes* are devoted to social stereotyping. The child portraits of Jacob Amigoni's suite catch the atmosphere of the streets of London. Though a suite, its prints bear no generic title, such as 'Parte of the Criers of London'; instead each print has an individual label: 'Golden Pippins', 'Shoe-Black', 'Lamp-Lighter', and 'Chimney Sweeper'.[8]

Laroon's and Amigoni's suites employ a bigger scale than any of the early broadsheets in order to express the new importance of their subjects and to respond to what William Ivins calls 'the informational pressure' on prints, that is, the escalating imperative to cram more lines and information into the same space.[9] The space previously allotted to thirty-six peddlers within pot sheets measuring 18 × 26 cm now holds single hawkers, who appear on sheets of 18 × 27 cm for Laroon and 19 × 25 cm for Amigoni. This magnification nourished greater formal intricacy, which Laroon lavished on costume and Amigoni on face. Such changes gentrified the London Cries. They replaced popular English cuts with what the bookseller Philip Overton classified as 'large superfine Prints, curiously engraven' in the continental tradition of Bonnart, Bosse, Mitelli, but especially Annibale Carracci (1560–1609), whose eighty peddlers of food and drink from 'fat Bologna', etched forty-one years before Laroon's designs, were imitated all over Europe for two centuries.[10] Among artists like Laroon and Amigoni, Carracci's prototypes shaped a decisive awareness of the aesthetic worth of ambulatory traders. Among audiences in England as in Italy, they satisfied the curiosity of the middle classes by their account of different types of work done in the streets of Bologna, but they also enticed the nobility with their technical dexterity.[11]

In other ways, Laroon's and Amigoni's ensembles reflect shifts in the purpose and direction of the London Cries, changes best understood in light of the works' artists, publishers, audiences, styles and contents. The fact that they are signed by their creators reflects a jump in the status of Cries. They are the earliest examples of the genre to carry names, assertions of authorship by artists claiming the theme as their own and proposing it as a feature of their professional identities, such as might advance their careers.[12]

Both foreign masters were familiar with continental printmaking, which had a long tradition of Cries in which certain styles of engraving could claim the status of fine art. Laroon, born in the Hague to a father who was a painter of French extraction, trained in Holland before coming to England where, after the Restoration of Charles II, he hoped to become rich.[13] He toiled in London as a portraitist, and though he once painted Charles II, he earned his daily bread both as a hack illustrator exploited by booksellers and as a drapery painter, a trade then esteemed 'the lowest Degree of a liberal Painter', earning between half a guinea and a guinea a day.[14] Amigoni, far more prominent, was a Venetian decorative painter, etcher, and portraitist to the court of George II; he was the first of four famous artists whose names Joseph Andrews garbles when parading his connoisseurship in Fielding's novel. It is not a coincidence, I will show in chapter 5, that three of Joseph Andrews's 'Italians' created Cries: 'Ammyconni' (Amigoni) painted a quartet of London Cries; 'Hannibal Scratchi' (Annibale Carracci) sketched the *Cries of Bologna*; and 'Hogarthi' (the very English Hogarth) engraved 'The Enraged Musician'.[15]

Laroon, on the commission of the bookseller Pierce Tempest (thinking of what would sell briskly), drew pen-and-ink sketches of his hawkers. Amigoni, on his own initiative (casting about for a subject having a broad sale), painted oils of his.[16] He passed them to his engraver before selling them; two went to the Italian castrato Carlo Broschi, then ruling the world of English opera under the stage name Farinelli.[17] Laroon's pen-and-ink drawings survive; Amigoni's oils have perished.[18] The two artists' respective print sellers, Pierce Tempest and Joseph Wagner, cut the compositions on copper and sold them in London.[19] Wagner (1706–80), a German apprentice to Amigoni, charged about two shillings for his master's suite; Tempest got half a guinea for Laroon's.[20] So while both ensembles appealed to rich buyers, Laroon's luxurious folio of seventy-four designs also targeted connoisseurs and *virtuosi* from a wealthier class than the purchasers of Amigoni's economical cycle.[21]

What we know about Laroon's buyers and can surmise about Amigoni's confirm what the prices of their suites suggest. Wagner sold Amigoni's designs from his print shop in Great Marlborough Street, where he catered to serious print collectors belonging to the middling sort and some of their 'betters'. Tempest sold his *Cryes* to the same buyers from his shop at the sign of 'the Golden Head' in St James Street, Covent Garden. A speculator in fine prints, the leading dealer in old master drawings, and a man of many markets, he also advertised it in *The London Gazette*, where he paid ten shillings per insertion to cultivate a specific – and unlikely – audience.[22] In his notice of 18 May 1688 (run over and over again, indicating its effectiveness), he describes his *Cryes* as 'fit for the Ingenious and Lovers of Art'.[23]

Who were Tempest's 'Ingenious and Lovers of Art'? And did they really buy Laroon's and Amigoni's hawkers? Cries, picturing by office the meanest, most miserable inhabitants of the urban world, would not seem likely to entice *virtuosi*, especially connoisseurs from the nobility, who shunned low-life images and viewed commoners in art as the objects of laughter. Art theorists held as axiomatic the view that coarse, mimetic reproductions of low subjects from daily life were suited only to vulgar artists and vulgar publics, just as noble subjects shaped by beautiful abstractions could only be fully apprehended by patrician audiences.[24] Following a tradition going back to Aristotle, scholars of art and literature linked the social pyramid with the hierarchy of artistic genres and treatments. At the bottom of that pyramid, commoners enjoyed crude imitations of mean things; at the top, elites relished images of perfect humanity.

The educations, interests and incomes of the five people who are known to have owned the *Cryes of the City of London* ratify the view that Laroon's ensemble appealed not to a single class of collectors, but two such classes, the first interested in the subjects of representation and the second in its techniques. Three of the five people were city men belonging to the rich part of the middling sort; at least one, Pepys, was anxious to define his status against the 'lower orders' from which he and his ancestors (tailors by trade) had recently arisen.[25] Their names are Samuel Pepys (1633–1703), Narcissus Luttrell (1657–1732), and Zacharias Conrad von Uffenbach (1683–1734), who visited England from Germany in the early 1700s and wrote a book about his trip. These men, by what they published about Laroon's *Cryes* or scribbled in its margins, offer clues to its early reception.[26] Von Uffenbach, in *London in 1710*, writes of walking into a print shop to buy Laroon's engravings, which he pockets without a worry about price:

> After this we went into a print dealer's and bought the 'Cryes of London' in seventy-four sheets for half a guinea. In these engravings all those persons who hawk cheap wares, crying them in the street are represented from life with the words that they cry. They are similar to the 'Cris de Paris'. One can also obtain them with notes, for the curious tones that they call or sing can be freakishly imitated on the violin. They had no copies left of this last variety with the notes.[27]

Pepys, Luttrell, and von Uffenbach are a homogenous lot. Unlike the chief consumers of the first English novels, all are men. All had university educations (two attended Cambridge) and cultivated politics, literature and the arts. They owned personal libraries and collected books; they wrote avidly and read voraciously. They belonged to that coterie of bibliophiles, intellectuals and aspiring connoisseurs who, by their appetite for drawings, etchings and engravings, helped suckle a native tradition in printmaking after the Restoration. All were well-off; in Daniel Defoe's seven-fold reconstruction of society, they were 'The middle Sort, who live well' or even 'the Rich, who live very plentifully'. If von Uffenbach's published response to the *Cryes* in his travelogue is representative, they relished Laroon's prints for their subject matter – their faithful report of 'all those persons who hawk cheap wares . . . represented from life with the words that they cry'.[28]

But the *Cryes* appealed also to Defoe's 'Great who live profusely'; it surfaces in the libraries of Sir John Mill (1681–1706), fourth Baronet of Mottisfont, and William Cavendish (1640–1707), first Duke of Devonshire.[29] No one in this period was greater or lived more profusely than the first Dukes of Marlborough, one of whom acquired, for the library at Blenheim Palace, forty-nine of the artist's original sketches in pen and ink from which the *Cryes* was engraved.[30] Something about the ensemble of Laroon's low-life studies caught the eye of the aristocracy and nobility. What was it?

The Cryes of the City of London was the brainchild of Pierce Tempest, a prosperous, crafty bookseller. To advance his trade, this man proudly recorded his name in big letters in the middle of the ensemble's title page. The artist's name, in contrast, has to be hunted down, for it is relegated to the bottom of the page, where, in tiny letters, it perches outside the design's border: 'MLauron delin'. Tempest's first edition of the *Cryes* was an instant success. Within a year, he boosted it from forty to fifty, then sixty, then seventy-two copper plates; he finally stopped at seventy-four in 1689.[31]

Tempest chose which of Laroon's designs would be engraved; in culling the artist's herd of hawkers, the publisher prefers fetching figures in the style of the balletic strawberry seller (**3.1**). Balancing men with women, he favours beautiful over grotesque figures and high characters over low.[32] His control also surfaces in the designs' formal borders, copied from Jean Baptiste Bonnart's *Cris de Paris* (1676). These three heavy lines, not present in the sketches, are understated by comparison with the baroque frames of early broadsides. By focusing the eye inside the frames, they emphasize the individuality of the portraits, distancing them from sheets that depict hawkers collectively.[33] They also imitate the formal characteristics of paintings in mats and frames, imparting what Sir Joshua Reynolds calls 'a more consequential air,' signifying aesthetic worth and cash value.[34] These are no fly sheets made for alehouses and taverns.[35] They are instead 'superfine Prints' fit for staircases but especially closets, those private rooms where wealthy people invited particular friends in moods of intimacy, engaged in 'closet meditation', or withdrew from the world, as Pepys did, to admire their 'plates, very neat'.[36]

Finally, Tempest's hand appears in the prints' legends, rendered in English, French and Italian. When London was a backward outpost in the international print trade (publishing little that a continental buyer would look at twice), Tempest designed his suite to sell in France and Italy, where a lucrative market for Cries flourished. So 'Madam Creswell' becomes 'Une Maquerelle', slang for an old procuress; and Colly Molly Puffe's fantastic sounding name turns into a baker's generic cry, 'Bonne Patisserie a vendre', evidence that these French and Italian captions really were aimed at overseas buyers and not designed as status markers to impress English buyers. Cleverly, the same French and Italian captions allowed the suite's publisher to snare foreign tourists visiting London, where pilgrims like von Uffenbach were eager to carry home pictures of the sights they had seen in England.[37]

So much for the cast that the publisher gave to the *Cryes*. But what about the artist? His stamp is the fluidness, the monumentality and especially the pioneering mix of aestheticism and naturalism in every print. But his most characteristic innovations are two: his flamboyant costume painting, a technique he plundered from high art to apply to the garments of hawkers; and the potpourri of bizarre or menacing characters banned from previous Cries.

A face painter in his own right, Laroon earned his bread and butter as a costume painter in the workshop of Sir Godfrey Kneller (1646–1723), who established picture-manufactory 'upon as regular principles as the fabricating of carpets at Kidderminster'.[38] Laroon won repute in his own day 'as an exact Drafts-man; but he was chiefly famous for Drapery, wherein he exceeded most of his contemporaries', according to Bainbrigge Buckeridge, England's first art historian.[39] Neglectful or incompetent in drawing hawkers' countenances, Laroon gave most the same round-faced head with the wide eyes, introducing beards, 'scarecrow' hair, and a few wrinkles here and there for diversity. Though a portrait painter, he had trouble even with this simple formula: for five characters, he had to glue new faces over botched old ones.[40]

By contrast, he pictured clothing with uncommon flair in an age when methods of portraying the dress of the rich favoured formulary treatment pioneered by his German employer, Kneller, whose assembly-line portraits all looked 'like copies of the same original' because they were manufactured as

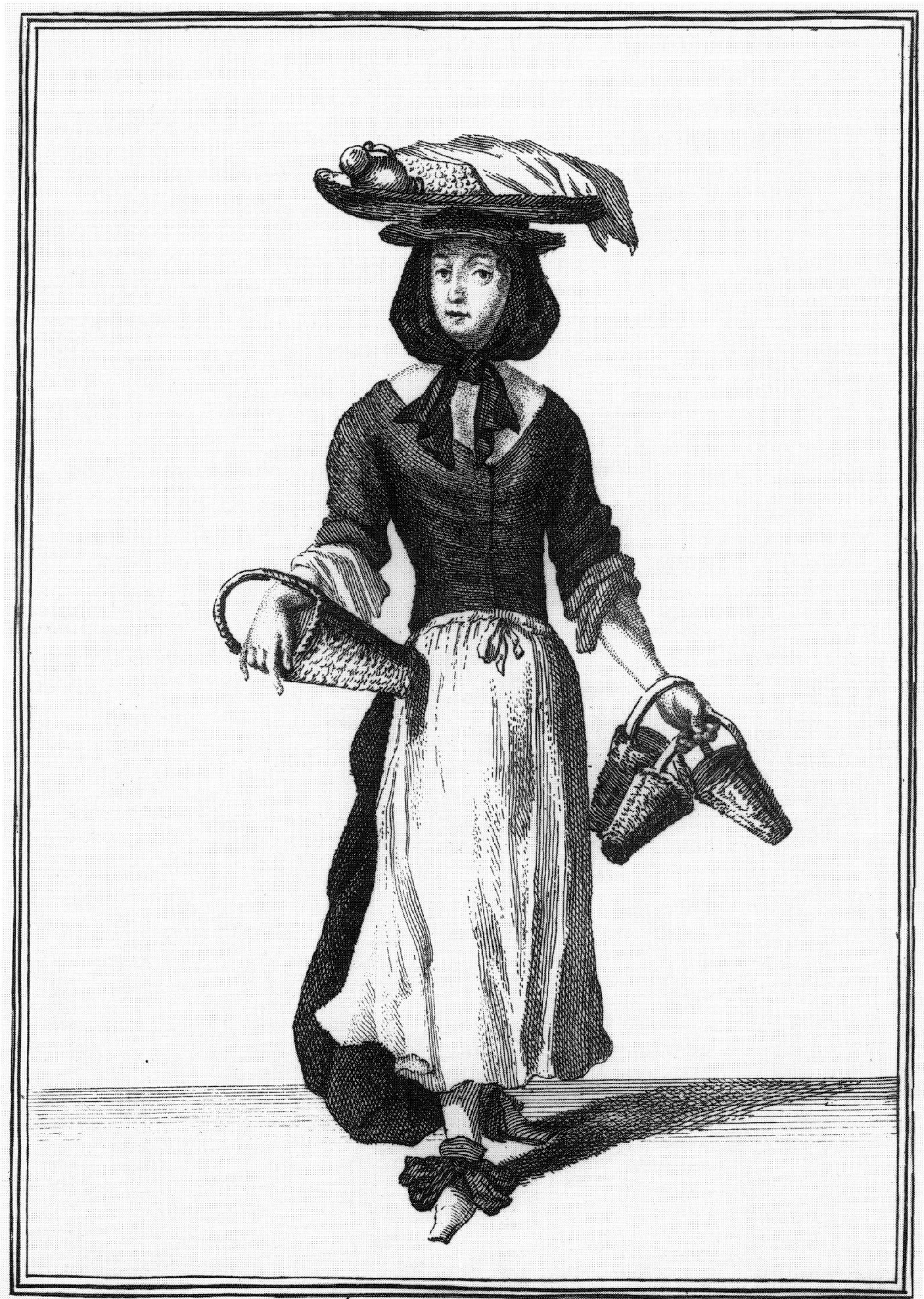

3.1 Marcellus Laroon, 'Ripe Strawberryes', 1687

such:[41] 'When he had finished the face and sketched the outlines of the shoulders, etc., the picture was given to the artist who excelled in painting a hat, and when the hat was fixed upon the head or tucked into the arm, the canvas was consigned to the painter of the periwig, who, having given eternal buckle to the flowing white curls which hung in ample ringlets on each shoulder, turned it over to another who gave the glossy blue velvet coat' and on and on.[42] Laroon, drawing on his mastery of drapery painting, sketched the jackets, trousers, and gowns of street characters with an expressive unity, rendering dress as an ensemble in which attention to what hawkers wore was balanced by concern for how they wore it. He fetishized dress, giving it, in addition to its functional role, displaced energy and social significance.

Dress in Laroon's suite, however, signifies not wealth and honour, as in contemporary portraits, but poverty and infamy in their many degrees. He makes *The Cryes of the City of London* into a suite of fashion plates picturing the styles of the wretched.[43] Laroon's virtuosity as an artist of costume (then called Habits) and posture (then called Action) was of paramount importance to Tempest, who understood the appeal of these subjects to elite audiences and made a calculated attempt to exploit them. In advertising the suite, he changed its title from *The Cryes of the City of London Drawne after the Life* to 'The Cryes and Habits of *London*, both Men and Women, drawn after the Life, in great variety of Action and Dresses'.[44]

Laroon's focus on Habits records a sartorial revolution as important as housing, diet, literacy or medicine. Early broadsheets use costume to fix calling, class and gender.[45] 'The Bellman of London' (**2.1**) differentiates dress by giving men breeches and women gowns. Abandoning the broadsides' rigid tableau of costume, the *Cryes* delineates dress dynamically; it offers a succession of widely different economic states and vivid local impressions that transform hawkers into figures of large social relations. Laroon's seventy-four peddlers fill up six of Defoe's scale of seven 'sorts'; their classes – the degrees of precariousness in which they exist – appear in the state and the repair of their clothes. Besides a taxonomy of 'native' London costumes, these images of hawkers are themselves a treatise on social hierarchy and its stereotyping as much as they are illustrations of how hawkers actually clothed themselves and lived.[46]

At the bottom of Defoe's ladder stand 'the Miserable, that really pinch and suffer Want'; they are represented only by the tinker (**3.2**), who covers his nakedness with his shredded jerkin and decayed breeches. Such images of intense misery are rare in all Cries. Just above him in this hierarchy of city types are 'the Poor, that fare hard', like the pregnant wax and wafer seller (**3.3**); indifferent to appearance, she goes in a torn apron and a skirt that is eaten up by wear. Next come the common poor, the urban version of Defoe's 'Country People, Farmers, &c. who fare indifferently', like the mackerel seller (**3.4**), whose clothes are intact, but shoddy and endlessly mended. Above her are the 'the working Trades, who labour hard, but feel no Want', described by Defoe as the sort who eat 'more Beef and Bacon'; their garb is not stylish, but it is plain and neat, like that of the dignified old woman plying forks and fire shovels (**3.5**).

Halfway up the ladder are the 'middle Sort, who live well'; they cultivate a Sunday-best look every day of the week, as does the peddler of lemons and oranges (**3.6**). Women like her are depicted as better dressed than men in support of the new cliché about the propensity of females for fashion.[47] Her swank gown of glazed wool, sketched from behind to reveal its architecture, is pinned back in a low bustle, and its distinctive square

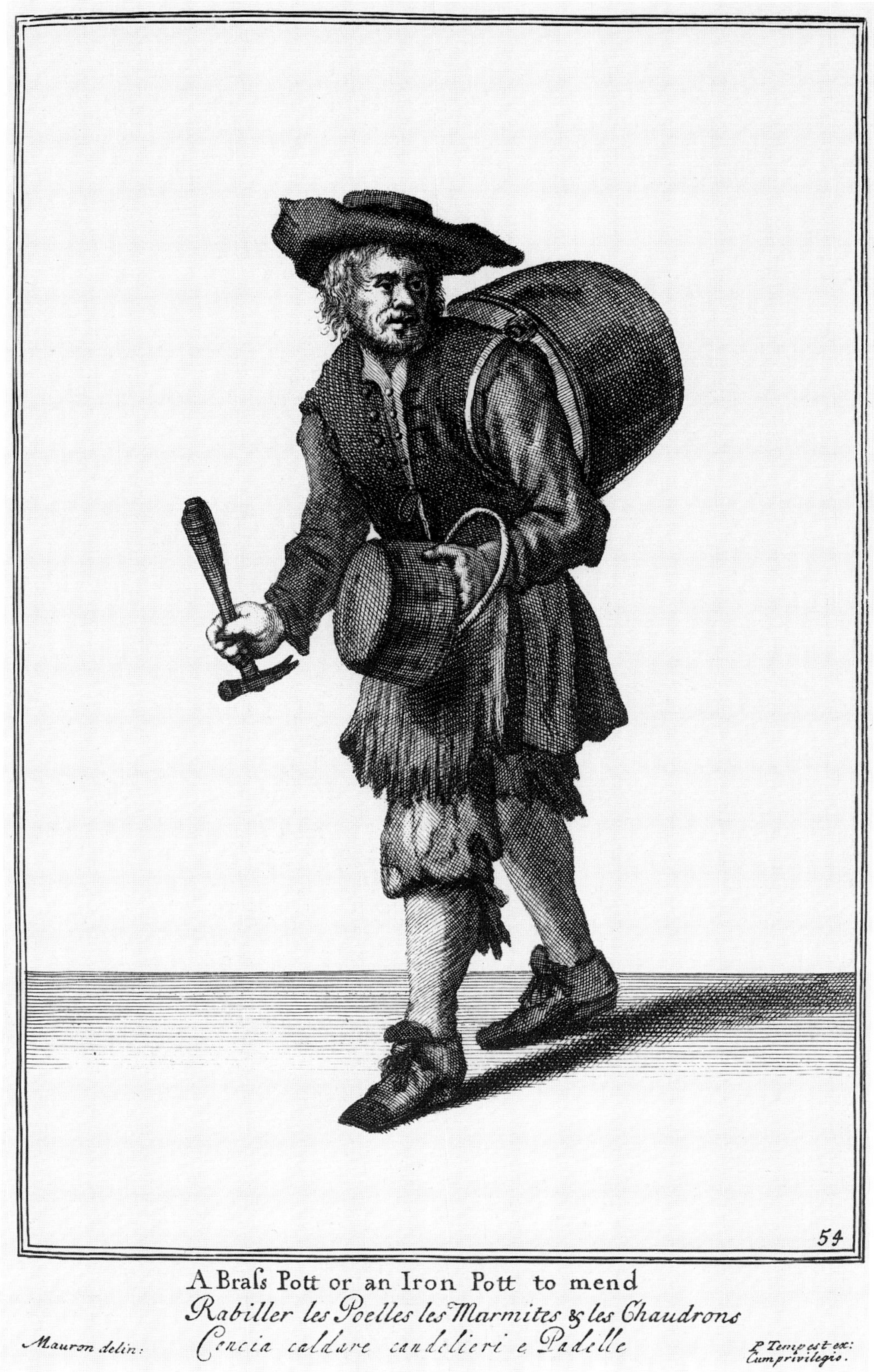

3.2 Marcellus Laroon, 'A Brass Pott or an Iron Pott to mend', 1687

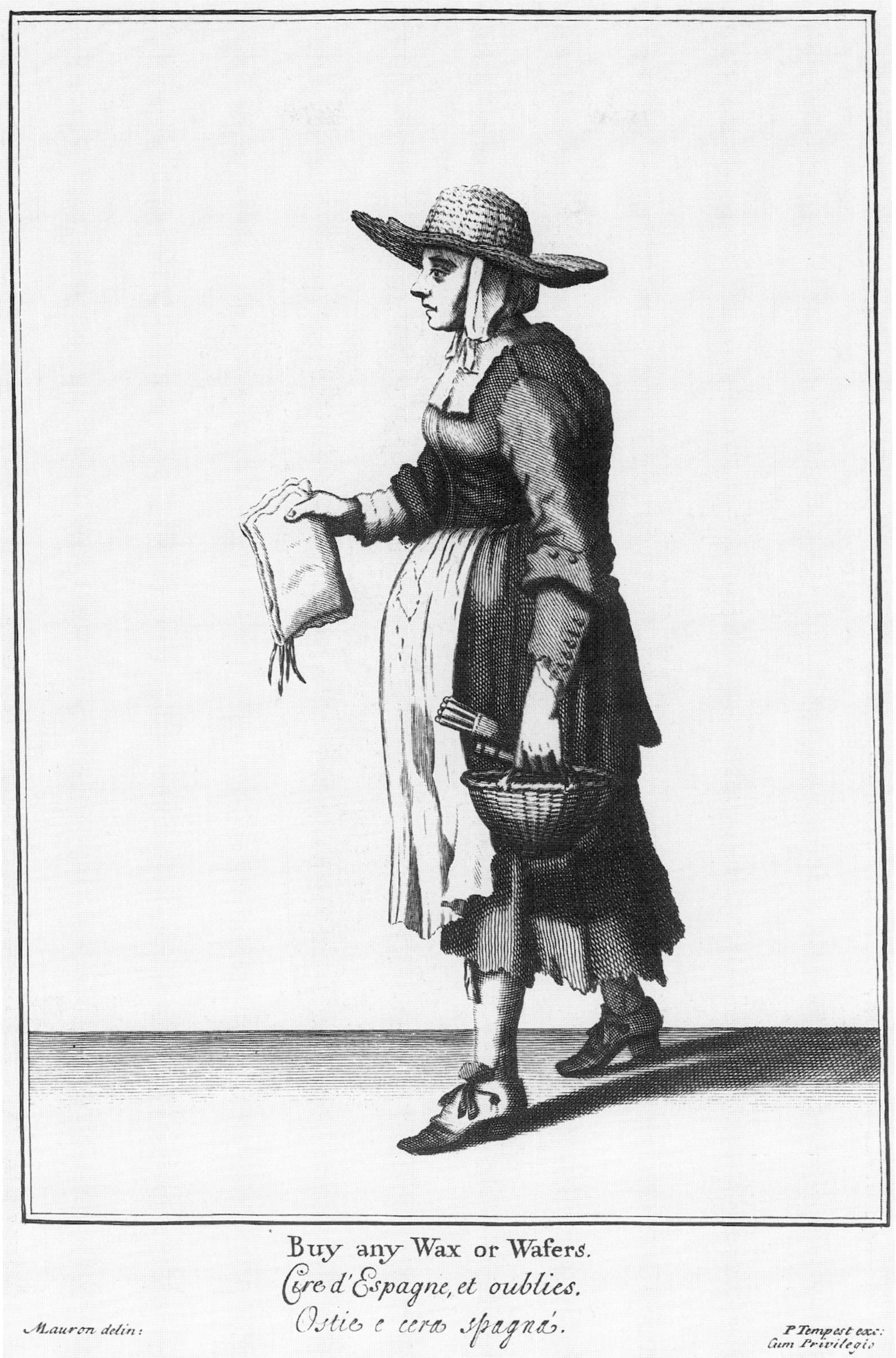

3.3 Marcellus Laroon, 'Buy any Wax or Wafers', 1687

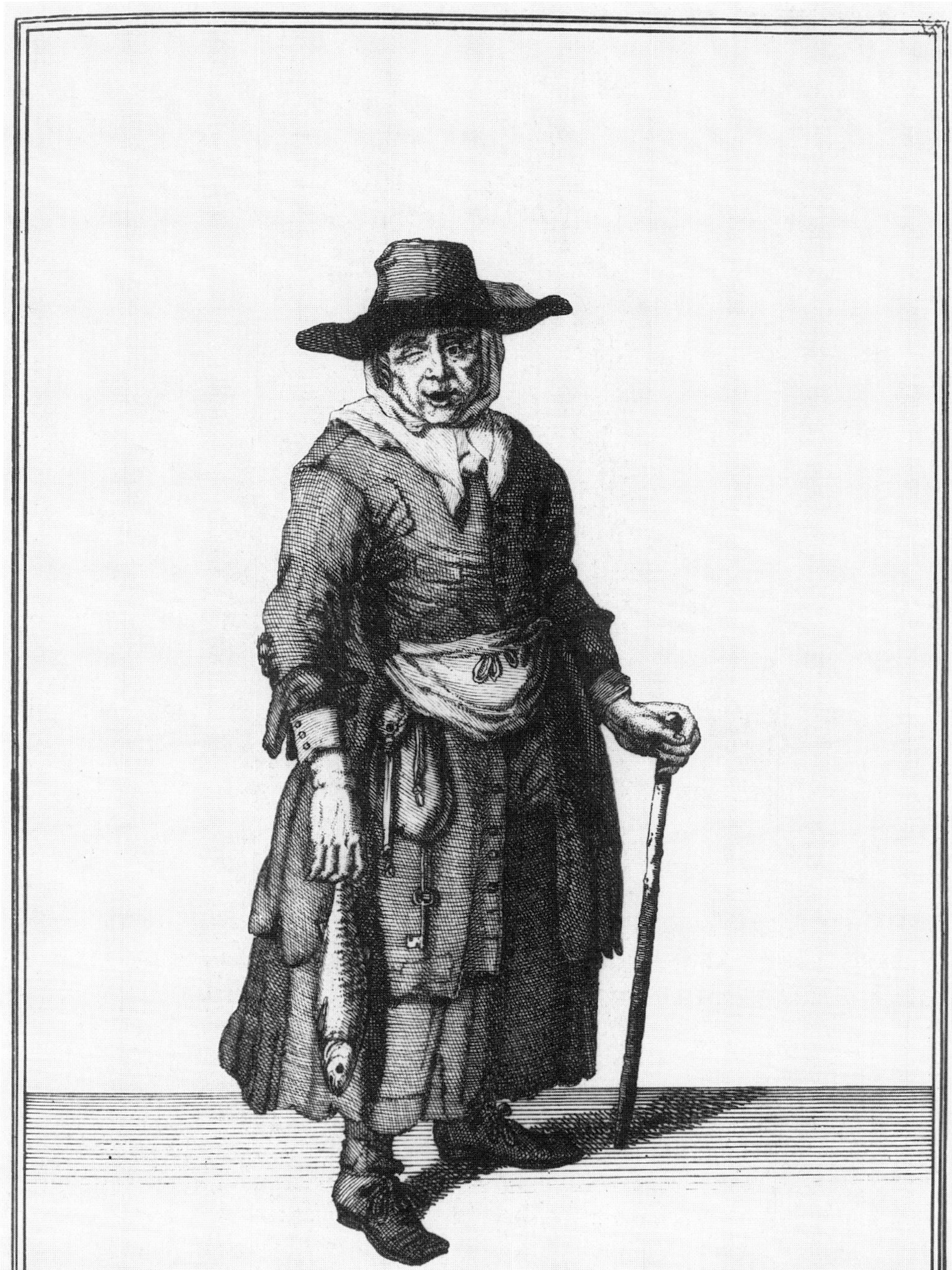

3.4 Marcellus Laroon, 'Four for Six pence Mackrell', 1687

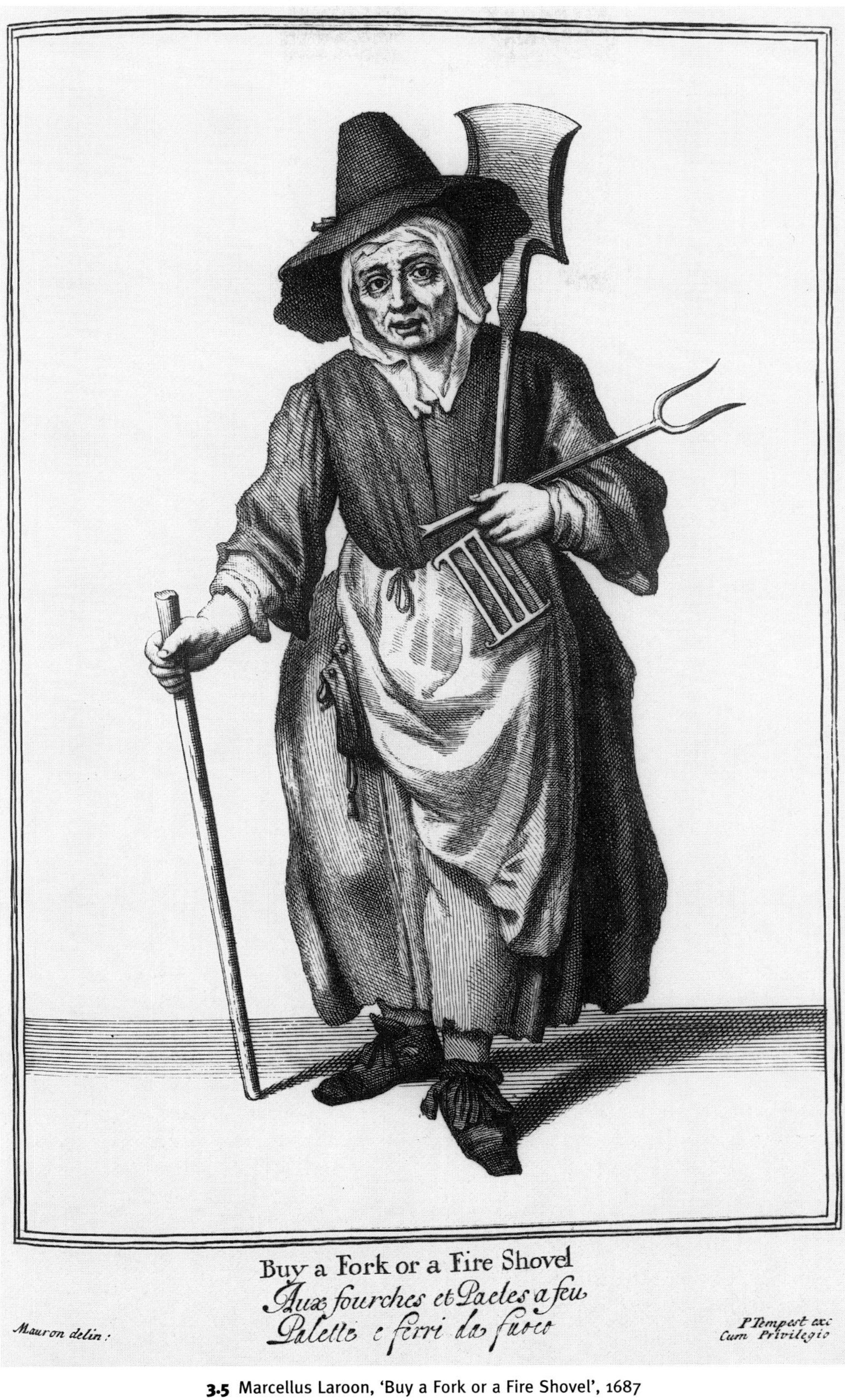

3.5 Marcellus Laroon, 'Buy a Fork or a Fire Shovel', 1687

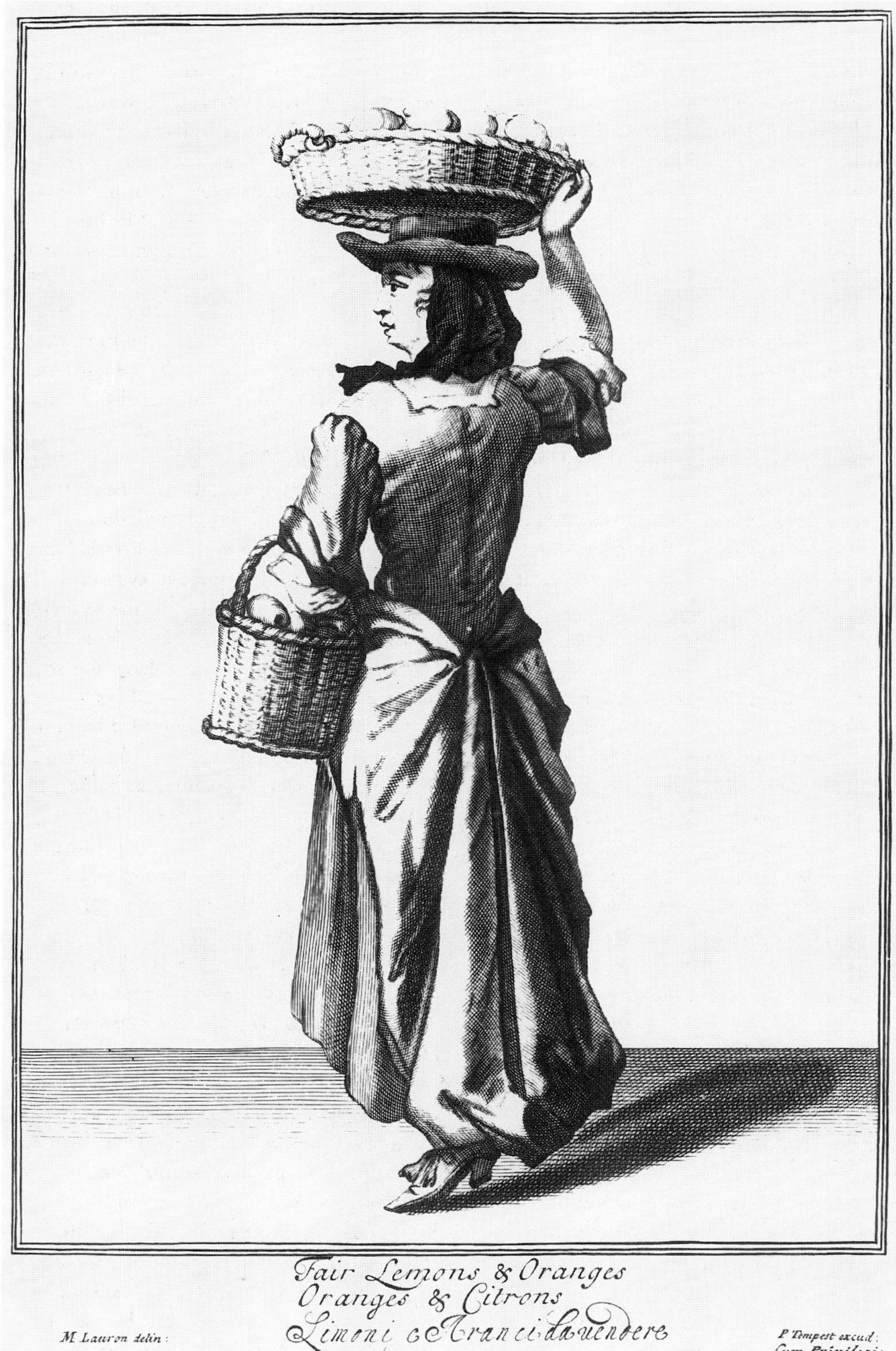

3.6 Marcellus Laroon, 'Fair Lemons & Oranges', 1687

neckline has a small border. Compared with the Dutch clogs worn by the hawkers from 'The Bellman of London' (created before footwear became a fetish), her shoes are glorious art forms with symbolic and decorative ornaments: she follows the style with half-moon toes and high heels, then coloured bright red. Laroon does not feature any of Defoe's top sort, 'the Great, who live profusely'. But surprisingly, he does include 'the Rich, who live very plentifully', linking them to his menacing figures, as I will show.

A portrait painter with his own studio and clients, Laroon uses dress not only for social and economic taxonomy but also for characterization. He catches dispositions and eccentricities in what his figures wear, but more subtly still in how they wear it. Coats and gowns personalized by men's and women's obsessions, quirks and rituals, some conscious and others unconscious, suggest an early psychology of clothing. The tatterdemalion coat of the mackerel woman (**3.4**) shows her deep poverty, but beyond that, the determination with which this resolute stoic has kept herself and her unique hand-me-down going, patch by patch. Her stout, padded look discloses something else: she is wearing several layers of clothing. Perhaps she has on her complete wardrobe because she has nowhere safe to store what was the most valuable of her worldly possessions? At the opposite end of the spectrum, the dealer in old satin (**3.7**), suffering a different professional deformation, wears an outlandish mix of the flamboyant garments she has picked up on her rounds. Its centrepiece is a dazzling stomacher in echelles, which she wears with elbow-length mittens, in a mood of smugness that tells how important a touch of class is to street vendors trading in fancy clothing, for whom it is part of their professional identity as well as a means of displaying status within their own social hierarchies. The most important garment of the kitchen grease buyer (**3.8**) is her long white apron. In a ritual that is both eccentric and intricate, she buries one hand under this 'safeguard' and hides the fingers of the other hand beneath her left arm – for warmth. But her short-sleeved shift has exposed the limbs of this fashion addict, and scooping up messes of clammy, frigid 'kichen stuffe' (tallow or pork fat sold to candle and soap makers) has chilled her arms and hands. Laroon, to show that her limbs are raw and blue, crosshatches them, proving that he has kept the promise of his title page to draw hawkers 'after the Life'.

Attending to accessories like headgear with their special powers of revelation, Laroon evokes aspects of criers' lives hitherto ignored: their politics, religion, even the places from which they hail. By the testimony of his bare head (in an age when the poorest of men, women, and children dared not step into the street without a hat), 'Oliver C: Porter' (**3.9**) is a Puritan, confirmed by how he shaves his skull (as well as by the letter C for Cromwell, whose ignominious name could not be spelled out in 1687). The long, curly hair and distinctive hat of John Kelsey (**3.10**) buttresses the legend's claim that he is a Quaker, a sect whose adepts shunned 'Babylonish' adornments in dress. Contemporaries read this hat, with its wide brim, moderate crown and flat top as a digest of the testimony of Friends in favour of humility and against frivolity.

Vendors' outfits even hint at their home towns, shires or countries: some wear regional costumes, others follow international fashions. The slouch selling chickens (**3.11**) is not, as we might first suspect, a forestaller, that is, a city hawker who buys cheap from farmers and trucks dear to townspeople. His shoes show him a rustic; they carry, in their heels, little tufts of grass lodged there when he walked across Norfolk's hay fields.[48] The vinegar seller (**3.12**) wears a rose in his dishevelled

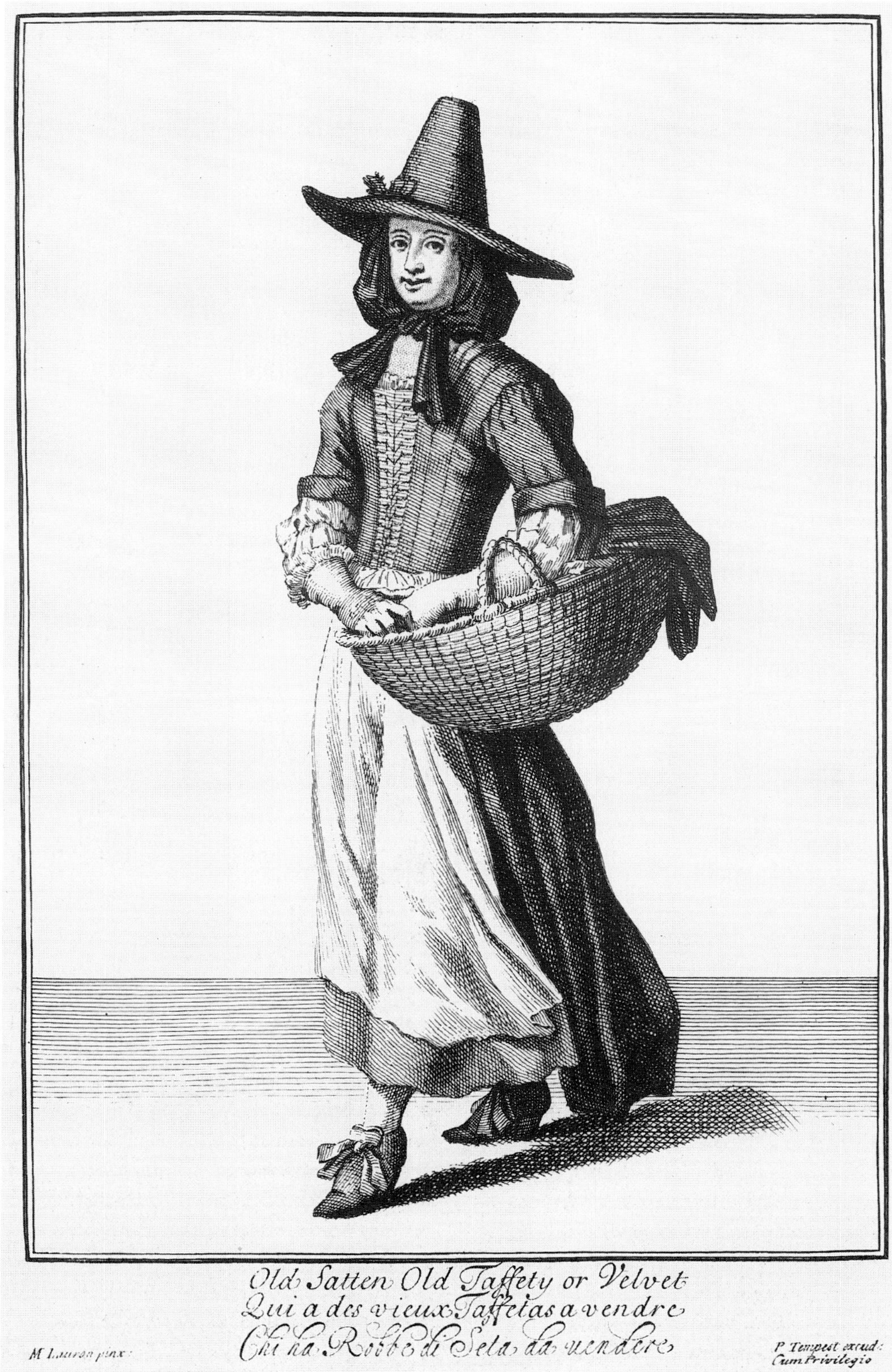

3.7 Marcellus Laroon, 'Old Satten Old Taffety or Velvet', 1687

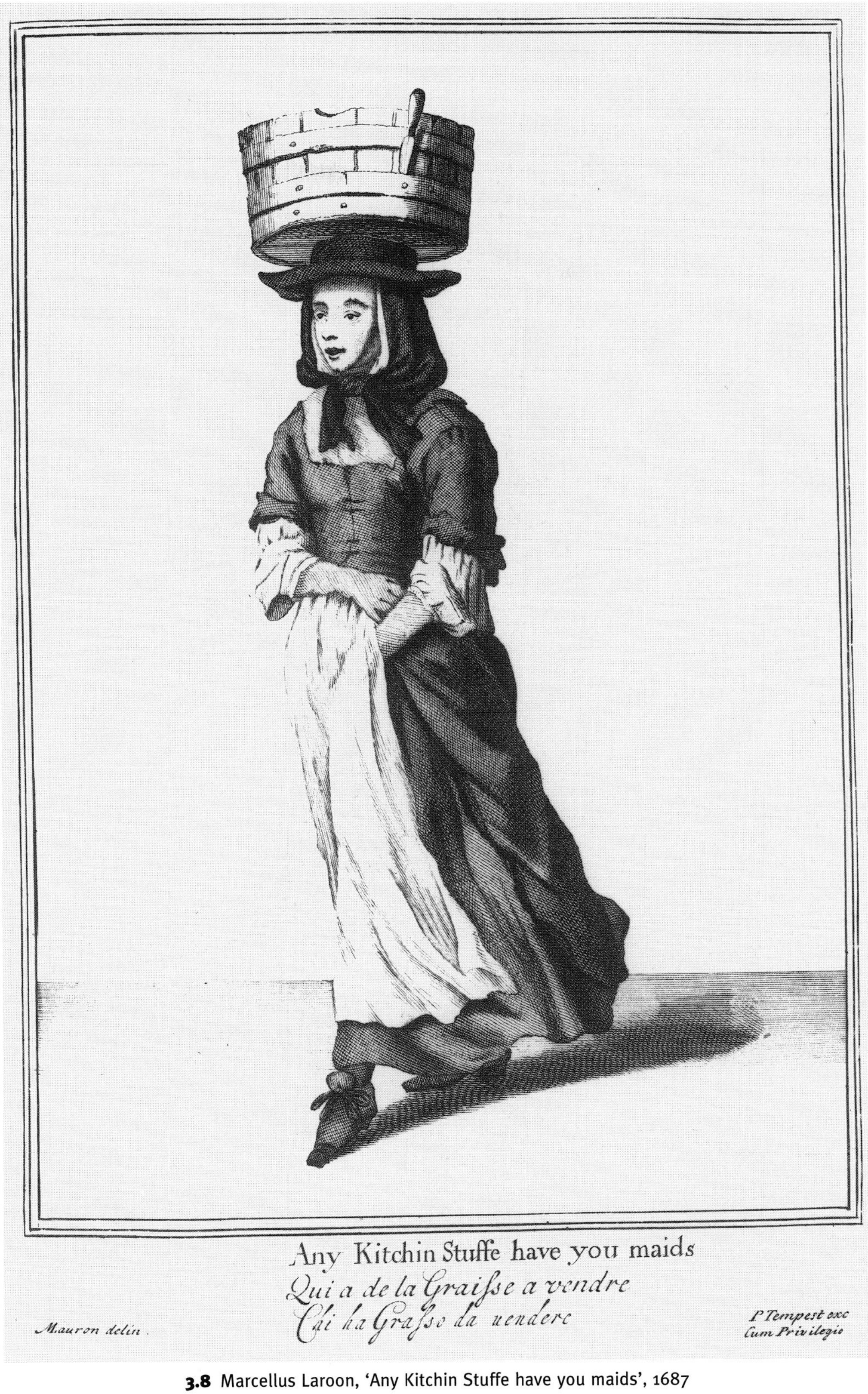

3.8 Marcellus Laroon, 'Any Kitchin Stuffe have you maids', 1687

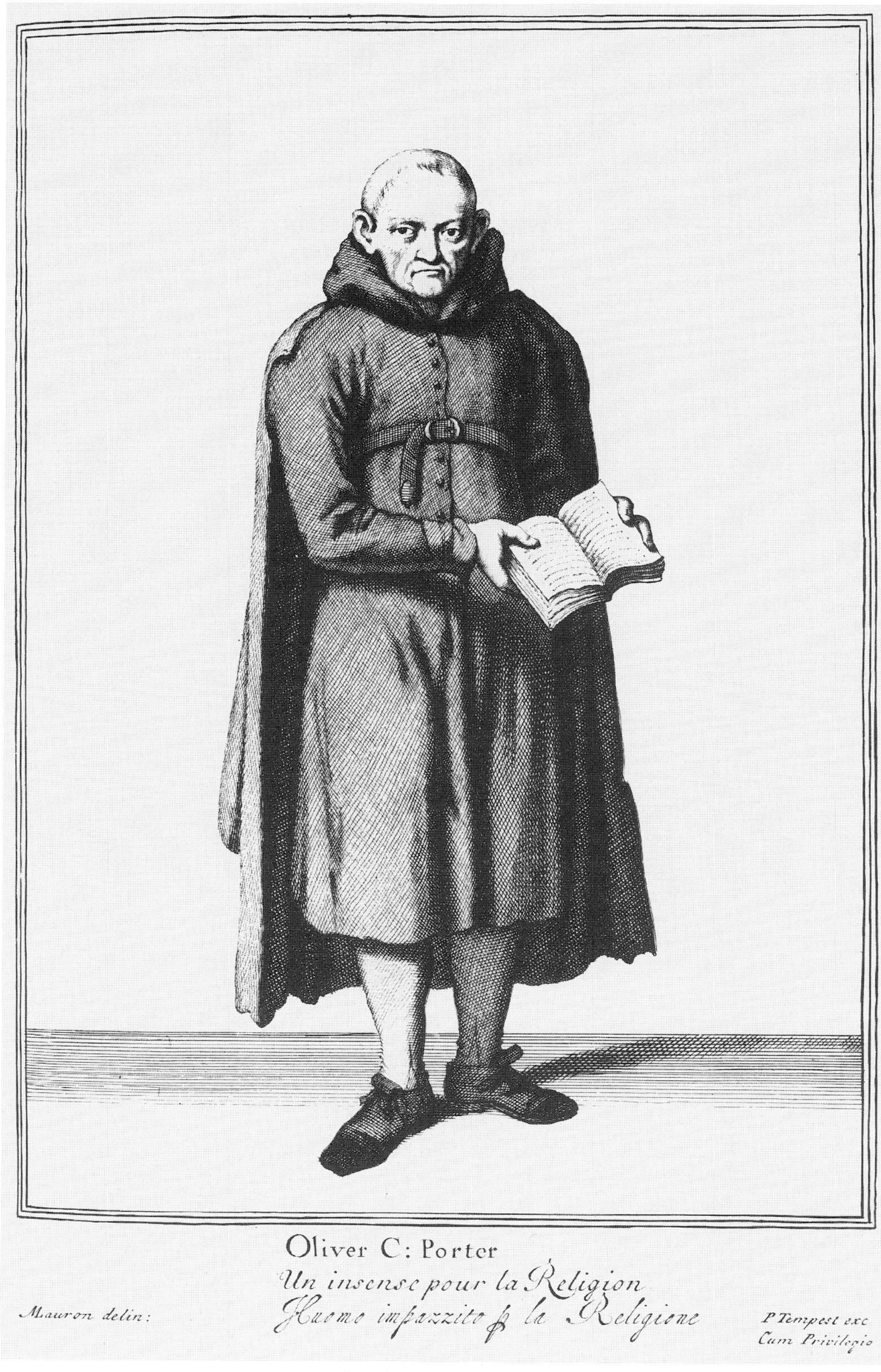

3.9 Marcellus Laroon, 'Oliver C: Porter', 1687

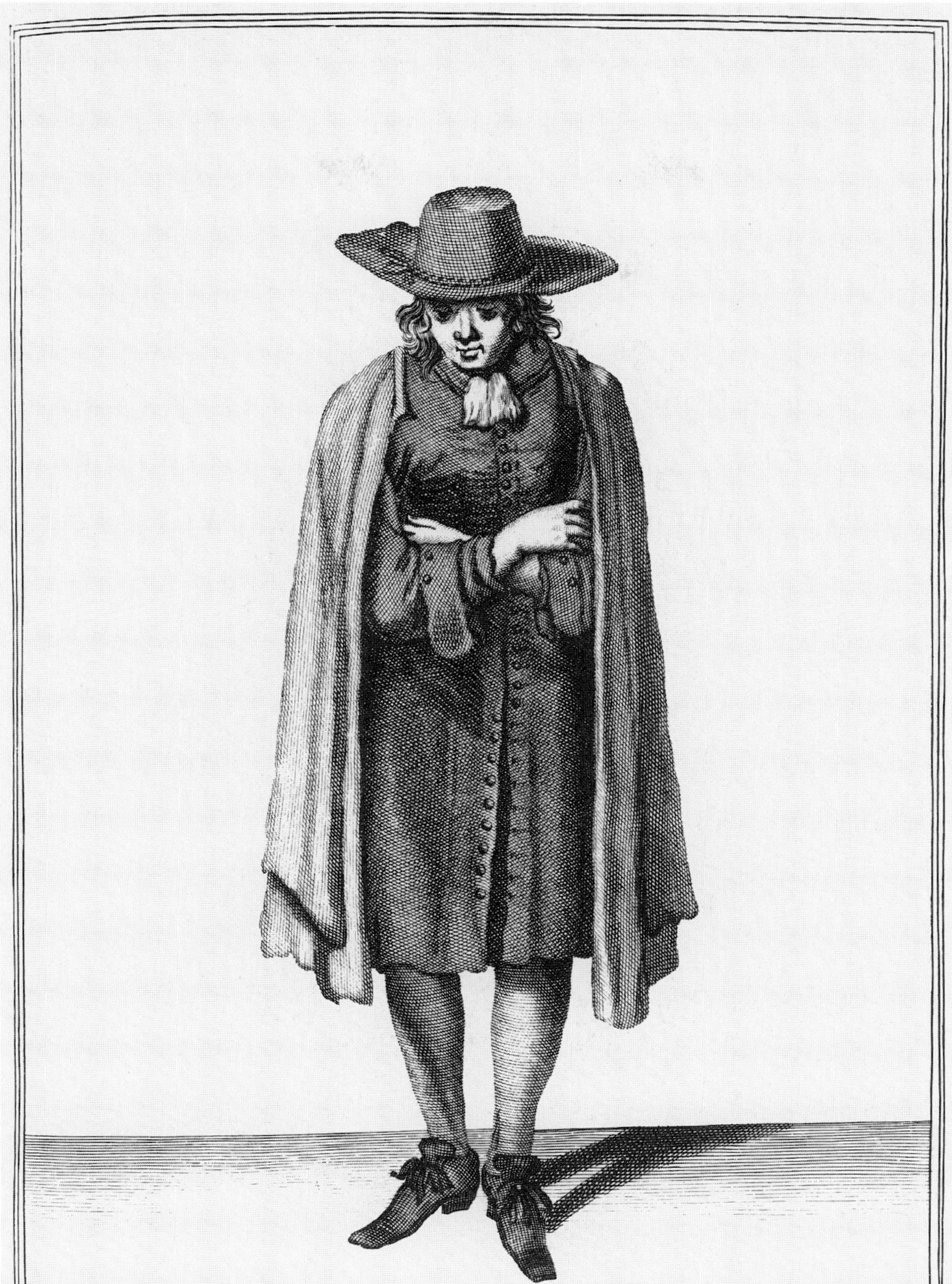

3.10 Marcellus Laroon, 'John the Quaker', 1687

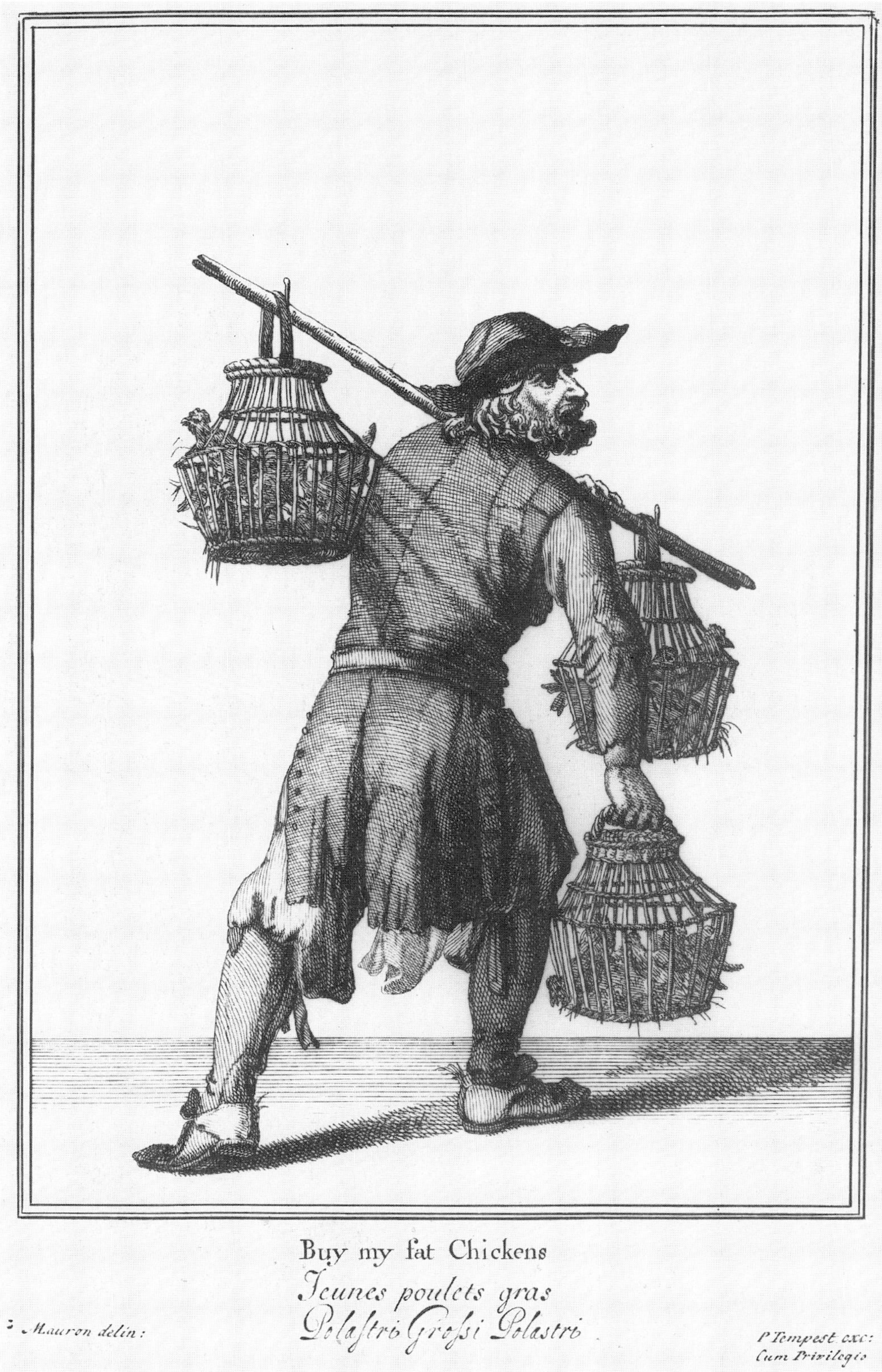

3.11 Marcellus Laroon, 'Buy my fat Chickens', 1687

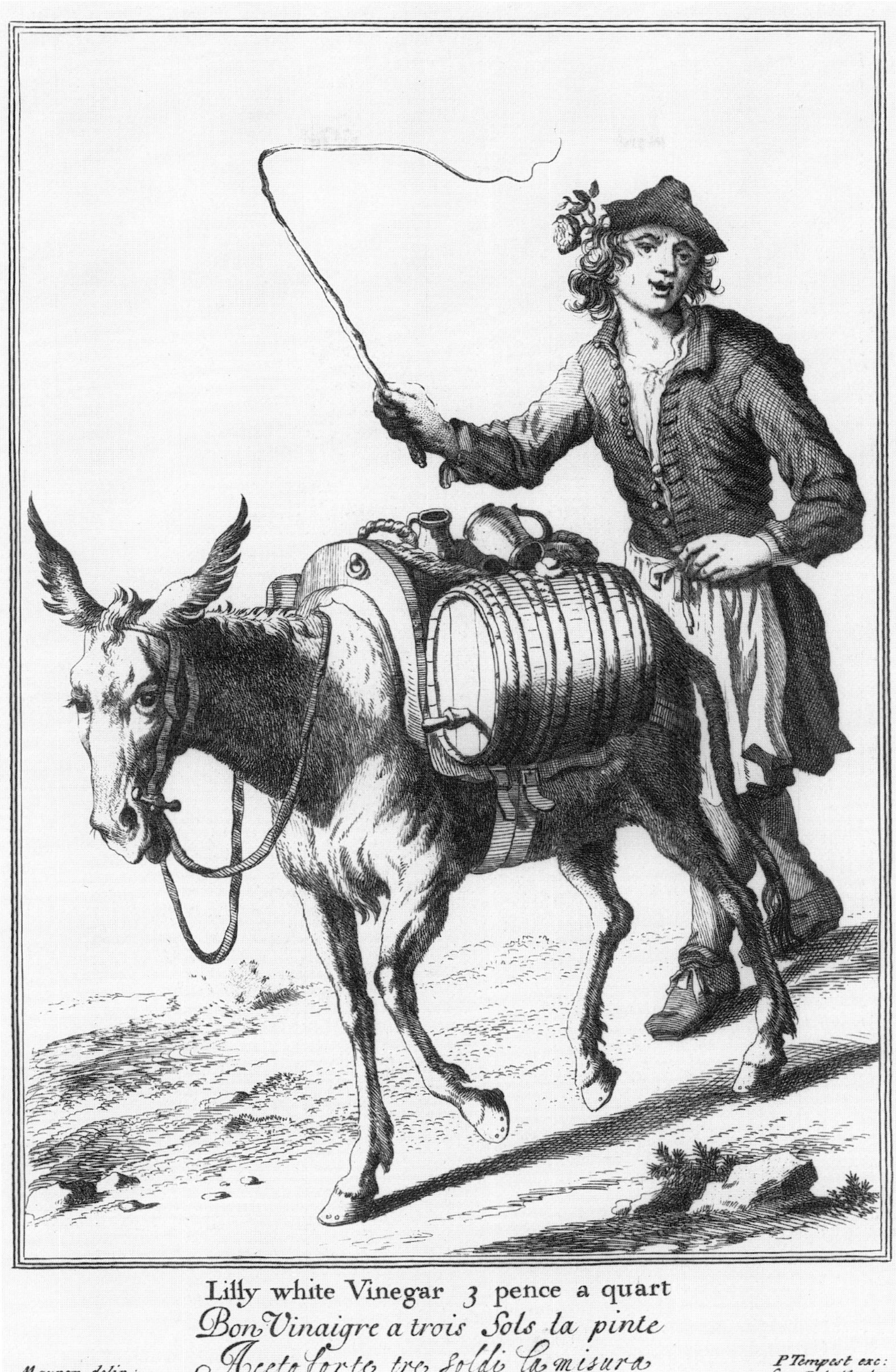

3.12 Marcellus Laroon, 'Lilly white Vinegar 3 pence a quart', 1687

hair, bringing to mind the country postilion travelling to London whom Carl Moritz noticed because he wore a bunch of flowers at his breast.[49] In addition to his rose, he wears his shirt and tunic unbuttoned in an age when constricting the neck was a sign of gentle birth; he is less a street character or a vinegar seller than a personification of England's peasantry. At the opposite end of the sartorial spectrum, the magnificent Don (**3.13**) follows a style combining careless ease and full control; his menacing Toledo rapier vies with his lace ruff, five scarlet rosettes and Spanish cloak tailored in diabolical black.

Laroon's characters from different economic, geographic and religious realms also include 'the Rich, who live very plentifully', exemplified by the Spanish Don, whose dress, stylish and opulent, conjures up gentlemanly wealth. But the Don is not the only envoy of affluence in the *Cryes*. The Squire of Alsatia (**3.14**), costumed even more richly than the Spaniard, wears a hat ornamented with white ostrich feathers and an enormous periwig, one chic ringlet of which cascades down his chest to demarcate him as an English aristocrat 'à-la-mode'. Among women, Madam Creswell (**3.15**), with her splendid petticoat, goes as a gentlewoman, while her 'niece' (**3.16**), waving a fan and wearing a petticoat of embroidered silk, appears as a fine lady traipsing off to a masquerade. Sandwiched between the ragged almsman crying 'Remember the Poor Prisoners' and the shabby London beggar (**3.17**), this platoon of splendidly costumed figures seems out of place here. What are such characters, Defoe's eaters of 'more Veal and Lamb, Fowl and Fish . . . more Butter, more cream, more white Meats', doing in an ensemble in which the dreary beggar freighted down with her still drearier children is a more typical and likely sight?

Notwithstanding their fine costumes, these 'wealthy' Londoners are not who they seem. In appearance, they are rich and respectable; in reality, they are all dastards. They misuse costume to conceal their villainous occupations, illustrating Fynes Moryson's jeremiad, that in his degenerate days, 'the very Bankrouts, Players, and Cutpurses goe appareled like Gentlemen'.[50] The Squire of Alsatia (**3.14**), though he appears to be a gentleman, is one of the scoundrels Moryson warns against.[51] His cozenage is chronicled by Robert Greene: booted, cloaked, and wigged after the newest fashion, he spies a country fellow, apprentice or sailor; immediately, the Squire 'letteth drop twelve pence in the highway that of force the Cony must see it'. When the gull snatches it up, the coney-catcher cries, 'Half-part' and quickly adds, 'Nay, faith, friend, 'tis ill luck to keep found money'. Away to the tavern they both trot, where out comes an old deck of cards. 'The first wager is drink, the next twopence or a groat and lastly, to be brief . . . he [the coney] loseth all they play for, be it a hundred pounds'.[52] Such trulls, foists, and stalls appear amongst Laroon's hawkers just after Londoners woke up to Greene's warning, 'Beware the cutpurse and cony-catcher'.[53]

Still farther beyond the pale of lawful society, Laroon features outcasts among the outcast, even though, like the Alsatian Squire, these figures also seem rich and respectable. Madam Creswell (**3.15**) represents a real-life Restoration panderer 'adept in all the diabolical arts of seduction'.[54] Her beautiful companion, the 'London Curtezan' (**3.16**), is a harlot going by the name of 'Mrs. Russel' who, like other strumpets, leads the field in women's fashions.[55] The two women, who play the 'aunt' and 'niece' gambit, are immoral as well as criminal. Their conduct, placing them beyond the boundaries of London's civil and religious communities,

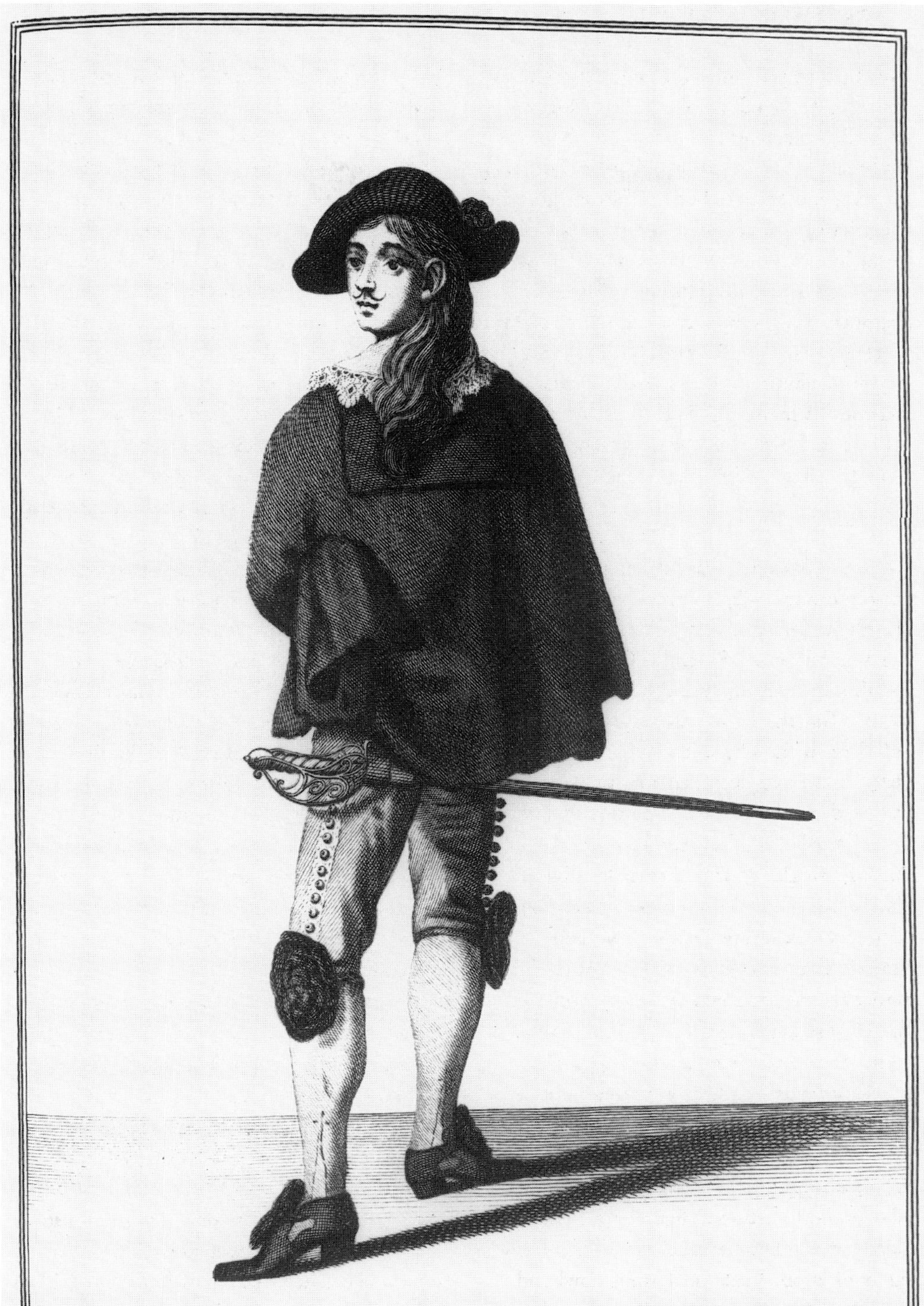

3.13 Marcellus Laroon, 'The Spanish Don', 1687

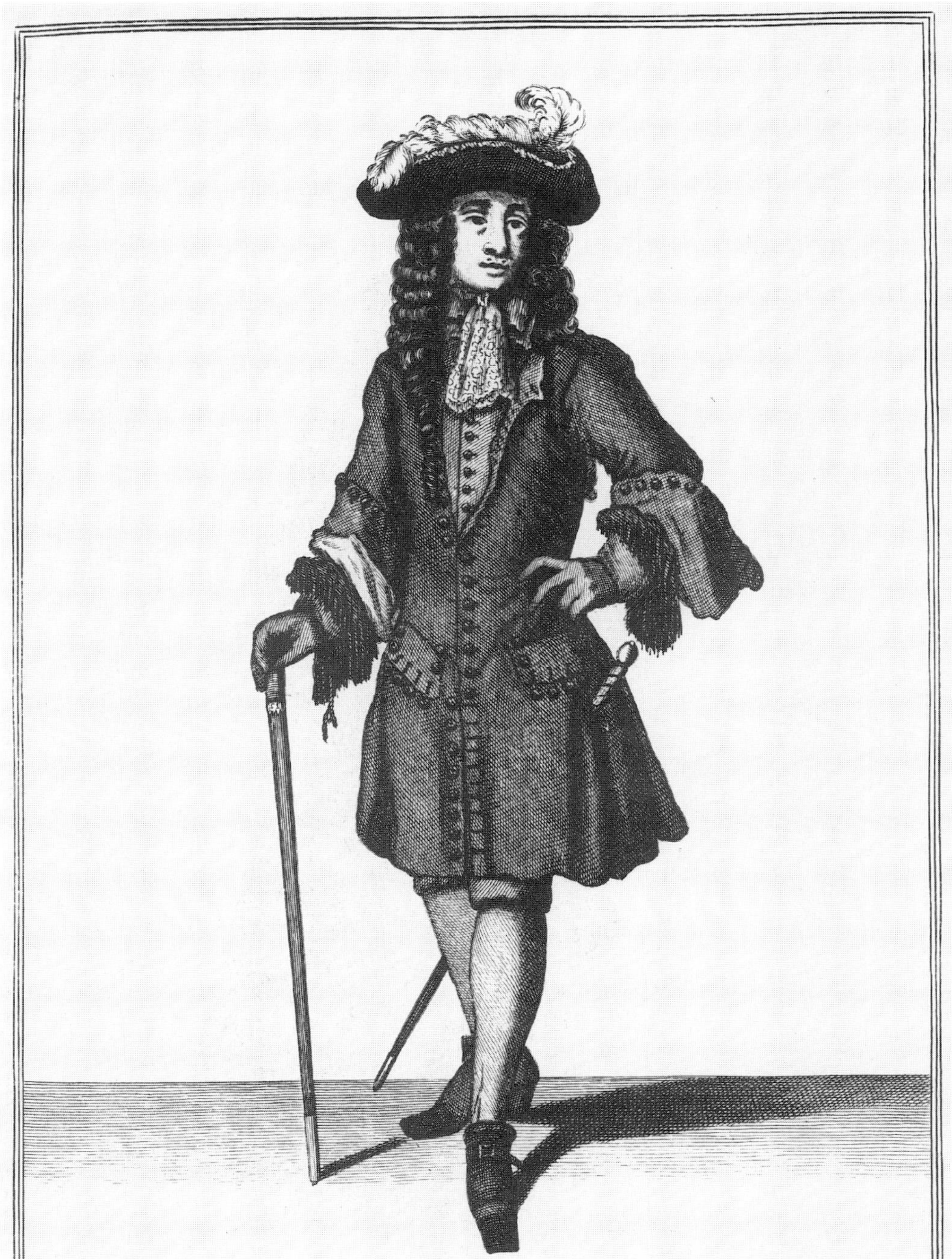

3.14 Marcellus Laroon, 'The Squire of Alsatia', 1687

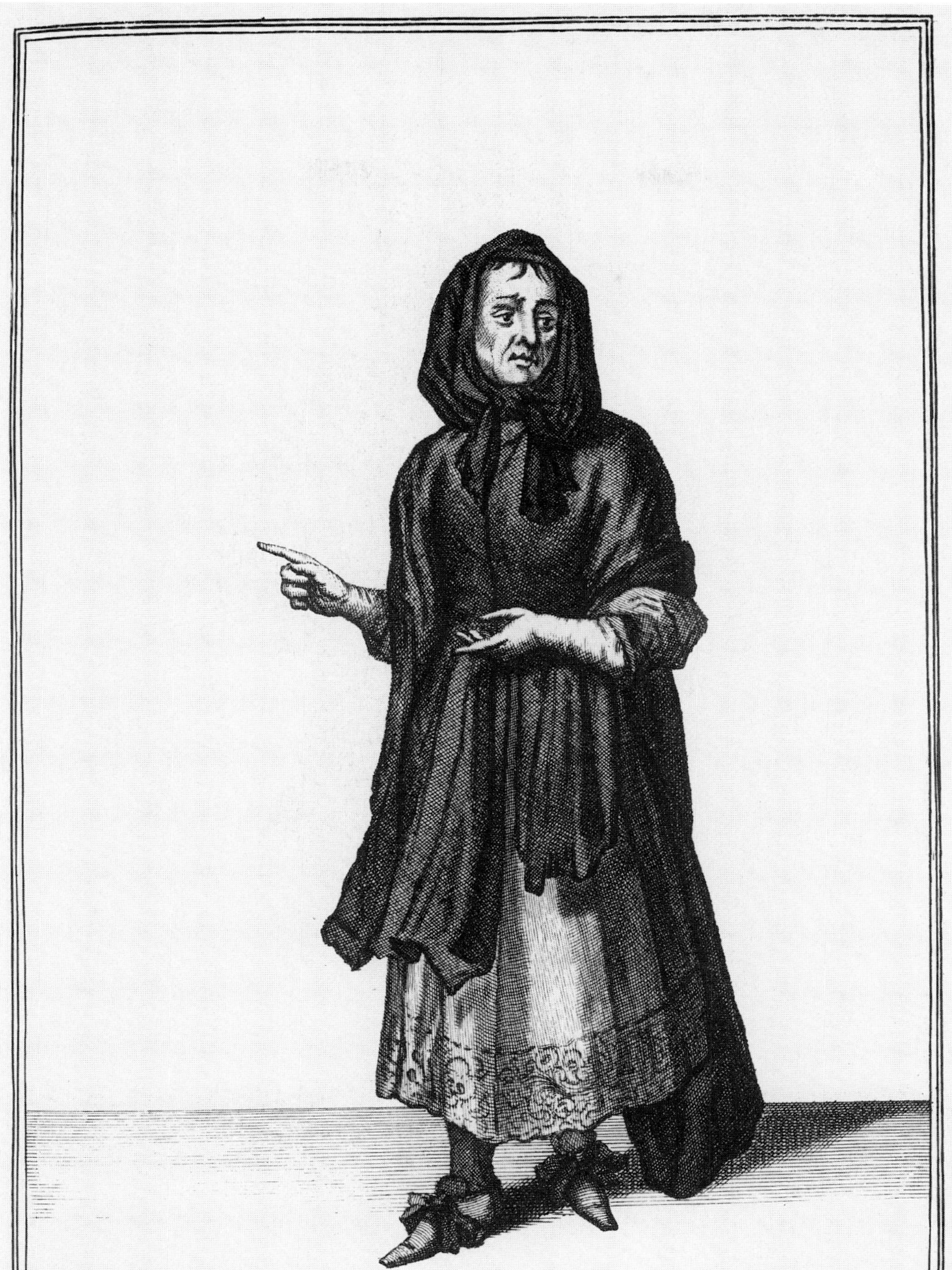

3.15 Marcellus Laroon, 'Madam Creswell', 1687

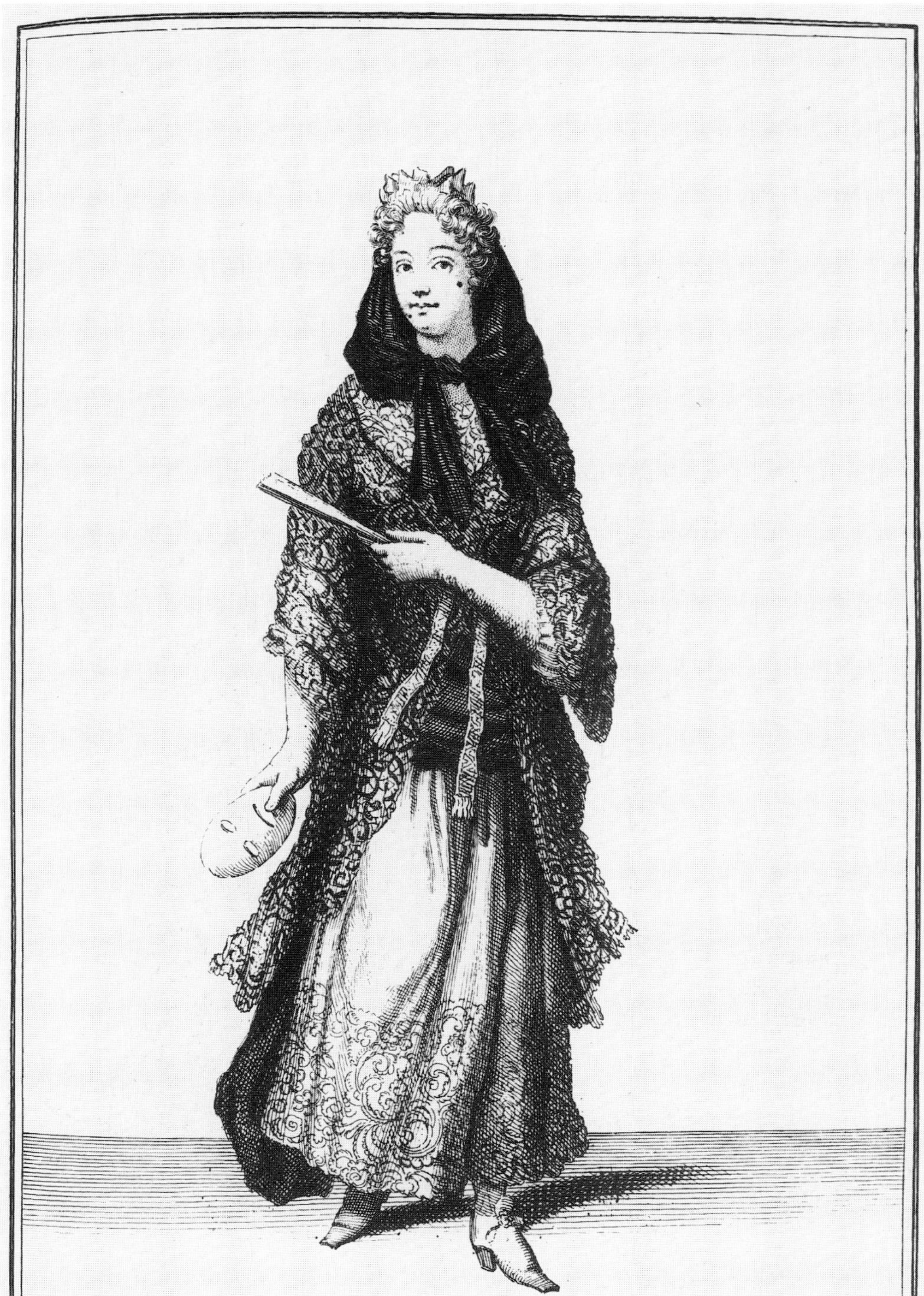

3.16 Marcellus Laroon, 'London Curtezan', 1687

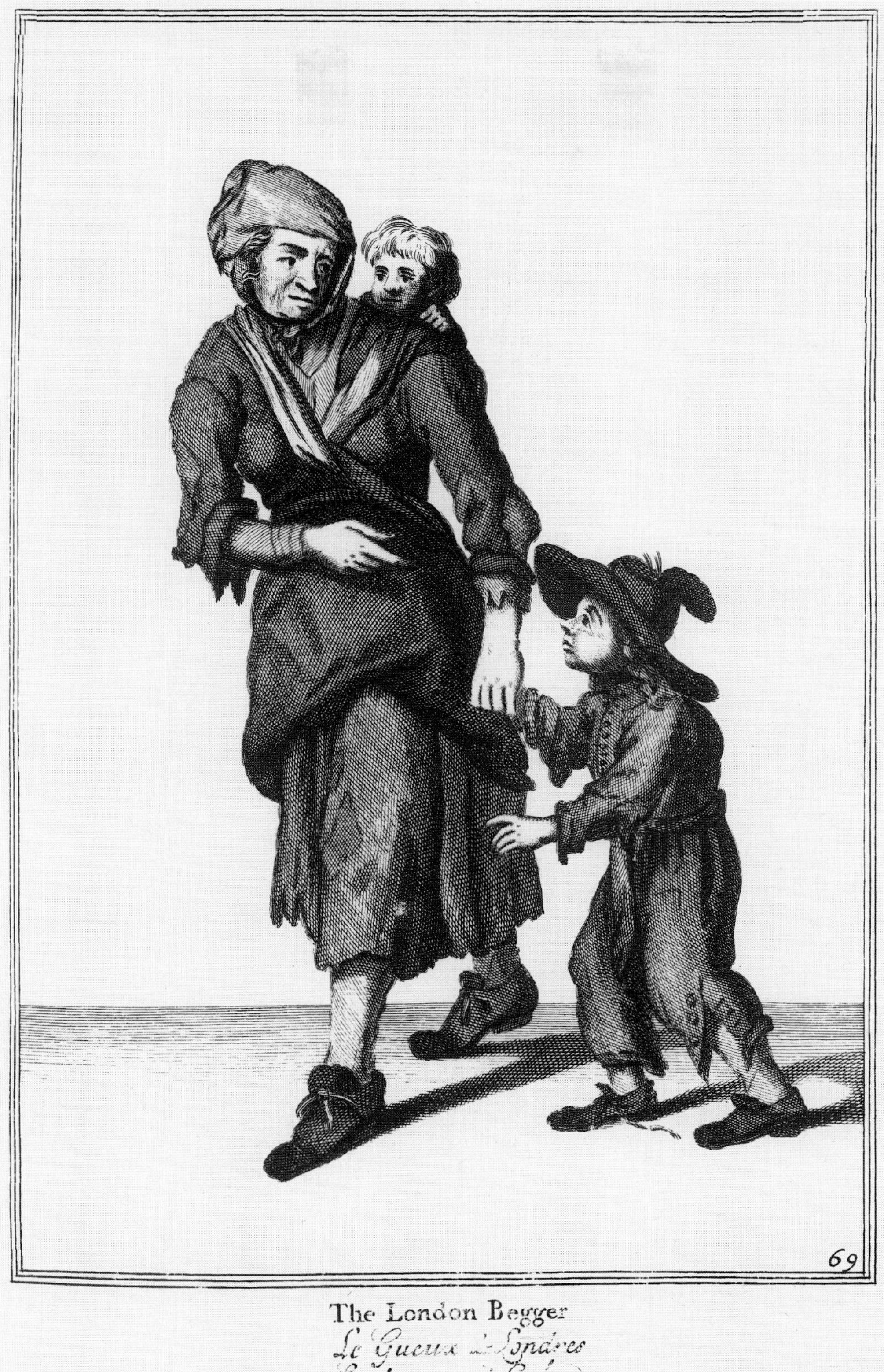

3.17 Marcellus Laroon, 'The London Begger', 1687

renders them doubly outcast members of a mobile, predatory, and sinister underworld requiring systematic explication to be properly understood.[56]

These types dress up to falsify their identities. But one figure dresses down. The London beggar (**3.17**) may look like a down-and-out on account of the black rags of herself and her children. She is not so. In Samuel Pepys's copy of the *Cryes*, the diarist identifies her as a false or 'sturdy' pauper going by the name of Nan Mills.[57] In the print, she betrays herself by the artful penury of the boy she showcases: his shoes are mismatched and the crown of his hat falls back to let a dramatic tuft of hair sprout through, adding up to a picturesque and eye-catching poverty. This boy has been rented to Mills and, not being ugly or deformed, has been dressed up to evoke sympathy; Johann Archenholz records that

> female beggars generally hire infants from those who are poorer than themselves, to rouse, by that means the charity of the passengers. They pay various prices for these children, from sixpence to two shillings a day, according as they are more or less deformed. A child that is very crooked and distorted generally earns three shillings and sometimes even more. I happened once to overhear the conversation of two of these women who were talking concerning their profession. One of them informed the other that she paid two shillings for the child in her arms: 'What!' replies her companion, 'are you a fool? Two shillings for that charming baby! – I would not give more for a monster'.[58]

In depicting the false beggar, the courtesan, Madam Creswell, and other London miscreants, Laroon shows that clothing is not just expressive of the identities of wearers, it is also transformative. Charged with dangers, dress reconstructs identities. It makes the rich poor and the poor rich, conferring on its wearers, even in the case of rags, privileges they do not merit.[59]

Laroon is the first artist to canonize, in Cries, those London whores, cutpurses and tricksters who assumed false identities. He also ushers in figures who follow marginal callings and challenge common social standards. Chief among these are his strolling players, who use the street as a stage; difficult to pigeonhole, some of these are quasi-respectable, while others are outcasts. The more decorous of these indecorous itinerants are contortionists like Clark the English Posture Master (**3.18**), who, in warping his body to outdo an ape, plays a comic role but is not himself the butt of wit or bestial humour, as the deformed are in baroque art. The most eye-catching of such wanderers is the 'famous Dutch Woman' (**3.19**), sexualized by the obscene jester drawing our eye to her underpants and stockings, often coloured bright red.[60] The erotic force of her garb, lost to us but thrilling to men accustomed to well-skirted limbs, is caught in the *Art of Dress* (1717) by William King, who writes of 'Those pretty legs, dress'd up with so much Art, / By which Men guess at ev'ry other Part'.[61]

Performers like the 'fast' young rope dancer and her pandering clown survived by mounting importuning, precarious exhibitions for fickle, stingy audiences. Figures like the Dutch rope dancer, offered the Dutch artist, himself a hawker of cultural wares, a reflection of his own marginal status as a foreigner and an impresario struggling to subsist.[62] Laroon 'had no great Success,' according to the contemporary art historian George Vertue; he eked out a living by painting flattering portraits, drawing dozens of sketches for exploitive booksellers, and peddling bawdy images to gentlemen printsellers like Pierce Tempest, who dabbled in erotica.[63] Effigies like these showmen and exhibitionistic women, rooted in an emotionally-charged observation of what the artist saw from his studio door in Covent

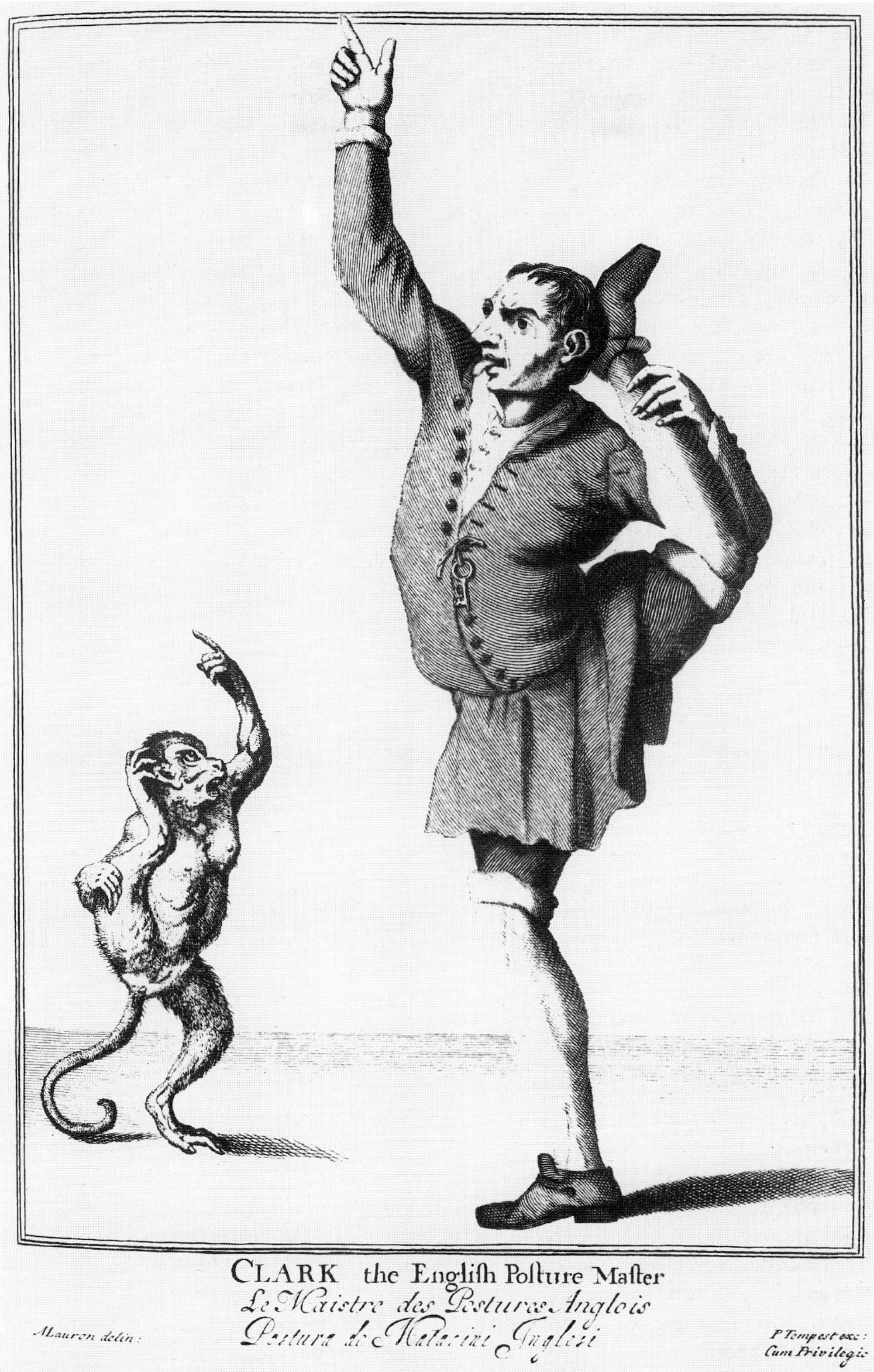

3.18 Marcellus Laroon, 'Clark the English Posture Master', 1687

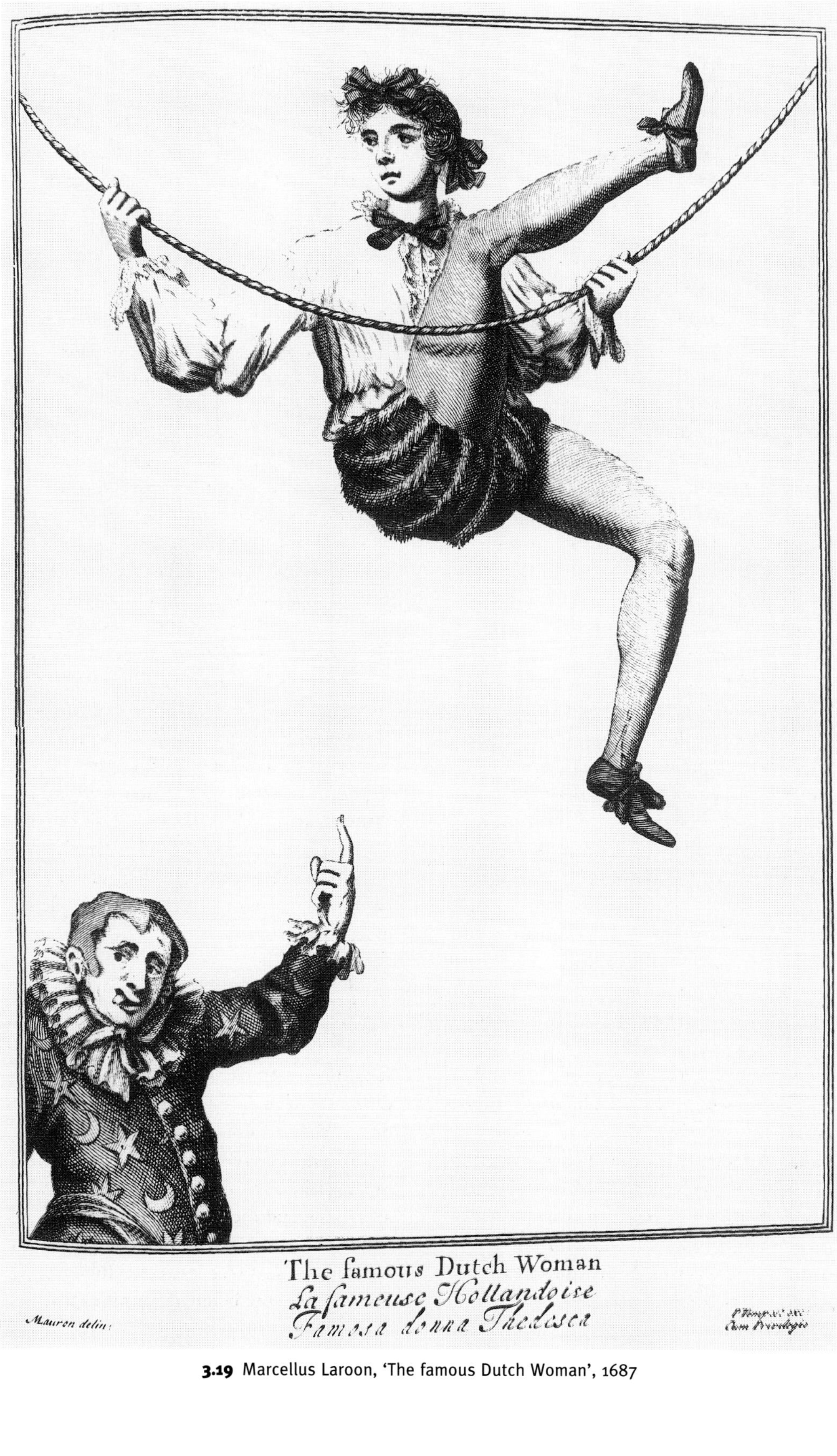

3.19 Marcellus Laroon, 'The famous Dutch Woman', 1687

Garden, are veiled self-portraits and displaced, collective likenesses of the artist himself.[64]

As Clark the contortionist (**3.18**) shows, Laroon links socially marginal entertainers to street characters whose bodies depart from ordinary physical norms. Maimed and deformed figures like the crippled ironmonger wearing the prosthesis (**3.20**) were once celebrated as expressions of nature's diversity or beneficiaries of God's favour.[65] By Laroon's time, the baroque obsession with ideal beauty made them look both repulsive and fascinating, especially to the voyeur who lurks in everyone who buys prints or studies them; in the seventeenth century, Moreno Villa lists nearly one hundred dwarfs and fools kept at the Spanish court.[66] Their new taxonomic status as illustrations of the world turned upside down or violations of cosmic order (comparable to the 7½ lb. radish and the exotic sea shell) explains the appeal of the contortionist John Evelyn admiringly called 'Proteus Clark'. Sketched twice by Laroon, Clark earned his living by appearing to be a freakish acrobat one moment (**3.18**) and a hump-backed, potbellied idiot the next (**3.21**).[67] Such an obsession with oddities describes nature by establishing its outer perimeters, not its norms and averages. In this scheme for arranging the visible world, identity lies in uniqueness more than in relatedness, an approach to classification that ultimately gives way to the more abstract and seemingly rationalized systems of relationships favoured by the early proponents of scientific method.[68]

Broadsides published a hundred years before Laroon's *Cryes* represent hawkers as decent, courteous, obliging and refined. No minstrels, half-wits, scourges, or varlets skulk among the energetic peddlers of 'The Common Cryes of London' (**2.3**) or the noble types in 'The Bellman' (**2.1**). These sheets observe the convention that street vendors must be depicted as typical, industrious and upright, whatever truth there may have been to the view of Lord Mayor Pritchard, who complained in 1682 that 'the Street of Cornhill and Passages about the Royal Exchange and Coffee Houses are much pestered with a sort of Loose and Idle People called Hawkers'.[69]

Laroon, tutored by Cries like Carracci's eighty designs (featuring a frontal view of a urinating Bolognese), swells the range of characters in his suite, which embraces cripples, swindlers and pariahs. That new range heeded a call for more verity of the kind reflected in the Lord Mayor's hostile pronouncement about hawkers, whose reputation for drinking, swearing, thieving, and lewdness was widespread. Such verity is singled out for praise in the interpretive responses of two 'readers' who bought Laroon's *Cryes*, von Uffenbach and Pepys. In his *Travels*, von Uffenbach responds to the Dutch artist's hawkers by affirming that they are 'represented from the life,' echoing, with approval, the pledge that Tempest makes to his buyers on the volume's title page. Pepys's response reflects the same interest in a subject matter that is lifelike and historical: he wrote the trades and names of the hawkers he recognized under their portraits, identifying eighteen as speaking likenesses of people then living in London.[70]

And yet, no matter how marginal or criminal or poor Laroon's figures are, they look poised, sometimes even elegant. A romantic nimbus clothes even the most wretched of them, distorted by a formalism originating in continental Cries like Annibale's, published in a luxurious folio volume 'for the use of all *virtuosi* and those who aspire to the profession of painting and of design'.[71] This formalism sometimes leads to falsification. For example, the bodily deformities that

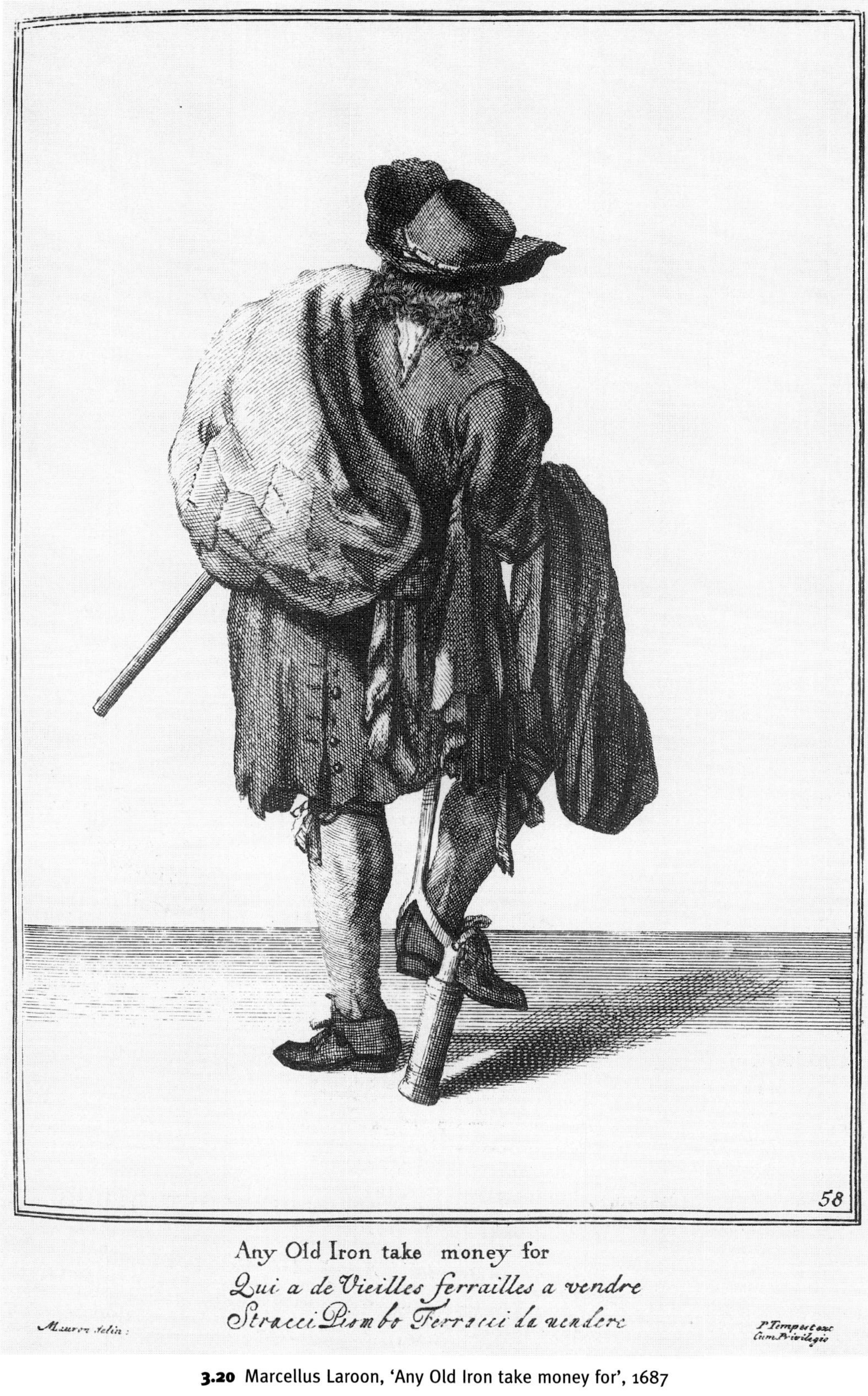

3.20 Marcellus Laroon, 'Any Old Iron take money for', 1687

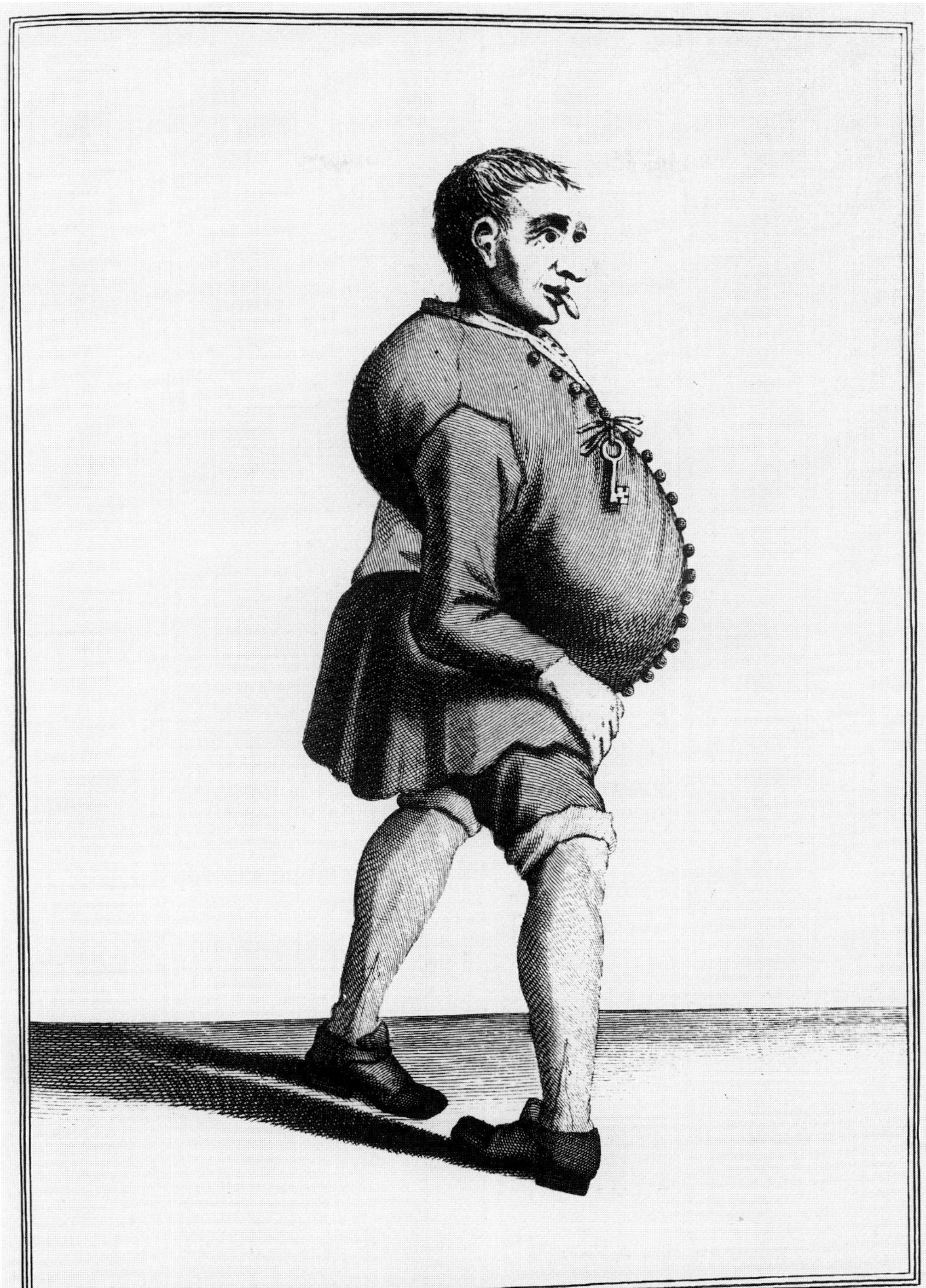

3.21 Marcellus Laroon, 'Josephus Clericus', 1687

Laroon's posture master Clark affects in order to amuse are absent in other peddlers, whose real-life counterparts contracted such physical afflictions from their labours. The stoop, the tilt, the herniated limp, are all chronicled in Bartolomeo Ramazzini's *Essay sur les maladies des artisans* (1777), though none appears in Laroon's *Cryes*.[72] His aged tinker (**3.2**), clothed in shreds, carries a big iron pot over his shoulder. Is it 40, 50 or 60 pounds? Whatever it weighs, it has little impact on the man's posture. Beating his hammer on his pan, the stiffly dignified figure strolls along, unbowed by the cauldron he carries. In such amiable images of toil free from woe, Laroon captures the rituals, postures and carriages of hawkers. But he misses the body's pain in the hawker's broken back or twisted face, pleasantly presented by generalizing techniques that engage a momentary and fleeting sympathy.[73] He purges misery and ache from physical labour, overlooking the tension it brings and the deformity it leaves. This blindness is a double surprise in light of prints and charades-style parlour games in which players, mimicking typical maladies of workers, challenged viewers to guess the occupations that deformed them.[74]

Why this indifference to actuality, which occasions an unconscious aesthetic joke in the portrait of the Dutch woman, whose magic rope (**3.19**) does not bend under her weight? Such matters of fact did not engage an important segment of Tempest's half-guinea audience made up of 'the Ingenious and Lovers of Art'.[75] While Pepys, von Uffenbach and other buyers of the middling sort purchased Laroon's prints chiefly to enjoy their subject matter by matching them with real-life figures or satisfying their curiosity – within limits – about the secrets of the lower orders from whom they had separated themselves in life, *virtuosi* belonging to the aristocracy collected them chiefly for their formal values. Thus, whereas Cries may mirror social life, according to a familiar and mechanistic view, they may also distort it in order to broadcast conventions and artistic techniques.

To noble owners interested in acquiring connoisseurial dexterity, the prints were not so much reflections of low-life subjects as they were instruments proffering instruction in the polite art of drawing. Functioning as a set of life studies, the prints played the role of a primer in the visual arts; from the time of Chaucer's squire, who could 'songes make and wel endite, / Juste and weel daunce, and weel purtreye [draw] and write', an English gentleman's ability to paint for pleasure added to his aura of cultural attainment.[76] A source of inspiration in the field of drawing, the ensemble offered patrician amateurs exercises of a technical nature to copy, imitate and vary, after the injunction of Edward Norgate (d. 1650), reputed 'the best illuminer and limner of his age', who advised amateur and professional draftsmen to ape 'the best prints cut in copper'.[77] Such artist/owners poured over the ink seller (**3.22**) to study not the faceless man's trade in goose quills but to copy the extravagant way he inclines his torso forward, the athletic extension of his right leg backward, and the expressiveness of his hand, uncommon in a mere hawker. Or they studied the vendor of fat chickens (**3.11**), not from any great interest in poultry workers, but to admire or copy the insouciant contrapposto by which this figure moves forward on one foot, swivels her head to look right, and balances three baskets in harmonious asymmetry. Studying but especially copying prints like this, with their contrived sense of plastic life and the dance-like grace of their figures, refined the taste, delighted the eye and finished the education of the noble patron in the fine arts. 'This [kind of copying] is one of the best and quickest ways to instill in young people good taste and a sense of perfection in design',

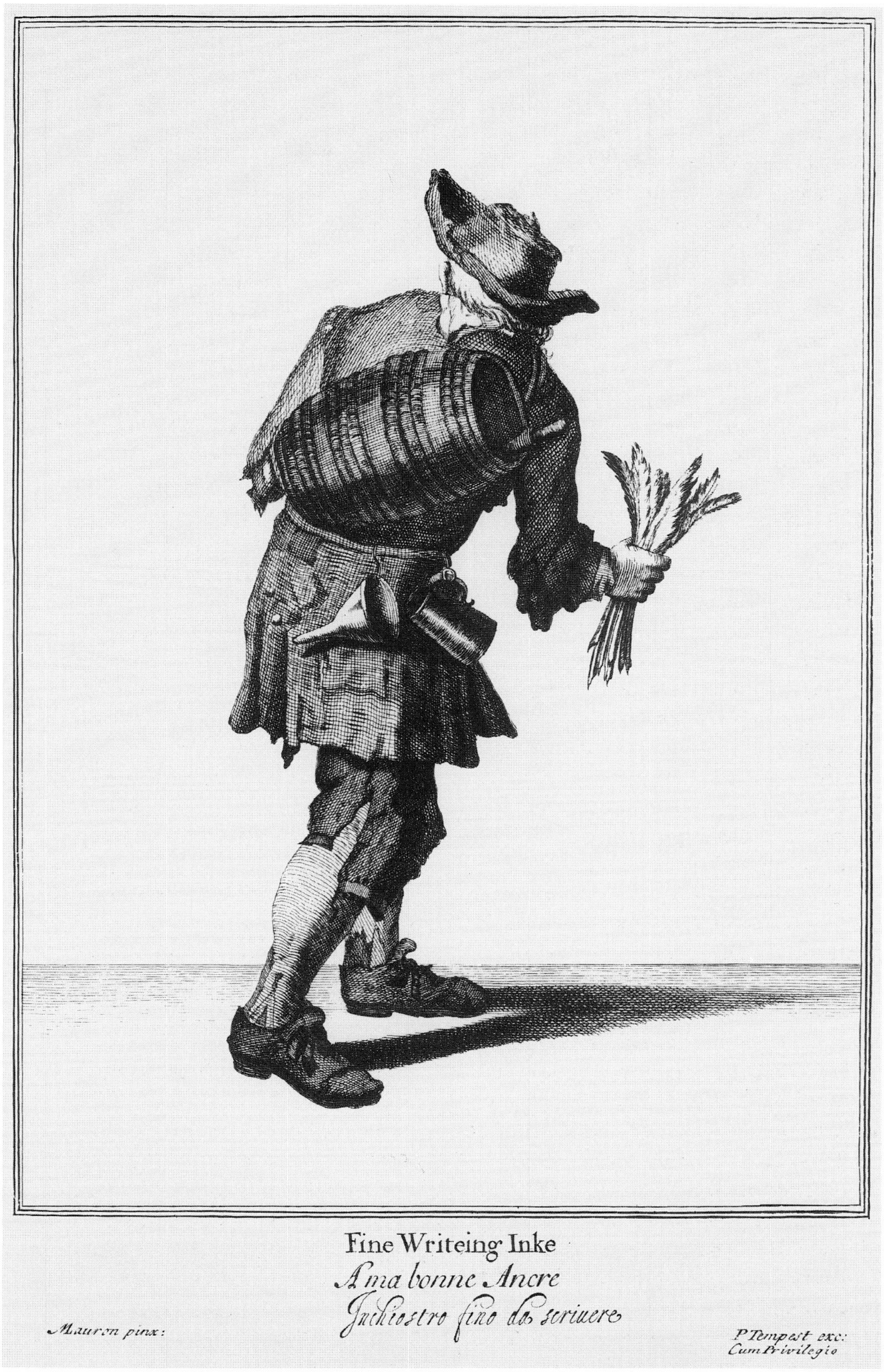

3.22 Marcellus Laroon, 'Fine Writeing Inke', 1687

according to the anonymous author of *L'Art de dessiner proprement les plan, porfils, elevations geometrales, & perspective, soit de'architecture militaire ou civile*, a technical drawing treatise from 1697. 'Fine pieces with their beautiful manner, are imprinted in their minds and leave their traces of perfection on which their imagination can later develop when it comes time to work without a model'.[78]

To these elite buyers, the *Cryes* resembled Annibale Carracci's *Trades of Bologna*, which Simon Guillain cut and struck off in 1646, fifty or sixty years after the artist sketched them. Issued as a luxurious folio by the Roman firm of Lodovico Grigniani, it carried a frontispiece describing Carracci's images as 'Diverse figures, 80 in number, drawn with pen in hours of recreation by Annibale Carracci . . . for the use of all *virtuosi* and those who aspire to the profession of painting and design'. The title 'Diverse figures', preferred over the alternative name, 'The Trades of Bologna', and bolstered by a lengthy preface dealing with idealist art theory, courts an audience of connoisseurs, noble Romans, scholarly amateurs, laymen of the arts and sciences, even rich members of the urban middle class.[79] In the eyes of such elites, Carracci's *Trades* and Laroon's *Cryes* belonged to the category of technical treatise; they were studies in volume, movement, attitude and graphic systems generally.

Another audience linked to these amateurs, not by class but by interest, also viewed Laroon's prints as manuals in the realm of fine art, rather like Caesar Ripa's *Iconologia or Moral Emblems*, which Tempest published in 1709.[80] This audience, whom Carracci's *Trades* identifies as 'those who aspire to the profession of painting and design', was composed of career artists and commercial publishers who bought engravings to build up a library of reference manuals, prompt books, and mechanic drills.[81] For these buyers, Laroon's *Cryes* served as anatomy investigations and drapery studies, but also graphic forumulae in general and the rules of art in codified form. Illustrating deportment or self-conscious display of the kind linked to courtly life, they shaped the taste of patrons, but they also advanced the education of such patrons' artists who supplemented their paltry incomes by decorating carriages, painting tavern signs and engraving designs on household objects, like the set of silver counters (*c.* 1640) used in games of chance and inscribed with likenesses of hawkers copied from *The Manner of Crying Things in London*.[82]

Artists, amateurs, and publishers left proofs of the mechanic and didactic purposes postulated here for the *Cryes*. Ebenezer Taylor, who cultivated an intense interest in figure studies, was such an amateur. As a young man, Taylor executed a drill to hone his skills as a draftsman: using pen and ink, he copied sixty-two of Tempest's engravings onto a set of pages which he first lined in red ink. He bound these leaves together to make a volume to which he added a title page proudly proclaiming his name, age and the year of his elaborate and time-consuming exercise: 'The Cryes of the City of London, Drawn in lxix Sculptures By Ebenezer Taylor. Aetat: xx: Anno Dom. MDCCCSSIV'.[83]

Evidence that the *Cryes* functioned as 'an artist's assistant,' a so-called 'vade mecum' serving to teach the craft, not just of drawing but of painting too, appears in the survival of copies coloured by hand, like the one in the Kress Library, Harvard University. Such copies have been the beneficiaries of a practice urged by a sarcastic Peacham, who advocated that gentlemen learn to draw 'by imitating the choicest prints' and that they learn to paint by 'wash[ing] scarlet, carnation, flame-colour, and violet over some plaine printes . . . without being beholden to some deare and nice professed Artist'.[84]

The *Cryes* was also copied by publishers, though these men's motives were heinous, compared to Peacham's and Taylor's. Four of them bought Laroon's book in order to plagiarize it. John Overton, John Bowles, 'JM' of London and Jacob Gole of Amsterdam each issued a 'spurious, Pyratical Copy' of Laroon's images to be sold to 'the lower class of Virtuosi' who could not afford the half guinea that Tempest demanded from his 'Ingenious and Lovers of Art'.[85] The earliest piracy, Overton's *Cryes of the City of London* (*c.* 1690), is a uniquely instructive work because it shows how prints that look dissimilar to us were closely linked in the minds of early modern artists and audiences. Overton's piracy, for economy's sake, reverts to the old broadside format, recasting Laroon's *Cryes* as six sheets, each measuring 28 × 19 cm.[86] Five of these sheets carry only street vendors; but the sixth (**3.23**) holds eight hawkers placed above spring, summer, autumn and winter allegorized as four women exhibiting the art of elegant feminine dress, in the manner of Hollar's *Four Seasons* (1641). This mix of hawkers and women who are half allegories and half habits looks incongruent. In fact, it exemplifies the harmony enjoyed by different kinds of programmatic art in the eyes of seventeenth-century viewers. Enriching Cries with seasons and costume figures, Overton's sheet also clarifies by concrete illustration the process of augmentation described in Walton's 1655 advertisement, offering a map of England 'inlarged with severall pictures, as the 5 Senses, the 4 Seasons, the 4 Elements, and the Cries of London and the like'.

Laroon's *Cryes*, imitated, pirated and reprinted, cornered the English market for peddlers in prints.[87] No artist challenged Laroon's monopoly until 1739 when Jacob Amigoni published 'Golden Pippins' (**3.24**), 'Shoe-Black' (**3.25**), 'Lamp-Lighter' (**3.26**), and 'Chimney Sweeper' (**3.27**). Aiming to displace *The Cryes* by exposing what is incompetent, obsolete, boring and repetitive about it, Amigoni's designs are shaped by three weakness in Laroon's images: hawkers pictured in a vacuum; a hodgepodge of characters lacking order or coherence; but especially, bungled countenances. Amigoni also avoids the hurdles of formal and stylistic monotony that caused one reader of this study to complain that all Laroons look alike.

The Dutch artist, in his *Cryes*, poses hawkers against white backgrounds to exoticise them but also to evoke the studio, with its dropcloth, rather than the city, with its buildings. In clear, uncluttered compositions, he censors staffage and settings to highlight hawkers' poses and costumes. Perhaps he deemed urban landscapes unnecessary; such landscapes – or the urbanity they embody – are more subtly enshrined in hawkers' dress and carriage, especially when these features are contrasted with the costumes and poses of peasants. By the evidence of his hawkers' attitudes and apparel, Laroon believed in the new culture of bodily appearances; he probably thought that London was mirrored more discerningly in the urbane pose of the strawberry seller (**3.1**) than it could ever be in a fictionalized London cityscape.

Amigoni, rejecting Laroon's faith in the power of gesture or costume to distill what is most metropolitan about London and its hawkers, sets his cherubic figures in naturalistic cityscapes. Though naturalistic, these cityscapes are not topographies but ficitve backgrounds, though the first sports one factual detail. Unified by time and place, Amigoni's ensemble moves from morning labour to evening leisure, focusing on increasingly close-up views of increasingly luxurious houses. In carefully differentiated scenes, it progresses from cityscape to public

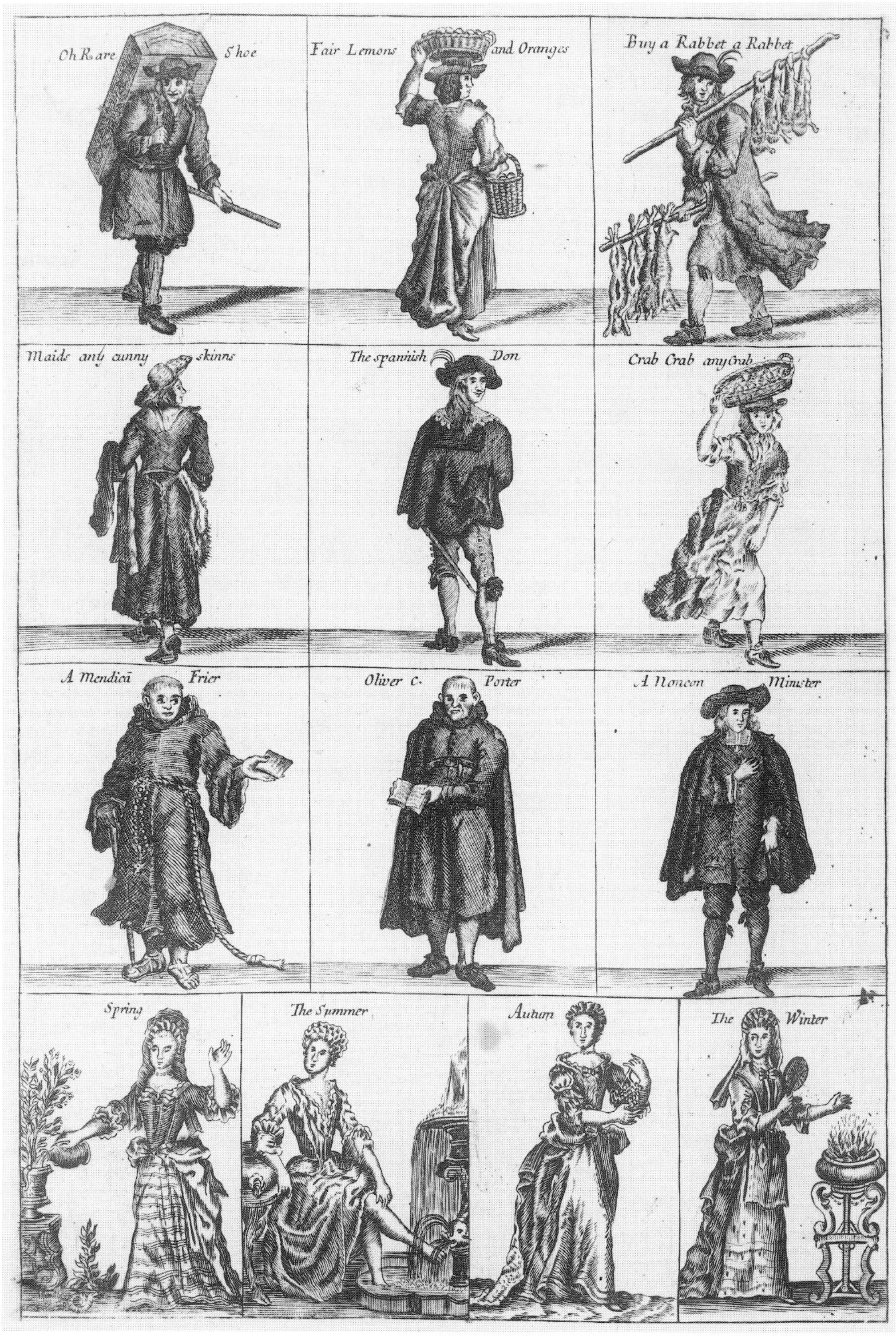

3.23 John Overton, Broadside of Hawkers with Four Seasons, from *The Cryes of the City of London*, late seventeenth century

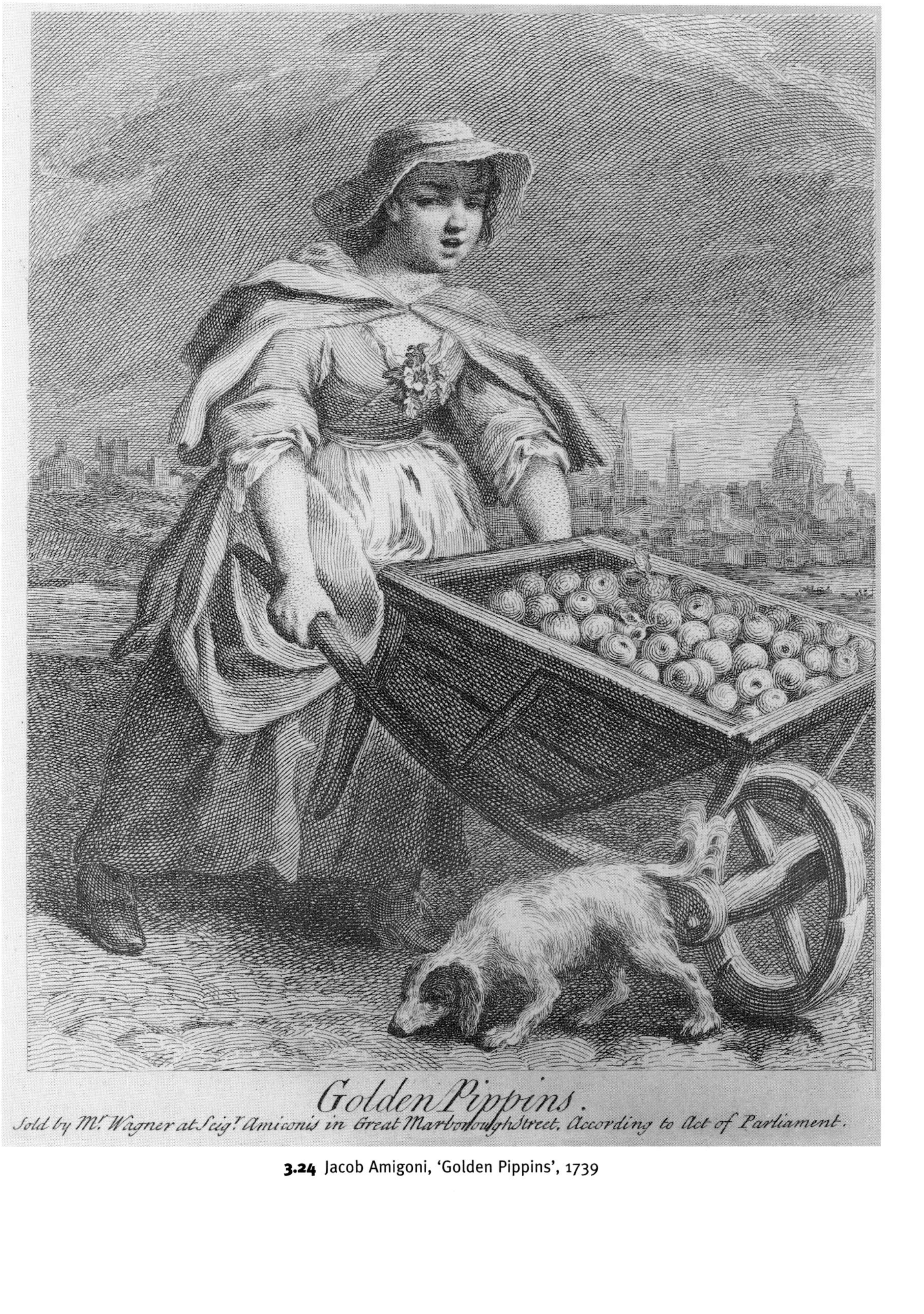

3.24 Jacob Amigoni, 'Golden Pippins', 1739

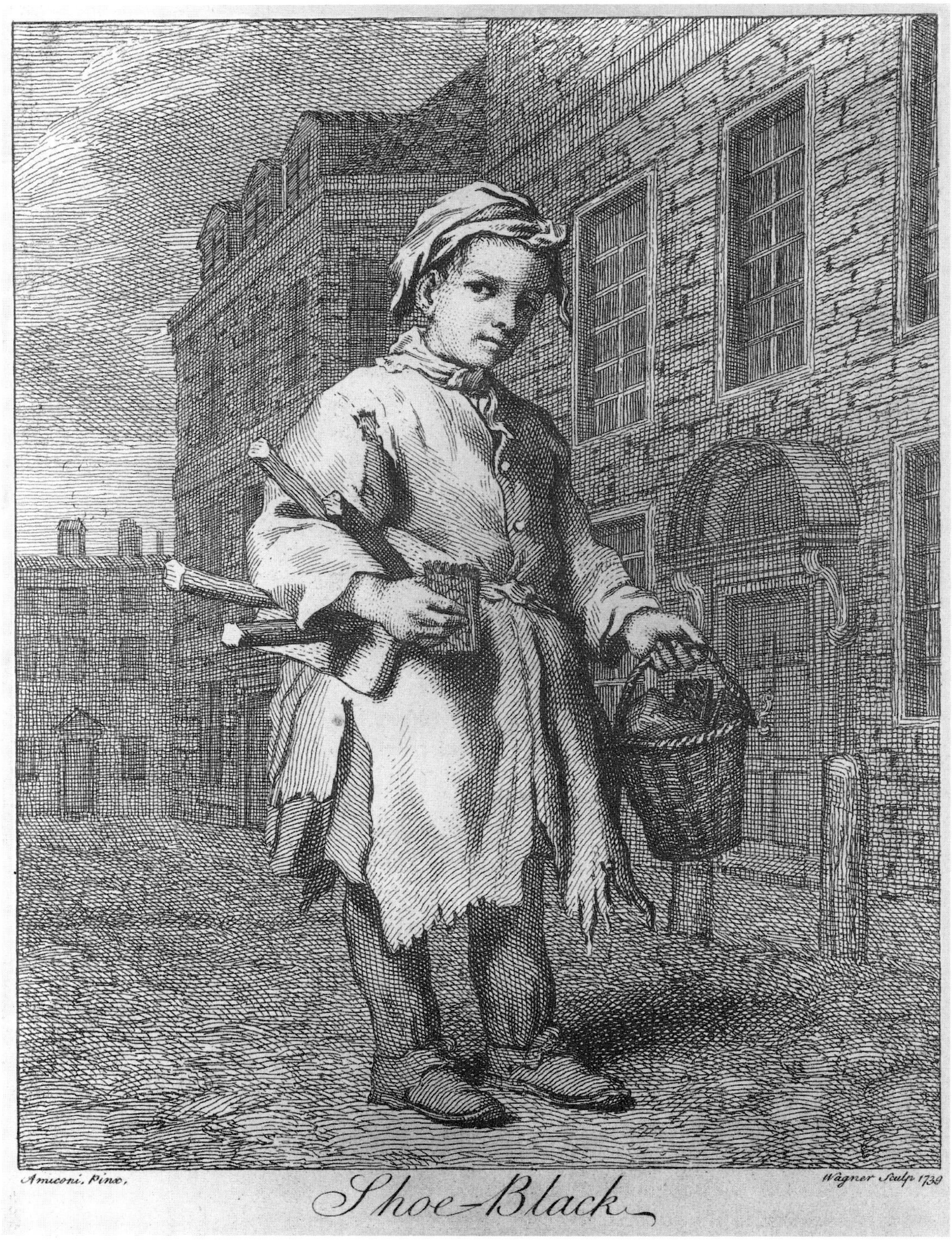

3.25 Jacob Amigoni, 'Shoe-Black', 1739

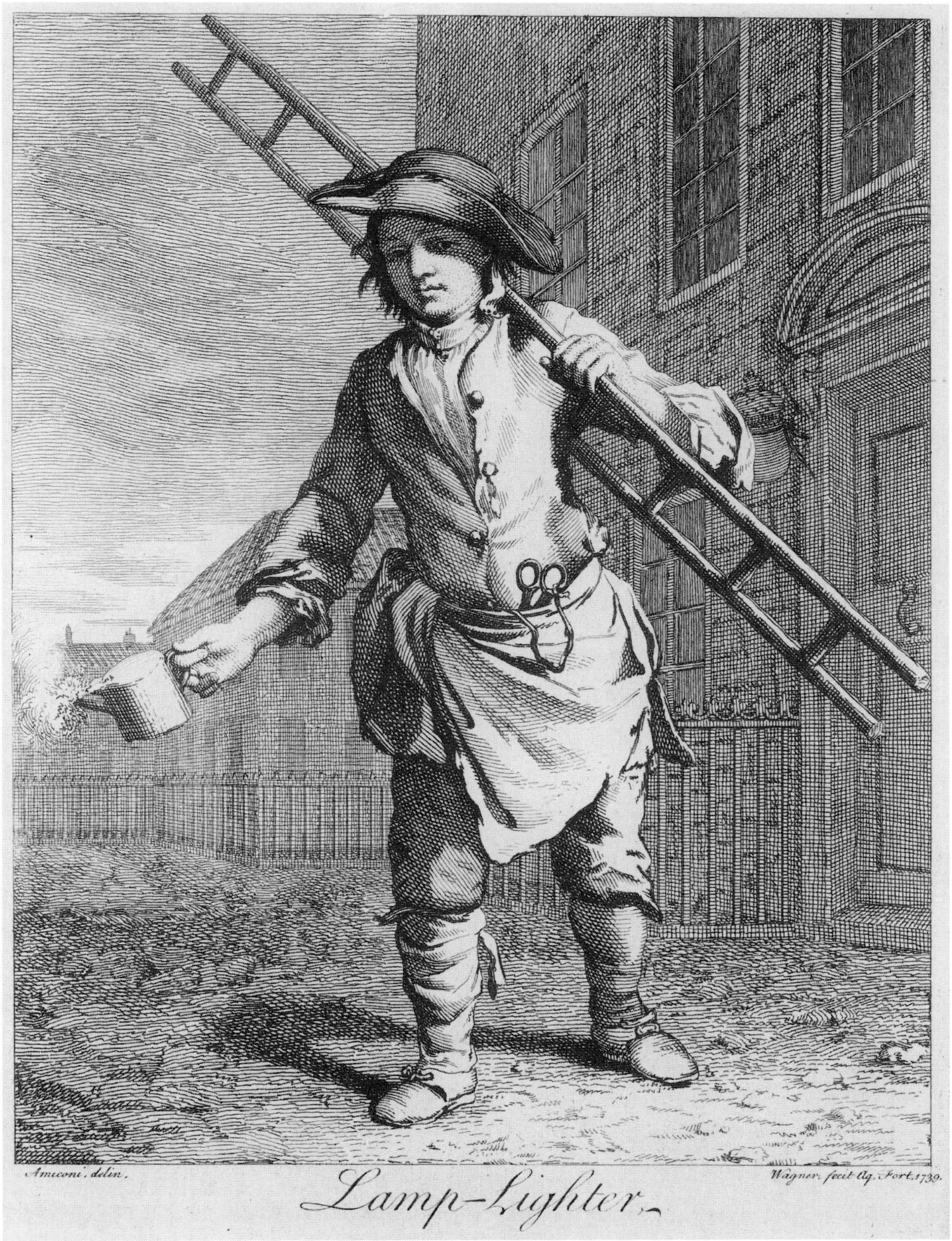

3.26 Jacob Amigoni, 'Lamp Lighter', 1739

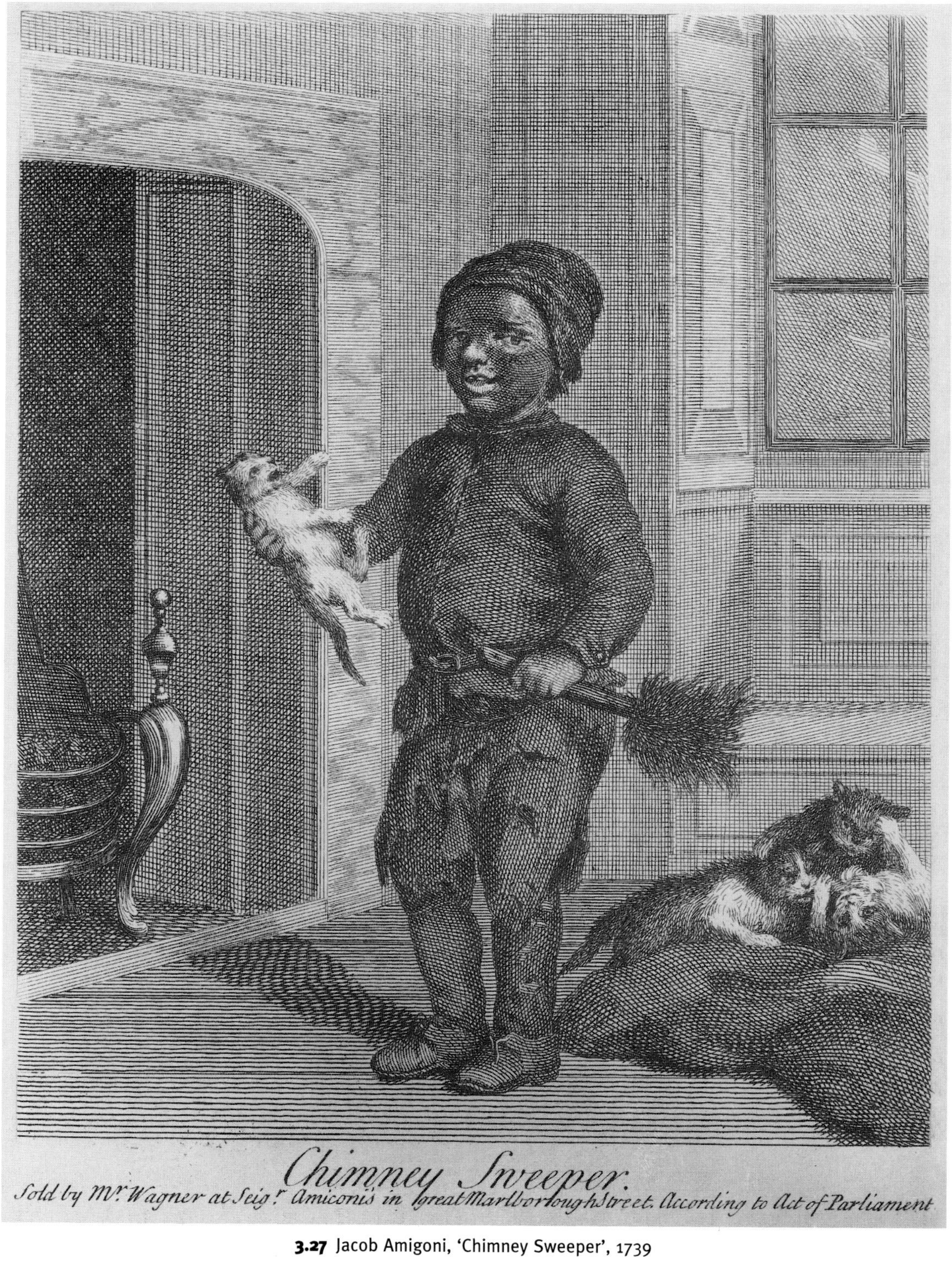

3.27 Jacob Amigoni, 'Chimney Sweeper', 1739

facade to private interior, from the capital's rural outskirts to its urban heart pictured at the four cardinal times of the day.

The city makes a panoramic entry into the Cries in 'Golden Pippins' (**3.24**), which shows a modern or mechanized coster trundling a wheelbarrow under a sky that heralds dawn, when hawkers sold the day's fruits and vegetables.[88] St Paul's on the horizon puts the hawker in titular Southwark, in a landscape with a rustic character established by two botanical notes: the primroses adorning the bosom of the country lass and the tree leaves attaching to her Kentish apples.[89] Amigoni's vendors are natives to the different quarters of town in which they work. 'Shoe-Black' (**3.25**), located in the city proper, pictures a child stationed before a row of anonymous townhouses whose leisured inhabitants he hopes to serve when they sally forth at noon. All three Palladian houses huddle together and open directly onto the street; they shut off this urban cul-de-sac and whittle down the sky, creating a mood that captures, for the first time in Cries, the claustrophobia of urban space.

'Lamp-Lighter' (**3.26**) is set in an even more prosperous neighbourhood: at twilight a youngster passes before the door of a mansion (it has more windows than the townhouse) that is protected from the wide street by a wrought-iron fence. But its best protection from crime is its acolyte and his new street lantern, which enlarge public space and restructure quotidian time: they turn evening back into day filled with pleasure for the rich and work for the poor. In 'Chimney Sweeper' (**3.27**), a night scene, the ensemble shifts abruptly from cobblestone streets to the reception room of a great house, a surprising and dangerous setting for public hawkers, who rarely appear in private interiors. In thus opposing character to setting, this design plays up the underlying perversity of the city and its confused estates, rich in sinister promise. The links between sweeps and night are more literal; they scoured flues cooled down at the day's end, when fires were extinguished, and they gathered 'night soil'.

The London of this quartet is odd in other ways. Its most striking aspect is that, like Hugo's and Atget's Paris of the late 1880s, nobody lives there: 'It was an inhabited spot where there was nobody; it was an abandoned place where there was someone; it was the boulevard of a great city . . . more gloomy by day than a cemetery.'[90] The four vendors enjoy neither the custom of shoppers nor the camaraderie of their fellow vendors, though the costermonger (**3.24**) is accompanied by a pet dog (reinforcing her affinity with nature), and the sweep (**3.27**) has collared a kitten (evoking childish cruelty but also, by animal analogy, hinting at a feral nature in the black boy). In 'Shoe-Black' (**3.25**) and 'Lamp-Lighter' (**3.26**), the mute streets with their abandoned houses make London look dead, as if stricken by the plague. Even the interior scene is strangely vacant, further accenting the incongruity of the destitute boy's presence in luxurious surroundings. No master or parent oversees the idle, mischievous sweep, whose impending but unspecified violence against the kitten speaks of the upper caste's growing anxiety about the outcast.

The four waifs and their defunct, anonymous city express a taste for isolation, loneliness and abandonment, an urban sublime intensified by the fact that 'Lamp-Lighter' and 'Shoe-Black' are twilight and night scenes. Their celebration of the crepuscular and elegiac, whether physical or spiritual, expresses the graveyard sensibility in vogue in the early 1740s, when Edward Young's *Night Thoughts* (1742) and Robert Blair's *Grave* (1743) heralded the Gothic Revival. The love of melancholy and fascination with death are tied to rural life and nature by Young, Blair, and most memorably by Thomas Gray in his *Elegy Written in a Country Churchyard* (1751), but they are here tied to the city and to children, especially the sweep. In the eighteenth century, infant mortality rates higher than fifty percent before the age of five rightly associate children with death.[91] The connection is particularly strong among climbing boys following a lethal trade. The mortal character of the sweep's calling surfaces in his missing teeth, his black 'mourning' clothes (Blake calls these shrouds 'the clothes of death') and the yawning fireplace, into which masters forced apprentices, before lighting straw fires under them or sticking pins in the soles of their feet to propel them into the jaws of the forbidding flues.[92]

Amigoni's four prints, in their progress from exterior to interior, from landscape to cityscape, from panorama to close-up, have a unity lacking in Laroon's ensemble, which sprouted chaotically from forty to seventy-four images. This unity is most striking in its homogenized hawkers, all poor children, a race of beings new to the Cries and to English art. Children seldom appeared in their own right without adults in genre art, even during the early baroque period.[93] But prints and paintings romanticizing cottage children, street urchins and infant beggars first appeared in the early eighteenth century; by the 1760s, they were a favourite subject at the yearly exhibitions of the Society of Artists.[94] Their popularity was due to Philip Mercier's fancy pictures assisted by Amigoni's Cries: both embrace city waifs who ranged in age from about six years (the sweep) to thirteen (the sturdy pippin girl). Indeed, fancy pictures as a class, which spotlight 'mean and vulgar' characters – ragged children, winsome market women, street vendors, musicians, and harlots – are the innovation of Mercier (*c.* 1689–1760).[95] A French émigré who apprenticed in Germany, worked in Italy and enjoyed a wide grasp of continental genres, he crossed Cries with the fête gallant to produce the new genre, illustrated by his provocative *Oyster Woman* (*c.* 1750–55) and frank *Venetian Courtesan* (engraved in 1739).[96]

Even though Amigoni's gamins follow the callings of grownups, they are emblems of childish virtue, one half of the virtue–vice opposition underlying the aesthetic of sensibility.[97] The mischievous sweep with a kitten in his clutches – the only figure who engages in youthful play rather than adult labour – may be a partial exception to this rampant goodness. Despite their childish identities, they are heroic in size and virtue, even more heroic than Laroon's figures. Posing in an aura of bright light, these little giants have a disturbing immediacy to them. Dominating the picture space, they are theatrical and monumental: the apple seller dwarfs the city behind her, and the brooding shoe-black overpowers the dark mansions at his back. Figure and setting together create a chain of romantic counterpoints: between living character and dead architecture, pathetic child and impassive façade, between the homeless and the well-housed, the visible poor and the invisible rich.[98]

But the most piquant counterpoint of the four prints is between the wretched, exposed hawkers and the comfortable viewer. This counterpoint is expressed in the way hawkers, looking us in the eye, establish their radiant faces and ardent gazes as their most striking aspect.[99] Their expressions, written on spiritual countenances, give these earth-bound cherubs a pathos that doubles their loneliness and physical vulnerability.[100] The elegant melancholy of the shoe-black who tilts his head wistfully, the noble, restrained dignity of the lamp-lighter, and naivety of the sweep, filtered through misery, cast them as envoys of intense feeling and urge us into a relationship with them.

Unlike Laroon's vendors, whose miens are petrified, Amigoni's figures personify strong emotion but especially heartache, borrowing the over-expressive and caricatured idiom of Francesco Villamena's Cries of Rome (*c.* 1626), which, in turn, derives from Carracci's *Trades of Bologna*.[101] In this respect and in one other, Amigoni's and Laroon's vendors are diametrically opposed. Laroon's figures are poker-faced and stereotyped, but they move in artful ways or adopt ingenious postures to show off complex, individualized costumes. Amigoni's wide-eyed figures wear refined, accessible expressions on their big faces, cast in half-shadows to intensify their melancholy. Except for the coster with the barrow, a female unable to carry the 'gravitas' of the males, they stand in simple, unvarying attitudes that bedim their costumes – stereotyped rags alike from one to another. What lies behind this contrast, by which the Cries of the two artists differ so systematically?

Amigoni's figures, to set themselves apart from Laroon's, accent 'what' over 'how'; they promote representation over invention, and reference over syntax. Within the realm of the referential, they show off hawkers' subjective appeal: their tenderness, sensitivity, and woe, but not the complication of their poses or the formal intricacy of the bodies, which they lack. Just when Hume declared that a taste for the polite arts 'improves our sensibility for all the tender and agreeable passions', these compositions focus on hawkers as agents of sentimental refinement; they stress the moral and emotional power of art over its technique and formal virtuosity.[102] Bonding hawkers to viewers, the images define the London Cries as an exercise in the exoticism of feeling and the purification of sensibility.

Laroon's ensemble, published at the end of the Restoration, stresses the forms of art; elucidating technique, it aspires to perfect the taste or gladden the eye of *virtuosi* among the nobility. Amigoni's cycle, published at the beginning of the Age of Sensibility, stresses art's tone and content; it aspires to evoke strong and lively feeling in buyers of the middling sort, viewed as connoisseurs in ennobling passions, the realm cultivated by that supreme bourgeois, Samuel Richardson. For this reason, when two of Amigoni's Cries in the collection of Farinelli were catalogued on 2 May 1783 after the soprano's death, they were praised as 'al naturale', meaning unstudied, artless, and expressive.[103]

In two respects, these ensembles shift the interest of the London Cries from where it was in early broadsheets. Laroon's and Amigoni's suites move the genre's focus from the thing sold to the seller; this change is especially clear in Amigoni's Cries where three of his four peddlers sell personal services, which pull the eye to the human figure, rather than wares, which push it away. Laroon emphasizes not the things sold but the sellers' attitude, 'actions', costumes, and identities, revealed in the prints' elaborate legends. Amigoni emphasizes the setting where the hawking occurs, revealed in the peddlers' complicated backgrounds; he also concentrates on hawkers' personalities, declared in their faces, expressive without being individualized. Both artists replace collective tableaus of 'public' hawkers with particular portraits of 'private' figures. Neither artist forsakes the general or typical in his treatment of character, even as they move the Cries in the direction of the historical and sentimental. Characters in both suites are cast as representatives of London's 'humblest classes'. Even when they are limned as historical personages, they are types.

Neither artist, in this focus on supply-side economics, examines the social links between buyer and seller. And neither scrutinizes the ties between the buying subject and the bought object, gifted with magical powers of transformation from the seventeenth century to our own day.

Laroon, in what is even more surprising than his innovative technical emphasis, sketches hawkers in the likenesses of living people – famous and infamous commoners – who would never have been the subject of traditional portraits. In the wake of the Commonwealth, which cracked the prestige of the aristocracy and briefly brought the toe of the commoner to the heel of the courtier, Laroon could picture, as persons, the many as well as the few, if not in oils, in iconoclastic prints. His 'English unworthies' are the very same people James Granger fears he has blundered to notice in his *Biographical History of England*'s twelfth class of subjects: 'Persons of both Sexes, chiefly of the lowest Order of the People, remarkable from only one circumstance in their Lives, namely such as lived to a great Age, deformed Persons, Convicts, &c'.[104] 'I have, perhaps, in the foregoing strictures, extended the sphere of it [biography] too far', he laments; 'I began with monarchs, and have ended with ballad-singers, chimney-sweepers and beggars'.[105]

In the legends to his prints, Laroon identifies eight of his hawkers as real people, disclosing their family names, given names, or sobriquets: Madam Creswell (**3.15**), John the Quaker (**3.10**), the famous Dutch woman (**3.19**), Oliver Cromwell's porter (**3.9**) and four others.[106] He also limns street people without revealing their names. Samuel Pepys identifies eighteen portraits as likenesses of men and women living in Restoration London, and Granger names four more. On top of this, the antiquarian and man of letters George Steevens saw 'a copy of Tempests Cries of London, with many more of the names inserted than are generally known, among which he remembered to have seen the Squire of Alsatia, called Bully Dawson, notorious gambler of his time'.[107] Whatever the accuracy of these identifications, they pay tribute to the newsworthiness, the topicality, the historical actuality and the democratic spirit of Laroon's portraits, more iconoclastic even than Hogarth's 'Heads of Six Servants' (*c.* 1750), called 'unique in the history of art' for the same reason.[108] When day labour was scorned and 'necessary' people – 'John Taylor's servant' or 'Agnes parson's servant' – lacked personal identities, sketching portraits of living hawkers was heresy or misguided pathos, even when such portraits tempered likenesses of individual sitters with genre art's dependence on types.[109] Endowing obscure street characters with recognizable faces and actual names (even Hogarth does not name his servants or his shrimp girl) gave status to those who had none; it argued that, though their social standing fell far below Bridget Holmes, Charles II's cleaning woman painted by John Riley (1646–91), hawkers were knowable human beings with a dignity conferred by their work, however mean and talentless it was.[110]

Amigoni's treatment of personality is as bold as his predecessor's thematic innovations. Reversing Laroon's emphases, he neglects hawkers' costumes and historical identities. Instead he focus on their faces, not to particularize or even differentiate but to idealize them. His peddlers' expressive eyes give them an angelic demeanour; precious and sentimental, they emote delicately. Despite settings that evoke the city for the first time, Amigoni's images tell little of what transpires on the streets of London and nothing about children – nothing about their history, psychology, and certainly nothing about their thievery or prostitution.[111] According to Samuel Curwen, the poor children of London were hardened 'in those pernicious practices of every species of vice the human heart can be tainted with, that renders them common pests and most commonly brings them to the halter'; the sight of dead and dying children abandoned by the roadside moved Thomas Coram to establish the Foundling Hospital in 1739.[112] Unlike the historical children Curwen and Coram saw, Amigoni's romantic urchins are not victimizers, nor are they complete victims. Quarantined in a world purged of grown ups, they are children posing as angels or angels posing as children.

In the broad context of eighteenth and nineteenth-century English art, Amigoni's figures anticipated and shaped the taste among Georgian audiences for the fancy pictures of Philip Mercier, Joshua Reynolds and John Rising. Mercier's *Oyster Girl*, Reynolds's *Cupid as a Link Boy* and Rising's *Ballad Singers* belong in this popular category. Among Victorians, they whetted the appetite for Lewis Carroll's and Julia Margaret Cameron's photographs of destitute infants idealized by their pathos and degraded by their poverty, objects of fantasy, secret desire and shame.[113] The most notorious example of this genre is Oscar Gustave Rejlander's 'Poor Jo', a portrait of Millais's son dressed up in rags and posed by the photographer as a street urchin, with coal used to blacken the soles of his feet. In the narrow context of Cries, Amigoni's designs stimulated new interest in the genre. Only Laroon's images were pirated more often.[114] As well as piracies, Amigoni's designs inspired two important ensembles of Cries that differ radically from each other; one of these, by a native artist, mocked the Italian's suite; the other, by a foreigner, imitated it in style, format, but especially in pathos. The images that mimic or ridicule Amigoni's and Laroon's Cries are the subject of the next chapter.

4

From representation to ridicule: Hogarth and the London Cries

BY THE FIRST quarter of the eighteenth century, the London Cries had become a commonplace of British art. The print seller John Evendon left at his death an assortment of engravings in his Leadenhall shop; a 1725 inventory, dividing his 1,800 prints into genres, deemed Cries so commonplace they required no further explanation than 'one book of prints of the Cryes of London'.[1] More striking still, a travelling auctioneer's preprinted catalogue dated 1716, but intended for repeated use, lists as one of its usual and customary subjects, 'London Cries'.[2] Despite its popularity, this thriving 'London' genre was nevertheless the property of foreign artists. In his 'Note books', George Vertue mentions English Cries as the work of continental artists only.[3] Such ironies must have galled Hogarth, who called native artists 'my Brothers' but branded foreign craftsmen 'interlopers' and 'Brazen Serpents'.[4]

Between 1660, when Laroon came to London, and 1739, when Amigoni left, a vital school of English printmaking began to sprout in the wake of Britain's rise as an economic force and a political power. The English school's manifesto may arguably be identified as the *Harlot's Progress* (1732), so popular that Abbé Le Blanc claimed he had 'not seen a house of note' without this and Hogarth's other moral prints, by which 'the whole nation has been infected'.[5] The aesthetic revolution launched by the *Harlot* and secured by Hogarth's other progresses was reported – and denigrated – by the Swiss artist Jean Rouquet, in his *Present State of the Arts in England* (1755): 'Mr. Hogarth has furnished England with a new kind of pictures, which contain a great number of figures, and are generally seven or eight inches high. These extraordinary pieces are properly the history of some vice, frequently a little too much *charged* for foreigners but always full of wit and novelty'.[6]

Shortly after Hogarth's pronunciamento, the London Cries changed hands and shape. Increasingly identified as an indigenous genre about a British city and its British inhabitants, it passed out of the custody of continental artists oriented toward art historical traditions from France, Italy, or the Netherlands and into the orb of native artists who opposed such 'foreign' conventions with English naturalism and satire. Led by Hogarth, these aesthetic nationalists championed 'common and unabstracted nature' in a vernacular style tied to familiar life. Devoted to the modern and the ordinary, this popular English style stood in deliberate opposition to the grand manner of continental painting which, in Reynolds's words, rises 'above all singular forms, local customs, particularities, and details of every kind'.[7] Instead of portraying heroic actions in the generalized language of classical idealism, native craftsmen, in a mood of xenophobic opposition, cultivated particularity, iconoclasm, comedy, and especially empiricism, laying the foundation of what, a century later, was criticized as 'the expressly materialistic, plebian, and democratic propensities of the English school'.[8]

They viewed art as a way to assert national interest, promote local spirit and clarify English identity. 'Everything requisite to compleat the consummate painter or sculptor may be had with the utmost ease without going out of London at this time', Hogarth decreed. 'Going to study abroad is an errant farce and more likely to confound a true genius than to improve him'.[9] Despite such patriotic bravado, native craftsmen were haunted by the stylistic authority of continental painters, with whom they were trapped in bitter economic rivalries. 'Nothing goes down but the Work of Foreigners', Campbell lamented in *The London Tradesman* (1747), usually a dispassionate source of factual information. 'Let our own Hands excell ever so much, their Work do [*sic*] not bring them one Tenth of the Price that is afforded to the meanest *Italian* bungler'.[10]

How, in such a climate, did the new British custodians of the Cries treat it and its hawkers? This chapter provides an answer by looking at the strikingly different ways one foreign artist and two Englishmen, active in the 1740s, responded to Laroon's and Amigoni's street criers. Examining a quartet of Cries by the little-known J. S. Müller, two prints by the unknown G. Child and a well-known engraving by William Hogarth, it chronicles a spectrum of formats and styles in which artists typically echoed, incorporated, rejected or satirized the Cries of their forerunners. Beginning with Müller, it reads a quartet of his prints as a flattering imitation of Amigoni's Cries, whose format and spirit it borrows. Moving to Child, it interprets two of his images as obscene travesties of Amigoni's designs. Ending with Hogarth, it reveals his 'Musician' and *Rake's Progress*, Plate IV, as unrecognized satires of Amigoni's and Laroon's London Cries. A work of art about the process and product of creating art works having hawkers as their subject, Hogarth's print is a treatise on representation and misrepresentation, but it is also as an evangelical exhibition devised by him in his role as the self-appointed spokesman of the first generation of indigenous craftsmen devoted to the English vernacular.

The heart of this chapter is a revisionist reading of 'The Enraged Musician'. However, the chapter also charts the shift in Cries from representation to pathos and satire, reflected in J. S. Müller's novelistic Cries and Child's satiric 'Golden Pippins' and 'Chimney-Sweeper's Boy'. It seeks to demonstrate the varied, ambitious, and experimental nature of printmaking in England at mid-century by capturing the high passions that surrounded the depiction of hawkers when the Cries of London thematized authenticity, intention and artistic epistemology as consequential topics, at the same time as it moved beyond its generic boundaries to inspire satires, burlesques and new designs of many different kinds.

Among the Cries inspired by Amigoni's ensemble, J. S. Müller's 'The Wretched Shoe-Boy' (**4.1**), 'The Milk Maid on May-Day' (**4.2**), 'Baby, Cloaths, & All for Three Pence' (**4.3**), and 'The Blind Musician' (**4.4**) are the most inventive.[11] Published in the 1740s, this quartet of images is indebted to Amigoni's foursome for its format, with its emphasis on make-believe settings and monumental figures. But it also draws upon Amigoni for its pathos, conspicuous in 'The Blind Musician' and 'The Wretched Shoe-Boy'.

If the format and tone of Müller's suite derive from Amigoni, its legends are original. These inscriptions, twelve or sixteen lines of heroic couplets, poeticize and novelize the Cries as never before. Moreover, their ornate calligraphy has a visual character independent of their messages. Indeed these cannibalistic 'appendages' threaten the balance between

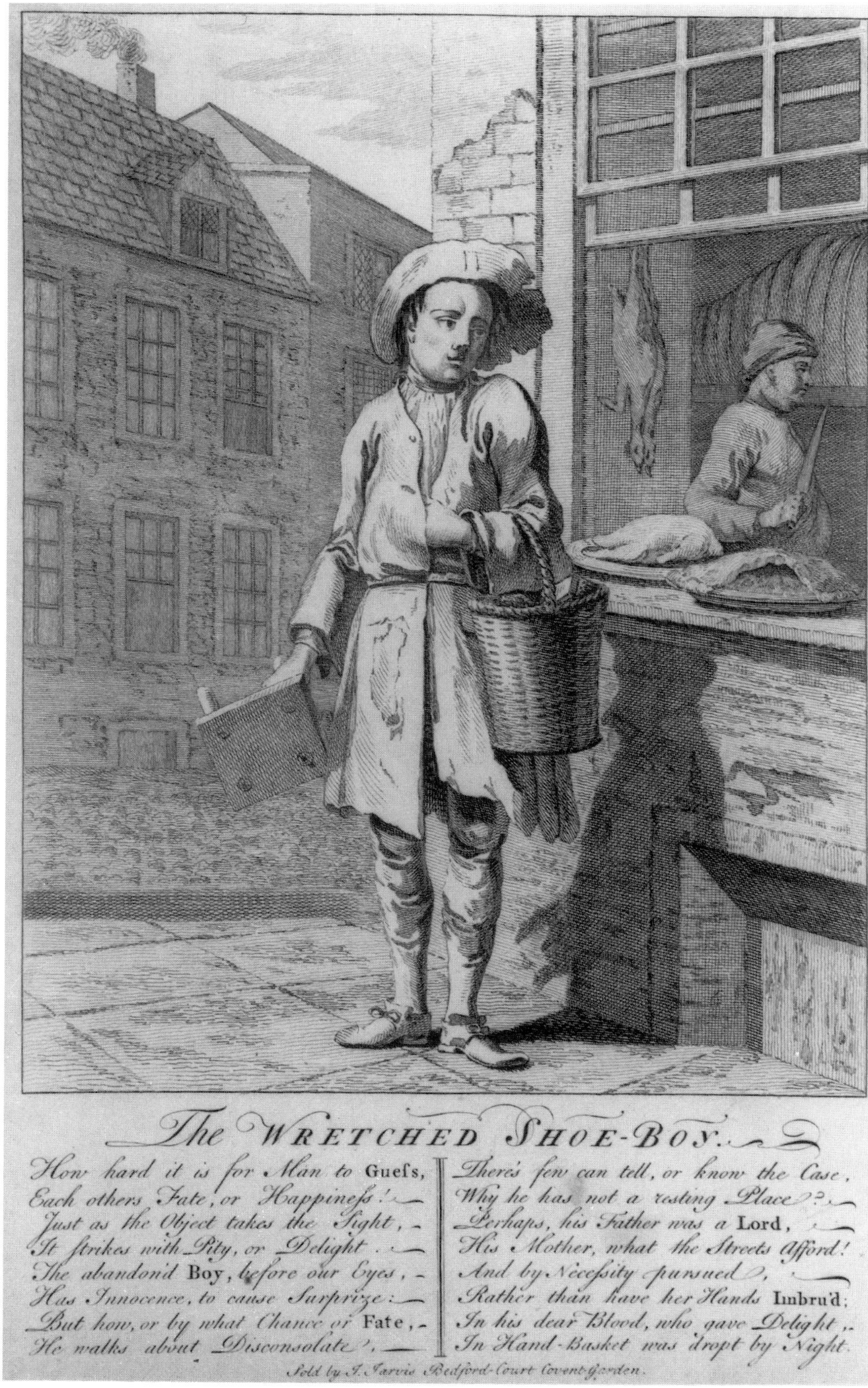

4.1 J. S. Müller, 'The Wretched Shoe-Boy', *c.* 1740

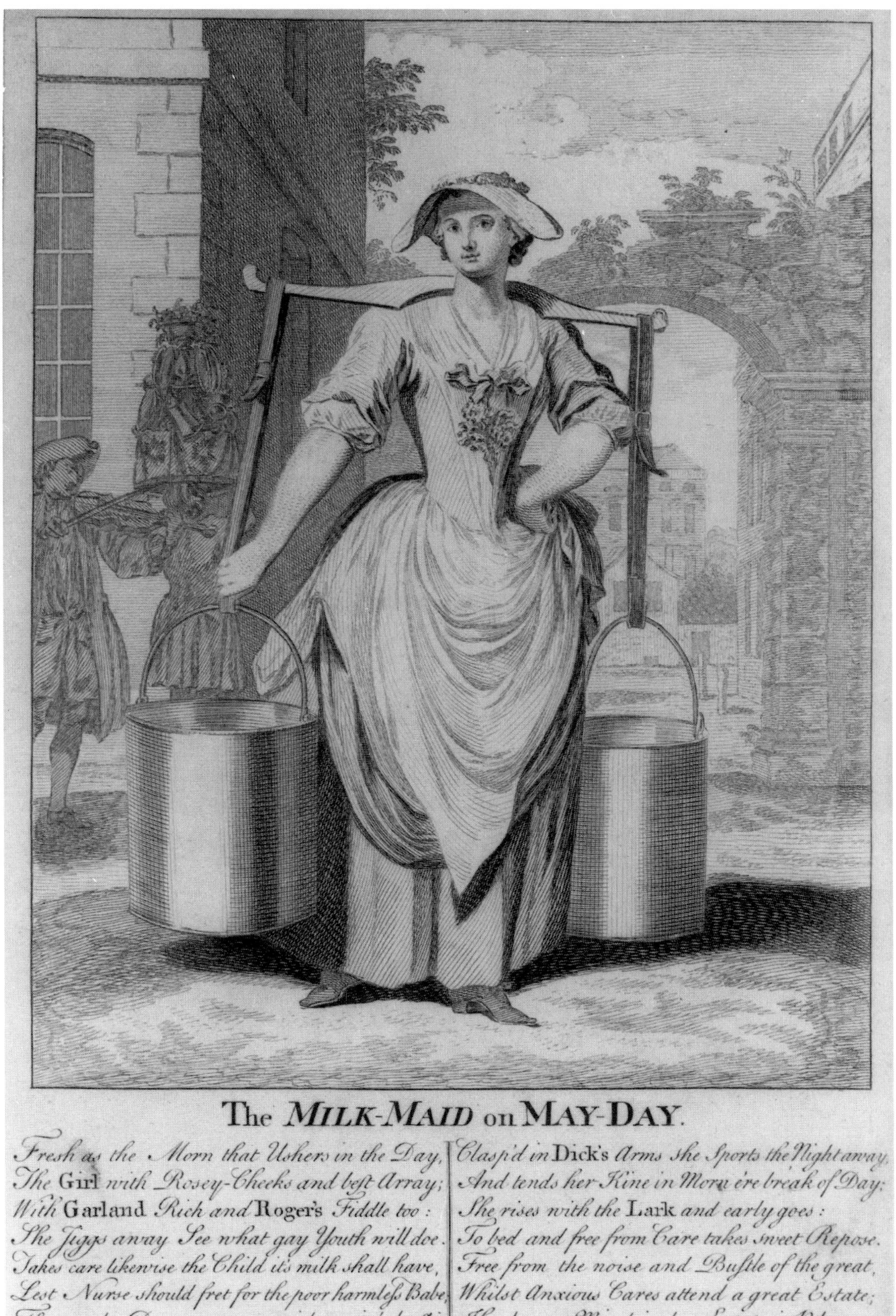

4.2 J. S. Müller, 'The Milk-Maid on May-Day', *c.* 1740

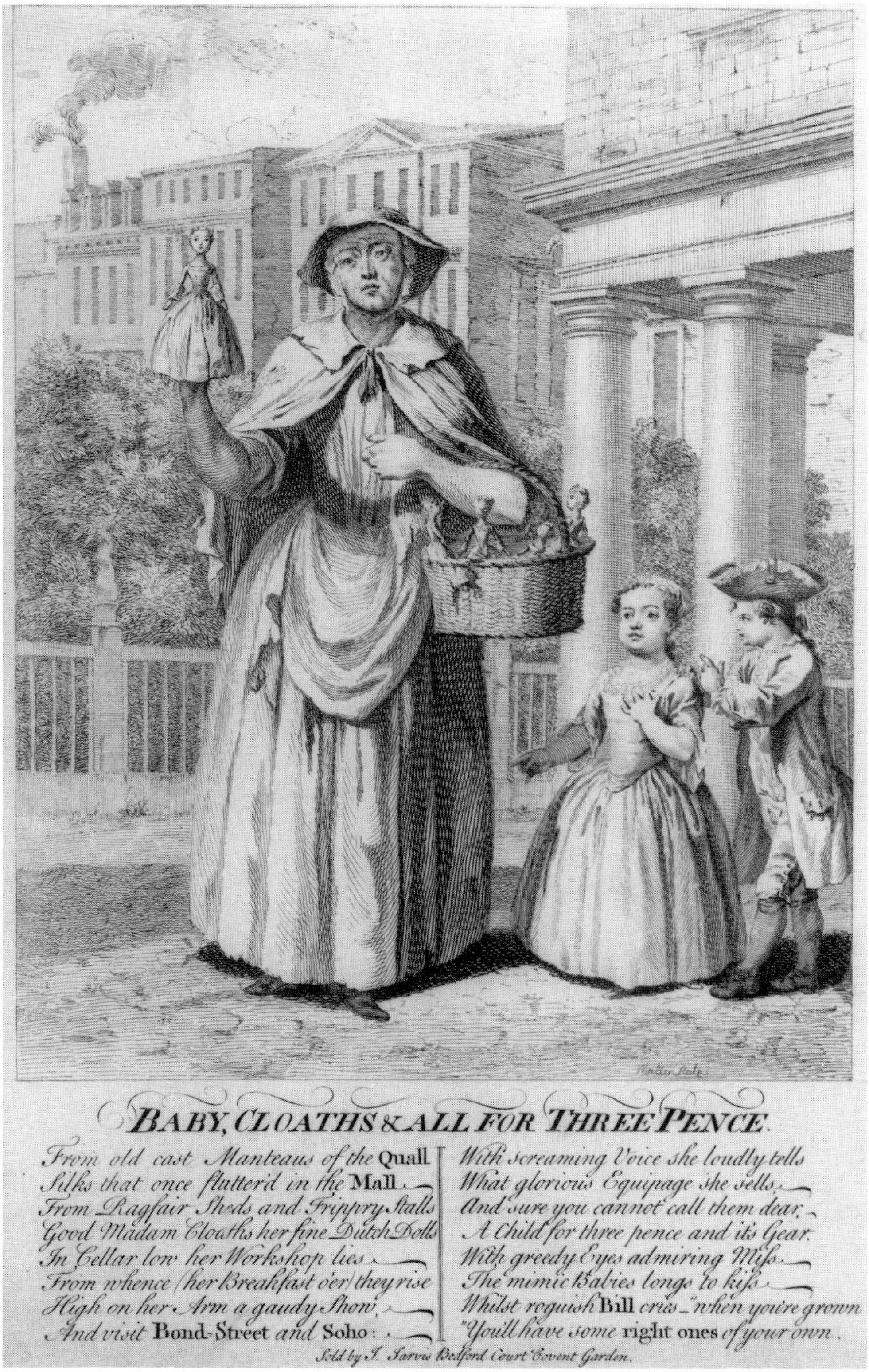

4.3 J. S. Müller, 'Baby, Cloaths & All Three Pence', *c.* 1740

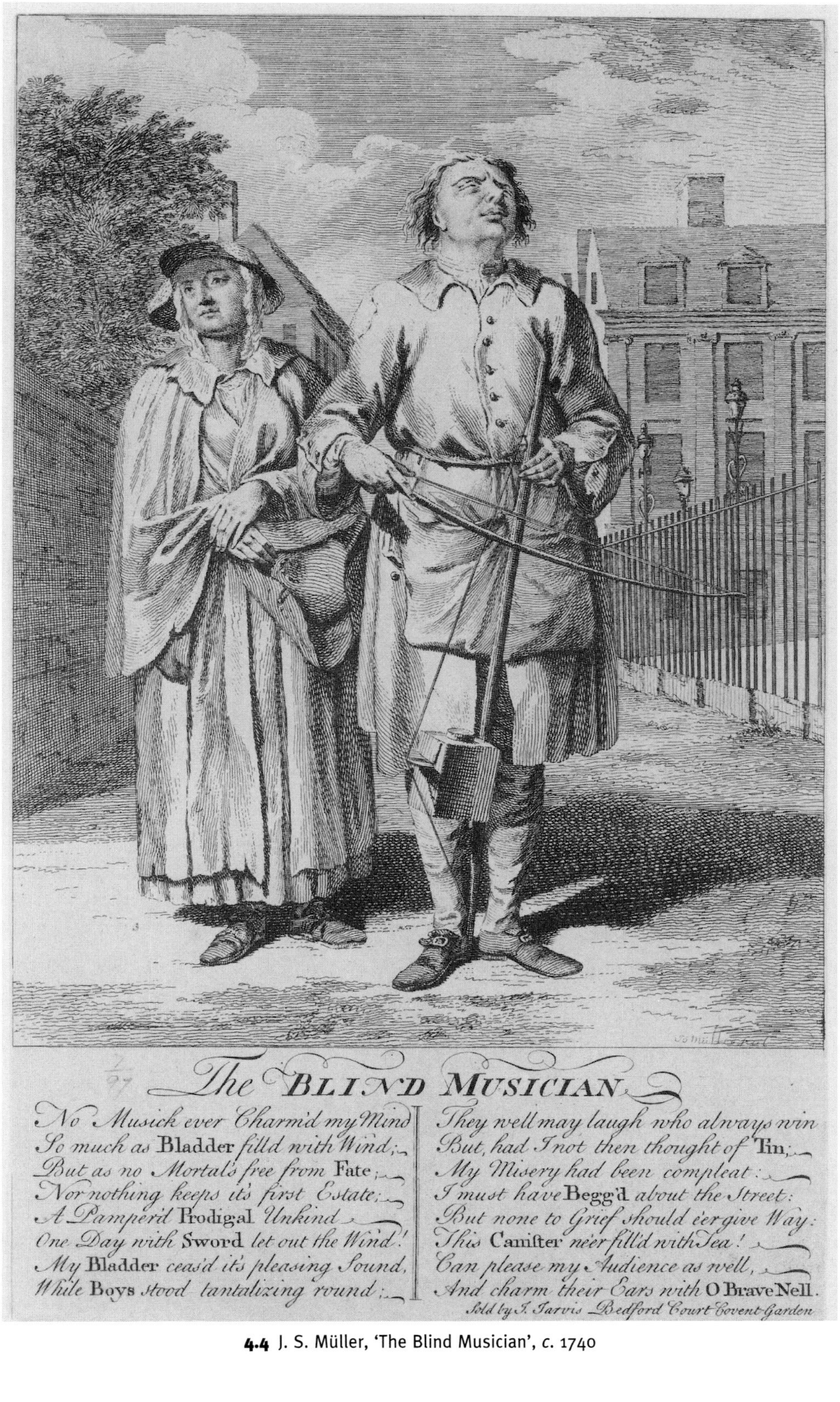

4.4 J. S. Müller, 'The Blind Musician', *c.* 1740

picture and poem. The texts drags the eye one way; the pictures pull it another.

These commentaries are, in content, every bit as iconoclastic as in form. Melodramatic, satiric or lyric verses, they transform hawkers from objects to subjects, making them characters in their own stories. The most ingenious of them invent anti-ecphrastic tales not told in the images. Like the plots of novels, they humanize hawkers by revealing thoughts, feelings and experiences not in Müller's emotionally flat or sentimental designs.

Take the portrait of the blind fiddler (**4.4**), a ballad monger and a ballad maker – copies of 'O brave Nell' spill out of the pouch of this plebeian Homer, whose lack of sight promises increased oral creativity, fulfilled by his autobiographical song with its dark vision regarding class conflict.[12] The print's caption is the song that this bard sings. It tells his life story in a ballad in which 'a Pamper'd Prodigal' punctures a musical bladder, requiring the instrumentalist to invent the 'tea-box and broom-stick fiddle' he plays. The ballad is remarkable for its concentration on social rank. Cries, though structurally devoted to the portrayal of 'low and base persons', hitherto evaded conflict between haves and have-nots; but the 'Musician' dramatizes such tension in an attack upon a beggar by an aristocrat, whose sword is a symbol of gentlemanly rank. The 'off-stage' attack is violent and unprovoked; its victim is poor, blind and submissive.

In making the wealthy character 'pampered', 'unkind' and 'prodigal' but casting the penniless fiddler as philosophic and industrious, this plot reverses the common practice of praising the rich and blaming the poor.[13] The fiddler, conscious that the indigent are not entitled to be idle (as the rich are), is eager to avoid beggary, as he tell us in his own startlingly 'authentic' voice:

But had I not then thought of Tin;
My Misery had been compleat:
I must have Begg'd about the Street:

An idealist who yearns to labour and equates beggary with 'compleat' misery, he evokes the stereotype of the deserving poor, the poor by destiny and order and not by idleness, extravagance or will, thereby opposing one stereotype to another one, which held that only the needy are debauched.[14]

In painting the vices of the rich and virtues of the poor, the 'Musician's' text propagandizes on behalf of the underclasses, making it the first Cries of London to espouse in words the cause of the destitute. But in warning that 'no Mortal's free from Fate', the text of this image offers a different message, phrased in the language of philosophical principle and aimed at the 'mechanics' for whom the fiddler stands.[15] It promotes subordination and long-suffering, exemplified by the musician's poverty, handicap, bodily toil and outcast life, dressed up to look natural and universal.

Trouble between London's haves and have-nots also surfaces in 'The wretched shoe-boy' (**4.1**), which, at first glance, seems to trade in pathos rather than in the colourful costumes and engaging city folklore of the 'Milk-Maid' or 'Baby, Cloaths & All for Three Pence'. In fact, this sombre print, the first Cries of London to juxtapose outcast and upper caste, presents a conflict between a cook and a ragged youth whose mother, 'by Necessity pursued', abandoned him on a London street instead of murdering him ('Rather than have her Hands Imbru'd; / In his dear Blood, who gave Delight'). The plump cook is surrounded by plucked chickens, a fat goose and a tempting pie. The thin boy is alone, hungry and unemployed, but not idle: though the street is deserted, this sentimental bootblack lingers in hope of trade.

His longing glance at the pie argues he is about to pinch it, making this image the first Cries to hint that the poor prey upon the rich, just as, in 'The Blind Musician', the rich savage the poor. Showing haves and have-nots heading for trouble, it treats the latter with more apparent sympathy and real condescension: the shoe-boy is 'Wretched'; he deserves our pity. And the print clothes its inflammatory theme in muted imagery. The rich are pictured only in their deputy, the cook, whose knife – exaggerated in immensity and raised to strike – promises blood. And the poor's envoy – powerless, passive and childish – is neither angry nor threatening. The boy contemplates a crime, but he does not yet commit it; so the picture casts rich and poor as people of contrast, not conflict. Still, the print nudges the London Cries closer to social art more than any other example before Paul Sandby.

In Müller's Cries, texts assume a dynamic role; they give peddlers 'private histories' recalling the lives of characters from the prose fiction of the same period: Jonathan Wild, Moll Flanders, Pamela, Joseph Andrews and Tom Jones, all marginal figures, thieves and even foundlings of noble parentage, like the shoe black. Making its debut at the same time as the first English novels of the 1740s, this ensemble registers the same interests as early fiction: social desegregation, class difference and sexual conflict, all the subject of keen interest following the revolutions of the seventeenth century. Novels and prints picture the city as a place of unseen connection and hidden alliance; both represent the poor as intertwined with people of the middling sort; both fear this intertwining, which subverts hierarchies.[16]

Such misgivings are palpable in the 'Shoe-Boy' and *Moll Flanders*. In print and novel, the middling sort use their characteristic cultural artifacts to war with the lower order as much with the aristocracy. The larcenous glance of the youth suggests a nervousness, among those who bought prints and read novels, about street hawkers as a source of offences against property. The boy's predicament and his inclination to crime, according to the print's text, are genetic, the consequence of a sexual offence hidden in his origins. The youth is a bastard, the spawn of a 'mixed' union between a lord and a whore, whose sexuality exemplifies what is mercenary about ties formed in London: urbanity makes possible and even promotes wickedness. But the other agent of corruption is the youth's mother, singled out for scrutiny and labelled 'what the Streets Afford'.[17] Whoring mother and thieving son, protean man and woman who are the nightmares of modern urbanity, incarnate the misgivings that closeness to have-nots inspired in haves.[18]

About the time that Müller drew inspiration from Amigoni's quartet, an English engraver called G. Child was outraged by the same prints. Venting his irritation, Child concocted a reply, which survives in the form of two prints picturing Amigoni's hawkers as scamps or worse. In contrast to Müller's quartet, which flatters Amigoni and imitates him, Child's engravings taunt the Italian, using scabrousness and personal invective. Published in the 1740s, 'M'st ye ha' some Golden Pippins' (**4.5**) and 'The Chimney-Sweeper's Boy' (**4.6**) appeared about the time the rich Venetian artist had returned to his native Italy.[19] Both were cut by the mysterious engraver who signs himself 'G. Child Sculps'. Child does not appear in any history of graphic art in England.[20] The only works by him in the British Museum's Department of Prints and Drawings are two book illustrations.[21] At first glance, his prints evoke the plagiaries that English craftsmen made of Laroon's *Cryes* in the 1690s and later. However, Child adds long, interpretative

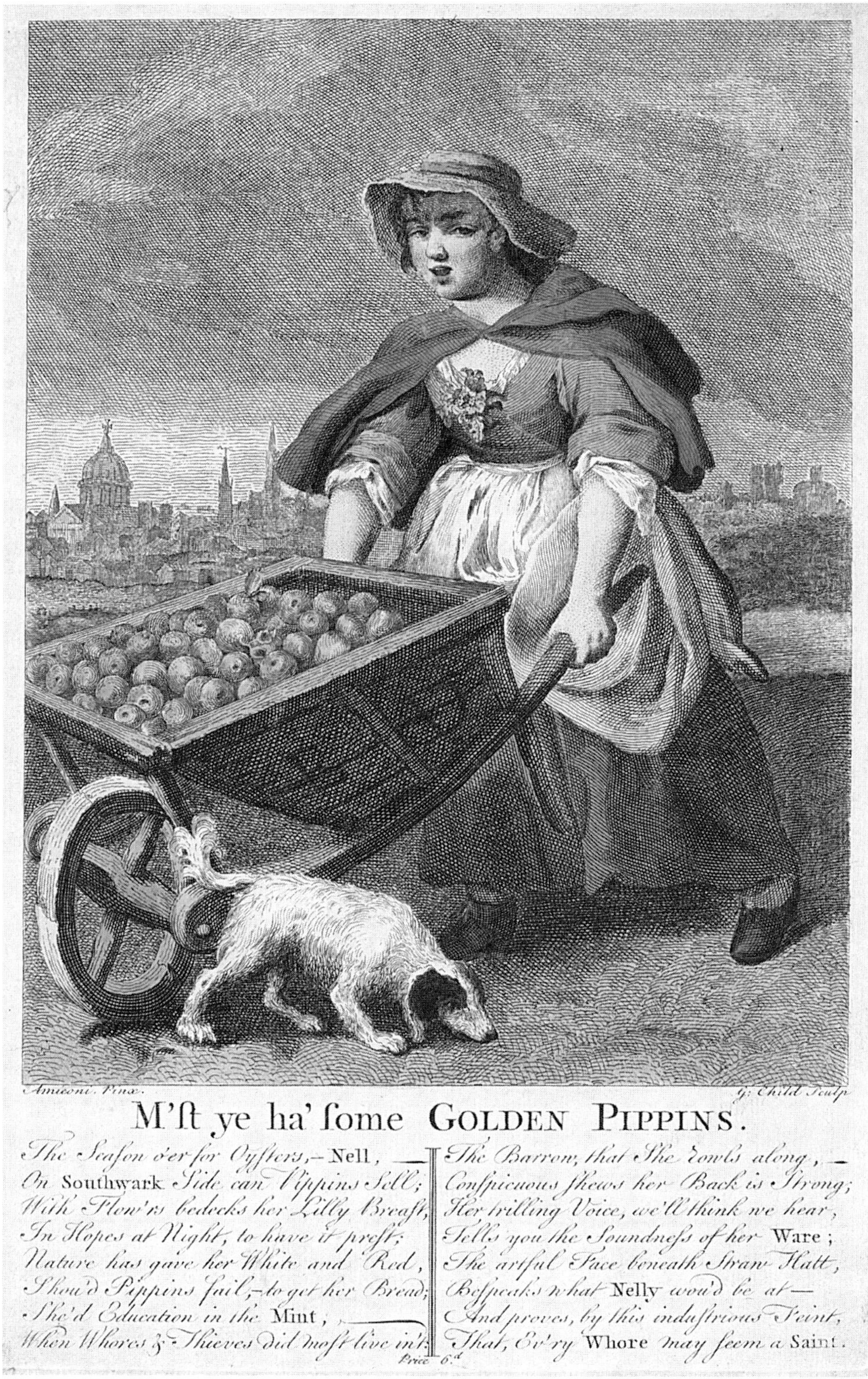

4.5 G. Child, 'M'st ye ha' some Golden Pippins', *c.* 1740

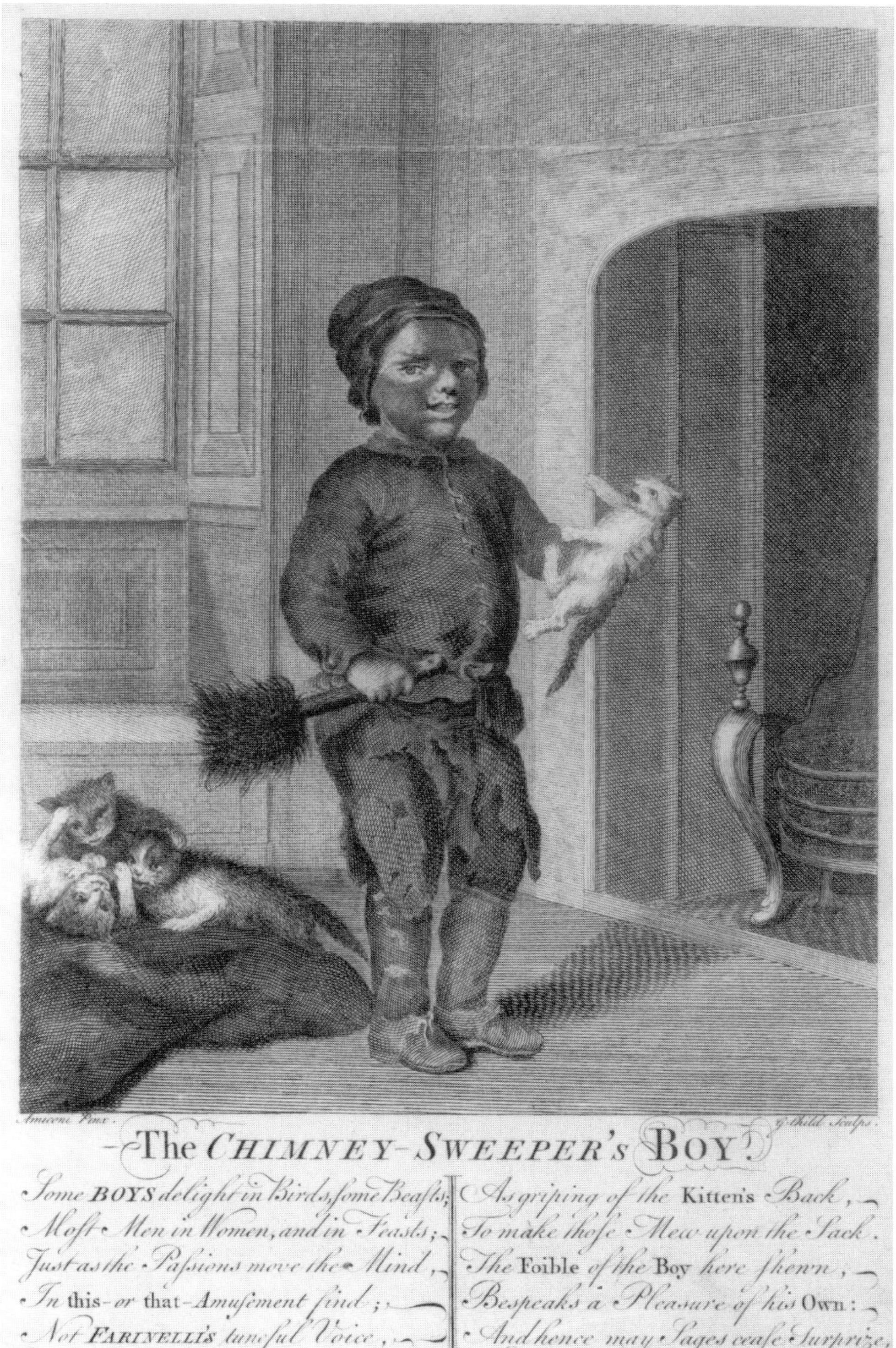

4.6 G. Child, 'Chimney-Sweeper's Boy', *c.* 1740

verses to Amigoni's original iconography, just as J. S. Müller does in his quartet.[22] He literally reinscribes the Italian's designs, adding to or replacing his short titles with long commentaries that resemble Müller's.

Formally, Child's 'The Chimney-Sweeper's Boy' (**4.6**) exactly replicates Amigoni's 'Chimney Sweeper', except for the transposition created by copying. But this palimpsest's mischievous text, comparing the sweeper to men who delight 'in Women, and in Feasts', attributes dissipated motives to the innocent-looking urchin, perverting the meaning of Amigoni's original iconography, which ennobles the youth. According to Child's new message, the boy is a knave who derives 'a Pleasure of his Own' from manhandling the kitten; that pleasure delights him (sadistically, by implication) more 'than Farinelli's tuneful Voice', a baffling reference to the famous Italian castrato worshipped by English opera lovers in the 1730s.

This vein of ribaldry turns erotic in Child's second image, 'M'st ye ha' some Golden Pippins' (**4.5**), which telegraphs its 'low' mood by the 'low' dialect of the coster's cry. The young apple woman, we learn, 'With Flow'rs bedecks her Lilly Breast, / In Hopes at Night, to have it prest'. But Nell (whose 'Back is Strong') wishes her breast pressed for money, not love:

Nature has gave her White and Red,
Shou'd Pippins fail, to get her Bread;
She'd Education in the Mint,
When Whores & Thieves did most live in't.

The frankest lines of the commentary paint Nell as a trollop and hypocrite:

The artful Face beneath Straw hatt,
Bespeaks what Nelly wou'd be at
And proves, by this industrious Point,
That Ev'ry Whore may seem a Saint.

With this lewd verse, Child transforms his Cries – and Amigoni's – into pornographic suites catering to the sexual fantasies of men. His transformation exploits the ill repute of fancy pictures and Cries as prurient genres, called 'Postures', 'wanton pieces', or 'Bawdies'. Cries and fancies earned that reputation because they sometimes equated buying and selling with striking sexual bargains.[23] Both featured, in their canon, harlots like the 'London Curtezan' or racy women trading on sexual allure like the famous Dutch rope dancer. Indeed, in any Cries, fetching vendors might be strumpets, or fetching strumpets might be vendors, especially when the objects these jades sell are suggestive, as chestnuts, leeks and a cornucopia of other fruits or vegetables are. This titillating ambiguity is illustrated by Charles Brandoin's 'A Ladies Maid Purchasing a Leek' (**4.7**), an erotic urban scene of buying and selling that evokes Cries but also parodies continental fête galantes, the refined pastoral form thriving in England in the 1770s. A scene of intrigue, it identifies

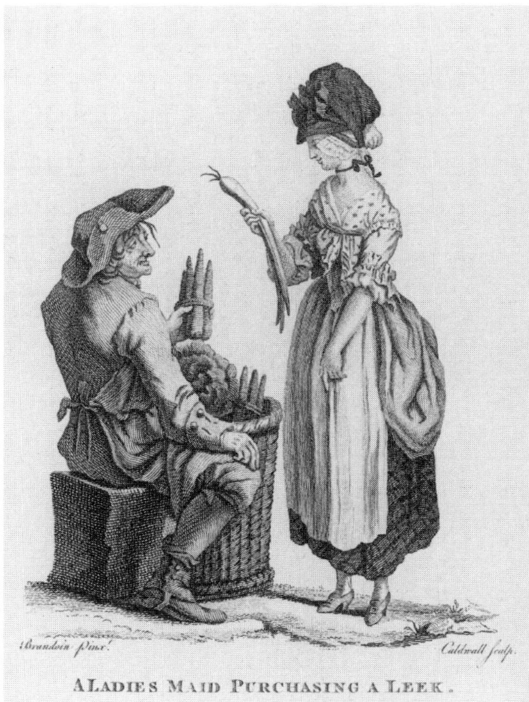

4.7 Charles Brandoin, 'A Ladies Maid Purchasing a Leek', late eighteenth century

street commerce with sexual negotiation. But it reverses the internal conventions of this kind of popular ribaldry: a seller of the lowest order who is male propositions a buyer of higher status ('a ladies maid') who is female and who regards his offer not with outrage but amused scepticism.[24]

Child's travesties, turning Amigoni's sentimental designs into lewd prints, represent an unknown skirmish in a well-known war waged against the Venetian painter. The war was begun in the 1730s, when Hogarth, with a set of English writers, formed a cabal to ruin the continental adventurer. Amigoni, when he first came to England in 1729, was patronized by English nobles and royalty.[25] His success irritated xenophobic natives, who held a low estimate of his painting, a judgement shared by contemporary connoisseurs and art historians. 'Amiconi's women are meer chalk, as if he had only painted from ladies who paint themselves', Walpole declared, echoing the view of Vertue who maintained that his portraits are 'neither like nor correct'.[26]

'Seingor' Amigoni, as he styled himself in London, quickly became a society darling by exploiting his links to the Italian opera.[27] He came to England with an opera singer, married an Italian mezzo-soprano nicknamed 'La Luccesina' in 1738, and formed a power alliance with Farinelli and Nicolo Porpora of Naples, the soprano's teacher who was also a composer with a new company in London called the *Opera of the Nobility*.[28] Their contemporary, the musicologist John Hawkins, records that the three were 'united in the bonds of a strict friendship and a communion of interests: at the same time as the nobility under the new subscription engaged with Farinelli, they also agreed with the composer Porpora as a composer for the opera and with Amiconi to paint the scenes'.[29] In two years, Farinelli made enough money to build an Italian villa, which Burney nicknamed 'The English Folly'.[30]

Amigoni was acclaimed too, in part because Farinelli patronized him by buying – perhaps 'acquiring' might be more accurate – his pictures.[31] The singer accumulated twenty-three of his designs; were some – or all – gifts from a self-promoting artist, perhaps?[32] In July 1735, 'a great concourse of persons of distinction [went] every day to his [Amigoni's] house to view his full-length portrait of Farinelli'.[33] Done in the best operatic style, this portrait (which Wagner engraved and sold at his shop in Great Marlborough street) shows Farinelli not as the fat, slouching castrato Hogarth ridiculed in a counter-portrait in *Marriage à la Mode* (**plate 4**), but as a demigod crowned by Euterpe, heralded by Fame, and attended by putti.[34] Thus Child's enigmatic reference to 'Farinelli's tuneful Voice' as less pleasurable to the boy sweep than his childish sadism. This mockery is rendered more piquant by the fact that the celebrated soprano, as everyone in the parochial art world of eighteenth-century London knew, owned two of Amigoni's Cries in oil: *Golden Pippins* and *Chimney Sweeper*.[35]

The clique of Englishmen who plotted to vilify Amigoni was composed of the painter John Ellys, James Ralph who edited the *Weekly Register*, Fielding the novelist, and Hogarth.[36] To this gang of xenophobes, the name of 'G. Child' must now be added. Who is this mysterious figure, whose prints have not been noticed until now? I do not think 'Child' is a pseudonym for Hogarth. Though he gave one of his surrogates in *Industry and Idleness* the name 'Goodchild', the English artist loved to avow his views publicly, even when this practice led to brawls. He was probably a crony of Hogarth's or a hireling of his friends. And what is to be made of the perplexing letters 'E' and 'D' carved on the side of the coster's wheelbarrow? This 'ED' monogram, not in Amigoni's design, may be the signature of the real artist, while 'G. Child' is the signature of the mere letter engraver. Whatever his identity, this prankster, by signing these two images 'Amiconi Pinx', casts his quarry as a servant of the debauched and depraved, whom he supplies with child pornography. With this characterization, he lands the best-placed blow of any member of his clique on the reputation of the Italian. The blow is especially well aimed because while Amigoni promoted himself as a practitioner of biblical frescoes, historical narratives, royal portraiture and other elevated genres, he traded in semi-pornographic prints. His *Five Senses*, sold by T. Jeffreys in the Strand and W. Herbert on London Bridge, all feature voluptuous women alluringly posed in degrees of nudity. The lewdness of these prints is clear in 'Feeling', showing a half-naked woman who looks at the viewer as she fingers the tip of a phallic arrow with one hand and caresses its shaft with the other.

Around the time Child attacked Amigoni, Hogarth advertised 'The enraged musician' (**4.8**). Recently singled out by David

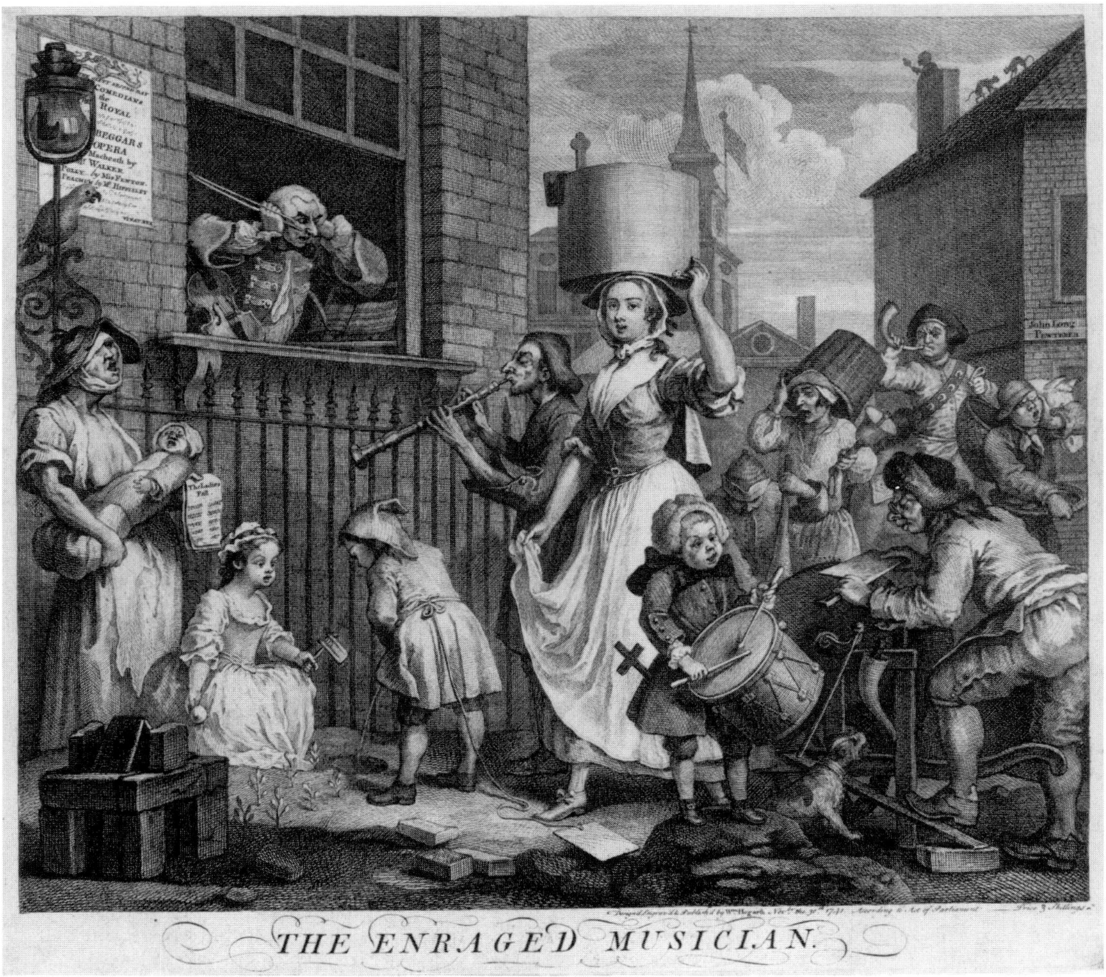

4.8 William Hogarth, 'The Enraged Musician', 1741

Bindman as 'the most richly comic of all Hogarth's prints', it shows a phalanx of raucous hawkers invading a city lane.[37] With the clarity of an historical document, it mirrors the pandemonium that gripped the streets of London in the eighteenth century, Hogarth scholars have shown. Here the city's nefarious street commerce erupts in a vocal/musical class war, waged between the proponents of euphony and of discord, between a 'high' foreign musician come from Italy to amuse the aristocracy and a horde of 'low' British labourers playing their overtures upon bells, grinding wheels, and horns, or – worst of all – screaming their vulgar operas of the street in cacophonous voices.[38]

So much for the engraving's social meaning, or one of its social meanings, which historians of art call its pre-iconographic subject and primary topic. But what about the print's secondary subject, that world of referents and formal links illuminating the image's conception, production and artistic meaning, about which scholars, except for Frederick Antal and David Bindman, have been silent? What about its contexts and its allusions to other art, especially popular art?

More than a transparent image chronicling the city's bustle in a lifelike way, 'The Enraged Musician' belongs to a network of images created by many different artists, all involved in the depiction of hawkers. Antal classes the 'Musician' as a design in which 'the continuation of the [Cries] tradition is clearly apparent', and Bindman asserts that 'it belongs to the genre of London cries but is organized into a composition instead of separate figures'.[39] Though emphatically not a Cries of London, it can only be fully and properly understood in the light of this genre. It responds directly to the pictorial conventions and habitual subject matter of Cries, using artful repetitions and dissonances of theme or style to rebuke that genre as continentals had practised it.[40] A picture about knowing and picturing, the print borrows from Cries, combining the 'big sheet' format of the early broadsides with the particularizing techniques of the later ensembles. In this it is both a satire and a manifesto. A satire, it ridicules the Cries of those foreign artists – chiefly Laroon and Amigoni – who, in Hogarth's self-promoting view, warped the depiction of London hawkers in the late seventeenth and early eighteenth centuries. When conceptions of national character were among the most highly charged myths of state and culture, it stands as a manifesto of popular British art and an 'exhibition picture' of what a Londoner could do when he took an old continental theme and gave it a new, delightfully original English twist.[41]

'The Enraged Musician' belonged to a 'Set': three prints treating the art of painting.[42] The set's first print was 'The Distressed Poet', issued in 1737; its second was the 'Musician', published 30 November 1741; its third is unknown. Who bought 'The Provok'd Musician', to call it by its advertised title? To subscribers who paid for his progresses before they were published, the artist gave small designs as receipts and keepsakes; surviving examples of these subscription tickets, some bearing the names of their owners in the artist's hand, have never been studied as evidence of Hogarth's audience, described by George Vertue as composed of 'persons of fashion and artists'. They demonstrate that his prints were purchased chiefly by middle-class professionals: lawyers, bankers, doctors and government functionaries, some of whom Hogarth identified as 'Esquires' to acknowledge them as gentlemen by birth, position or education. Men rather than women, these buyers are typified by the following individuals whose names survive on subscription tickets: Joseph Andrews Esq.,

William Dale, John Danby Esq., Alexander Dobson, Nicholas Fazakerley, Henry Gray, Mr. Hackton, John Huggins Esq., James King, George Lambert, William Windham Esq., and Thomas Wrisht.[43] But these tickets also show that Hogarth's prints charmed some aristocrats like Lord Biron, the Duke of Richmond, the Duke of Queensborough and Horace Walpole (1717–97), though he disliked 'The Enraged Musician'. Comparing it with two other Hogarth engravings, the Earl of Orford was troubled at what he viewed as the print's mood of horseplay: 'His Bartholomew-fair is full of humour; the March to Finchley, of nature, [but] the Enraged Musician tends to farce', he proclaimed.[44]

Hogarth's engraving was gestating in the late 1730s, when Laroon's ensemble was still making money by selling to the same audience the satirist cultivated.[45] It was advertised seven years after another reissue of Laroon's *Cryes* in 1733 and one year after Amigoni's quartet of 1739. These two foreigners' ensembles, the first trading on costume and the second on pathos, constitute its artistic background. In a more subtle and original way than Child's travesties, the 'Musician' rebuts and willfully deforms the intricate images of the Dutch artist and the sentimental ones of the Italian.[46] Throughout the 1730s, that Italian was Hogarth's nemesis. In 1736, feeling especially beleaguered, Hogarth engineered his own election to the Board of Governors of St Bartholomew's in order to deny Amigoni the commission to paint the hospital staircase. Next the belligerent Englishman, whose own allies branded him 'the little Game Cock of Covent Garden', did the St Bartholomew job for nothing.[47]

Three years later, in another artistic mugging, Hogarth published 'The Enraged Musician'. He sold it for three shillings and formatted it as a large broadside. The broadside format, updated by the addition of narrative, offered Hogarth an economic edge as well as useful historical and ideological ties. By 1740, ensembles like Laroon's, featuring seventy-four engravings cut in what Vertue calls a 'neater and finer' style, as opposed to a 'loose and open' one, were extravaganzas of the past.[48] The copper and the skilled labours of engravers needed to produce such a suite would have cost a sum of money so astronomical it could not have been recouped.[49] The copper alone for seventy-four engravings, at 25/– per plate, would have cost almost £100.[50] In 1750, the French artist Bernard Baron charged one hundred-and-fifty pounds to scrape a large copper plate and thirty pounds to engrave a small one. Seventy-four of the smaller plates, about the size of Laroon's, would have cost £2,220.[51] Hogarth's print, issued as a single sheet selling for three shillings, undercut Laroon's *Cryes* at half a guinea and challenged Amigoni's quartet at about two shillings.[52]

Hogarth distanced the hawkers in his 'Musician' from those of his continental rivals not only by reviving the unfashionable broadside but also by linking his peddlers to an actual London setting and giving them palpable British identities in order to illustrate his dogma that English art should be English. He contended that the paintings of foreign rivals were self-referential and out of touch with everyday English life. To expose their 'monsters of Heraldry' and create an art 'something like Nature' he aimed to produce 'Modern Moral Subjects'.[53] These modern moral subjects had two features. They represented 'a Field unbroke up in any Country or any age', meaning they were not enchained by artistic convention, an early example of the conviction that later turned into the battle cry of Romantic poets and painters.[54] Unlike myths, often international and cosmopolitan, they were national and provincial, even chauvinistic; they were not only 'descriptive of the peculiar manners & characters of the English nation', they were specific to London and to the neighbourhood of St Martin-in-the-Fields, where he lived.[55] In mirroring 'the customs, manners, fashions, Characters, and humours of the present age in this country', Hogarth made the 'Musician' British by peopling it with British types, locating it in a British setting, and above all filling it with British noise.[56]

The first target of the 'Musician' is the nationality of Laroon's and Amigoni's peddlers. Laroon's hawkers, posed in white space, float in a no man's land free of city bustle and barren of clues about their national origins or place of work. Without a street, church or house to link them to the capital, they could be Romans or Parisians, Scots from Edinburgh, or Irish from Dublin, as so many 'Londoners' really were. They 'speak' three languages; their shouts are scratched in English, French and Italian; but they themselves are pictured outside time, place and culture. The nationality of Amigoni's vendors is only a little less vague: their stereotyped urban backgrounds evoke no historical locale. They derive from the common practice of continental printmakers who represent Segovia, Prague, Nurenberg and Valencia by the same generic urban view, an interchangeable *typus* meant to convey, not an individual town, but the idea of a town.[57] Except for 'Golden Pippins', which represents London by St Paul's dome, these placid, fictive scenes are mute about the national identity of their child hawkers or the name of the city where they labour.

By contrast, Hogarth's street sellers are English, and their place of work is a jumbled London. His 'Enraged Musician' is the first picture of hawkers to evoke an historic neighborhood in a way that makes it recognizable. The street where John Long practices pewter-making, even the house where the violinist fiddles, have historical identities. The scene's conspicuous steeple belongs to St Martin-in-the-Fields.[58] George Stephens verifies the traditional identification by pointing out that St Martin's Church hoisted a flag (flying in the print) on its steeple to mark certain holidays when its bells were rung, a custom Hogarth knew from living in Leicester Square, two streets to the northwest.[59] According to eighteenth-century commentator John Ireland, the exact setting of 'The enraged musician' is St Martin's Lane. That real 'thoroughfare', in contrast to Amigoni's faux streets with their broad, orderly, static lines, is represented as the narrow, crowded alley it truly was.[60]

Balancing reportage with dramatic conviction, the engraving shows a street so confused in layout and architecture that its buildings battle each other for what elbow room there is. The most prominent of these buildings is the musician's house.[61] It is not devised by a scene-painter as a theatrical background, a genre of artificial locations illustrated by the stagy dwellings in the Cries of Amigoni, who painted sets for Farinelli's Italian operas. Rather, it is conceived in response to an historical building and executed as a satiric topographer might draw it. Indeed the identity of the house is recorded on the strength of its appearance. The violinist's address, by a Hogarthian conceit alluding to the design's artistic theme, was the home of William Huggins (1696–1761),[62] who drafted the Engraving Copyright Act of 1735.[63]

'The Enraged Musician's' English setting is peopled by English hawkers whose national identity appears in their rough visages interpreted by contemporaries as characteristic of London's lower orders; Abbé Le Blanc claims, in his *Letters*, that British audiences preferred 'the print of a game-keeper, whose sole merit lies in his carbuncled face' before a portrait of one of the handsomest sopranos in Europe – Farinelli.[64] The 'buttocks-of-beef' looks of the fishmonger with the squint and the cyclops-like gelder with the bulging eye are trenchant critiques of Amigoni's soulful, angelic faces; hardy, rough-hewn 'originals' like these anticipate the nationalism of a commentary on George Morland's figures: 'His sailors are British, and have braved many a storm . . . His fishermen, postboys and ostlers are *English – English, Sirs, from top to toe*'.[65]

Within Hogarth's print, these plebeian faces contrast with the Roman nose and full lips of the mediterranean violinist, of whom Jean Rouquet remarked (upon the artist's authority), 'Le Musicien est un Italien que les cris de Londres font enrager'.[66] The effete man's foreign looks are underlined by his style of dress: the bag wig, solitaire, elegant ruffled shirt, and, decorating his coat, the ornamental loops known as 'frogs', here turned into a Francophobic pun of the sort Hogarth relished.[67] Protected from the mob by a spear-like fence, he is the prototype of 'imported' impresarios, artists and painters as well as musicians and composers encroaching upon the livelihood of English performers.

But double irony is the soul of Hogarth's wit. He proposes norms only to subvert them, and gives characters identities that turn out to be the opposite of what they first seem. A scrutiny of the 'Musician's' Londoners exposes them as British in the manner of Defoe's famous 'True-Born Englishman', a 'Het'rogeneous Thing' who was no more English than William III and the first two Georges.[68] The paver is Irish; he wears 'the peculiar cap of his people, being of a bee-hive shape, having the lower edge turned up to form a brim'.[69] The milkmaid is neither a Londoner nor English. Dairy women came to the capital from farms where they serviced cows and endured punishing manual labour; their duties were so physically demanding that the seventeenth-century reformer, Peter Chamberlen, proposed assigning such tasks to men, 'in regard of women's tenderness, and danger of going in the wet, besides the labour of bring it [milk] home'.[70] The milkmaid's trade was dominated by the hardy stock of Wales and Ireland, the likely home of this woman.[71] Woodwind players in London during the first half of the eighteenth century were chiefly foreigners.[72] The hautboy player is a Jew come to England under Cromwell's dispensation; perhaps he hails from France, where the woodwind was invented.[73] His nose is hooked (following the practice in anti-semitic caricature), and he is the only bearded fellow in a picture filled with clean-shaven men.[74] The little drummer is French, according to John Ireland, who based his assertion on the child's fashionable clothing: his bag wig, grand bow tie, and shoes with buckles.[75]

Of the eight street traders peopling 'The Enraged Musician', three come from Laroon's *Cryes*, which Hogarth knew well.[76] Writing of the tie between Cries and 'The Enraged Musician', Antal asserts that, even though a continuation of the tradition appears in the print, it 'is seldom possible to recognize the literal origins of figures from the Laroon set in Hogarth'.[77] In opposition to Antal, I argue with Bindman that Hogarth deliberately purloins Laroon figures that are, in fact, identifiable. These three figures – the ballad woman, the milk seller, and the knife grinder – constitute the print's structure, a pyramid projecting (with comic irony) a society of the London vulgar, hierarchically graded. The ballad monger, the most wretched figure, moors the picture on the bottom left; the knife grinder anchors it on the bottom right; the milkmaid, the most statuesque figure, forms its apex. The musician, to typify continental artists Hogarth detested, appears in a rectangle, off-centre and outside the admired form of the Renaissance pyramid.

This triangle of peddlers is important to theme as well as structure.[78] By it, Hogarth deforms Laroon's idealized figures, moving them out of individual portraits into communal dramas that are clamorous, quarrelsome, laborious and competitive. Picturing hawking as an encounter rather than a pose, he theatricalizes the push-and-pull that is the trade's pith. Compare, for example, Hogarth's knife grinder with Laroon's, from 'Knives or Cisers to Grinde' (**4.9**). Smoking a pipe, Laroon's grinder expresses, in his face and pose, a surprising ease and relaxation, as if he performed an urban version of what the more romantic of England's georgic poets called, without irony, 'happy labour' or 'grateful toil'.[79] In contrast to this blithe figure, Hogarth's peddler doubles over his wheel, leaning forward to concentrate better on his exacting chore; the intensity of the fellow's drudgery is underlined by the fact that he requires eye glasses to angle the blade across the spinning wheel. Here is a fellow whose nose is to the grindstone.

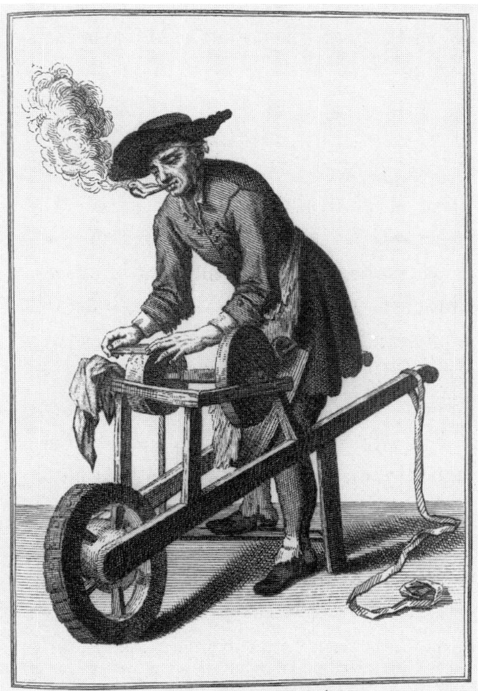

4.9 Marcellus Laroon, 'Knives or Cisers to Grinde', 1687

Knife grinding takes such a toll that he has parked his contraption in a shady patch of St Martin's Lane, though better light would aid his labours. He grinds so violently that his machine's wheel – three times bigger than Laroon's – fires off a shower of sparks, which evoke the 'steel-on-stone' rasp that made his calling more hated than any other type of street vendor.[80] Such knife sharpeners did not minister to householders, as the tiny blade in the hands of Laroon's figure implies. They served commercial people and heavy users: Hogarth's man hones a big meat cleaver. This tool evokes stinking slaughterers – and their wailing victims; the worst of these were the dog-and-cat's meat sellers, who purveyed a fetid stew of horse flesh, bullocks' guts, and tripe tied together in bunches agreed to be 'the most disagreeable and offensive commodity cried for sale in London'.[81] Laroon's figure represents knife-grinding as a restful trade, followed in quiet while puffing contentedly on a pipe of tobacco. Hogarth's man pursues an arduous calling with the din of London ringing in his ears. On his right, he is bedeviled by a dustman, a sow gelder, a fishmonger, and a paver; on his left, he is beset by a milkmaid, a drummer boy, and a barking dog, the witty reversal of the affectionate pet in Amigoni's 'Golden Pippins'.

Laroon's ballad monger (**4.10**) and Hogarth's (**4.8**) are, in formal ways, even more distant from each other than the two artists' knife grinders, but like them are

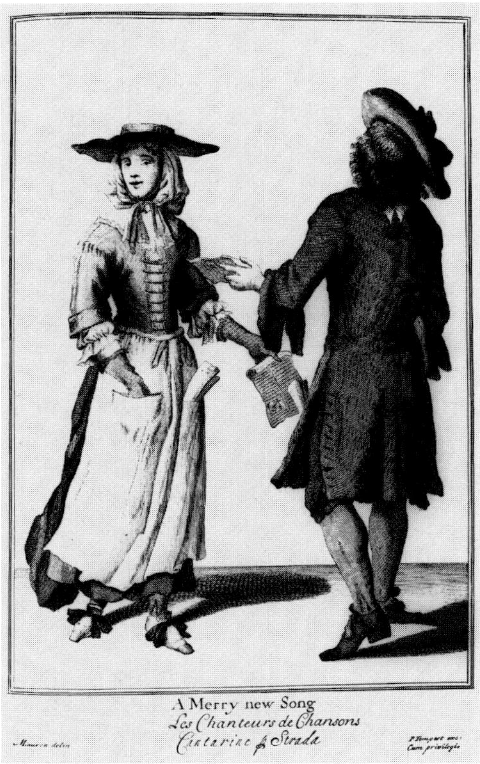

4.10 Marcellus Laroon, 'A Merry new Song', 1687

linked by the same contrast and critique. In the eighteenth century, ballad trucking was little more than an excuse for panhandling. The American loyalist Samuel Curwen (1715–1802), sightseeing in Bath in 1780, met

> a man whose haggard looks and tattered garment denoted [a] variety of wretchedness, having a long squalid beard, his face dirty and wrinkled, his hair through which, in appearance, a comb had not passed for many years, his garment of every possible colour and shade, each piece of the bigness of one's palm, tackt together by thread of a different colour and in stretches ½ as long as ones thumb. This man, answering to the name of Selby, earned a wretched livelihood by begging and selling ballads.[82]

Nothing of Curwen's narrative appears in the prosperous, fashionably dressed couple gracing Laroon's 'A Merry new Song' (**4.10**), in which a pair dance and sing to lure customers. The man has an elegant coat with buttoned vents and hounds-ears cuffs; the woman a kerchief fringed with lace, a chemise of frilled sleeves and an extraordinary pair of elbow-length gloves of the kind perfumed with cloves or nutmeg. Hogarth's woman, the antithesis of Laroon's, is a female Selby. Toothless and stupefied, she is naked above the waist and ragged below. Whereas Laroon's hawker is young and shapely, vivacious and stylish, and dances merrily with a man, Hogarth's is old and abandoned, evoking the class of 'horridly ragged, dirty and disgusting' London prostitutes, who, according to Francis Place, 'used to take any customer who would pay them twopence behind a wall' in Charing Cross Street.[83] Offering moralistic proof of love's 'progress' in her pregnant belly, squalling baby and autobiographical ballad ('The ladies fall'), she represents a radical disfigurement of Laroon's hawker, whose portrait overflows with conjugal lyricism.

Of all the hawkers in *The Cryes of the City of London*, the most theatrical and picturesque is the milkmaid (**4.11**); the same 'daughter of May-day', as Ireland calls her, is also the most striking hawker in 'The Enraged Musician'.[84] She alone rises above the discord of the print, in which she is a counterweight to the grotesque ballad wench. She closely resembles Laroon's milkmaid, more closely even than Müller's milkmaid. The Hogarth and Laroon figures' monumental posture and similar body type, the common attitudes of their limbs and torsos, their youth and good looks all support David Bindman's view that Laroon's figure 'was undoubtedly an influence on "The Enraged Musician"'.[85]

These correspondences, however arresting, do not obscure the two figures' crucial differences, epitomized by the Sunday-best

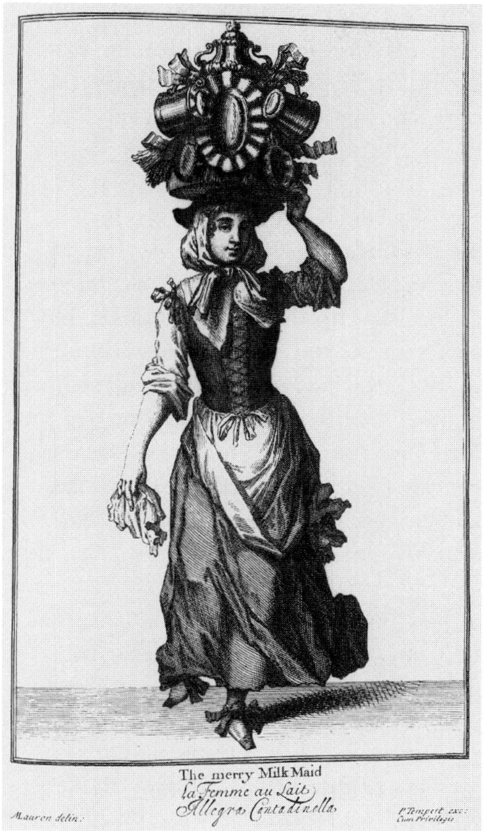

4.11 Marcellus Laroon, 'The merry Milk Maid', 1687

clothes of Laroon's merry maid and the drab occupational outfit of Hogarth's vendor, remarkable only for her apron. While Laroon's elegant maid is dancing (notice the flight of her right foot) to the music of the merry fiddler in celebration of May Day, Hogarth's is lugging a pail of milk up St Martin's Lane, impeded by the hautboy player and obstructed by the urinating pupil. Totting the milk pail has given her arms that, unlike the limbs of Laroon's figure, are brawny.[86] Such arms were the milkmaid's hallmark. According to *The Modern Husbandman* (1750), the milkmaid 'may be known by her red plump Arms and Hands, and clumsy Fingers; for in most great Dairies they are forced to milk their Cows abroad, a great Part of the Year; I may say, almost all the Year, even in Frosts and Snows, while their Fingers are ready to freeze in the Action'.[87]

The most eye-catching feature of Laroon's merry milkmaid is her fantastic headdress, a garland of flowers before 1680 but afterwards, as milkmaids abandoned their rural origins for the suburbs, a pile of silver.[88] Joseph Addison calls this ornament a 'Pyramid'; his mock-heroic account is a fitting gloss upon Laroon's poetic print celebrating the culture of the lower orders:

> It is likewise on the first Day of the Month that we see the ruddy Milk-Maid exerting her self in a most sprightly manner under a Pyramid of Silver Tankards, and like the virgin *Tarpeia* oppress'd by the costly Ornaments which her Benefactors lay upon her.[89]

Henri Misson finishes Addison's story:

> In this Equipage, accompani'd by some of their Fellow Milk-Maids, and a Bagpipe or Fiddle, they go from Door to Door, dancing before the Houses of their Customers, in the midst of Boys and Girls that follow them in Troops, and every Body gives them something.[90]

In Addison's fable, 'Benefactors' lent milkmaids the silver they needed for their pyramids. In reality, Addison's 'Benefactors' were pawnbrokers.[91] Milkmaids rented sterling or even ready-made garlands of plate on security from bondsmen.[92] One usurer was particularly resorted to because he leased his plate at so much per hour under surety from 'respectable' housekeepers for its safe return. From him and his brethren, one set of milkmaids hired the silver from 10:00 o'clock in the morning until 1:00 in the afternoon and a second set from 1:00 pm until 6:00 in the evening, and so on, during the first of May and the following days, when the bondsmen's silver was safeguarded by a constable who accompanied the women on their rounds.[93]

The merry milkmaid's silver pyramid, by its picturesqueness, turns the image she graces into an illustration of the quaint culture of the lower orders, viewed from the perspective of their high customers, surrogates of those who bought Laroon's *Cryes*. An early example of folkloric curiosity, the design pictures the ritual it features from a superior vantage point. Whatever its purposes, one of the effects of this antiquarian perspective is to aestheticize that ritual so as to obscure its coercive edge. In practice, the ritual amounted to a license to extort money, coloured as merriment. The execution of the ritual appears in the conduct of a noisy gang of sweeps who, armed with shovels and brushes, danced a May Day jig before Lord's Bute door in 1763. When their demand for cash was refused, they grew angry. But they confined their retaliation to joining the Opposition, *The Whitehall Evening Post* joked.[94]

The pail that Hogarth's woman carries on her head is no silver pyramid. Indeed this iron tub, by its plainness, mocks the ornament borne by Laroon's woman. And yet the two pails serve comparable purposes within their designs. The exoticness of the first conceals, while the commonness of the second reveals, even exaggerates. The pail that Hogarth's maid totes is striking for its immensity, which Hogarth bathed in light to catch the eye and overstated to suggest that selling milk was drudgery. With a gaze trained to calibrate the volume of such containers, John Ireland complained: 'The milk-pail is much too large.'[95] In addition to being enlarged, this bucket is particularized like no other pail in any other Cries; a closer analysis of it reveals the spirit of English empiricism in which it was executed.

At its top, the cruciform handle evokes the trouble involved in fetching the empty vessel, twice a day, back from Covent Garden to Islington. The handle on the bottom of the tub (depicted so particularly, its rivets can be counted) evokes the skill she needs to balance the pail on her head without spillage. The small measure hooked into the vessel's rim evokes the Sisyphus-like exertion required from the milkmaid when, with every patron, she drops the pail to the ground and then hoists it back up on her head again. Finally there is the size of the container, which probably held seven or eight gallons. Such a volume of milk would have weighed more than 55 pounds; with another fifteen pounds for the pail's heavy metal, the milkmaid's burden comes to seventy pounds. Laroon, by hiding this tub behind a mound of silver, obscures and idealizes the milkmaid's labours. Highlighting the same tub, Hogarth demythologizes these labours, even as he idealizes her English – more accurately, Welsh or Irish – bloom.

Laroon and Amigoni portray hawkers individually, one to a sheet, proposing that street sellers worked in isolation – and silence.[96] But in Hogarth's print, a fishmonger howls, a sow gelder blows his horn, a dustman rings his bell and a boy bangs his drum. All reflect the grievances of Londoners who complained of the city's cacophony, then as now among urban life's most distinctive woes. What made London a 'Prodigious and Noisy City, where Repose and Silence dare scarce shew their Heads in the Darkest Night'?[97] Street peddlers, according to their critics. Tom Brown painted the capital as a confusion of many throats, all roaring at once:

One Tinker Knocks, another Bawls, '*Have you Brass Pot, Iron Pot, Kettle, Skillet, or a Frying-Pan to mend*': Whilst another Son of a Whore yells louder than *Homer's* Stentor, '*Two a Groat, and Four for Six Pence Mackarel*'. One draws his Mouth up to his Ears and Howls out, '*Buy my Flawnders*', and is followed an Old Burly Drab that Screams out the Sale of her *Maids* [fish, usually skate] and her *Sole* at the same instant.[98]

Like Brown's peddlers, Hogarth's vie with each other in an all-out war of noise. Aggrieved contemporaries classified these contending noisemakers as instrumentalists and vocalists, but some of Hogarth's crew are instrumentalists and vocalists simultaneously, like the dustman who out-shouts the singing drummer but also peals his bell so loudly that he himself must turn his head away from its clangor. Among the vocalists, the gelder blowing the cow horn wars with the girl cranking the noisemaker, and both of these instruments are outdone by the hautboy, which produced the most discordant of all orchestral sounds, according to the eighteenth-century ear. Ned Ward, in his *London Spy* (1699), offers this operatic and over-embellished tale of the hautboys he heard played by a Bartholomew Fair orchestra:

> the next instrument they betook themselves to were hautboys, which, ill played, are undoubtedly the best windpipes in the world to scare a man out of his wits, and I dare swear would raise the Devil, the father of all discord, much sooner than ever Friar Bacon or Cornelius Agrippa could by their diabolical invocations. For my part, I declare, their disproportion'd notes and imperfect cadences had such an effect upon my ears that I thought their noise would have burst my head in as many pieces as gunpowder does a grenado-shell, and put my whole microcosm in such a disorderly trembling that had they tooted a little longer, I believe I should have been all disjoined, for such music is enough to make a man's bones dance out of their sockets and put his whole body under a painful dislocation.[99]

Far more numerous and even more vociferous than these instrumentalists are London's vocalists. The ballad seller, who sings 'The ladies fall' in a loud, doleful voice, is drowned out by the fishmonger using one hand as a sounding board by which to magnify his cry, as Ireland shrewdly notices.[100] This fishmonger, in turn, is surely out-shouted by the sweep, 'issuant' from a chimney, where, to announce his deliverance from darkness, he customarily whooped with all his might and clattered his brush.[101] These vocalists are outdone by the picture's central figure, the milkmaid. Although Hogarth shows her mouth delicately half-opened, milkmaids were infamous for uttering a cry more horrid and 'barbarous' than the shout of any other London vendor.[102] Francis Grose (1731?–1797) claimed, at the end of the eighteenth century, that his hawker sang milk 'in an inarticulate scream, seemingly uttered as if her posteriors were then actually being pierced by a cobbler's awl'.[103]

But there is more. Beyond their internecine wars, Hogarth's figures contend against the background noise of London. One part of this hubbub comes from animals. Horses neigh and clatter, dogs bark, cats fight (on the pewterer's roof), and a 'city' bird, escaped from its cage, squawks. This witty species of *rara avis* from the Indies is, in telling ways, the reverse of native birds. While wild songsters from the English countryside make music, this tame parrot makes 'human' speech, but speech that is without meaning. Imported from an exotic climate to amuse a wealthy patron, the repetitious, expensive bird most resembles the scraping, expensive fiddler (who in turn most resembles repetitive, expensive foreign artists) flying to England from abroad to gratify what were in Hogarth's view the mindless tastes of the rich.

The other part of London's general clamor comes from human beings: a weeping baby, a careless schoolboy banging his slate on the ground behind him as he walks, and the stone-thudding paver who, Ireland records, 'to every stroke of his rammer, adds a loud, distinct, and echoing HAUGH!'[104] But the greatest villain of the scene is the invisible John Long, whose pewterers, wielding thirty or forty hammers ringing incessantly on metal, followed the noisiest manufactory in London.[105] And London's bells are pealing. The flag flying from St Martin-in-the-Fields signals a holy day so that the iron tongues of London's churches would have been tolling all day long in a 'perpetuity of ringing'.[106] There were eighty-three churches in the three square miles within the walls of London, and three hundred in the City and its Liberties.[107]

In picturing London as Pandemonium, Hogarth demonstrates his print's correspondence to life, specifically, its correspondence to English life. He believed that the Laroons and the Amigonis of the age had, like visual gossips, copied themes from each other and from continental art, ignoring the Englishness of life in London to favour instead 'wonderful copies of bad originals' or 'dismal dark Subjects, neither entertaining nor ornamental'.[108] He is the first aesthetician to call upon British collectors to 'see with their own Eyes', and 'Let but the Comparison of Pictures with Nature be their only Guide'.[109]

Day in and day out, Londoners heard their city's criers before they saw them, if they saw them at all through their tiny windows. For them, criers were sounds more than sights – and loud, obnoxious sounds. Few Londoners remarked on the details of dress, emphasized by Laroon, but many echoed Swift when he complained, in his journal to Stella, of 'a restless dog, crying cabbages and savoys, plagues me every morning about this time; he is at it now. I wish his largest cabbage was sticking in his throat'.[110]

Those not annoyed by peddlers' noise loathed their accents and dialects, which were legion and incomprehensible.[111] Welsh, Irish, Scots, French, and Italian 'vocalists' contend in 'The enraged musician', as well as a smattering of Londoners, the latter speaking the impenetrable dialects of 'Change-Alley, Covent Garden, and the different regions of the city, comically mimicked by the phonetic title to Child's apple seller: 'M'st ye ha' some Golden Pippins' (**4.5**). Together these hawkers cast the nation's capital as a modern Babel.[112] Just as *Night* evokes a London suffering the biblical cleansing of fire as a punishment for its corruption, so the 'Musician' evokes a London cursed by the biblical 'confusion of tongues' as punishment for its mad enterprises.

Hogarth's 'picture' of the London noises underlines the visual nature of musical performance, its spectacle. But it accomplishes a more imaginative feat yet, one which no other print of street vendors approaches, even remotely. Instead of pursuing artistic inventiveness by reshuffling the internal elements of Cries like costume or background, the 'Musician' records vendors' sounds in spatial form. It reproduces vendors' voices, instruments, and the din of all London on paper, where they come alive to the ear through the medium of the eye. By that feat, the print depicts sound so that an audience can perceive it, leaping over the boundaries of a deaf medium in a way continental Cries had not. The 'Musician's' achievement, whereby it represents what was previously unrepresented, establishes British art's claims to originality and greatness. No foreign work had enlarged the Cries or used it to create this kind of revolutionary effect, by which viewers are taught to listen with their eyes. Furthermore, in showing the visual replicating the auditory and usurping its effects, the design establishes the supremacy of British art over the entirely distinct realm of music, native as well as continental.

Few contemporaries understood Hogarth as deeply as his friend Henry Fielding (1707–54), that other quintessential Londoner. Writing about 'The enraged musician' in his *Journal of a Voyage to Lisbon* (1755), he caught

Hogarth's exposition of London's noise perfectly when he observed that this print is 'enough to make a man deaf to look at'.[113] Alive to city sounds, Fielding saw no farce in Hogarth's 'Musician'. Walpole, pastured in Twickenham or rural Norfolk, saw little else. Laroon makes us see hawkers – and their costumes – more clearly than any artist before him. Amigoni makes us feel for them. But in the noisiest picture in English art, Hogarth makes us hear them.

If Hogarth abducts three hawkers from Laroon and sentences them to hard labour in his 'Musician', he ignores Amigoni's children. Not a single boy or girl vendor appears in 'The Enraged Musician'. The two children in the print, pictured with a scatology that is a hallmark of Hogarth's satire, are a far cry from Amigoni's.[114] Whereas Amigoni's children trundle barrows and haul ladders with spectacular enthusiasm, Hogarth's mischievous urchins play with childish intensity. The shameless boy from the lower classes urinates down a coal hole. The sheltered girl from the regent classes (a contemporary called her a 'young lady from a boarding school') gets a first lesson in sexual anatomy.[115] Across from them, a better-off child dressed in the style of an adult beats a costly military drum and sings a song in isolation – is he the musician's child or just his surrogate? All these figures complete an ironic inversion typical of Hogarth: the children who work in Amigoni are made to play, while the adults who play in Laroon – the milkmaid, for example – are put to work.

No child hawkers appear in 'The Enraged Musician'. But about 1742 or 1743, seven of them unexpectedly surface in Plate IV of Hogarth's *Rake's Progress*. Withdrawing the original design of 1733 from sale, the artist undertook a recutting (**4.12**) that added a tableau featuring a newspaper vendor, a vote canvasser, two youths of shady callings, a chimney sweep and two shoeblacks, the last three repeated from Amigoni. Since these afterthoughts play no role in the rake's story, they may refer to a different work of art. Perhaps they mock the elevated view of childhood proposed by the Italian painter in his London Cries?[116]

Amigoni and Hogarth agree in picturing London's children as orphans, unfettered by family or institution. However, while the Italian painter shows passive waifs singly, denying they are a social threat, the English engraver depicts energetic ragamuffins forming a gang, demonstrating they constitute a social menace. Amigoni's children, saintly in their poverty, seek work energetically but vainly; Hogarth's shun work to play. Amigoni's are innocent victims; Hogarth's are victimizers preying upon each other and grown-ups. Experienced, dangerous, and talented, all act and look like adults. One resembles an elder: stooped over *The Farthing Post*, he indulges in the delights of old men – tobacco and politics.

These blackguards – in 1736, the word 'blackguard' referred specifically to shoe blacks – do not, like the 'Musician's' children, build houses or crank noisemakers.[117] Their pastimes are the most corrupt of adult distractions cultivated by the likes of the *Rake*'s anti-hero Tom. Sallying forth in the afternoon, Tom Rakewell takes a chair to White's coffee house and betting den; like him, the eager young peddlers, squandering the shank of their work day, gamble in their own school, a moveable 'academy' for hazarding, which, with a mixture of childish imitation and professional pride, they have named 'Blacks' to rival 'White's' and reflect the calling of their chiefs, who shine shoes.[118] One bootblack drinks gin while he throws dice. Liquor has so befuddled him that he has literally lost his shirt, the absence of

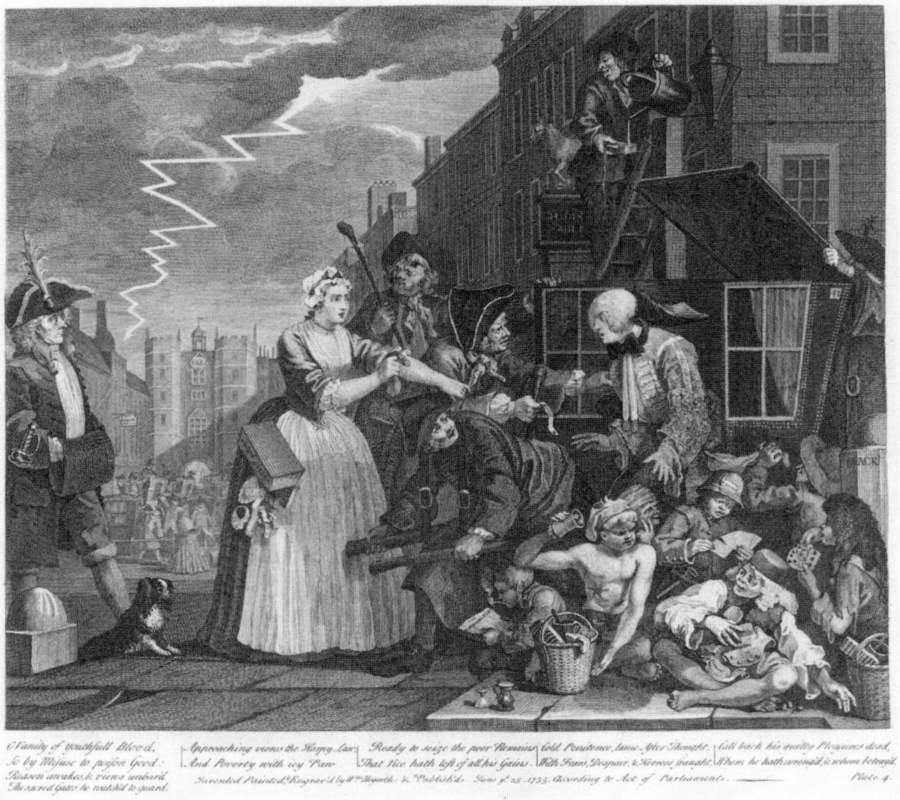

4.12 William Hogarth, *Rake's Progress*, Plate IV, *c*. 1743 (late state)

which reveals a gangland tattoo. He now wagers the tools of his trade in a bet that menaces his own means of production and the livelihood of his opponent.

Amigoni's children, hard-working and innocent, are uniform figures; but Hogarth's are differentiated by the forms of profligacy in which they specialize. Some cultivate vices like gambling, drinking, and smoking; others break the law by exploiting talents unique to children. One youth uses his tiny hands and nimble fingers to whip away Tom's handkerchief. Whatever his avowed calling, his real trade is thieving. Another capitalizes on his small stature to hide behind the vote canvasser in order to telegraph to his confederate that their victim has two honours.[119]

In the matter of London's orphans, Hogarth had first-hand experience: he and Jane had adopted two from the Foundling Hospital. For this reason he is of one mind on the topical subject with Daniel Defoe, who also knew the dark wisdom of the proverb: 'Hell is paved with infants' skulls'.[120] In *Everybody's Business*, he singles out shoe blacks and errand boys for condemnation; they belong with 'the 10,000 wicked idle, pilfering vagrants . . . called blackguards'.[121] 'Tis scare credible what a black Throng they are', he adds elsewhere, concluding in a mood of Swiftian irony that 'many of them indeed perish young, and dye miserable, before they may be said to look into Life; some are starv'd with Hunger, some with Cold, many are found frozen in the Streets and Fields, some drowned before they are old enough to be hang'd'.[122]

Müller's four prints, Child's two satires, and Hogarth's single sheet offer instructively different and increasingly imaginative reactions to the Cries of London at mid-century. Even though Müller's and Child's prints belong to the genre while Hogarth's sheet lies just beyond it, the images of all three artists grow directly out of the Cries and feed back into it to shape its history. Of the three responses, Müller's flattering echoes and Child's irreverent parodies of Amigoni are the most literal. Child's two images, for all their cleverness, iconoclasm and new tone of mockery, express their antagonism, from a formal perspective, by a duplication that amounts to plagiarism. Facsimiles of Amigoni's designs, they steal his imagery. From this viewpoint, they are retrospective rather than prospective. Operating within the generic parameters the Venetian had established, they fail to expand or enlarge the conventions by which hawkers are depicted in art. They propose narrow satiric purposes, which they achieve by recourse not to new motifs or pictures, but to new words, a characteristic English strength. To the extent that they do not create a fresh visual vocabulary or devise an original English iconography, they are literary satires that vindicate the jibe Gravelot made to James Basire: 'De English may be very clever in deir own opionions but dey do not de draw'.[123]

By contrast, Hogarth's 'Enraged Musician' advances a more creative and original response to Laroon. Indeed, Hogarth's is a searching, wide and scornful critique of the genre from its beginnings to 1740. It starts out as a mockery of Laroon's and Amigoni's designs, but it ends up playing a formative role in the direction Cries take. While Müller's narratives and Child's travesties operate inside the accepted conventions of the genre, Hogarth's 'Musician' operates outside; it expands the range of the Cries and revolutionizes its history in three different ways.

Distantly alluding to the first single-leaf Cries, Hogarth's 'Musician' which Antal calls 'a compressed cycle of various street vendors', recasts the traditional arrangement of the broadside, replacing its harmony with conflict and its order with chaos.[124] Instead of marshalling dignified hawkers in neat rows arranged by calling or sex, it pictures men and women anarchically elbowing their way along a narrow London lane. Instead of representing each hawker alone, it makes them into a horde so dense and swarming that its individual members are difficult to untangle, count or classify.

In addition, the 'Musician' transforms the depiction of peddling by replacing a static idiom with a dynamic one. Instead of Laroon's genre portraiture, Hogarth's design embraces drama. But it rejects Müller's romantic May Day spectacle in his 'Milk-Maid'. For while Müller's incident is lyrical and high, Hogarth's is comic and low. 'The Milk-Maid on May-Day' pictures a carnivalesque folk festival in which a fiddler and his companion bear a pyre across an arcadian landscape. The 'Musician' pictures a scene of daily drudgery in which vendors shout and sell but nobody listens or buys.

Though hawkers shout and their patron stops his ears, everybody in the 'Musician' hears and, for the first time in images of hawkers, everybody reacts to and interacts with everybody else. Despite this interaction, the 'Musician's' vendors demonstrate no camaraderie; they bestow no social character upon the work they do. On the contrary, they engage in fratricidal rivalry, vying for the ears of their patron. Perhaps their lack of mutuality is due to their remarkable diversity, which is moral, economic and social. No sentimental uniformity unites this crew, who range across a moral spectrum that 'progresses' from the noble milkmaid to the sordid ballad seller.

The introduction of customers – or, ironically, a single customer – into images of hawkers is the sheet's third and most vital innovation, underscored by the print's title as well as by its formal organization, especially its rectangular frame, drawing the eye to the 'provok'd' violinist. Laroon and Amigoni shift the focus of Cries from the thing sold to the individual seller; Hogarth moves it from the individual seller to the individual buyer. But in a reversal of the historical balance of power between an underclass of supplicating hawkers and an upper class of aloof customers, the violinist is victim and the hawkers are victimizers. Passive, impotent and enraged, he is vanquished but abhorrent, the instrument of a divorce between the artificial harmony of high leisure and the natural discord of low labour – the 'concerts of every day living'.[125] Active, powerful and unselfconscious, they are sympathetic victors; for they represent a native folk whose festive energy triumphs in a print allegorizing the conquest of elite, foreign culture by popular English tradition.

As an allegory of the victory of low culture over high, the oboist and the fiddler replay the legendary musical competition between Marsyas and Apollo, each representing two different instrumental harmonies, one terrestrial and corrupting, the other celestial and ennobling.[126] The Jewish oboist stands below the violinist's window, facing him directly, as if challenging a rival in a musical contest. In this pose, with his bearded, satyr-like appearance, he evokes Marsyas, who loved 'low' wind instruments, which appealed to the body's passions. Above him, the 'superior' violinist calls up Apollo, who favoured 'high' stringed instruments which appealed to the mind's principles.[127] In the old myth popular in continental art, Apollo defeats Marsyas and flays him; in this comic modern version, the classical outcome is reversed. Hogarth's Marsyas of the street, standing for all those peddlers who use wind instruments – either their natural voices or manmade devices – defeats the Apollo of the court to win the competition.

'The Enraged Musician' exercised wide influence on English prints of the late eighteenth and early nineteenth centuries. Its publication in 1741 affected the depiction of hawkers on single sheets, but it also impinged upon the portrayal of vendors in ensembles. Regarding single sheets, the 'Musician' inaugurated a stream of lookalike designs that borrow from or allude to Hogarth's prototype. Between 1655, when Walton's broadside appeared, and 1741, when Hogarth's print was published, no surviving sheet of hawkers came to market. Between 1741 and 1818, twelve such designs appeared. The last single sheet to call itself a Cries was Charles Williams's 'New London Cries or All the Talents making themselves Useful', a political allegory published in 1808. After that, the closest title to a broadside of hawkers is Thomas Jones's 'London Cries or addition made easy' (*c.* 1836–48), a pedagogical toy sold as a jigsaw puzzle or a single leaf. The last sheet to ape Hogarth's 'Musician' was George Cruikshank's 'Les Savoyards: A little music à la Françoise' (1818), which treats ethnic stereotypes under the guise of treating urban music. The most slavish of these copycat designs is Isaac Cruikshank's 'Enraged politician' of 1799 (**4.13**) which borrows Hogarth's iconography and adapts his title to ridicule Lord Belgrave's Bill to Suppress Sunday newspapers, alleged to corrupt the poor. This fable about parliamentary business illustrates the last stage in the evolution of broadside Cries and their spinoffs across three

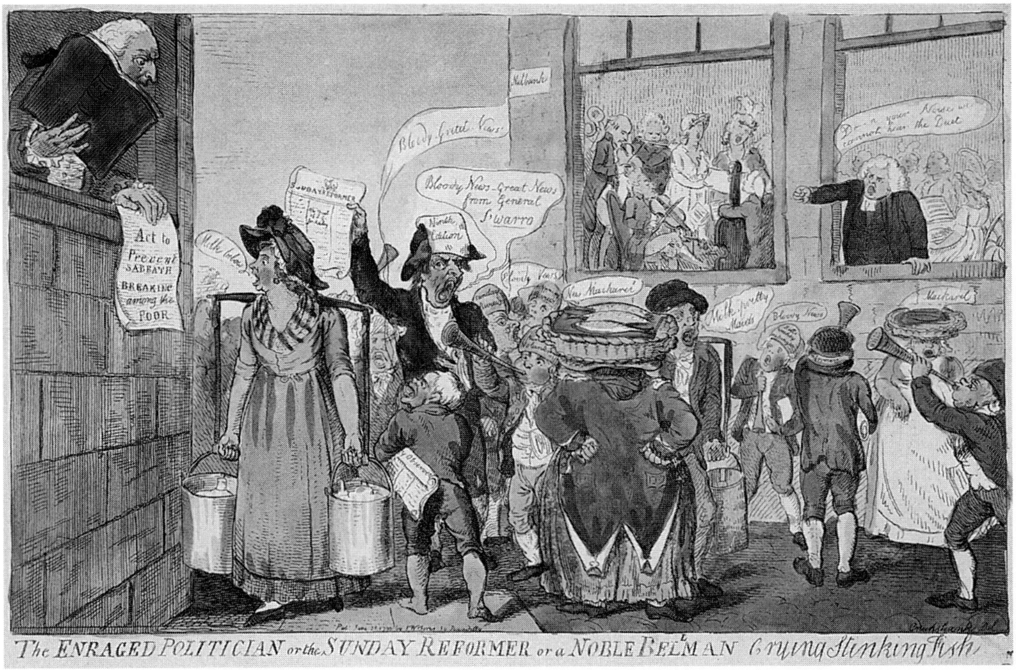

4.13 Isaac Cruikshank, 'The Enraged Politician or the Sunday Reformer or a Noble Bellman Crying Stinking Fish', 1799

centuries: these designs begin as static, serious tableaus, shift to comic dramas under Hogarth's influence, and end as political allegories or satires.

'The enraged musician' also reshaped and reinvigorated Cries configured as ensembles, the ascending format between 1740 and 1821. With the help of Child's images, Hogarth's print effected this renewal by introducing into suites of Cries new techniques, themes, tones, subjects, and arrangements that moved them away from genre portraits toward theatrical images peopled by carefully observed social types. These dramatic changes – and the resistance they met – are the subject of the next chapter.

5

Retailoring the lower orders: ensembles from 1740 to 1821

BY THE SECOND half of the eighteenth century, Hogarth's ambition that his Copyright Act (1735) would be 'an encouragement to engraving and printselling' had, Sir John Hawkins reported, been 'pretty nearly gratified'.[1] As a result, London dealers in fine prints 'suddenly increased to some hundreds: and if we consider the number and abilities of the engravers who are now in that metropolis, we must allow that, of all arts relative to design, that of engravings has made the greatest and quickest progress in England', according to the Swiss Jean Rouquet's *Present State of the Arts in England* (1755).[2] William Blake (1757–1827) captured this metamorphosis in English printmaking when, in 1800, he cast an anti-nostalgic glance back to his own youth:

There are now I believe as many Booksellers as there are Butchers & as many Printshops as of any other trade. We remember when a Print shop was a rare bird in London & I myself remember when I thought my pursuits of Art a kind of Criminal Dissipation & neglect of the main chance, which I hid my face for not being able to abandon as a Passion which is forbidden by Law & Religion, but now it appears to be Law & Gospel too.[3]

Long before Blake's statement, the British school rivaled the French, according to John Lockman's 'To Mr. Woollett, the Engraver, on his Print of Niobe' (1761):

Here, emulous, they form'd an English school
Which, animated by the royal smile,
Must flourish, and do honour to our isle.
In fame, it now with that of Paris vies,
And may, in time, still more resplendid rise.[4]

Lockman's boast was only part poetic hyperbole. Print selling in Britain was already shifting from an import to an export business. This trend increased when art was displayed not irregularly at taverns but annually at exhibitions of paintings, even when these shows, like the Royal Academy's, banned prints: engraver's could only be Associates of that organization.[5] The following trade note comes from the year 1787:

The export trade of our engravings to France far exceeds the trade at home. The trade at home is chiefly in low-priced prints – little ovals and furniture decorations. Of the more costly production, the French exceed by three to one the buyers in England. In Paris alone to Sir Robert Strange's last print, the subscriptions there exceeded ours as seventeen to three . . . For valuable prints, the supply of Great Britain was till very lately from abroad. The balance is now turned entirely in our favour, for with our immense exports in the print trade, the imports last year were less than a hundred pounds.[6]

In 1805, David Macpherson summarized the progress of British art across the course of his own life, recording in the *Annals of Commerce* that he had witnessed British craftsmen 'elevated from humiliating inferiority to acknowledged superiority over the rival artists of the continent, and British prints sought for in every part of the globe enlivened by any rays of taste and science'.[7]

Against the background of English prints' rising fortunes, Cries in ensembles flourished, developing along two different paths. Inspired by the images of Laroon, one Cries took a lyric turn; reacting against this lyricism, the other took a satiric twist. The French artist L. P. Boitard led the lyric development. During the late 1750s, he romanticized Laroon's designs, reworking the copperplates that Robert Sayer acquired to print a new edition of the *Cryes*. In a furious response, Paul Sandby ridiculed the Boitard–Laroon designs, but he also mocked Amigoni's images. Attacking both these foreigners' works, Sandby, who apprenticed as a military draftsman, created a suite of lampoons that, in their cool savagery, outstripped even Hogarth's mockery.[8]

Like Boitard, Francis Wheatley sought to modernize the Cries of London. Labouring in his own smooth, romantic style, he created an ensemble of Cries that drew their inspiration from Laroon, whose formal refinement he intensified, sentimentalized and feminized.[9] In sweetening Laroon, he moved away from the mordant satire of Sandby, drawing instead on the voguish picturesque prevailing in the late eighteenth century. His saccharine ensemble provoked Thomas Rowlandson's *Cries of London*; this cycle revives Sandby's caustic ridicule using a style for which the word 'brutal' is not too strong. Fierce competition marks the popular art of the late Georgian age; despite the flourishing state of printmaking, too many continental and domestic craftsmen chased too little fame and money. Hogarth wrote that the 'misery among the unsuccessful' was so intense that they 'often have wished that they had been brought up cobblers'.[10] The outcome of that competition is the wittiest, most irreverent, but also the most darkly brilliant images in the history of the London Cries.

Boitard's, Sandby's, Wheatley's and Rowlandson's ensembles appear along a spectrum running from picturesque revival and romantic invention to erotic satire and artistic spoof. All cater to elites enthralled, until the Impressionists, by programmatic imagery like the seasons, the temperaments, the continents and the London Cries. In shaping programmatic images of the underclass to provoke the sympathy or delight of elites, Boitard and Wheatley (in opposition to Sandby and Rowlandson) shift the Cries of London in the directions that Bouchardon, Boucher, Tillard and Watteau move the Cries of Paris, examples of which appear in the cabinets of rich collectors like Pierre Crozat, Baron de Thiers and Abbé de Fleury, Canon of the Church of Paris.[11]

Among the lively, blasphemous designs produced in Georgian England, Sandby's stand out. His hundred watercolors, twelve etched *c.* 1759 as *London Cries done from the Life Part 1st* and others published here for the first time, represent the most distinguished achievement of ensemble Cries in scope, power and insight. They are the heart of this chapter, which argues that, despite economic and popular failure, these images offer at once the most sympathetic and most caustic likenesses of hawkers in English art.

Marcellus Laroon's suite, a 'blockbuster' among Cries, enjoyed a long, eventful life. It sold so well that it went through six editions from 1687 to 1709 and four more reprintings from 1711 to 1733.[12] The suite's coppers, after changing hands several times, became the property of Robert Sayer, who republished them about 1759, when he listed them under the heading 'Sets of Fine Prints. Proper to collect in the Cabinets of the Curious' and charged seven shillings for the complete series. But in a dramatic switch, this London bookseller marketed the suite to add two new audiences, both of them slightly down-scale, perhaps provincial, and though not poor, insufficiently rich to buy the big ensemble all at once. Following a strategy of parts-publication begun by English print sellers in the 1730s, he serialized the *Cryes* in six segments, each containing twelve prints, noting in his catalogue, 'N.B. *This Set may be had divided into six Parts, any of which may be had singly. Price 1s*'.[13] He overhauled it in big and little ways: he added a new title page and new images, but he also refurbished a selection of Laroon's compositions, seventy years behind the times in hawkers' costumes and bodies.

The suite's eight new and forty-one refurbished images cast it as a source about what, in matters of costume and looks, was eye-catching in London. The suite's representation of London fashions, increasingly accepted as normative for all of England, appealed to adults who were either keen to live a stylish modern life or curious to acquire knowledge of the world. The suite's

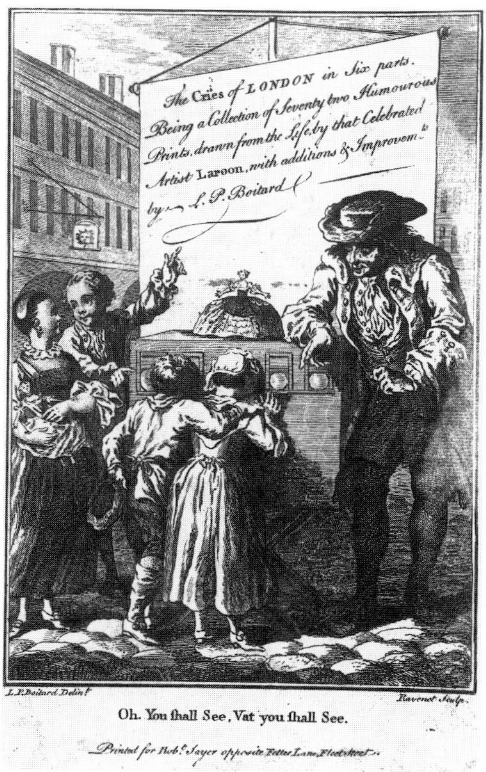

5.1 L. P. Boitard after Marcellus Laroon, title page to *The Cries of London in Six parts*, *c.* 1759

pretentious and wordy new title, *The Cries of London in Six parts. Being a Collection of Seventy two Humourous Prints, drawn from the Life by that Celebrated Artist Laroon, with additions & Improvements by L. P. Boitard* (**5.1**), appeals to buyers wanting a school book for children: it changes the archaic '*Cryes*' to '*Cries*', erasing the patina of old age and retrospection clinging to the ensemble and giving it a blush of up-to-the-moment literateness. More important by far, the title advertises the prints as coming with 'additions & Improvements' carried out by Louis-Phillipe Boitard (died *c.* 1760). Boitard, the book's impresario, was a Parisian artist working in England, famous for his stylish line and his mastery of the human figure – but infamous for his pirating of Hogarth's *Rake*.[14] His French monograph was still able to establish the fashionable status of the suite and set it apart from – and above – mere English prints.

To court Francophilic English buyers, Boitard created a new title page, which another Frenchman, Simon François Ravenet, engraved. On to that elegant page, Boitard introduced a gathering of genteel youngsters between six and ten years old who summon up the ensemble's new consumers. These little people are supervised by a 'teacher–artist' of aristocratic carriage and especially dress, an avuncular savoyard suggesting the book's new buyers: aunts, uncles, mothers, and godparents. Such buyers could view the *Cries* not only as a diverting costume book for themselves but also as an educational investment for children, who could learn to read and reckon by grappling with conundrums like '4 pair for a shilling Holland socks'.

To appeal to adult buyers – chiefly women, including provincial women – Boitard 'improves' Laroon's images by reshaping vendors' clothing and bodies to give them the look, motivations, and sensibilities of the late 1750s. Focusing on women, the French engraver makes female dress clean, neat, respectable; and he modernizes its cut and accessories to reflect the mid-century's new zones of interest on the body: the neck, head and feet.[15] Linking changing tastes in clothing with changing tastes in physical beauty, he poeticizes women's faces and torsos to make them young, expressive and shapely. He also eroticizes hawkers, exploiting erogenous spots on the body: eyes, mouth and especially breasts. In this Frenchified Cries, women don new bodies as effortlessly as new gowns and, for the first time, the human form is self-consciously cast as fashion's counterfeit.

Boitard's amalgamation of dressmaking and plastic surgery leaps off the page in 'Buy my Dutch Biskets' (**5.2**). The pastry woman's 'Improvements' include, in place of the dark hood of her forbear (**5.3**), a new bonnet in a petite shape and light colour. Her face, purged of its solemnity and impassiveness, is flirtatious and coy. Instead of crying Dutch biscuits, she smiles and invites: her cupids-bow lips are bee-stung and pouting. In the most eye-catching change of all, she abandons a kerchief and warm, closed gown for a low cut dress that exposes her bosom. Such alterations carry an erotic spark now lost due to pornographic inflation; they transform the hawker from a seventeenth-century baker's drab allegorizing winter to an eighteenth-century coquette masquerading as a pastry girl.

Among those additions which the title page credits to Boitard, the nosegay vendor (**5.4**) stands out by reason of its French tone and artificial figure. This design was created by François Boucher and cut

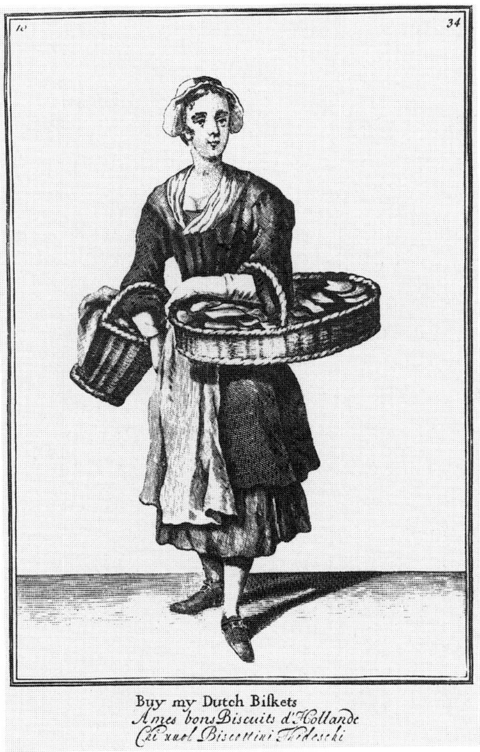

5.2 L. P. Boitard after Marcellus Laroon, 'Buy my Dutch Biskets', *c.* 1759

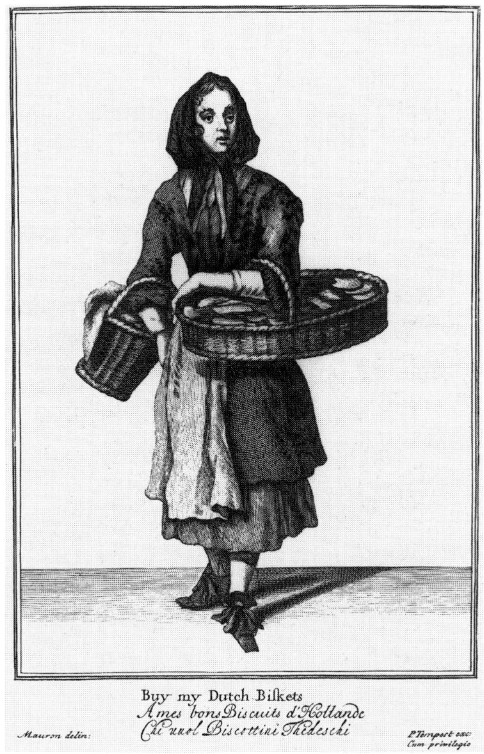

5.3 Marcellus Laroon, 'Buy my Dutch Biskets', 1687

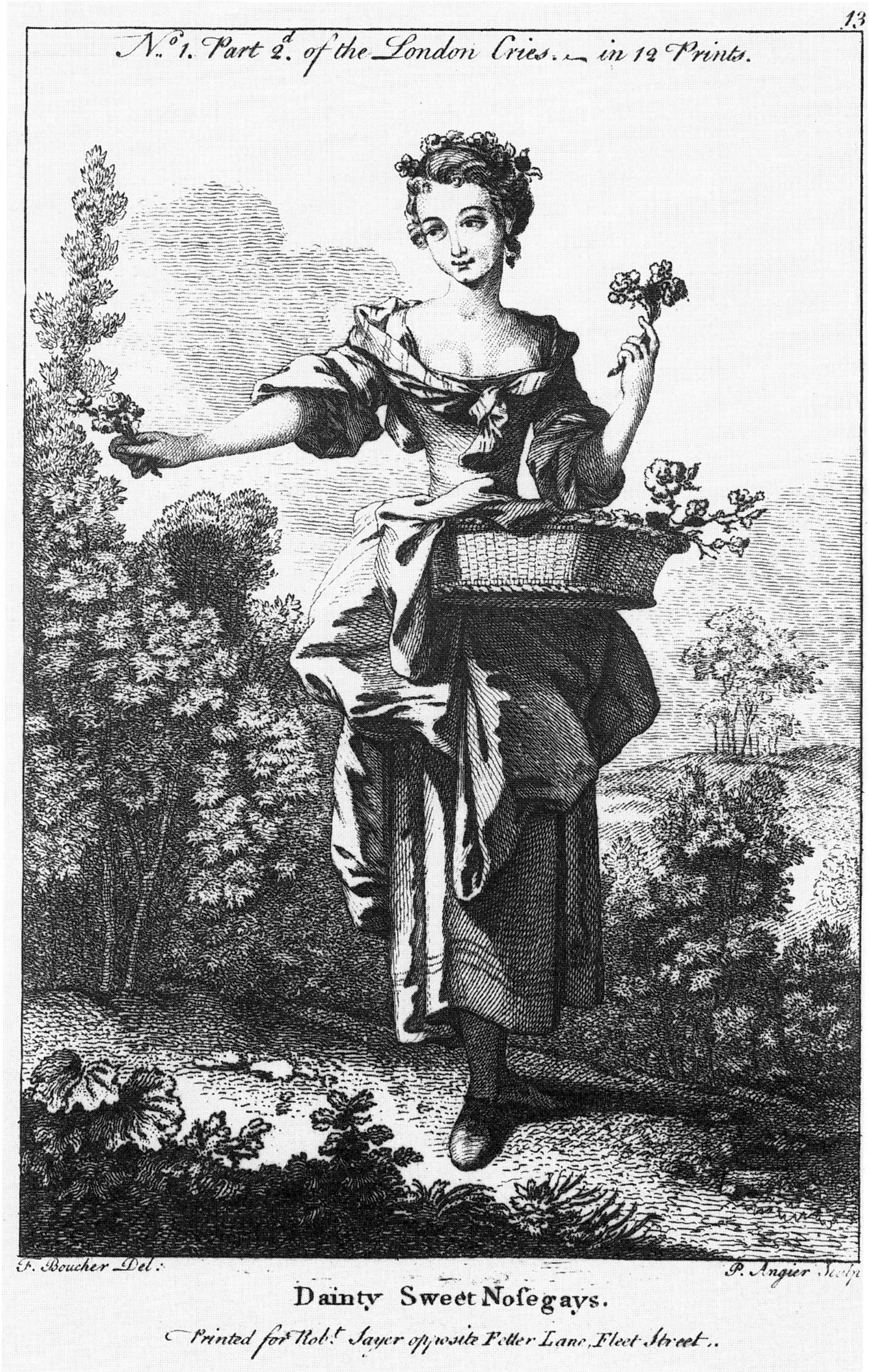

5.4 L. P. Boitard after François Boucher, 'Dainty Sweet Nosegays', *c.* 1759

by Paul Angier and Ignace Fougeron, Parisian engravers working in England.[16] In subject as well as tone, the image differs from Laroon's originals and Boitard's modernizations. Laroon's hawkers garb themselves in street clothes, cast-offs, or work clothes with an everyday regional English cut; some of these garments are shamefully ragged, ill-fitting or outdated. The working garb of Boucher's peasant looks more elegant than occupational, more Parisian than English.[17]

The young lady in 'Dainty Sweet Nosegays' (**5.4**), instead of a hat, wears a *parure* of flowers in her hair and, in each hand, carries bouquets evoking innocence, naturalness, fertility and purity, virtues seldom admired in hawkers. Her gown separates, molds and bares her breasts by means of a decollete neckline, the mark of aristocratic dress before the French Revolution.[18] But the most spectacular of her garments is the skirt that cinches her waist to the point of deformity, and then billows round her hips in a storm cloud of cloth. Women labouring in fields lifted their skirts, as the nosegay seller does; but her gown is too narrow at the waist and too full at the hem for work, just as her revealing bustline is inimical to either hawking in the city or toiling in the country.

Of course, she does not really toil. This actress flourishes two bouquets, not to sell them but for the ecstasy of it all. Not for her the humiliation of city women soiled by the suspicion of whoring because they worked on the street for money.[19] Pantomiming her way through an unpeopled landscape in bloom, this 'opera' peasant evokes the pastoral life of the Golden Age. She is not one of London's 'disorderly lewd women and maids fitted for painful and labourious service', but a Gallic allegory of morning, spring and the sanguine humour from the lush dreamworld of Boucher who created this anti-urban caprice in the spirit of the French 'fête champetre'.[20]

'Dainty Sweet Nosegays' and a companion print titled 'Ground Ivy, Ground Ivy' (personifying evening, winter, and melancholy) are rural idylls unprecedented in the London Cries. Both appear at odds with the urban subject matter that is the theme's meat and drink. But these fantasy figures and landscapes, however muddled the substitution of the country for the town renders them, are the logical outcome of Amigoni's hallucinatory cityscapes.[21] Amigoni's designs are peopled with poor, deserving children; Boucher's with romantic young women, refined sisters of the barrow bunter from 'Golden Pippins'. Staged in bucolic Southwark and deserted London, Amigoni's designs suburbanize the Cries; moving his figures even farther afield, Boucher countrifies the genre, as he did his own *Cris de Paris* (1737), published as twelve etchings having no other similarity to these two images. Linking the city with sentimentality, pathos, the elegiac, the wistful and the picturesque, Amigoni sketches London as a place of rustic urbanity. Banishing the city entirely, Boucher replaces it with images of urbane rusticity in which romantic, buxom women are part of nature's bounty.

Boitard's revivification of Laroon's *Cryes* was so successful he hawked it as an annual; his new and enlarged catalogue for the year 1766 offered *The Cries of London for the present Year 1766. Being a collection of Humourous characters in eighty six-Prints, done under the Direction of Mr. Boitard and neatly engraved.* The book's success goaded Sandby into creating a counter ensemble of a hundred or more watercolours, a selection of which he etched as *Twelve London Cries done from the Life Part 1st.*[22] Published about 1759, this suite sold for three shillings from Sandby's own house 'Next door to the Fountain in Broad Street Carnaby Market' and through 'F. Vivarez, Engraver, in Newport Street'; Vivarez was a pupil of Wagner, who etched Amigoni's Cries.[23] These twelve etchings and Sandby's unpublished watercolours both use derisive realism to topple Laroon's ensemble, Boitard's revision of it, and the realism-as-romanticism that both suites embrace as their idiom.

Sandby began his career as an artist about 1747. In the wake of the 1745 rebellion, he was appointed to the Military Drawing Department of the Board of Ordnance which, having first trained him in its Drawing Room at the Tower of London, posted him to Scotland to map, for purposes of subjugation, the north and west Highlands.[24] There he learned to combine refinement with mathematical exactitude, an achievement that ultimately made him the indisputable master of artists working in watercolour, a domain in which he was called 'the monarch of the plain'.[25] Back in England about 1752, he turned to mapping the 'primitive' hawkers of London, using his newly acquired skills not only as a watercolourist but also as a surveyor/observer of Scotland and its natives.[26]

As well as possessing uncommon artistic talents, the 'father of modern landscape painting in water-colours' had a wicked wit and a vile temper.[27] A founding member of the Royal Academy, he lived close to the centres of patronage and political power in Georgian England, so he saw connoisseurship as morality and bad taste as depravity.[28] His cut-throat attacks on Hogarth, who also approached aesthetics with moral fervour, were provoked by the narrowest of artistic squabbles over his *Analysis of Beauty* and 'The Times, Plate 1'. While Sandby's assaults on Hogarth are legendary, his vicious, witty strike against Laroon and Boitard, also provoked by 'bad taste', is an untold tale.[29]

Sandby knew Laroon's *Cryes of the City of London* from its reprintings. The suite's popularity surely maddened the satirist, who likely viewed its idealization of hawkers as artistic prostitution. His was a gloomy vision of London, intensified by his work as a watercolour artist of nature and by his residence in Windsor Forest (where he lived with his brother). Active in the rivalries of the contemporary art world, the oppositional artist brooded over his dead rival's images in the decade following his return to London, when he saw the city with the acuteness and fresh discernment of a man who had not eyed it in six years.[30] About 1758, he dashed off fourteen tiny vendors (signing one 'M. Lauron F') in *Rustic Scenes, Figures, Landscapes*, an etching exercise packed with his obsessions.[31] When Boitard's *Cries of London in Six parts* appeared in 1759, the impetuous Sandby sketched about a hundred hawkers in red chalk, pencil, or pen and ink. The opposite of his tidy landscapes, these spontaneous figure drawings, coloured in a palette of grays, browns, blues, lemon yellows and greens, are freely sketched with a supple humour and an eye for social behaviour.[32] They are said to illustrate his figure drawing at its best.[33]

Using a secret technique he paid money to learn, Sandby etched and sold a medley of his polemic designs himself.[34] He aimed these twelve etchings at new buyers and old connoisseurs, the circle of sophisticated and monied print lovers who, in 1760, represented an expansion of that nucleus of English art patrons described by Buckeridge in 1706 as composed of 'some few illustrious Persons and Men of Worth and Honour, who are solicitous for the Prosperity of the Arts, and contribute, by their Studies and Bounty, towards making them flourish and prevail among us'.[35] These buyers belonged to the upper middle class or aristocracy, enjoyed an influence out of all proportion to their numbers, and included people like the botanist Sir Joseph Banks, Sandby's well-to-do patron, Maria Walpole of Englefield

Green, and her uncle, Horace Walpole, all of whom bought *Twelve London Cries*.[36]

Along with his unpublished watercolours, *Twelve London Cries done from the Life by P. Sandby* proposed both destructive and constructive goals. They aimed to destroy the standing of both Laroon's *Cryes* and Boitard's bucolic additions to it. To do this, they recreated the vulgarity, the feel, even the smell of hawkers, exposing Laroon's images that pictured street vendors as uniformly gracious, pliant and deferential. Their second goal was to construct a new tradition for picturing criers in English art. Sandby's twelve etchings, together with his unpublished watercolours, strove to revolutionize, update, and actualize the idioms used in previous Cries by reabsorbing the historical actualities of street hawking from daily life into the expressive canon of the genre. They aimed, as readings of the title page and five designs show, to replace Laroon's old picturesque realism and Boitard's French pastoralism with a new urban antipastoralism founded on an up-to-date technique marked by caustic naturalism.

Every artist of the London Cries uses his title page as a manifesto by which to expound or justify his particular outlook on hawkers in art, and Sandby is no exception. His title page (**5.5**), promising to picture hawkers 'from the Life', dramatizes and verbalizes how this rivalrous man spins his ensemble out of his forerunners' suites. Alluding to the title page by which Boitard reanimated Laroon's *Cryes*, Sandby deliberately refashions the French artist's 'peepshow-operator-waiting-on-customers' motif to advance sentiments contradicting those of his Gallic rival.

In Boitard's design, one figure merges with another to create a chain of harmony: two children chat companionably, a boy and girl embrace, the benevolent hurdy-gurdy man hovers over his delighted and delightful customers. But in Sandby's inverted scene, discord rules. To the left of the pagoda-like peepshow, three pedestrians jostle one another; all are disabled: one hobbles on a crutch; another is stout and slow; the plump man's servant reels under his load. Sandby's peepshow impresario, a young woman, lacks the elegant bearing of Boitard's engineer. An awkward figure, she cranes forward, staring blankly at the viewer, wielding the charms of her face to lure customers. The eagerness of her patrons – two young men – raises suspicions about the propriety of her 'show'.

Unlike Boitard's male savoyard, who mothers his flock, Sandby's unmotherly (but pregnant) woman ignores the dishevelled boy who anchors himself to the leg of the machine. This boy is also a peepshow hand, perhaps a diminutive barker. Is he her neglected son or brother? If Boitard's London is a land of milk and honey where Frenchified children gambol, Sandby's is the capital of tribulation. Here a clumsy English gamin fights a starved dog for his supper, which he eats alone, an image of child poverty set against a backdrop of adult wealth, luxury and conspicuous consumption, represented by the 'fat cat's' footman who wobbles beneath a mountain of packages.[37]

Expanding these themes and intensifying their force, Sandby creates a cluster of pictures belonging to low burlesque, one of the most popular genres in the literature and art of Georgian England. These unbridled travesties delineate hawkers 'from the Life' to imitate and parody Laroon's/Boitard's pictures. Where his predecessors paint fishwives or flower girls in a solemn style that makes them appear dignified, indeed heroic, Sandby sketches the same characters as grotesque, criminal and sometimes murderous. To distinguish Sandby's lenience toward the dead Laroon apart from his severity toward the living Boitard, I turn first to the English artist's satire of the Dutch draftsman.[38]

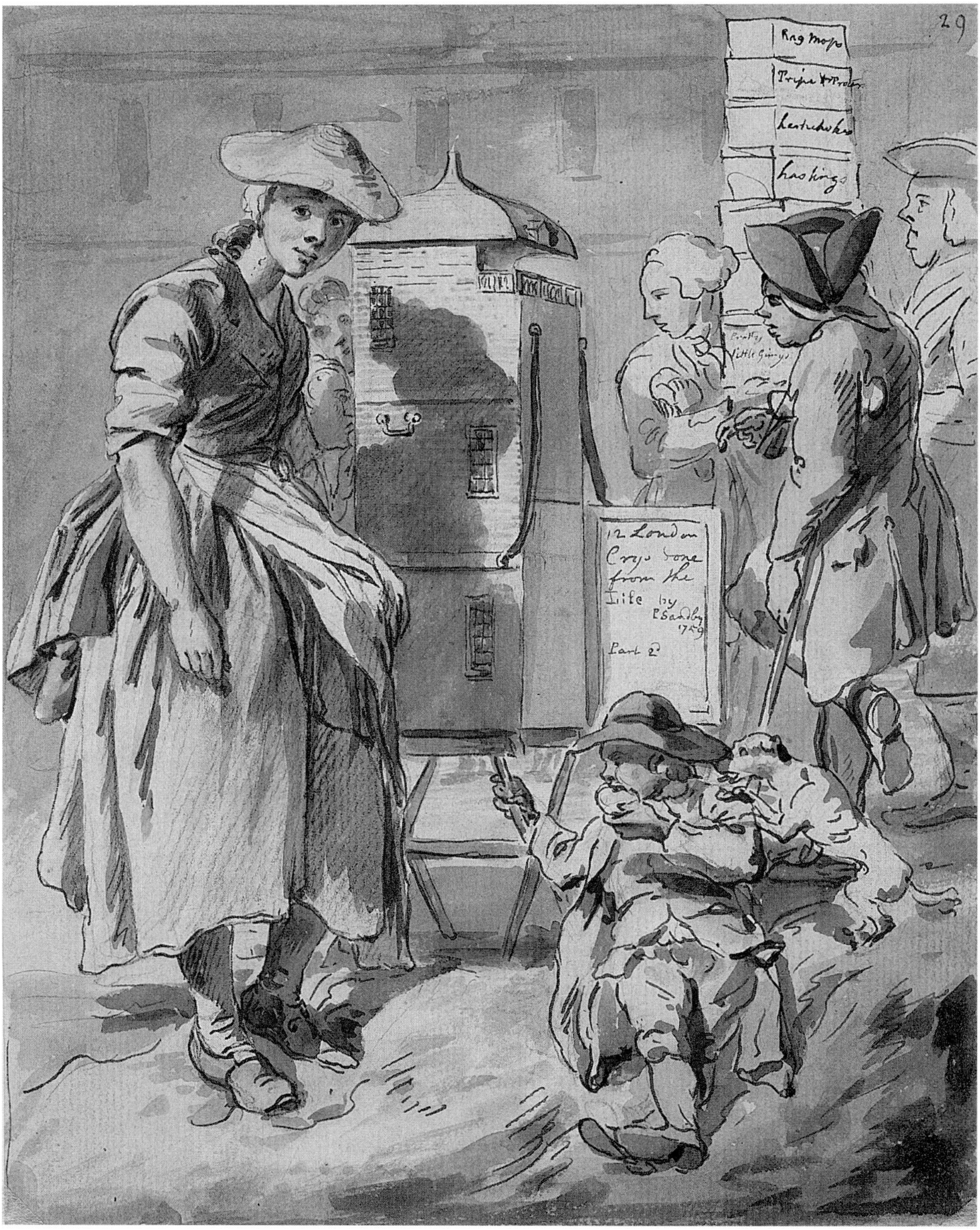

5.5 Paul Sandby, title page to *Twelve London Cries*, *c.* 1759

In his pen-and-ink sketches, Sandby attacks Laroon's romantic prints to reveal the 'true' nature of street vendors. His 'Last Dying Speech' (**plate 2**), an untitled watercolour at Yale, assails Laroon's 'Merry new Song' (**4.10**).[39] Dutch print and English watercolour both depict a team of vendors, man and woman, selling ballads; the likenesses of the two images extend to how the men look away while the women look toward us. But there all kinship stops. Laroon's pair dance with grace and intimacy. Sandby's awkward peasant plants both feet on the ground and bawls her ballads from her cavernous mouth. In the distance, her man works the crowd without sentimental reference to her.

But the greatest difference in the two ballad vendors lies in their garb and places of business. Laroon's fashionable hawker wears a laced bodice, a kerchief trimmed with fancy work and a brocaded chemise, bespeaking money. It is not easy to describe the hodgepodge of rags that Sandby's ballad seller wears. She has on the remains of a cape, half or more eaten away. Her bodice is a shapeless wrap; her tattered apron, also amputated by wear, is hard to tell apart from her skirt, a dirty rotting rag. Her right shoe is tied with a twig; her stockings are wrinkled and befouled. Sandby is the first artist of the London Cries to depict peddlers so filthy that they reek on the page, just as Hogarth's bawl on paper.

Laroon's hawkers float in a white space with utopian and sanitizing tones. Sandby's couple hawks at a spot where the call for 'last dying speeches' is loudest: a public execution where they exploit, with brisk indifference, the literal death of their 'author'. This gallows image reflects the prevailing bias against ballad sellers (whose real trade was often criminal, since they teamed up with pickpockets, for whose benefit they gathered crowds). It disputes Laroon's lyrical 'Merry new Song', which argues that the true business of ballad sellers is musical, a view also contested by the ballad hag in Hogarth's 'Musician' (**4.8**), which contends that the commerce of ballad singers is sex.[40]

Sandby's satires of Laroon in his pen-and-ink sketches are tame compared to the savage travesty he reserves for Boitard and the French designs he imports into England from Paris. The English artist published his anti-French lampoons as part of his twelve etchings. Giving public expression to his anti-Gallic animus, Sandby issued 'Will your Honour buy a Sweet Nosegay or a Memorandum Book' (**5.6**) as No. 4 of *Twelve London Cries* to ridicule Boucher's 'Dainty Sweet Nosegays'.

The nosegay sellers in Sandby's and Boitard's *Cries* are leisured, elegant, young and pretty. Both go in skirts hiked up to great fullness and low bust lines that reveal their breasts. However, their decolletages, interpreted by their contrasting poses, suggest characters that are quite different from each other. The low-cut dress of Sandby's flower girl flaunts her breasts, which, though small and flat, are more provocatively bare than the full, shapely ones of Boitard's. Hand perched on her hip, she adopts an expressive, insolent pose considered the prerogative of socially powerful men, for whom it was a statement of pride and assertive might.[41] By an attitude of aggressive ease, this English street walker exudes a taunting, defiant sexuality. Casting a half-predatory, half-inviting eye at 'your Honour', she hides her memorandum book behind her back and shelves her flower basket on her hip, where it is lost in the billowing skirt.

But Sandby's hardened, young 'pennyrent' does not merely defame Boitard's innocently languorous nymph. This print undermines the traditional fabrication of the flower girl in all Cries by changing her from a symbol of innocence endangered to one of dangerous experience. A figure of depravity,

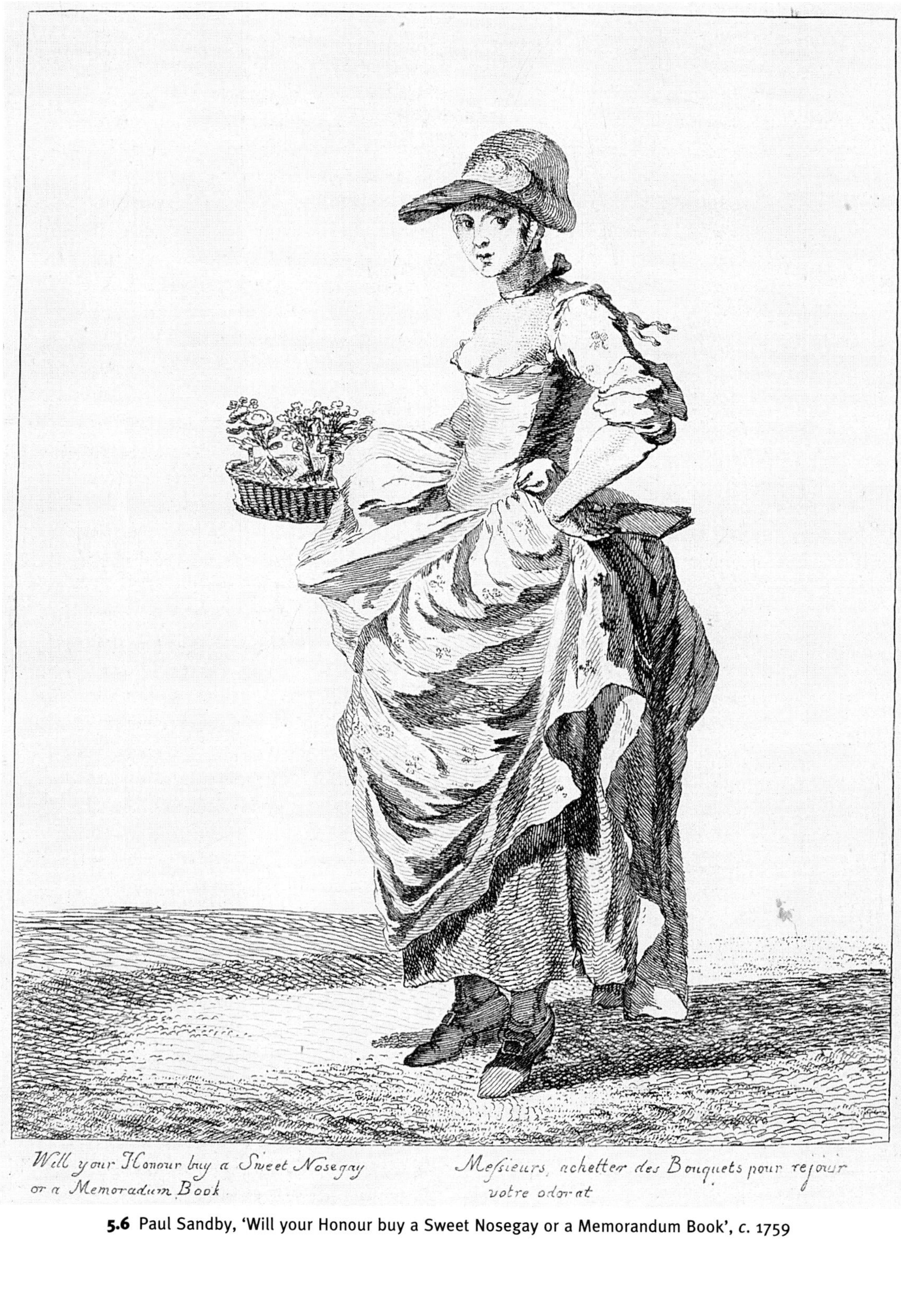

5.6 Paul Sandby, 'Will your Honour buy a Sweet Nosegay or a Memorandum Book', *c.* 1759

she is the first female in English art to represent the lower class as sexual threat to the upper class ('Will your Honour?'), instead of the other way around. Selling flowers one moment and herself the next, she is, by reason of her speech and brazen stare, one of the least euphemistic, most unsentimental trollops in art, created when the depiction of prostitutes borrowed from the formulae of goddesses and mythological nudes.[42]

Sandby's ambition was to alter the dominant paradigms for depicting criers in art. Like Hogarth, he wanted to make London Cries not continental but English, not fanciful but actual. In the work of Laroon, Amigoni and Boitard, Cries follow a 'soft' paradigm; they are sentimental, pastoral and bucolic interpretations of city life derived from continental art. Sandby aims to replace these with satiric, anti-pastoral and naturalistic interpretations drawn not from art but the realities of life in London – Hogarth's London. Using staged contrasts, sometimes between one character and another but at other times between figure and background, he presents England's capital as a place of division and conflict: men and women, rich and poor, master and servant, patron and vendor. To illustrate these broad goals, I will analyse three images in which Sandby works to create his own London Cries rather than to pummel adversaries. These English watercolours, without precedent in continental art, possess a clarity and an independent authority that increase from one to another. All are marked by a surprising switch in sympathy that declares Sandby's pioneering social vision.

'Bootblacks' (**plate 3**), showing how social, sexual and psychological motives converge in a scene from daily labour, contrasts the division of shoeshine work by sex.[43] In the background, a man blackens the shoes of an aristocrat in a tableau that sets the rich, elegant client over against the poor, uncouth shine; the leisured, insouciant gentleman against the toiling lackey; the purse-proud, erect aristocrat above the humble, stooped labourer. The bootblack, bent over his taskmaster's shoes, is shorn of personal identity, defined not by his invisible face but by his anonymous labour. In the foreground, a young woman cleans boots dropped off by customers; slumping over a pile of old shoes, she works her brush mechanically, staring at the ground. Is she pensive or drunk? Estranged from her task, isolated from her counterpart (with whom she has neither talk nor sight), and stupefied by repetitive work, she is the first hawker in the London Cries to evince symptoms that modern sociologists call alienation and describe as a feature of city life over the past three hundred years.

'Bootblacks' contrasts the quiet alienation of a young woman with the social humiliation of a man and the high station of a well-born customer with the low rank of his hireling. Open warfare between hawker and customer breaks out in 'Rare Mackerel, Three a Groat Or Four for Sixpence' (**plate 4**), a dissertation on the threshold as a site of ritual war or welcome. Etched for *Twelve London Cries*, 'Rare Mackerel' pictures a psychological, social and physical confrontation between a savage fishwife and two reluctant customers. Who can say if the invasive fishwife pesters the retreating tavern-keepers more than the tavern-keepers vex the fishwife? The fishwife's rapacious snarl, bristling with teeth that evoke cannibalism, is hostile, menacing, and loud: is she crying mackerel or damning her customer or doing both at the same time? The more forward keeper's piercing, furious gaze is also deeply fearful. Hostility and physical alarm erupt in how she clenches her fist and sticks her head through a narrow aperture while shielding her body behind the door, barred with a chain. The stand-off between fishwife and tavern-keepers in 'Rare Mackerel' pioneers, in the London Cries, the frank portrayal of hatred, anger and envy, dividing haves from have-nots.[44] This image is the first Cries to cast Londoners as split between the contemptuous, fearful, derisive rich and the wrathful, insolent, threatening poor.

The noisy clash between fishwife and tavern owner treats animosities between propertied householders of the middling sort and unpropertied vendors of the lowest orders. A companion sketch, 'Buy my Muffins' (**plate 5**), rehearses the same scene between more disparate classes, represented by a pastry vendor and three aristocrats. Compared to 'Rare Mackerel', 'Buy my Muffins' is a scene of low-voltage contrast; its mood of gentility and indifference is governed by the civilizing presence of aristocrats, too far above hawkers to be threatened by them in the way the alehouse keeper and her servant are. This watercolour presents a split between mean and noble or inside and outside. Inside the house, two ladies and a gentleman take tea and cakes in high ceremony. Framed by a window, the opulent private scene comments on the gloomy public spectacle. Unlike Amigoni's muted antitheses of rich and poor from which the wealthy are absent, this scene juxtaposes low character against high. It identifies the lives of the rich with their secure townhouse and counterposes the exposure, insufficiency and isolation of the vendor, whose home is the deserted street. The spiked fence suggests that the gap between rich and poor is unbridgeable and even policed, by contrast with 'Rare Mackerel', where householders meet hawkers face to face.

In 'Buy my Muffins', the wealthy are better off than the poor: better housed, better dressed and better fed. But they are different in ways more fundamental still; they eat different foods in different quantities with different utensils. More important, they eat in a different style: they dine. They angle their heads, wave their hands and hold their torsos in distinctive ways – more vertically, more rigidly, more ceremonially than stooped hawkers. This speech of the bodies, part of the 'art of conversing agreeably', unites the diners with one another by means of a common discipline.[45] It sets them in opposition to and above peddlers like the solitary muffin man, irretrievably different from and more passive than his sociable customers. Bent by his basket, he seems rancorous and bitter, perhaps defeated, as he quits the dwelling of the well-to-do. Has he been rebuffed by the rich, passing over his muffins for more delicate, less suspect and more assuredly sanitary treats of their own, as his overflowing basket argues?

Though his expression is hard to read, his downturned mouth harbours a sour disaffection that acknowledges his own powerless condition versus the high and mighty state of his customers. The formal organization of this image and 'Rare Mackerel' suggest the same point. Both designs picture householders from afar or incompletely, technical impediments to identifying with them. But they portray vendors from below and close up, which, by monumentalizing and particularizing them, generates sympathy between them and the viewer. In formal terms, these two images of discord are narrated from the slant of drifting vendors rather than their settled customers, reduced to shrieking heads or distant staffage. This unprecedented shift in sympathy, repeated in certain other etchings and watercolours, makes Sandby's the first Cries to depict hawkers and their customers from the bottom up. Profoundly unconventional, they oppose the interest, not only of vendors' customers, but of their surrogates, the artist's buyers and patrons. In espousing this 'inverted' perspective, they stand as the most original images in Sandby's *oeuvre* and in Cries of London as a genre.

Sandby's designs, those that expose hawkers as well as those that espouse them, are united in an effort to reverse the genre's sublimation of social life to artistic form, its prettification of its subject to the exclusion of naturalistic interest or lifelike detail.[46] Sandby's compositions resocialize the genre, by incorporating into it what is repulsive and truly frightening about hawkers, as well as what is contemptuous, hostile or indifferent in their customers. These designs show, for the first time, sympathy both with customers who regard vendors as unsavoury, even threatening and predatory, and with vendors who regard customers as irate, haughty or unconcerned about the welfare of those that do their heavy lifting. They thus create a new fable for Cries that is actualized, naturalistic and distinctively English, much as the 'Enraged Musician's' is. That fable links the hatred, fear and cruelty of the rich to the villainy and anger of the poor in an unbroken cycle of mutual cause and effect.

Sandby's *Twelve London Cries* failed either to win an audience or make disciples. His suite of etchings was the first of six serializations he planned to compete with Boitard's suite in six parts. Title pages to the second and third installments, ready for the etcher's needle, survive among his watercolours, which mysteriously vanished after the artist's death, but reappeared on 13 June 1961, when Sotheby's auctioned them off as seventy-seven 'costume drawings', the property of 'a gentleman'.[47] The preliminary study for a subsequent title page (**plate 6**) executed in the spirit of the first title, shows another engaging young woman 'entrepreneur' proposing to 'Turn your Copper into Silver now before your Eyes'. A counterfeiter, this hawker offers a service that was not only felonious but capital too; in 1788, the last woman in England to be hanged and then burned was Margaret Sullivan whose crime was to colour copper coins so that they appeared silver.[48] The watercolour also bears an inscription identifying it as Sandby's third title page: 'Twelve London Cries done from the Life by P Sandby 1759 Part 3d'. Because *Twelve London Cries done from the Life Part 1st* miscarried, neither this preliminary study nor any other watercolour was cut.[49] The result was public humiliation for this artist whose quarrelsome temperament and irritable personality appear in every one of his Cries, which employ the techniques of satire and inversion to advance themes of enmity and antagonism.[50]

Why did Sandby, esteemed 'one of the most inventive and varied of all English printmakers', blunder in his attempt to shift the genre of Cries from continental to English, from lyric to satiric and naturalistic?[51] A key to the failure of his artistic program to establish new protocols for Cries emerges in a comparison with Francis Wheatley's (1747–1801) *Itinerant Trades of London*. Wheatley's *Trades*, prized by buyers when they first appeared, have kept their popularity with today's collectors. They are not only the most successful suite of hawkers ever published but 'perhaps the most enduringly popular of all English prints', according to Stephen Calloway's *English Prints for the Collector*.[52]

The Wheatley paintings engraved as *Itinerant Trades* were either commissioned or snapped up by the firm of Colnaghi & Company. In either case, the artist, who was reputed 'a very personable man, fond of dress', executed these oils when his 'habits of expense became too unbounded for his means and . . . he was compelled to paint and draw for the print-sellers': his house and its contents were sold to satisfy his creditors in 1793; four years later, he pawned his Royal Academy Diplomas for £22.[53] So Wheatley's

Itinerant Traders owes its inspiration to a commercial art publisher – and poverty. Despite the importance it grants to incident, the suite is, in tone, least like Hogarth's 'Enraged Musician' and Sandby's *Cries*, the satires of belligerent artists expressing felt ideological positions. It is most like Laroon's *Cryes* and Boitard's recast *Cries*. *Itinerant Traders*'s mood is formed by late Georgian buyers having tastes that the artist likely shared. Its theme is the civilizing powers of buying and selling.

Between 1792 and 1795, Wheatley showed his *Cries of London*, fourteen small oils, at the Royal Academy, an apotheosis that indicates the genre's extraordinary rise in status from ephemeral broadsides cut for taverns to paintings executed for England's premier exhibition.[54] Before they were even hung, they were puffed in the press as 'advances' on the 'old' subject of the Cries of London', for instead of making single figures, he [Wheatley] has introduced the itinerant tradesmen in small groups, and represented them subservient to humorous incident', as did Müller, Hogarth and Sandby.[55] At this early point, they were announced as 'intended for the "Engraver"' and not any engraver but a foreign craftsman named 'Schiavonetti, a very ingenious Italian artist [who] has already began upon those which are finished in a very promising style', according to the same puff. Between 1793 and 1797, Colnaghi had thirteen of the paintings engraved by French and Italian craftsmen: Francesco Bartolozzi, G. Vendramini, A. Cardon, T. Gaugain and, of course, L. Schiavonetti.[56] The firm then sold the paintings to art collectors from the aristocracy and elites of the middle class.[57] Colnaghi's halftones were printed in coloured stipple, imparting the effect and status of the original oil paintings in order to lure new buyers. Bearing titles in French and English for an international market, the prints came in a paper wrapper bearing the letterpress, *The Itinerant Trades of London in thirteen engravings, by the first artists, after paintings by Wheatley*; the set cost 'fifteen shillings colored or seven shillings and sixpence plain'.[58] The demand for these 'furniture prints' was so enormous that it quickly wore out the copperplates; in 1812, Colnaghi advertised a new set of engravings recut by Thomas Alliprandi.[59] Their price and sale by subscription conjures up city elites adorning their homes with subjects inculcating a reverence for middle-class benevolence in the same way that their high-born counterparts decorated their palaces with historical or mythical paintings extolling patrician virtues.[60] Increasingly these urban elites were represented by women challenging the patriarchal bias of connoisseurship by buying art that showed domesticity, religious morality and female benevolence as the characteristics of their culture.[61]

Wheatley's designs shift the tone of Cries from the comic or satiric of Hogarth, Child and Sandby back to the serious mood of Laroon and Boitard. With a few exceptions, the theme remains either serious or sentimental from Wheatley's time through the Victorian period, when the depiction of the poor in ensembles of Cries becomes more benevolent and more repressive at the same time.[62] Though they are the antithesis of Sandby's Cries, Wheatley's designs are not deliberate reactions. Rather they are flattering responses to Laroon's images, which they modernize, reinvent and polish in a style that pays close attention to picturesque formality and still closer attention to costume, which, seesawing between the simple neatness of the theatrically rustic and the positive elegance of the urbane, no longer signals class, occupation and social status but instead indicates character, personality and virtue. If Laroon's images appealed to men and Boitard's 'improved' versions targeted children, Wheatley's aim to please women.

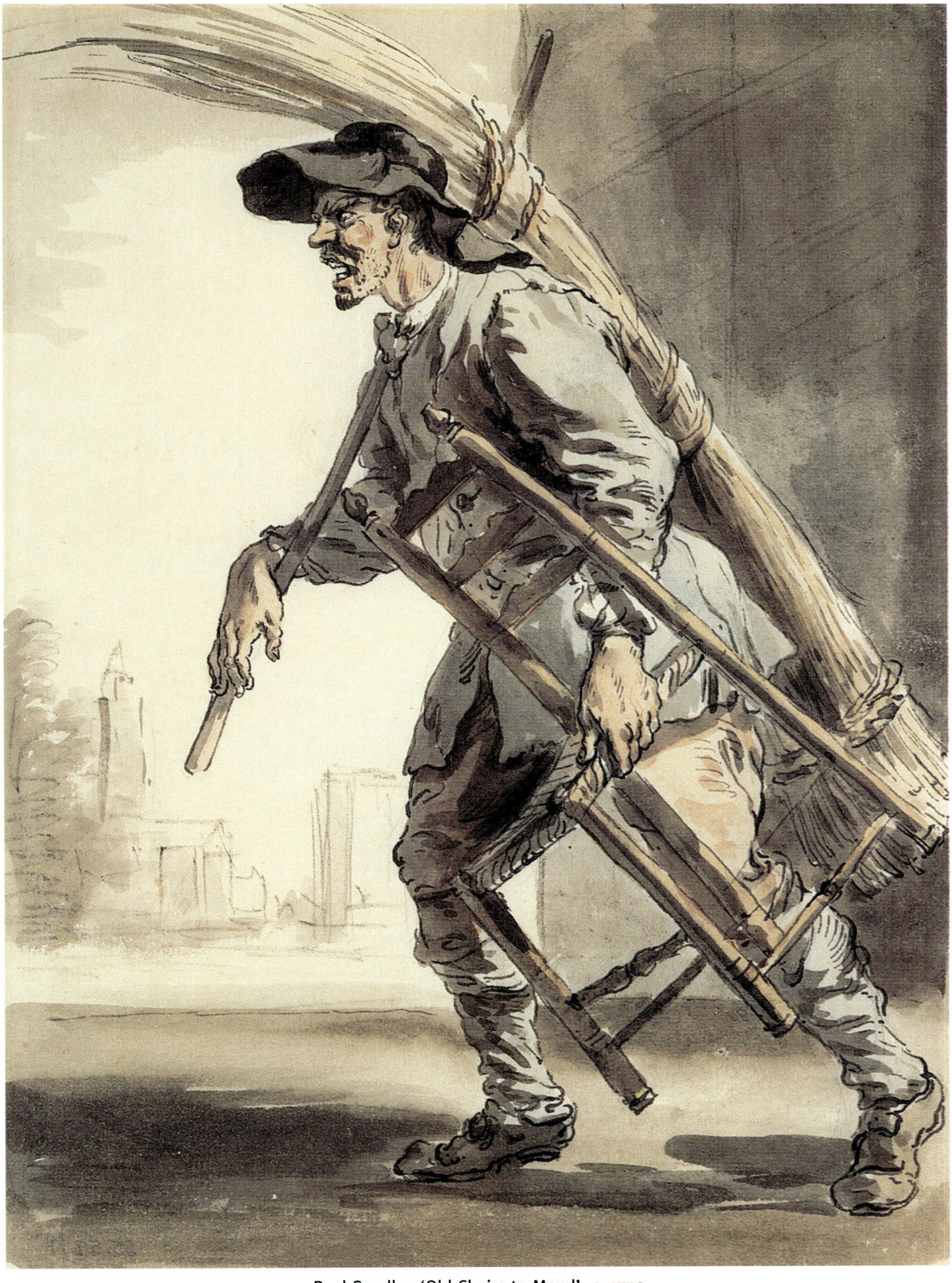

Paul Sandby, 'Old Chairs to Mend', *c.* 1759

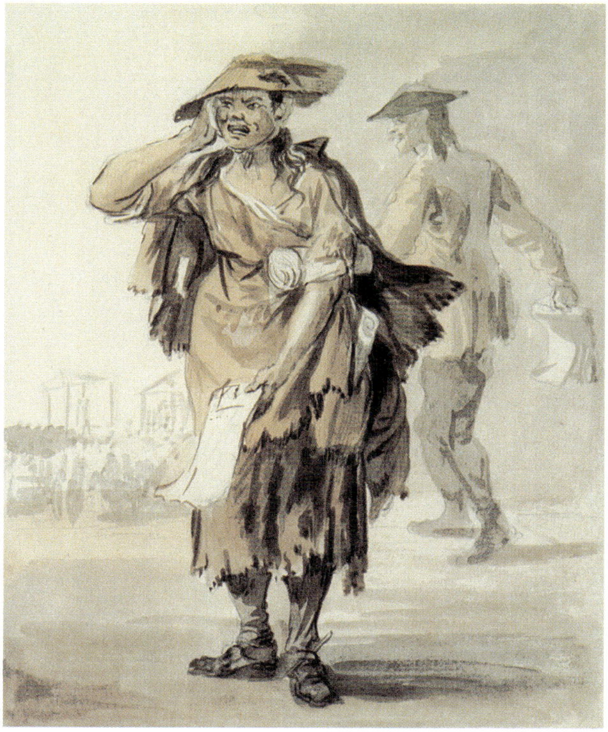

Paul Sandby, 'Last Dying Speech', *c.* 1759

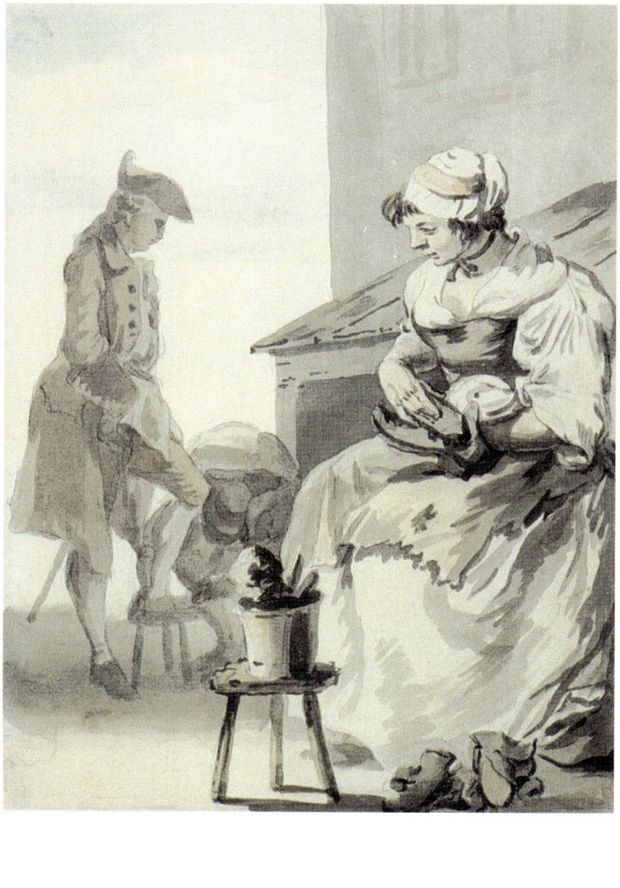

Paul Sandby, 'Bootblacks', *c.* 1759

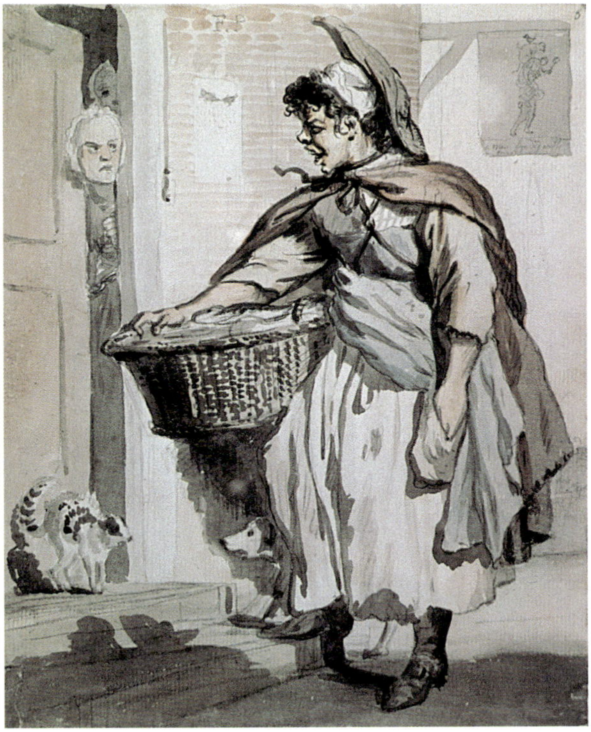

Paul Sandby, ‘Rare Mackerel, Three a Groat Or Four for Sixpence’, *c.* 1759

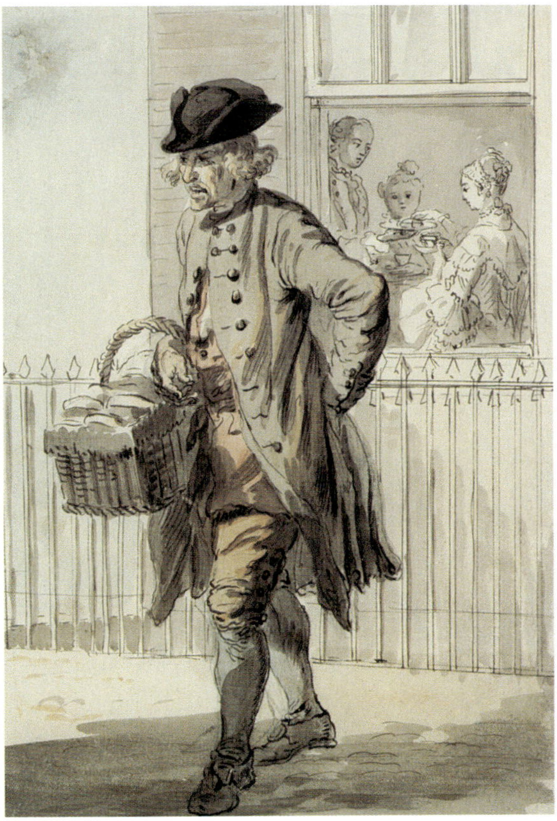

Paul Sandby, ‘Buy my Muffins’, *c.* 1759

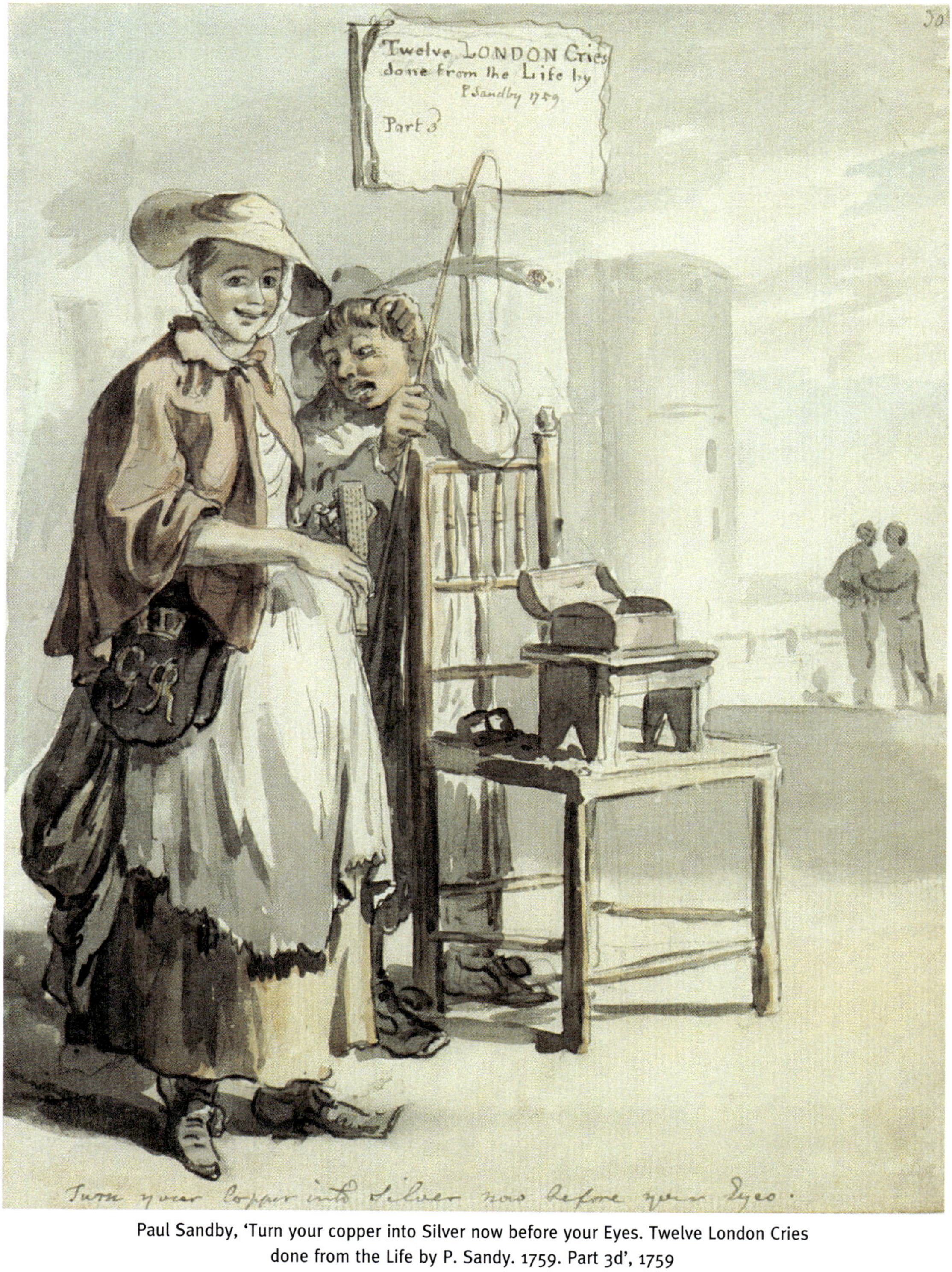

Paul Sandby, 'Turn your copper into Silver now before your Eyes. Twelve London Cries done from the Life by P. Sandy. 1759. Part 3d', 1759

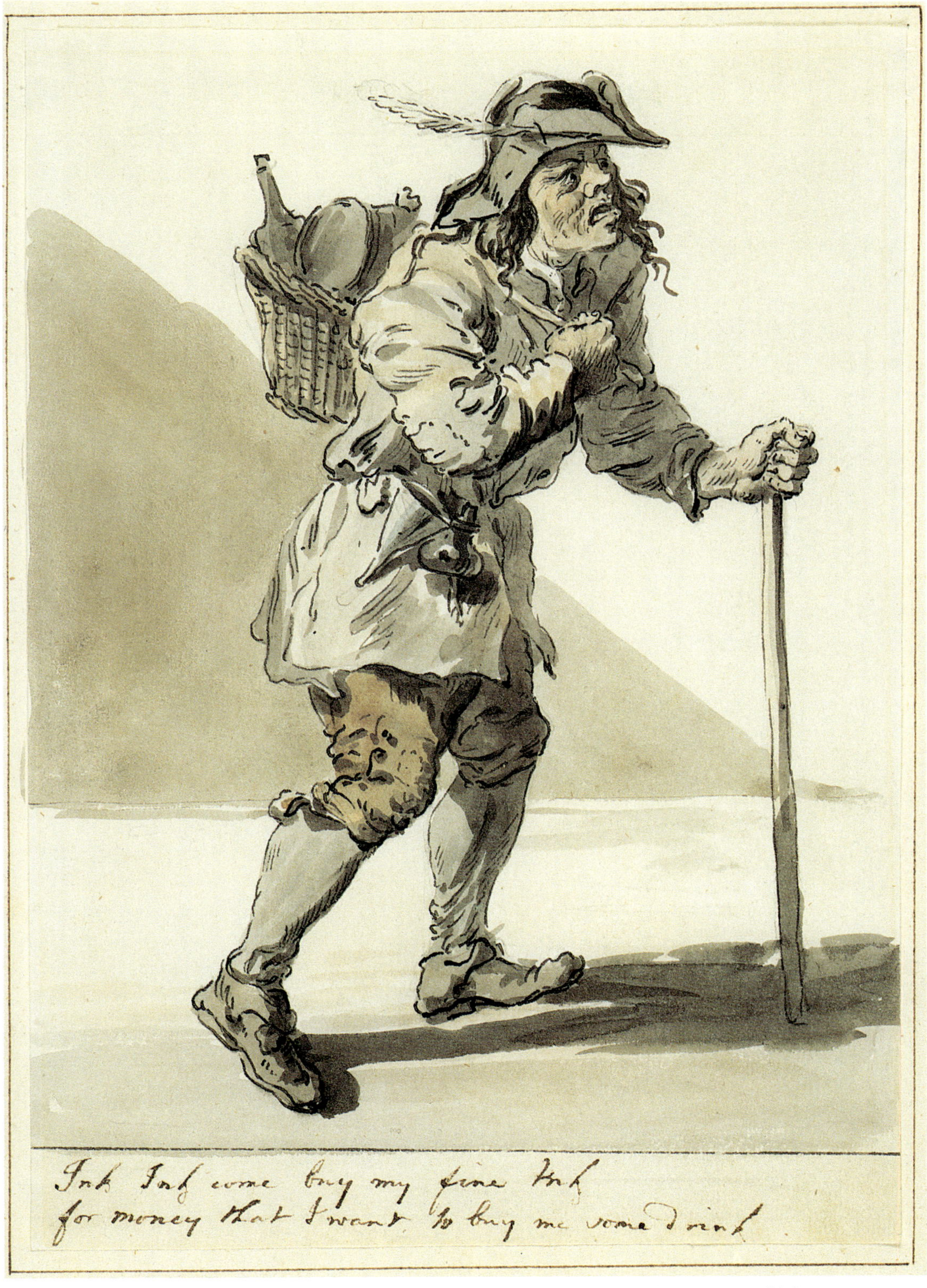

Paul Sandby, 'Ink, Ink, come buy my fine Ink for money that I want to buy me some drink',
c. 1759

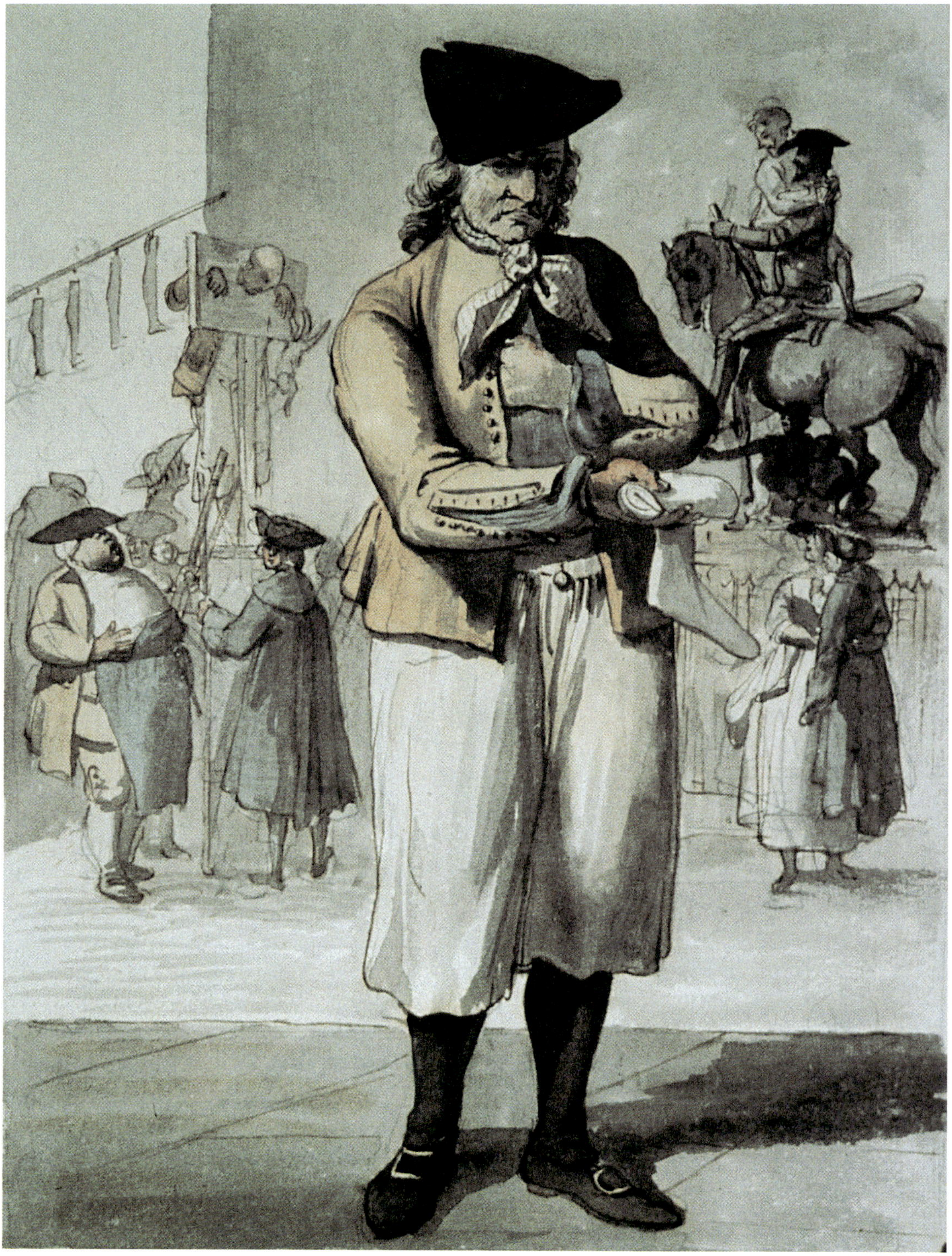

Paul Sandby, 'Sock Vendor', *c.* 1759

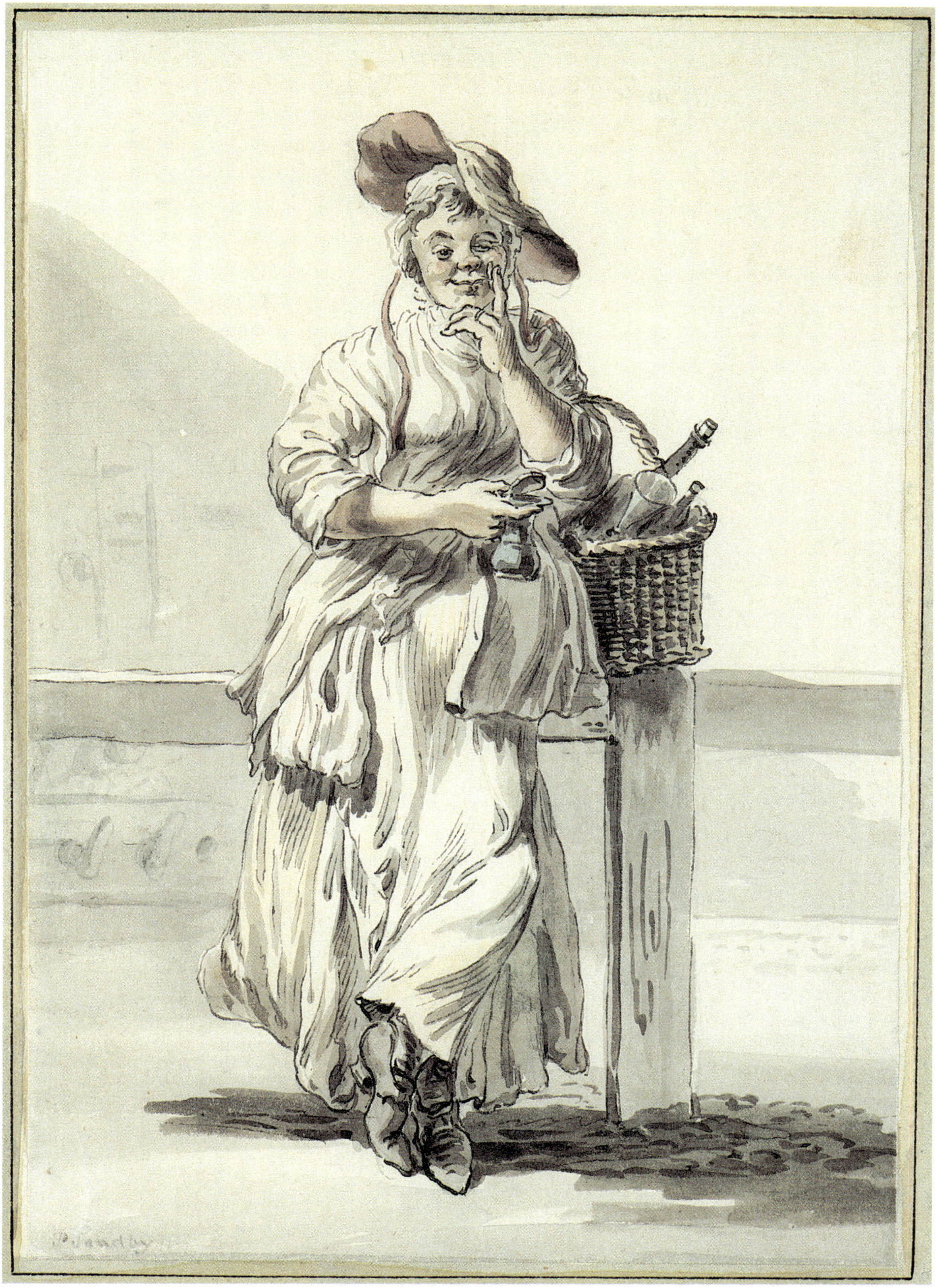

Paul Sandby, 'Wine Seller', *c.* 1759

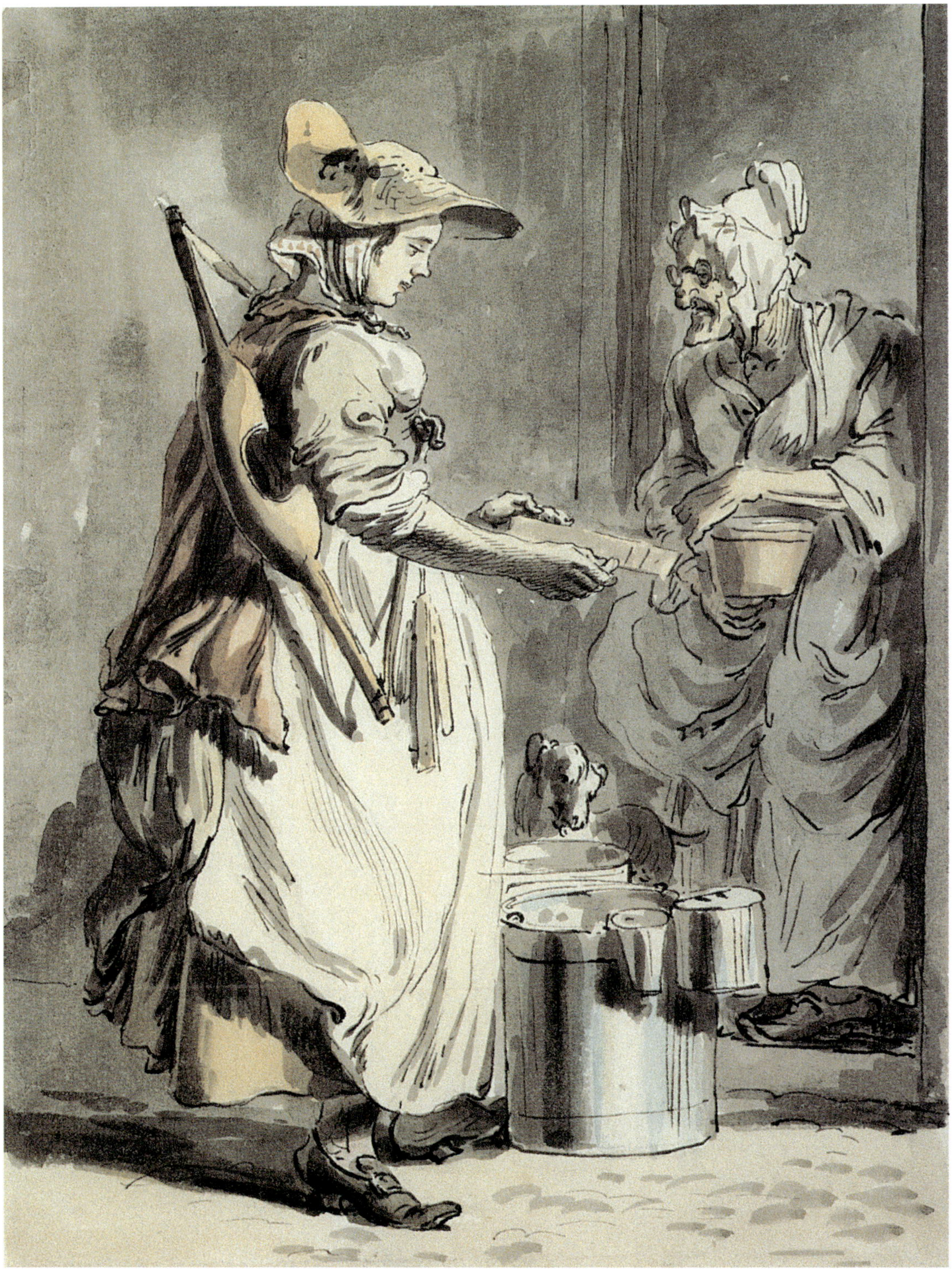

Paul Sandby, 'Milkmaid', *c.* 1759

In technique, the engravings employ stipple, which John Landseer, savaging Bartolozzi in a lecture to the Royal Institution in 1806, stigmatized as 'effeminate' and 'peculiarly expressive of softness', in contrast to the 'manly' style of line engraving.[63]

In substance, these costume prints favour female characters whose task is to advance ideals of Christian and womanly conduct both at the bottom of the social pyramid and at the top. What stands out most about Wheatley's characters is the large number of rich, elegant patrons who trade with hawkers at a point in history when the role of such vendors was to 'accommodate the less affluent with the necessaries of life in the smallest quantities'.[64] These characters, surrogates for Wheatley's rich, elegant buyers, transform Cries like 'New Mackrel, New Mackrel' (**5.7**) from reflections of street life to discursive sermons by which print buyers are encouraged to admire the behaviour of their own class.[65] The action of 'New Mackrel', in which a lady ostentatiously donates a coin to a fishwife, unfolds before a door that invites comparison with the chained entrance in Sandby's print of the same subject, 'Rare Mackerel'. Unlike Sandby's tavern entry with its clamorous hawker, this townhouse door is open wide to welcome such wretches as the grateful fishwife, in the tradition of aristocratic guest-friendship and hospitality long dead by 1790.

Of the three figures standing at the threshold, the lady and her maid are the celebrities. Unlike the customers in 'Rare Mackerel', who recoil in fear or anger, these heroines cross over the doorstep to welcome the hawker, transformed from a repugnant victimizer to a victim with a carriage that makes explicit the engaging servility everywhere implicit in Laroon. Lady and maid incline toward the pretty hawker, imaginatively switching places with her as offerer versus receiver. All three are bound by those ardent feelings of charity that, according to Thomas Bernard, writing in the late eighteenth century, fostered the 'mutual good will and connexion, which *ought* to subsist between the rich and poor'.[66] Romantic costume prints like Wheatley's 'New Mackrel', establish how humanely 'the Quality' administer to the deserving poor, identified as Jews, Irish, children, and virtuous country folk. More important, they demonstrate why the 'meaner sort' ought to defer to their betters, who treat them so angelically.[67]

In Wheatley's designs, rich and poor are coupled, whereas in Sandby's images the two classes are separated spatially by iron fences or doors, psychologically by outlook and conduct, corporeally by action, posture and bodily appearance, and materially by costume. Indeed the costumes of street vendors and their customers are interchangeable in Wheatley's fancy pictures like 'A New Love Song' (**5.8**). The antipode of Sandby's 'Last Dying Speech' (**plate 2**), this print is a revelation of elegant character and elegant female dress. The tall, beautiful ballad seller goes in a romantic version of English common dress, notably a 'round ear' cap of white muslin under a straw *bergere* bonnet, its crown trimmed with a blue ribbon and its brim fashionably rolled. Dressed in a new russet shawl that speaks of her provincial origins, she curtsies condescendingly to her customers, who seem awestruck, perhaps by her low-cut bodice. This bodice, like her immaculate petticoat, is white, a colour preferred by elites but seldom used by hawkers. Most remarkable, she lacks the only garment indispensable to hawkers, an apron to protect, transport, store and show her wares. With stylish clothing in a palette of bright hues, this ballad monger rivals her wealthiest customer, the lady in black period costume buying a love song to croon to her baby. No gallows' speeches or murderers'

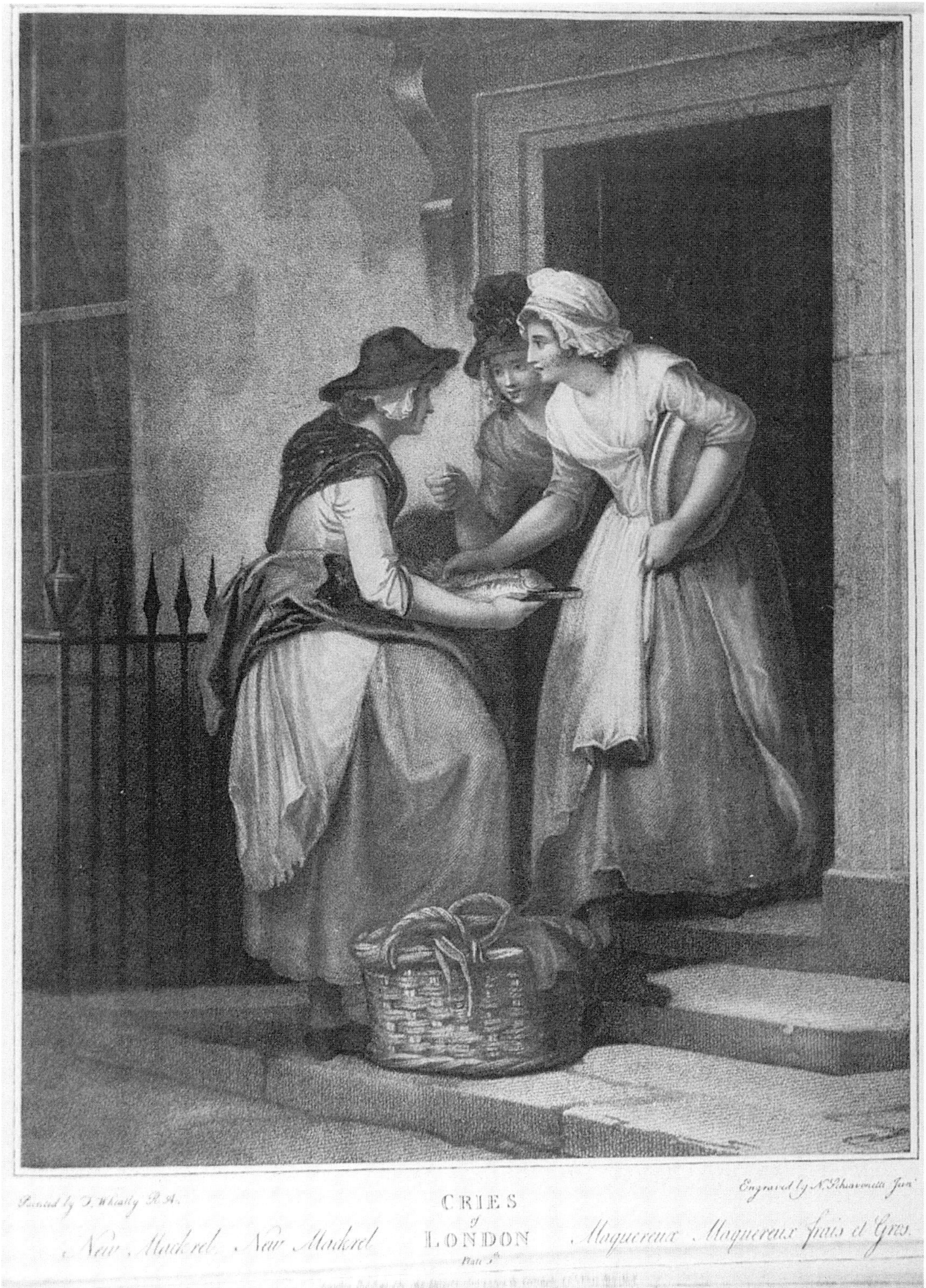

5.7 Francis Wheatley, 'New Mackrel, New Mackrel', 1796

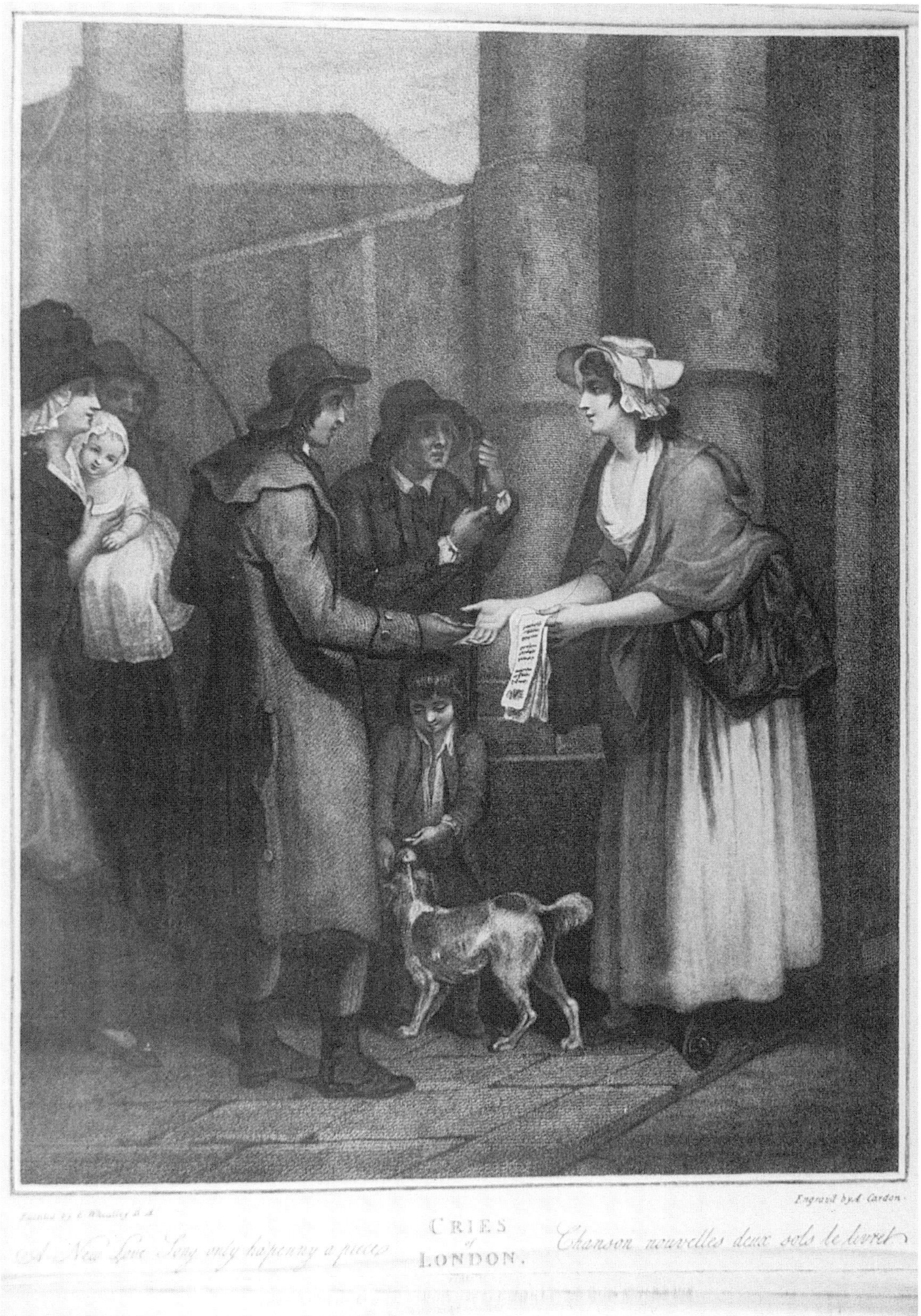

5.8 Francis Wheatley, 'A New Love Song', 1796

confessions among the stock of songs hawked by this docile vendor, understood at the time to be a necessary idealization, because a less exemplary figure would be so much less a pattern of how the poor should behave.[68]

In art, idealization generates either further idealization in spiralling degrees or else burlesque. The characters exiled from Wheatley's pictures hold centre stage in the *Cries of London* by Thomas Rowlandson, whose *Imitations of Modern Drawings* (*c.* 1780) indicates the centrality of mimicry in his art. Rowlandson's eight aquatints were engraved by the Swiss, H. Merke, coloured by refugees from the French Revolution, and published between 1 January and 4 May 1799 by the German-born Rudolph Ackermann, whose Repository of Arts was Colnaghi's rival among print-selling establishments in the capital.[69] Published three years after *Itinerant Trades*, Rowlandson's *Cries* aped Colnaghi's 'large print' format, inviting a costly frame and wall space; it was the big ensemble's swan song. When Wheatley's suite of thirteen prints cost about one shilling and two pence each coloured and half that plain, Rowlandson's ensemble went for two and sixpence per print coloured and one and sixpence plain.[70] It vied commercially with the *Itinerant Trades*, whose aesthetic principles and motifs it attacked, at the same time as it affronted the memory of the *Cryes of London done after the Life*, then out of print and not an economic threat. It substitutes urban conflict for rural harmony to ridicule Wheatley's lyricism, much as Sandby mocked Laroon. It appealed to those connoisseurs Buckeridge describes as 'waggish collectors', men who relished erotic wit and satire.[71]

The specificity with which Rowlandson's energetic naturalism takes aim at Wheatley's frozen, high manner appears in how the satirist turns his predecessor's harmony into conflict. For example, Rowlandson's 'All a growing, a growing, here's Flowers for your Gardens' (**5.9**) burlesques Wheatley's 'Two bunches a penny primroses' (**5.10**) by changing that print's sentimental vignette into a droll narrative of sex and money played out between a city ingenue and an urbane country gardener.[72] The gardener, a swaggering cad, having sold the gullible, lovesick woman one small flowering plant, urges a second, bigger pot on her, while reaching into his cart for a fruit tree bearing lemons.

This bucolic rogue is typical of the quick wits who populate Rowlandson's teeming *Cries of London*. More often men than women and children, these figures prove hawking to be self-interested, exploitive, and tension-ridden – in a word, characteristically urban. At their best, Rowlandson's figures are 'necessary' people who testify to London's filth and dirt: the Irishman (**5.11**) hawking brick dust; the yokel (**5.12**) carrying cages housing two fat rodents – ironic allusions to the picturesque dogs Wheatley favoured. Other characters expose the debased tastes and morals of city dwellers or evoke the daily annoyances of life in London. A Hogarthian ballad seller (**5.13**) bawls broadsides so loudly she must muffle her ear against her own howls. Mocking Wheatley's delicate ballad woman selling 'A New Love Song', the buxom, ragged singer deals in 'Last Dying Speech and Confession of the unfortunate malefactors who were executed this morning'. At their worst, these characters are nakedly exploitive, seeking sex, as does the hideous lecher offering dust for love (**5.11**); or money, like the grotesquely caricatured Jews (**5.14**) gesturing obscenely through the crotch of torn breeches in order to swindle a country servant girl by crudely embarrassing her.[73]

This or that peddler may be wicked, but their customers are no better, so that

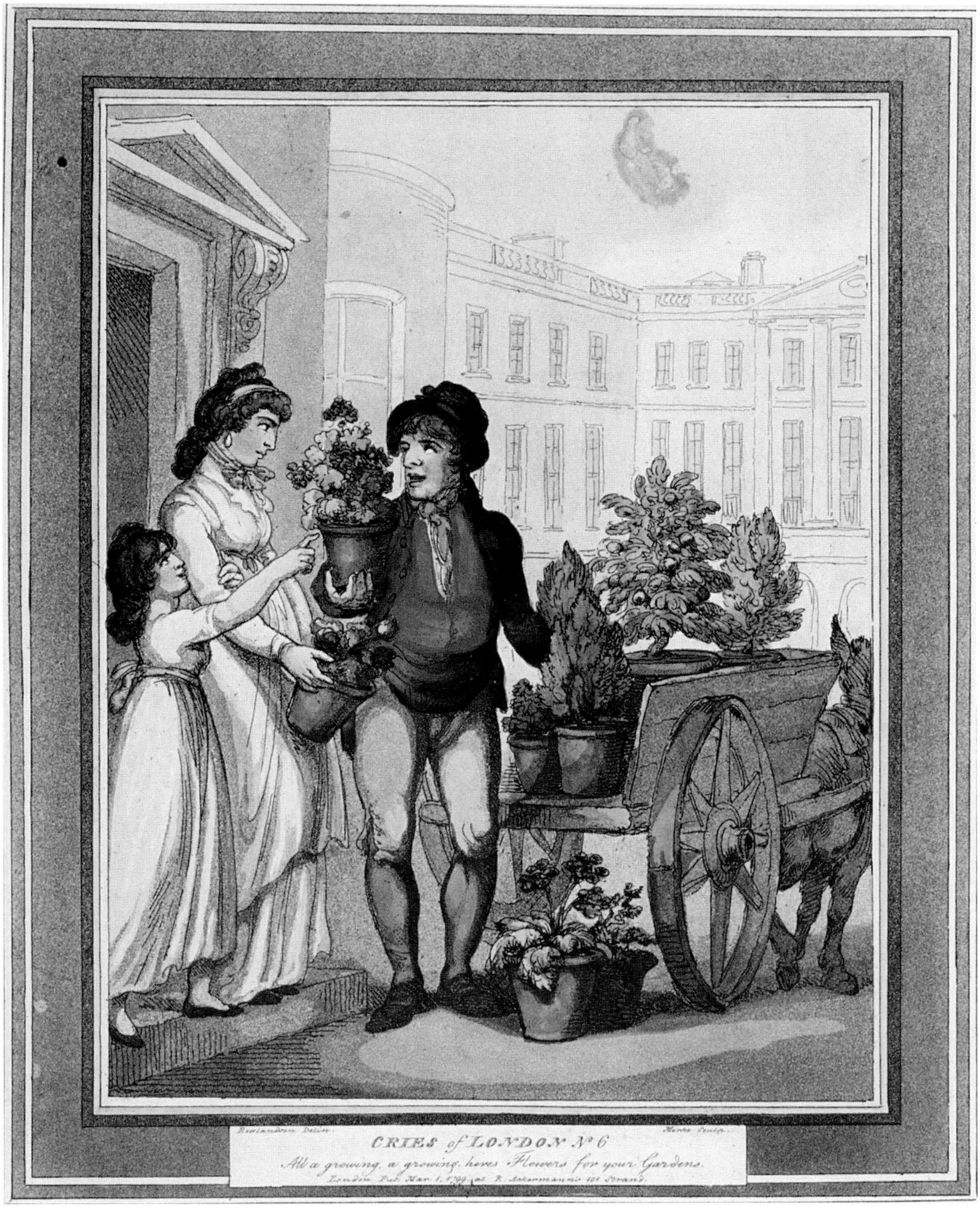

5.9 Thomas Rowlandson, 'All a growing, a growing, here's Flowers for your Gardens', 1799

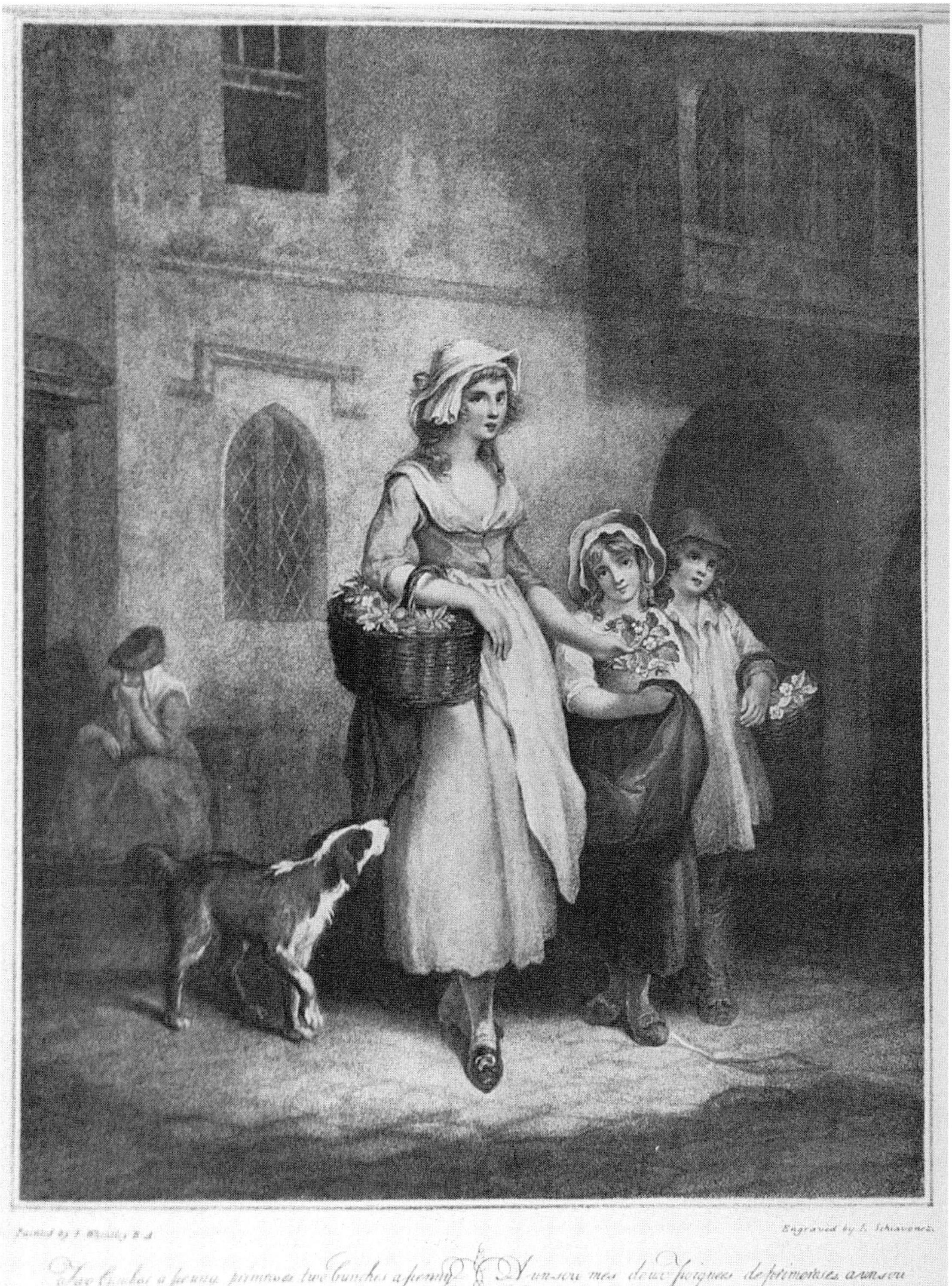

5.10 Francis Wheatley, 'Two bunches a penny primroses', 1793

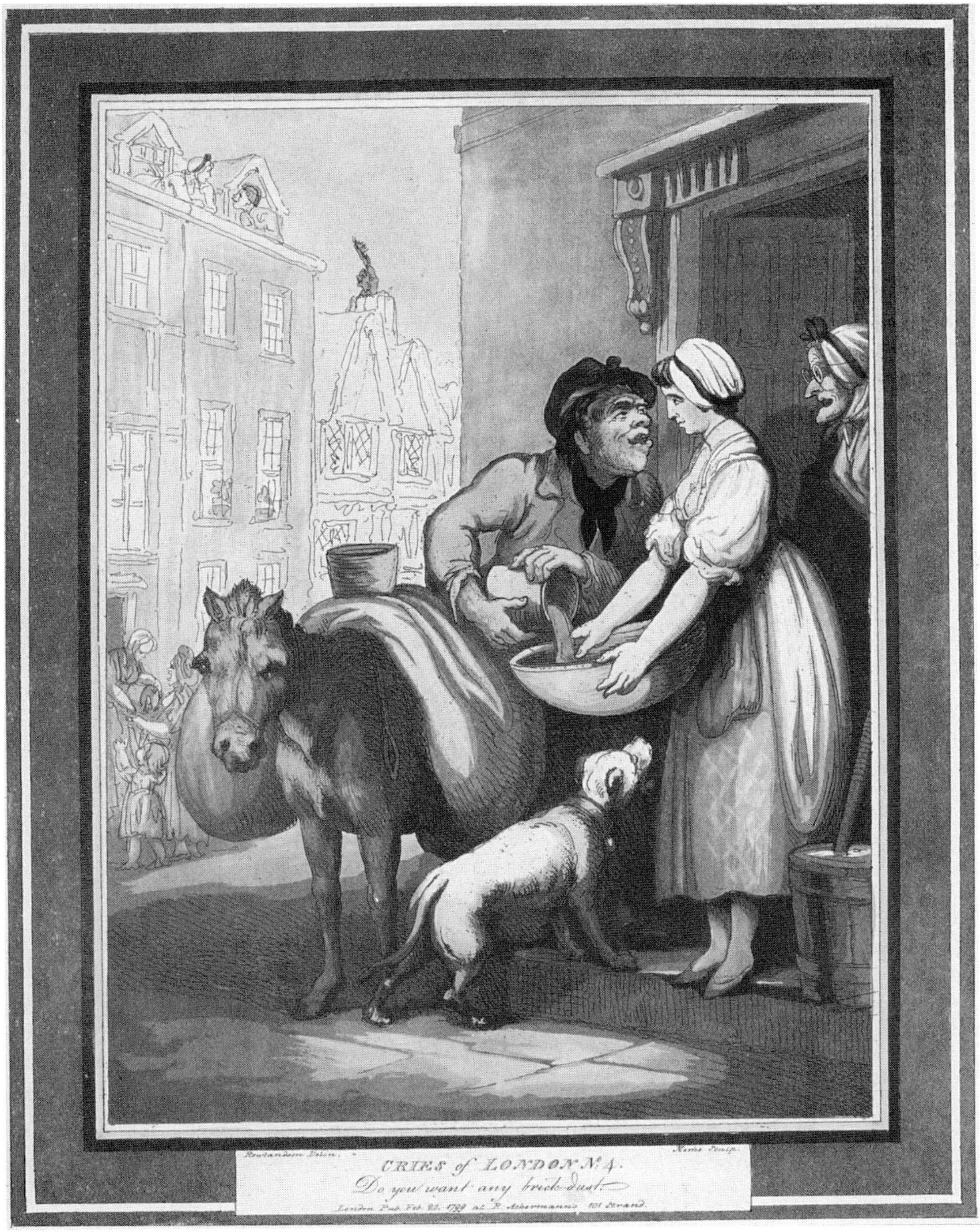

5.11 Thomas Rowlandson, 'Do you want any brick-dust', 1799

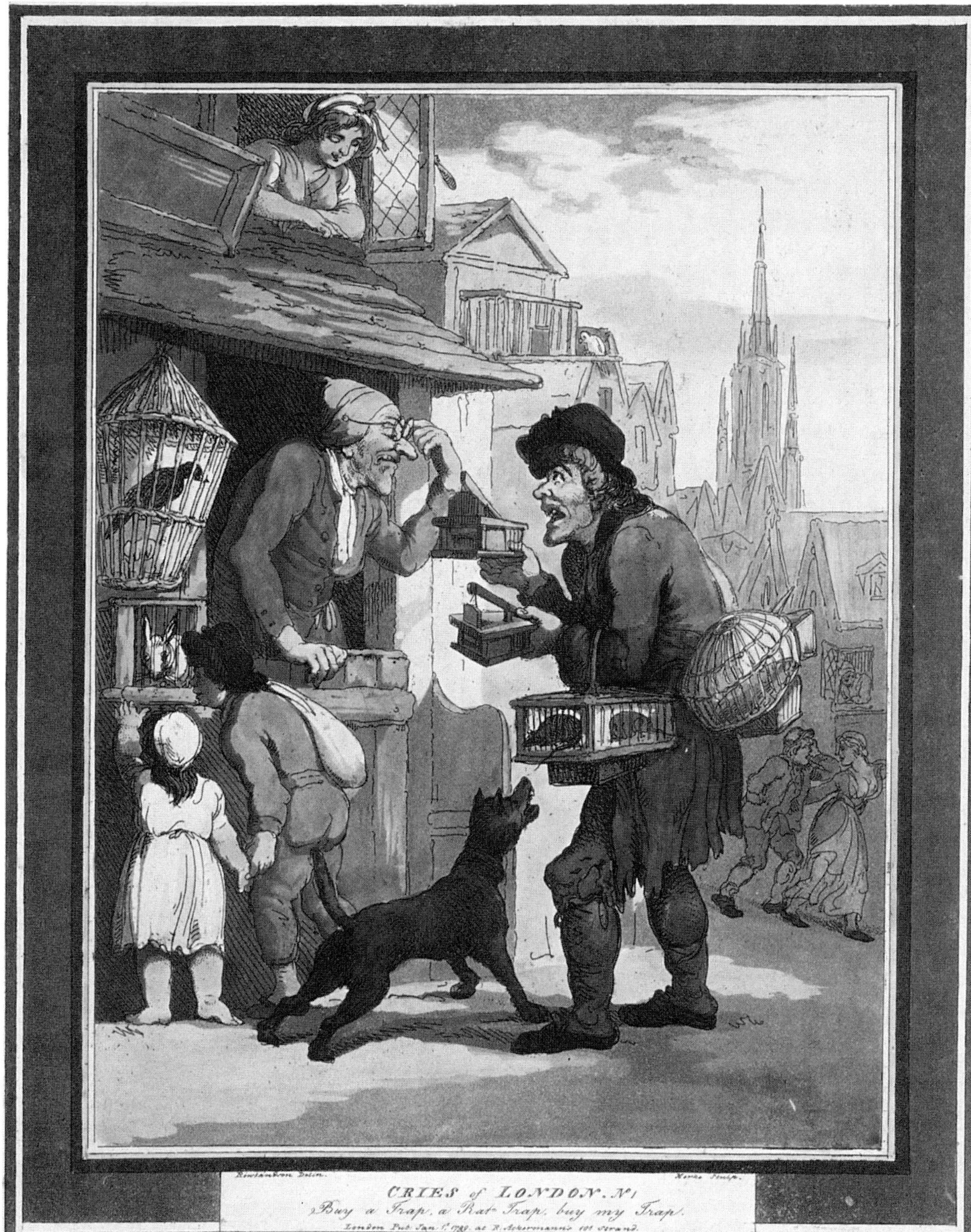

5.12 Thomas Rowlandson, 'Buy a Trap, a Rat-Trap, buy my Trap', 1799

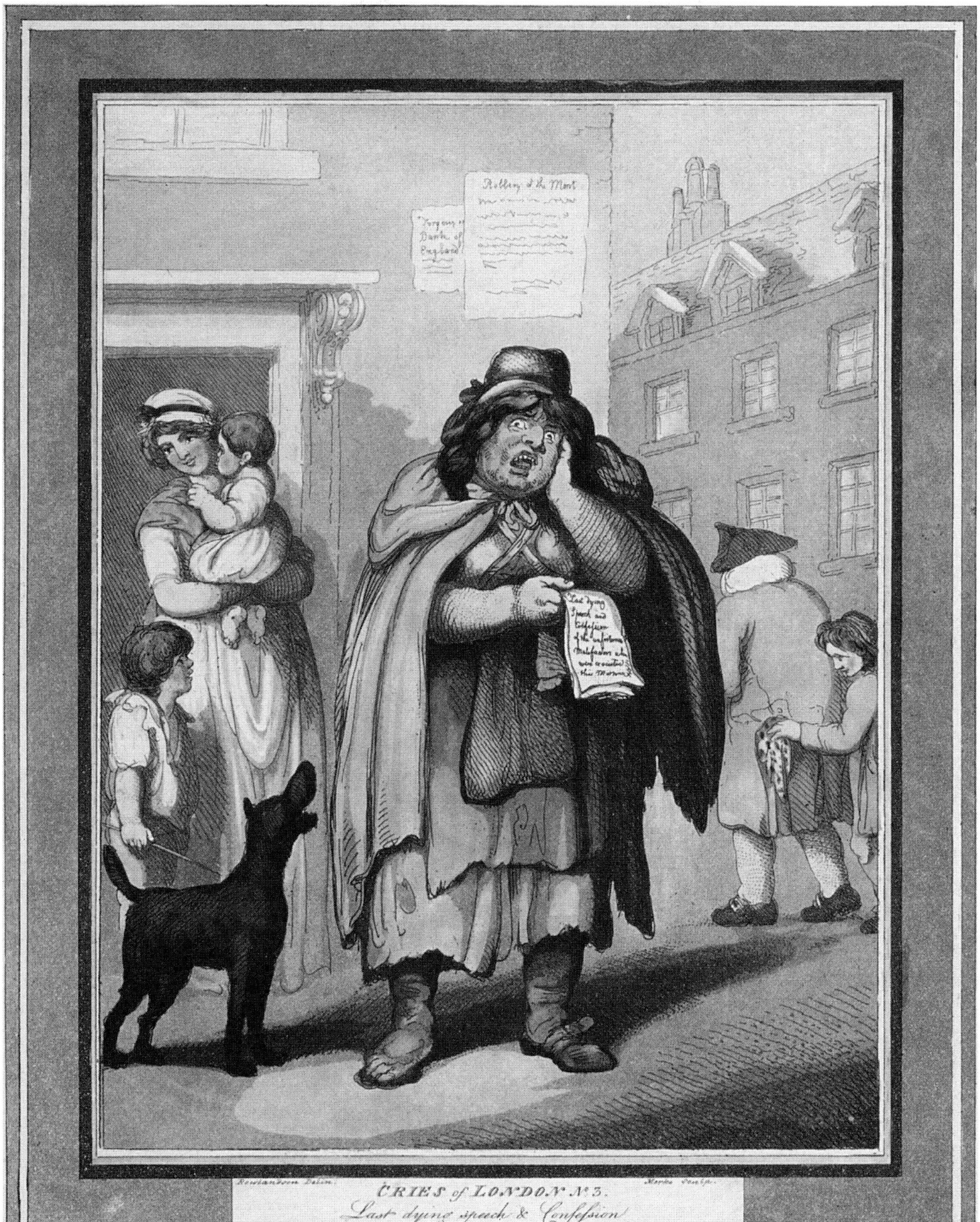

5.13 Thomas Rowlandson, 'Last dying speech & Confession', 1799

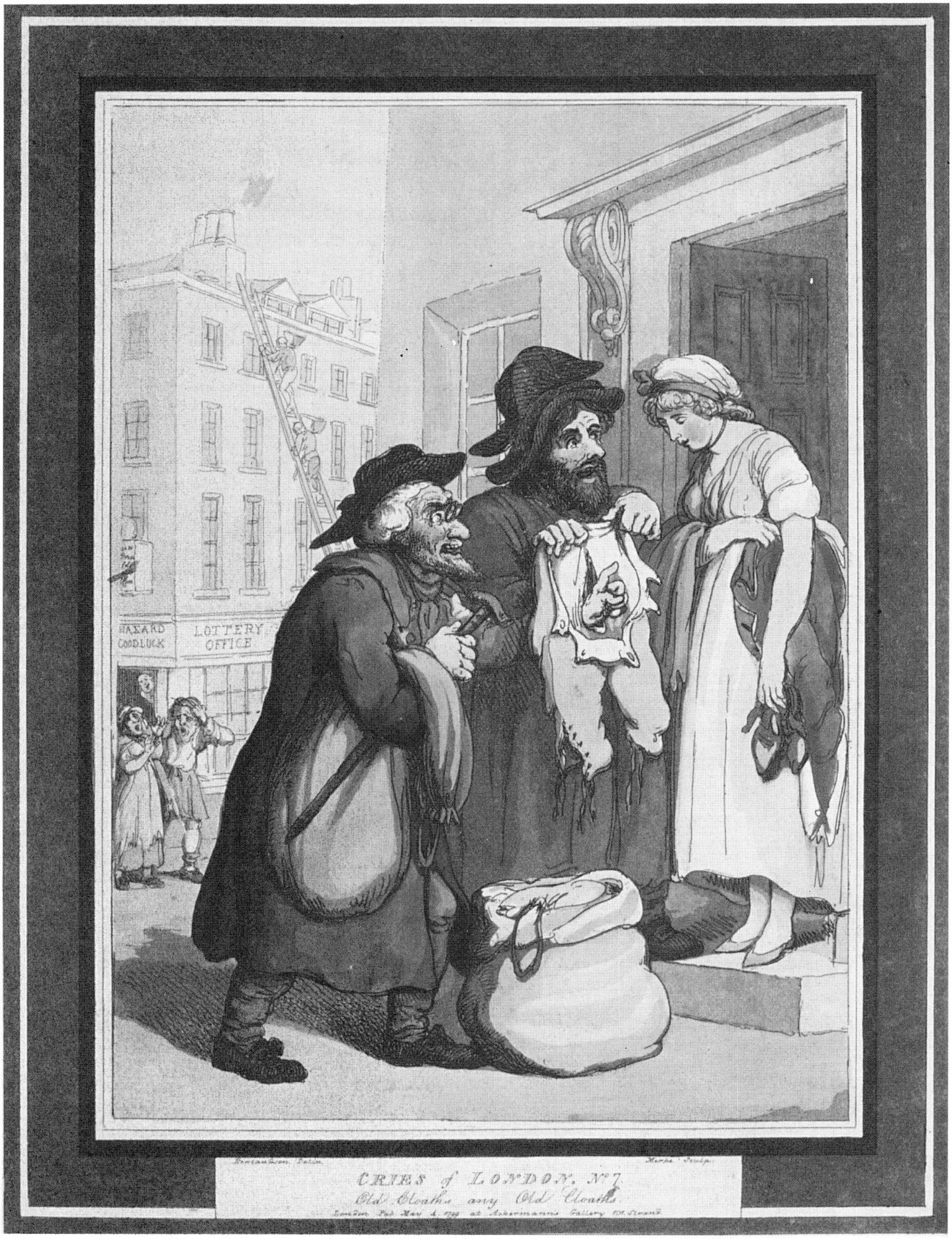

5.14 Thomas Rowlandson, 'Old Cloaths, any Old Cloaths', 1799

Rowlandson, ridiculing rich and poor alike, turns Wheatley's even-handed flattery into even-handed satire. In staged contrasts, the hallmark of his comic street theatre, he juxtaposes cynical, debased types from the city against innocent, naive ones from the country. Next to the skeptical pet seller (**5.12**), the peasant selling rat traps is a simple buffoon, not a churl. 'Water Cress' (**5.15**) reverses this kind of simple stereotyping by offering urbane country figures and naïve citizens in a chain of contrasts. The first contrast links the withered roué entering Mrs. Burke's 'house' to two young costermongers who appear to sell the old whoremonger watercress but really mean to shame him so he will buy them both off to be gone. The second unites the two 'virtuous' costermongers with the two beautiful 'city ladies'; these two spectators, whose whorehouse boredom is relieved by the drama below, serve as ironic surrogates of the viewer who help expound the print's instructional narrative. Here, as in Rowlandson's other Cries, the designs overflow with conflict and sex. Class conflict is overt and politicized, expressed in how the child, barefooted and angry, brandishes her watercress at the man in a hostile, aggressive way. No 'Please Sir' from this threatening, unpredictable gamin. Sex is covert, shown in symbols and gestures that are strictly iconographic, so that the prints' legends are free of carnality.

The least attractive, most criminal types in Rowlandson's *Cries* are the wayfarers in the background. They include, in 'Last Dying Speech', a young handkerchief thief (**5.13**) who mocks Wheatley's model children and perhaps also taunts the respectable youths selling laces in Laroon, who inspired them.[74] These and other such figures are self-seeking, exploitive, hustling, aggressive, venal and lascivious; they redefine the moral character of hawkers, shifting it from good in Wheatley to bad in Rowlandson.

But they are not angry, crazed or homicidal like the menacing lace vendor (**5.16**) or the deranged ink seller (**plate 7**) of Sandby, who renders Laroon's good hawkers not only bad but mad.[75] His lace vendor is a psychopath, who suggests, by the sinister way he loops his cords to look like snares or nooses, that he would as soon strangle his customers as sell them cord to tighten stays. Is this figure, pictured without a hint of comedy or satire, a compatriot of the real-life Thomas Dwyer and his Irish confederate James O'Neal, who, when examined by the law in 1723 about what trade they followed, declared they sold laces but were found guilty of robbery and hanged at a Tyburn?[76] Unlike Laroon's ink seller, who walks away from us in a graceful, academic pose, Sandby's peddler (**plate 7**) lurches threateningly across our path, beating his breast and grimacing wildly. Here is a figure of terror over whom we have no control. He is a street vendor, of course, but he also has private pursuits of his own, and one of these is far more important than his social identity as a seller of ink. He is pictured in the throes of a medical crisis, the nature of which is revealed by his shout, not a street cry but the taunting confession of an alcoholic who works to imbibe: 'Ink, Ink come buy my fine Ink for money that I want to buy me some drink'.

The sins of Rowlandson's figures are venial, not mortal; more often than not, they are weaknesses of the flesh. He is the first artist to cast the London Cries as battles of the sexes or erotic skits, though the instinctive animality of his characters, especially their womanizing, makes them more laughable than depraved. They are not madmen or nihilists, but scoundrels and roustabouts who harbour no grudge against society; V. S. Pritchett thought them 'lumps of animal horror or stupidity'.[77] They are sexual predators and economic opportunists, over-energetic, half-genial agents of London's

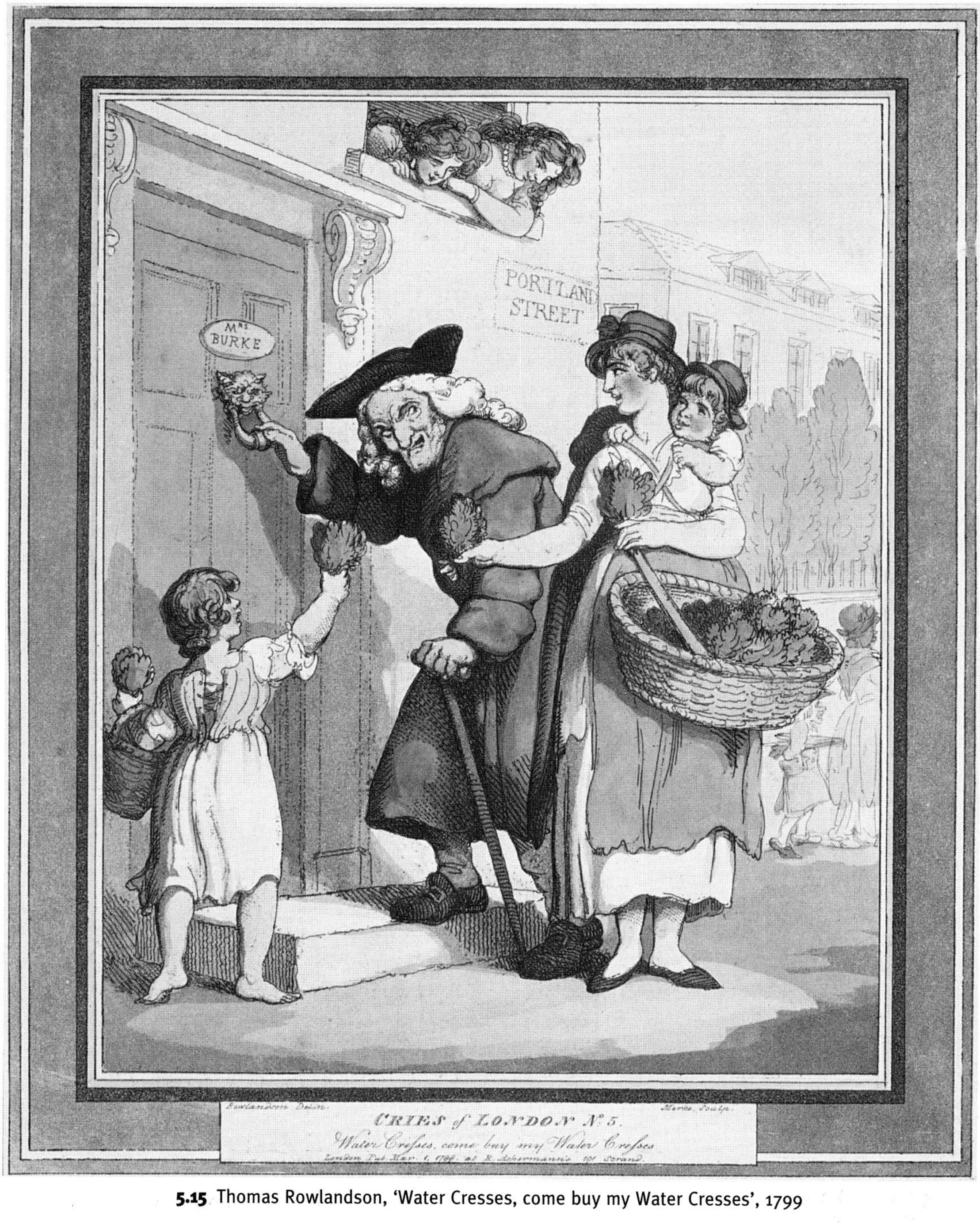

5.15 Thomas Rowlandson, 'Water Cresses, come buy my Water Cresses', 1799

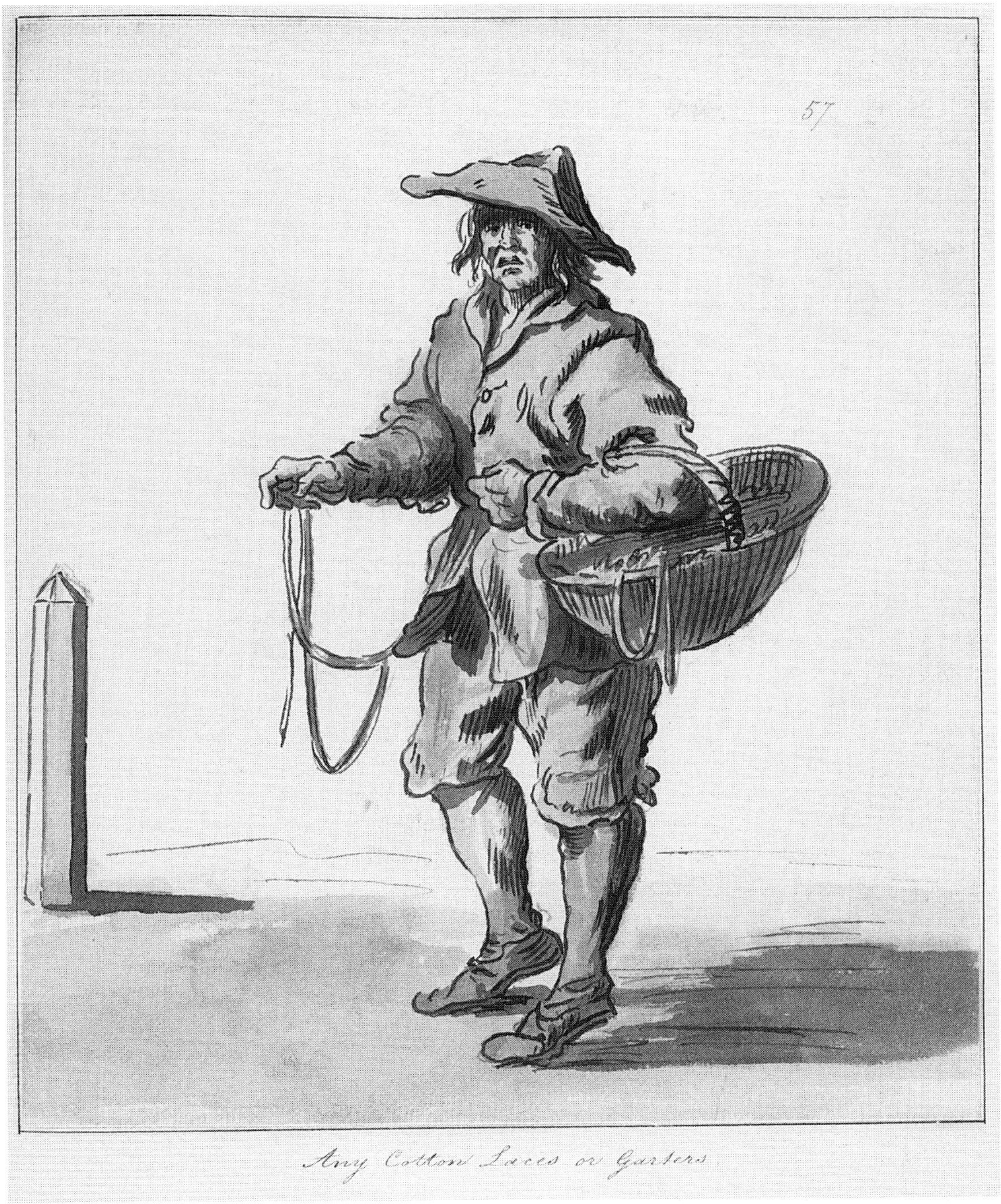

5.16 After Paul Sandby, 'Any Cotton Laces or Garters', *c.* 1759

nefarious commerce eager to seize the moment and its ill-gotten gains – a few extra pennies for a pair of ripped trousers, a shilling for a purloined handkerchief, a wet kiss, or something more. A social satirist, Rowlandson hatches figures who violate good taste, politeness, and discipline. He makes no attempt to create or analyse new stereotypes; his characters are more vibrant than original. He introduces the English burlesque style into the Cries. In the manner of comic strip artists, he mixes irony with coarse humour and raillery, all in the service of a simple anecdote. He is not a moralist or a scholar of human nature. And he is certainly not a pessimist like Sandby, who, following in the footsteps of Swift or Hogarth, represents English comedy at its most darkly philosophic.

Between Laroon's *Cryes of the City of London* (1687) and Rowlandson's *Cries of London* (1799), ensembles of hawkers undergo consequential changes in their aesthetic programmes, expressed in prints' backgrounds and characters. Regarding backgrounds, early ensembles pose hawkers against settings that are blank or sketchy; later ones, sophisticating the practices of Amigoni and especially Hogarth, introduce hints of place but also people who are not vendors. Such metonymic treatments of the city render the genre circumstantial, social and urban. More important, settings shift from passive markers in early Cries, like Boitard's and Amigoni's, to active agents in later ensembles, especially those of Sandby and Rowlandson.

But compare Boitard's backdrop in his title page (**3.1**) to Sandby's theatrical scene for his sock vendor (**plate 8**). Boitard's setting designates the place where the savoyard works as a generically urban landscape. Sandby's features a man in the stocks, a handful of curious bystanders, and, behind them, a clump of houses. Though sketchier than Boitard's mechanical scene, Sandby's is dense in allusions that reverse the reader's understanding of the image. By himself, this vendor seems honest. But the scene behind the man suggests otherwise. From that scene it is clear that this fellow, a discharged sailor, has pilfered the socks he is selling from the clothes line of a proto-industrial factory beside the pillory he stands perilously close to – and will soon occupy. He has aroused the mistrust of two beadles, one of whom turns around to eye him with professional suspicion, perhaps as a prelude to arresting him. Is the criminal in the stocks the sock dealer's former accomplice? And has the accomplice not 'fingered' this thief to the watch, perhaps to win early release? In backgrounds like this, Sandby not only conjures up the material and spiritual conditions of hawkers' lives, he amplifies their characters and histories, telling their past while foretelling their future.

The figures in ensembles of Cries follow a similar pattern whereby their ties to each other grow closer over time. Early suites, like Laroon's, feature one hawker per sheet while later ones, like Sandby's, Wheatley's and Rowlandson's, offer multiplicity and diversity in their characters: one or two hawkers, perhaps a customer, sometimes a few hangers-on, all entangled in their own parallel farces or witnessing the street dramas from vantage points that are physical or moral. More important, early ensembles show vendors in attitudes that are public, fixed and posed, later ones in attitudes that are dynamic and fluid. In Laroon's 'Four for Six pence Mackrell' (**3.17**), the wife plants her feet on the ground, dangles a single fish at her side and waits for a customer. In Wheatley's 'New Mackrel' (**5.7**), three characters take part in a scene that has two different levels, one manifest and the other latent. At the manifest level, an obsequious fishwife sells her catch, mixing elegance and hygiene – her mackerel come on a plate, not in her filthy hands. At the latent level, a lady and her maid act out a drama of humanity in which, paying scant attention to the mackerel, the first bestows a coin and the second pity, which the vendor acknowledges with gratitude. In Rowlandson's 'Buy a Trap, a Rat-Trap' (**5.12**), eight figures and a small zoo of animals – a dog, two rats, a rabbit, a crow, and a dove – take part in three different dramas. In the foreground, a repulsive bumpkin, observed by a beautiful young woman at a casement window, importunes a stall keeper who rebuffs his solicitation.[78] In the background, the same dynamic is repeated, but it is varied by means of a double inversion in which a whore, observed by a portly man at a casement window, dragoons a reluctant hayseed. In counterpoint to these two dramas of experience, a parable of innocence fills the conceptual middle ground, where two children covet a rabbit.[79] In prints like these, static identities, orderly relationships and fixed metiers play no role. Instead, knotty public actions intersect with private melodramas unfolding between peddlers, their customers and a host of human and animal bystanders. These figures' relationships to one another, acted out with increasing degrees of bodily exhibition, are dynamic, disorderly and embroiled rather than stable and hierarchical.

In late Cries by Sandby, Wheatley and Rowlandson, such exchanges are not only intricate and dynamic, they are also interactive: encounters, trysts, confrontations or clashes abound. Hawkers in early suites sell, but nobody buys. Hawkers in late ensembles sell, customers buy, hesitate or resist; sometimes bystanders observe, comment on, or meddle in the complicated ways of everyday life. Rowlandson's flower vendor uses his virile aura to sell blooms, but, observing the lovesick gaze of a vulnerable customer, he also seems about to 'buy' the unspoken proposal of the young woman. Such is the layered, theatrical nature of these kinds of give-and-take that they sometimes look allegorical. Their texts allege buying and selling but their subtexts divulge a spectrum of quite different themes: charity in Wheatley; sex and money in Rowlandson; sex, status and power in Sandby.[80]

From the publication of Laroon's *Cryes of the City of London* (1687) to the debut of Rowlandson's *Cries* (1799) more than a century later, ensembles' vocabularies shift, reshaped by the growth of popular English art, especially Hogarth's. After Laroon, the first English Cries, petrified by his powerful influence, repeat his figures over and over, as JM's and Overton's piracies show. In the same way, Child plagiarizes Amigoni, though he ultimately replaces a tone of mimicry with a new mood of travesty. The language Child's designs use to slur their Italian rival is, nonetheless, the English language; they do not create a fresh visual lexicon. Not until Hogarth's 'Enraged Musician' do native artists generate a visual vocabulary by which to create authentic English images of hawkers or satirize the Cries of foreign artists. The formal visual language pioneered by Hogarth is enlarged by Sandby and, less imaginatively, by Rowlandson following in both men's footsteps. Sandby creates an original iconography with which to dispatch his adversaries and voice his profound revulsion as well as equally profound compassion for outcasts. Sometimes that iconography alludes to the figures of his predecessors, as in 'Will your Honour buy a Sweet Nosegay or a Memorandum Book' (**5.6**). More often it is radical and unprecedented. One of the hallmark's of Sandby's designs is their independence from words, arguably the most compelling testimony to their visual power. Sixty-three of Sandby's watercolours have no titles of any kind, as the case is with a bemused young woman leaning against a fence (**plate 9**), the first female hawker to be shown drunk. And it needs none. The flagon in the young woman's hand shows she is a wine seller, but her glazed eye, euphoric smile and relaxed pose all conspire to reveal her 'secret': she is her own best customer. Are these peddlers lushes, whores and thieves, victimizing scoundrels whom the Cries of London ought to expose to their 'betters'? Are they oppressed and victimized characters whom the Cries ought to espouse against oppressors? Or are they deserving, grateful, compliant, and sympathetic figures whom the Cries ought to praise? These are the debates that, between 1687 and 1820, make the London Cries a riveting genre of popular art, especially in the hands of artists like Sandby, who forsook stock character types from allegory and personification in favour of sharply observed social and psychological figures like this tipsy hawker. He probes her alcoholism by studying its impact on her private 'virtue' and public vice (note the stocks behind her), and by contrasting her mellow addiction with the half-mad *delerium tremens* of the male vendor howling, 'Ink, Ink, come buy my fine Ink, for money that I want to buy me some drink'.

6

Hawkers infantalized: Cries as illustrated books

WORDS ARE everywhere in the London Cries. They appear inside the designs and out, above them and below, where they evoke the age-old link between work and song, which eases travail and dispels sorrow.[1] They surface in the designs of native and continental artists alike, taking the shape of titles, verses, words in cartouches, chants in banderoles and big blocks of explanatory prose, all using language to rekindle, frame or vie with pictures.[2] Every Cries is a literary picture, not just because it tells a story, but because it marries word and image, elements that are hard to unite, especially in the West, where letter and picture do not always communicate.[3] Though rife with shifts, ruptures and fissures, the Cries's blend of the verbal and visual is its characteristic feature, intensifying its appeal in a way not explained by its decorative charms, sometimes meagre. It shapes the development of the genre and illuminates its history.

Between 1590 and 1861, when the last London Cries appeared, interest switches from pictures to words in the genre, though not in a linear trajectory. This shift correlates with the movement of Cries from broadsides to suites to illustrated books, the special focus of this chapter. In early broadsheet Cries, words play subservient roles. Though their importance ebbs and flows from the late 1500s to the middle 1600s, it increases in later broadsides, which also add a second category of commentary in the form of publication lines. In early ensembles, as in early broadsides, words play a corroborative role. About 1740, the subordinate role of words changes in two suites: J. S. Müller's prints (**4.1–4.4**) imitating Amigoni's pathos-filled images; and G. Child's satires (**4.5**, **4.6**) ridiculing the same design. Müller's and Child's suites, featuring prints that carry a hundred words of intricate verse, illustrate and promote the cannibalization of designs by legends in Cries.

Two decades after Müller's and Child's cycles, legends achieve dominance with the publication of the first London Cries to call themselves books. Edward Ryland's *Cries of London; or, Child's Moral Instructor* (*c.* 1760), a tiny volume aimed at the very young, is the first to include texts for which illustrations are excuses. At the hands of publishers like Ryland, Turpin, Roberts and the energetic Newbery family, the Cries of London changes from a work of art into a book of popular literature and a primer for children. But in the nineteenth century, books of Cries also targeted adults. Created for gentlemen cultivating anthropology, domestic politics and colonial affairs, these books yoke elaborate coloured prints to commentaries of a page or so offering 'potted' accounts of the doings of the lower orders. The most prophetic have elaborate introductions, continuous texts or narratives in which images are overshadowed by analyses of all sorts: demographic, forensic, statistical, linguistic and ethnographic.[4]

When the debut of neighbourhood greengrocers and the gathering thunder of Victorian self-righteousness turned criers into outcasts, artists stopped mythologizing them in the old formats.[5] Gradually vendors vanished from illustrated books for adults and finally even from children's volumes, as they vanished from all but the most destitute London streets. They reappeared, however, in the work of a new breed of picture makers, photographers, who divested them of the pelt of artistic life and rendered them as the sullen, lifeless lumps that peer out from Henry Mayhew's *London Labour and the London Poor* (1861–62), 'a cyclopaedia of the industry, the want, and the vice of the great Metropolis'.[6]

Cries as books made their debut in England during the second half of the eighteenth century, when a constellation of forces reframed images of hawkers for a new audience then shifting from the periphery of social scrutiny to its centre: children.[7] Women in their roles as mothers and governesses formed a new class of buyers eager to put books into the hands of offspring or pupils. Evangelicalism, with its drive for self-improvement and Protestant literacy, created a zealous assembly of consumers and academies interested in books likely to prod young people to read the Bible. John Bunyan, George Fox and Isaac Watt were prescribed for children of the pious in the eighteenth century, when literacy rates were higher among nonconformists than other segments of English society.[8] Finally, modern domesticity, shaped by the personal example of George III and his wife (famed for their 'Germanic' or bourgeois tastes), brought about a new sense of children as passing through stages of human development, each with its own needs.[9] Among the most urgent of these needs were books with forms and contents that would improve by entertaining.

The rise of modern domestic life – what the title to an early London Cries calls 'Private Families' – and the debut of Cries configured as small tomes are linked by the fact that, whereas prints are public forms of art, books are personal objects. Prints are linked to sociability. They are hung on walls in homes or alehouses, where they can be viewed both publicly and collectively, by many people at once. Or they are preserved in cabinets and folios where they are the subject of the communal gaze of viewers, typified by the men caught in the act of corporate connoisseurship in Charles-Nicolas Cochin's frontispiece to Edmé-François Gersaint's *Catalogue raisonné des diverses curiosités de feu M. Quentin de Lorangère* (Paris, 1744). Indeed the title of 'print collector' automatically conjured up gregariousness and sociability, for it granted its owner promiscuous access to the most celebrated collections of the Enlightenment without regard to rank or class, according to Gersaint, whose claims were no doubt exaggerated:

> His title as collector of curiosities grants him entrée to the most famous cabinets where he can go amuse himself. As such, he becomes the equal of those who happen to be of a higher estate, whether because of their station or condition, but who, like him, have given themselves over to this noble passion. As such, he is called on and received with pleasure at their gatherings, held for the purpose of sharing their discoveries or their acquisitions.[10]

Books are tied to isolation, by contrast. They are held in the hands of a single person, who reads them alone or to another person with whom the owner is intimate – a tutor, grandmother, younger sister or uncle – the appeal of Cries among aunts and uncles appears in an American version called *The Uncle's Present: A New Battledoor* (1809) illustrating each letter of the alphabet with a hawker. The smaller the book, the closer its ties to domestic life. This axiom is especially relevant to Cries, which, when they first appear in this form, resemble a modern credit card in size. Their diminutiveness links them directly to the culture of the closet, which promoted private reading and devotion.

In the 1750s, these trends were cultivated by booksellers especially inventive in marketing to commoners. Their books teemed with pictures and were therefore well-suited to the instruction of children, according to John Locke in *Some Thoughts Concerning Education* (1693), which championed illustrations in teaching literacy: 'If his *Aesop has Pictures* in it, it will entertain him much the better, and encourage him to read, when it carries the increase of Knowledge with it.'[11] These publishers marketed their illustrated books in clever new ways, selling Cries serially or volume by volume. Ryland built his first *Cries* into a three volumes set designed to transform children into book collectors; he sold each small tome individually for a shilling plain and two shillings coloured. Others broke their books down further, retailing them by sheet, so that all but the destitute could afford them. Kirk, whose bound *Cryes* sold for a shilling a volume, retailed the same pictures separately in uncut sheets at three pence each. But he also sold them as packs of playing cards and as panoramas encased in glass-faced boxes covered with Dutch floral paper.

The earliest example of this popular literature bore an instructively long title: *The Cryes of London Engraved and Sold by I. Kirk in St Paul's Church Yard. Also all sorts of English and Dutch Toys. Engraving of Seals in Stone Steel or Silver Also Silver & Copper Plates in the neatest manner and at the most Reasonable rates. a Grotto & Water Works to be seen free* (**1.7**). It was published in 1754 by John Kirk, who advertized it explicitly as 'very fit to amuse children'. Its 'Nice Yorkshire Limon Cakes' (**6.1**) is formatted as part of an abecediary in a panorama, a pedagogical merriment to teach literacy. Kirk's book was imitated by Edward Ryland, who published his rival miniature with the fulsome title, *The Cries of London; or, Child's Moral Instructor: for the Use of Schools, Private Families, Governesses, Tutors, &c. Decorated with 32 Copper Plates, Elegantly Engraved; with a Moral and emblematical Description of each particular Story; Intended at once to make Instruction Pleasing; and unite Humour with Decency* (**6.2**). Ryland's volume appeared about 1760, when the popularity of children's Cries was established. Writing to her

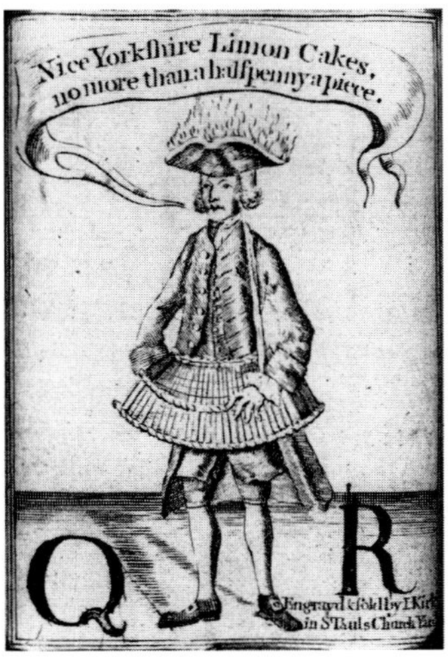

6.1 John Kirk, 'Nice Yorkshire Limon Cakes', 1754

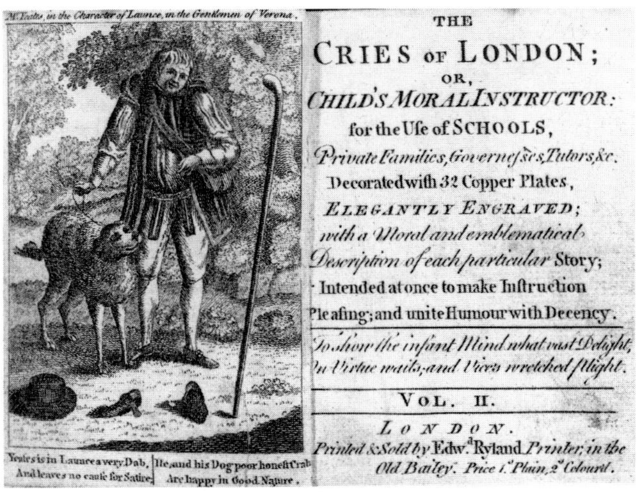

6.2 Title page to Ryland's *The Cries of London; or, Child's Moral Instructor*, c. 1760

husband in 1755, Mrs. Boscawen explained how she amused their son during his recovery from inoculation against smallpox: 'The chief service I can do him is to provide him with such amusements as will keep him still and quiet. So that, instead of waggons, carts and post chaises, we shall deal altogether in mills, pictures, dolls, London cries, and such sedentary amusements.'[12] Her language suggests that images of hawkers – in books designed for children or in ensembles (such as Laroon's but especially Amigoni's) featuring children and therefore easily recycled for young people – were familiar amusements in the nursery by the letter's date, when, lumped with dolls, they were classified as 'sedentary' and gendered as feminine in opposition to 'athletic' or masculine amusements.[13]

Literate women, questers after Christian knowledge and adepts of modern private life, helped define the audience and shape the format of the London Cries. But they also molded its new literary tones and contents, which differ dramatically from the overtly politicized commentaries of Müller's ensemble. Turning reactionary in spirit, Cries in little books preach the orthodox pieties of the 'Private Families, Governesses, Tutors, &c' of their titles, identified – with pathbreaking specificity – as their new buyers. Such pieties are moral, religious and educational. They seek to discipline the individual human body, not correct the body politic, to stem thieving in boys or lasciviousness in girls.

In tone and content, books of hawkers for youngsters divide into pedagogical and religious or moral. John Kirk's and Edward Ryland's Cries illustrate these differences. Kirk's *Cryes of London* (**1.7**) is the manifesto of books for children with an amusement-cum-pedagogical bias.[14] Though Kirk advertised his *Cryes* as 'little books', they are in fact ensembles of miniaturized prints bound with a title page. 'A White Line, Jack line, or a Cloaths Line' (**6.3a**) is typical: most of its space is bestowed on a figure while its few words are relegated to banderoles.[15]

Half of Kirk's designs are copies of Laroon's in reverse, as the sellers of white lines, jack lines, and clothes lines show (**6.3b**). The other half are original and have an actualized aspect that evokes the social life of the times; the black vendor selling a wine quart of 'perrewincles' for a penny (**6.4**) is the first woman of colour to appear in Cries. All the pithy texts are original. Most have a 'nursery-rhyme' flavor that is oral rather than written. Some are tongue-twisters, playful word games and nonsense rhymes, like 'a Longtail Pig, or a short tail Pig, or a Pig without a tail, a Sow Pig, or a Boar Pig, or a Pig with a Curling tail' (**1.7**). Others introduce basic concepts in weights, measures and currency, as does 'Fine Wood Strawberrys, six pence a pottle S T', also

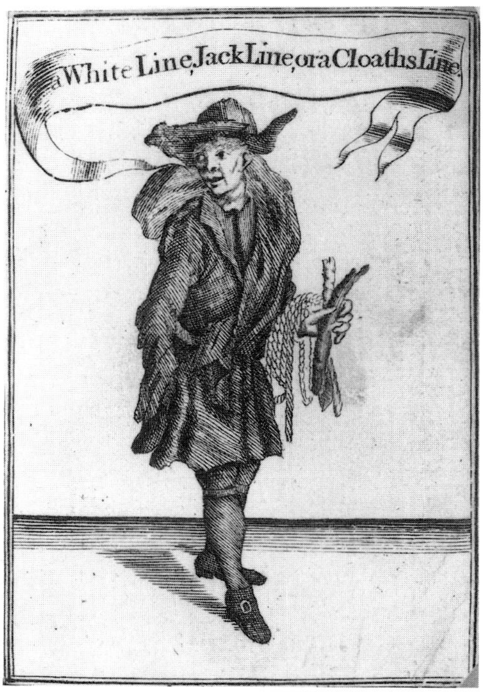

6.3a John Kirk, 'a White Line, Jack Line, or a Cloaths Line', 1754

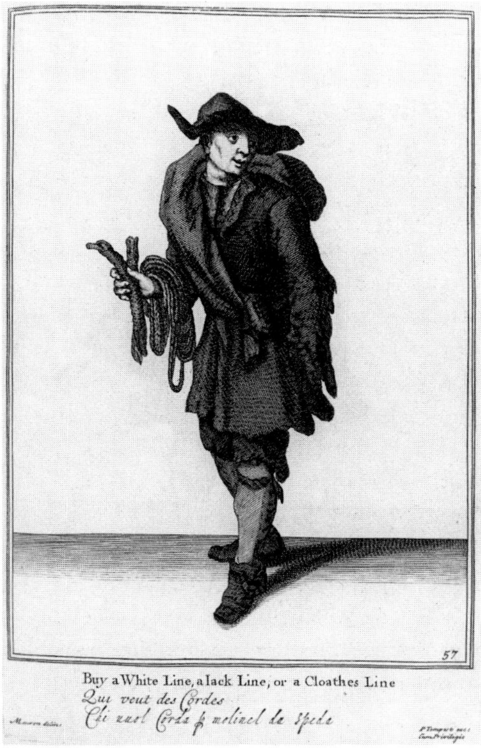

6.3b Marcellus Laroon, 'Buy a White Line, a Jack Line, or a Cloathes Line', 1687

Edward Ryland's *Cries of London* repudiates Kirk's preference for pleasure and instruction. Instead, it favours ethics and piety of the kind pioneered by the followers of George Fox, whose *Primer and Catechism for Children*, published with Ellis Hookes in 1670, was the prototype. Like Kirk's primer, Ryland's *Cries* marries text to images, but in this pioneering English union, words finally prevail. His is the first Cries to appear as a true book, albeit a book of verse. His thirty-two plates are plagiarized from Laroon (with backgrounds added), using a chapbook shorthand that has none of Kirk's neat line. But unable in themselves to carry much ethical cargo, they are overwhelmed by seven stanzas each of original doggerel written to civilize children. These sober stanzas, adding up to two pages of texts (as opposed to one for the picture), take no interest in the designs except as excuses for sermonizing; they give Ryland's *Cries* the feel of a morality book disjointedly illustrated.

Like so many books published for children in the late eighteenth century, this miniature conveys, through its proverbial or parabolic commentaries, simple lessons in utilitarianism and Calvinistic morality that assume the essential sinfulness of the 'youth of both Sexes'. Ryland's is the first children's volume to distinguish 'lads' from 'dear Miss'; it genders instruction, offering girls 'polite' narratives of domestic existence urging them 'To save the *market penny*' or 'become an happy bride', while presenting boys public narratives 'Of peace and war, of court intrigues/Duels, and dancing bears'. Directed at readers in the throes of puberty, it seeks to tempt or scare them into toil, thrift, reputation or temperance.

The book's verses begin with an allusion to the hawker and advance by free association to sundry species of good and bad behaviour. The commentary accompanying the singing-glass vendor is typical: his toys

from Kirk's alphabetical panorama.[16] Yet other mottos pose word problems to help 'weak accomptants'.[17] These range from the simple, 'Two a groat & four for sixpence Whitings', to the perplexing, 'Two Pound three Half pence three Pound two pence large Potatoes' (**6.5**), an intricate image with a Dutch background, a female customer and a publication line that shows it is the title page to 'volume two'. The purpose of these festive legends, spelled out in Kirk's advertisement, is 'to amuse Children and help them forward in their Learning'. This statement, putting 'amusement' before 'learning', makes *The Cryes of London Engraved and Sold by I. Kirk in St Paul's Church Yard* one of the first 'shilling merriments' to link schooling with pleasure and to value both above morality.[18]

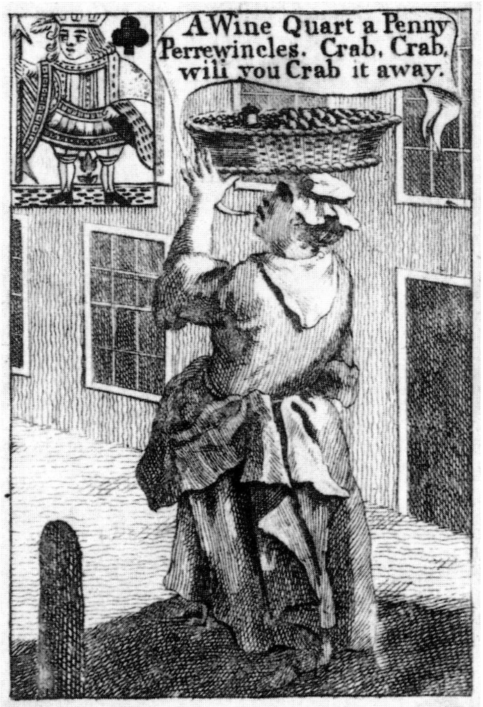

6.4 John Kirk, 'Perrewincles', 1759

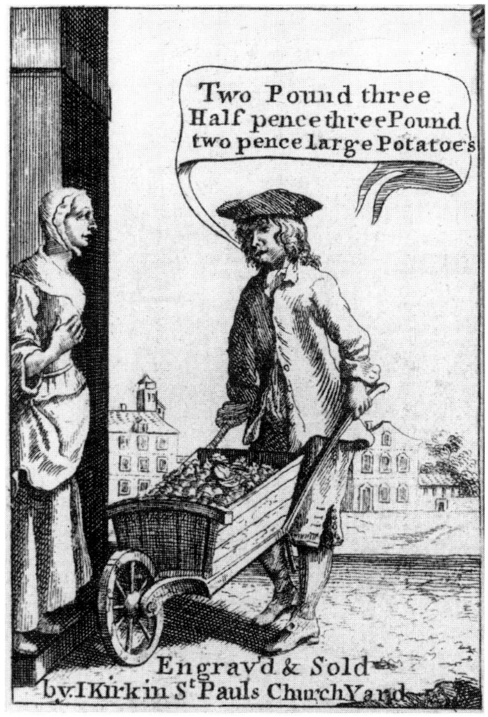

6.5 John Kirk, 'Two Pound three Half pence three Pound two pence large Potatoes', 1754

are proper rewards for the studious; they can 'trumpet' the praises of such boys, who don't 'sing away' their time; recreation is good in moderation, but those who pursue nothing else will grow up vicious; a bad reputation is a curse; and fame, like glass, cannot be mended. Some commentaries associate a vice with a crier, more or less at random. The mountebank who practices fraud is a plausible 'cheat' and 'rapscallion'. So is the lace-seller (**6.6**), a 'tartar' who, trading in the snares of personal adornment, 'wounds the infant mind' by selling sexy lingerie to girls:

The Mottos on her garters plac'd
Are 'siduously design'd;
To make a pretty Miss disgrac'd,
And wound the infant mind'.[19]

But the rabbit seller is made an atheist, the asparagus seller an overcharging deceiver fond of cursing, and the lobster woman a snuff addict, for no better reason than that the poet takes a notion to blacken hawkers' characters by alleging these vices. In sum, the world that the verses evokes is one of reward and punishment relentlessly conditioned on good or bad behaviour, to which are added occasional references to piety or impiety like the rabbit seller's disbelief. The commentary to the cherry seller promises that good children will reap 'golden fruits'; the caption to 'Buy a Jack Line' (**6.7**) warns that bad ones should expect to hang (but not burn in hell):

Shun ev'ry character that's black;
By study strengthen hope;
And round your neck, or on your back,
You ne'er need dread a Rope.

Leigh Hunt (1784–1859), raised on these books, saw them as 'Hogarth's pictures taken in their most literal acceptation. Every good

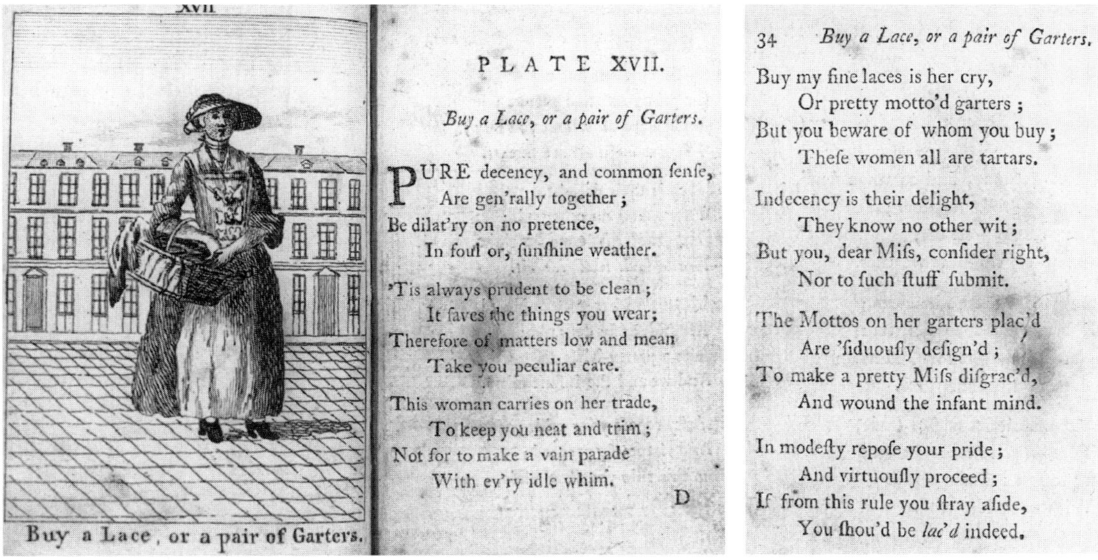

PLATE XVII.

Buy a Lace, or a pair of Garters.

PURE decency, and common ſenſe,
Are gen'rally together;
Be dilat'ry on no pretence,
In foul or, ſunſhine weather.

'Tis always prudent to be clean;
It ſaves the things you wear;
Therefore of matters low and mean
Take you peculiar care.

This woman carries on her trade,
To keep you neat and trim;
Not for to make a vain parade
With ev'ry idle whim.

D

34 *Buy a Lace, or a pair of Garters.*

Buy my fine laces is her cry,
Or pretty motto'd garters;
But you beware of whom you buy;
Theſe women all are tartars.

Indecency is their delight,
They know no other wit;
But you, dear Miſs, conſider right,
Nor to ſuch ſtuff ſubmit.

The Mottos on her garters plac'd
Are 'ſiduouſly deſign'd;
To make a pretty Miſs diſgrac'd,
And wound the infant mind.

In modeſty repoſe your pride;
And virtuouſly proceed;
If from this rule you ſtray aſide,
You ſhou'd be *lac'd* indeed.

6.6 John Ryland, 'Buy a lace, or a pair of Garters', *c.* 1760

boy was to ride in his coach, and be a lord mayor; and every bad boy was to be hung, or eaten by lions'. He called their lessons 'sordid and merely plodding morals – ethics that were necessary perhaps for a certain stage in the progress of commerce'.[20] Such 'Awful Warnings', the defining quality of Ryland's censorious *Cries of London*, politicize everyday life in mass art and make Kirk's *Cryes* seems whimsical by contrast.[21]

Whatever the differences between Kirk's cheerful primer with its polished designs and Ryland's stern tract with its simplified images, together they rocketed the London Cries into

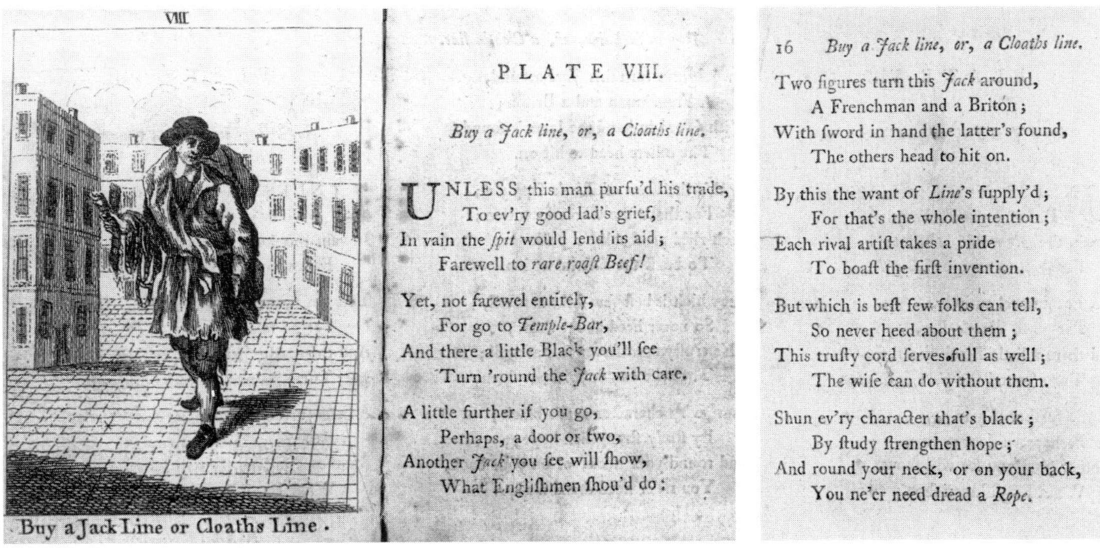

PLATE VIII.

Buy a Jack line, or, a Cloaths line.

UNLESS this man purſu'd his trade,
To ev'ry good lad's grief,
In vain the *ſpit* would lend its aid;
Farewell to *rare roaſt Beef!*

Yet, not farewel entirely,
For go to *Temple-Bar*,
And there a little Black you'll ſee
Turn 'round the *Jack* with care.

A little further if you go,
Perhaps, a door or two,
Another *Jack* you ſee will ſhow,
What Engliſhmen ſhou'd do:

16 *Buy a Jack line, or, a Cloaths line.*

Two figures turn this *Jack* around,
A Frenchman and a Briton;
With ſword in hand the latter's found,
The others head to hit on.

By this the want of *Line*'s ſupply'd;
For that's the whole intention;
Each rival artiſt takes a pride
To boaſt the firſt invention.

But which is beſt few folks can tell,
So never heed about them;
This truſty cord ſerves full as well;
The wife can do without them.

Shun ev'ry character that's black;
By ſtudy ſtrengthen hope;
And round your neck, or on your back,
You ne'er need dread a *Rope*.

6.7 John Ryland, 'Buy a Jack Line, or, a Cloaths Line', *c.* 1760

the orbit of children's books, replacing the Bible, *Pilgrim's Progress* and the 'good godly' tracts used to teach young people to read when schooling shifted first from religious doctrine to moral improvement and afterwards to educational and social betterment.[22] During the second half of the eighteenth century, the formative years of children's bookmaking in England, twenty-three out of forty London Cries targeted boys and girls. In the Victorian period, when little books became an integral part of child rearing up and down the social pyramid, 150 out of 180 picture books of hawkers – over 80 per cent – did so.[23]

The popularity of children's Cries after 1750 appears not just in burgeoning numbers and percents, but also in pedagogical toys and amusements. Kirk sold his pictures of hawkers 'stitched in little Books' and in three other formats as well: as uncut sheets of four images, 'likewise made up in Boxes' at a shilling, and in 'Rowlers at 1s a Piece'.[24] He even sold Cries configured as fifty-two playing cards, exploiting the fact that both are programmatic and serial. Copying the ingenuity of Robert Morden and William Berry who served god and satan by turning this devil's tool to ethical ends in their *Pastime Improved by a New Pack of Cards* (1692), Kirk offered, for five shillings in 1759, a pack of 'diverting Cards' curiously engraved with 'the Cries and Humours of London; finely copied after Nature, with their Proper Motto's'.[25] To reach a full set of cards, he recycled some images from his own little books. And he pirated twenty-three designs from the prints of Laroon, Amigoni, Hogarth, Bosse and Bouchardon, making his pack into an anthology of English and continental Cries by various hands. He copied the four of clubs (**6.8**) – plus two other designs – from Amigoni's quartet; and he took the king of spades (**6.9**) from Edme Bouchardon's *Cris de Paris* (1737–46), the most sculptural and best-known suite in eighteenth-century France.[26] The six of hearts (**6.10**) is noteworthy as a self-reflective scene suggesting Cries were bought and sold at auction: 'Gentlemen, nine Volumes of the London Cries, very fitt to amuse Children of all Sizes; two Shillings They'r a Going; a Going; a Going'.[27]

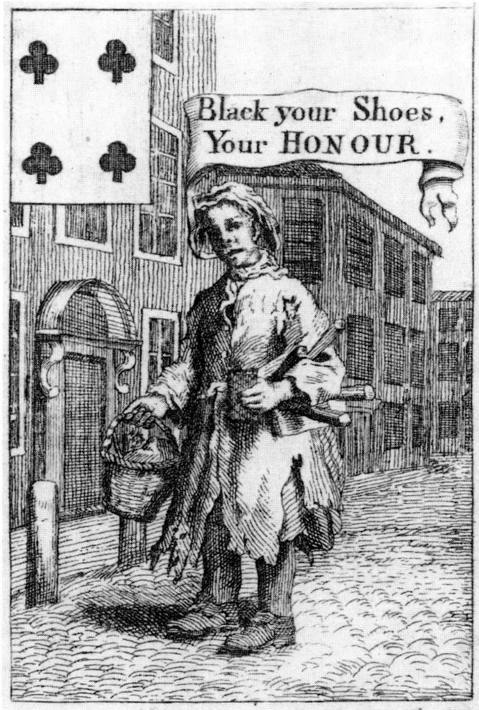

6.8 John Kirk, Four of Clubs, 'Black your Shoes, your Honour', 1759

Books of Cries for grown-ups first appeared in 1804. But they targeted specialized buyers, as will appear from three examples drawn from across the nineteenth century, when Cries as a genre surged in popularity and then plummeted in a decline illuminated by two of these books. All three volumes, employing original images that shrink and texts that expand, are directed at rich bibliophiles, antiquarians, connoisseurs and print collectors; they return depictions of

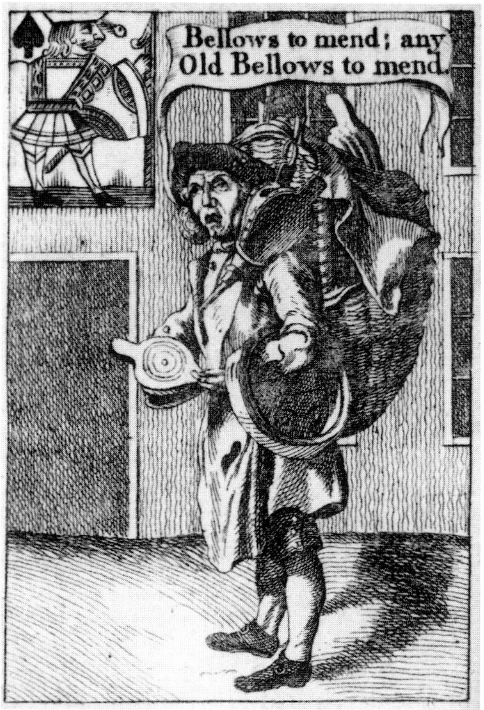

6.9 John Kirk, King of Spades, 'Bellows to mend; any Old Bellows to mend', 1754

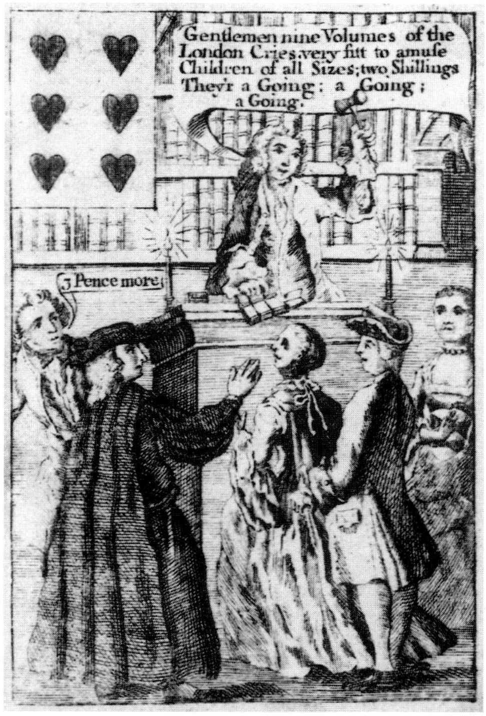

6.10 John Kirk, Six of Hearts, 'Gentlemen, nine Volumes of the London Cries', 1754

hawkers to favour among cultured men of the sort who bought Laroon's *Cryes of the City of London* in 1687. The first of these new books of Cries for adults is William Craig's *Itinerant Traders* (1804), thirty-one neatly manufactured, brightly coloured miniatures. The second and third, John T. Smith's *Vagabondiana* (1817) and *The Cries of London* (1839), base their appeal on their texts as much as their black-and-white illustrations, which evoke early photographs.[28]

Craig's (*c.* 1765–*c.* 1818) *Itinerant Traders of London in their Ordinary Costume with Notices of the Remarkable Places given in the Background* takes as its purpose the promotion of London as a city of beauty and order by reason of its monuments and noble buildings, which derive scale and human purpose from a brood of picturesque outcasts.[29] It unites topography with portraiture in pointillist designs explicated by two essays per image. Three of the book's images, borrowing the matter and manner of Amigoni's Cries, cast hawkers as little boys. Craig's inclusion of these youths makes his book look like a children's volume.[30] However, its price, about one guinea, was high; and its intricate prose assumes readers who know Rubens is an artist and Scagliola a precious marble.[31]

Itinerant Traders stands out for two innovations, the lesser having to do with images and the greater with texts. Craig's designs reverse the normal priority of foregrounds over backgrounds; its figures, posed and decorous, are pretexts for their settings: historic London buildings rendered in the factual manner of architectural drafting. This reversal shifts the focus of Cries from human to material concerns; it reduces hawkers to sentimental stereotypes, cast-offs of industrialization and relics of a bygone age.[32]

The match boy (**6.11**), plump and ruddy when London's gutter children 'were all pale and nearly all lean', poses alone against an orderly facade displaying the cheer and the servility expected of the deserving poor.[33] Generating a contrast between architectural grandeur and human impoverishment, he stands before the Lord Mayor's Mansion House, pictured by a geometry that highlights its pilasters, fluted Corinthian column and architraves. Such landmarks, flattered by Craig's neat classicism, eclipse their hawkers. This imbalance between cityscape and staffage is intensified by the social distance between the two. Hawkers, however affable, are nameless, servile and 'low'; settings are familiar and 'high', from civic edifices like the Pantheon (**6.12**) to stately private homes of nobles like Lord Harewood's townhouse in Hanover Square (**6.13**). As hawkers are relegated, in life, to rookeries where they serve the poorest of the poor, their habitats in art grow ever more elegant and noble, following the principle by which art redresses history's depredations and compensates for them.

The advantage setting enjoys over character is still clearer in the book's commentaries, which, matching the two-fold division of Craig's images, address backgrounds and figures in two blocks of prose using two type fonts. In length, these mini-essays fall somewhere between Ryland's two-page commentaries in verse and Smith's later book-length analyses in prose. The first essay explains hawkers' 'mysteries', and sometimes stigmatizes the hawkers themselves, whom the recent Terror had

DESCRIPTION OF THE PLATES.

MATCHES.

THE criers of this convenient article are very numerous, and among the poorest inhabitants of the metropolis, subsisting more on the waste meats they receive from the kitchens, where they sell their Matches at six bunches per penny, than on the profits arising from their sale. Old women, crippled men, or a mother followed by three or four ragged children, and offering their Matches to sale, excite compassion, and are often relieved, when the importunity of the mere beggar is rejected. The elder children of a poor family, like the boy seen in the Plate, are frequent traders in Matches, and these generally sing a kind of song, and sell and beg alternately.

THE MANSION HOUSE is a stone building of considerable magnitude, standing in Mansion-house-street, at the west end of Cornhill; it is the residence of the Lord Mayor of London. In the front is a portico of fluted pillars, with two pilasters on each side the portico, which is raised above, a lower story opening to the offices. A flight of steps, enclosed with a stone balustrade, leads to the grand entrance under the portico. When it was first resolved in the Common Council to build a Mansion-house for the residence of the Lord Mayor, Lord Burlington, zealous in the cause of the arts, sent down an original design of *Palladio*, worthy of its author, for their approbation and adoption. The first question in Court was not whether the plan was proper, but whether this same *Palladio was a freeman of the city,* or *no*. On this great debates ensued; and it is hard to say how it might have gone, had not a worthy Deputy risen up and observed gravely, that it was of little consequence to discuss this point, when it was notorious that *Palladio* was a *papist,* and *incapable* of course. Lord Burlington's proposal was then rejected *nem. con.* and the plan of a *freeman* and *protestant* adopted in its room. The man pitched upon (and who afterwards carried his plan into execution) was originally a shipwright; and, to do him justice, he appears never to have lost sight of his first impressions. The front of his Mansion-house has all the resemblance possible to a deep-laden Indiaman, with her stern-galleries and gingerbread-work. The stairs and passages within are all ladders and gangways, and the two *bulk heads* on the roof, *fore and aft,* not unaptly represent the *binacle* and *windlass* on the deck of a great north country *catt*.

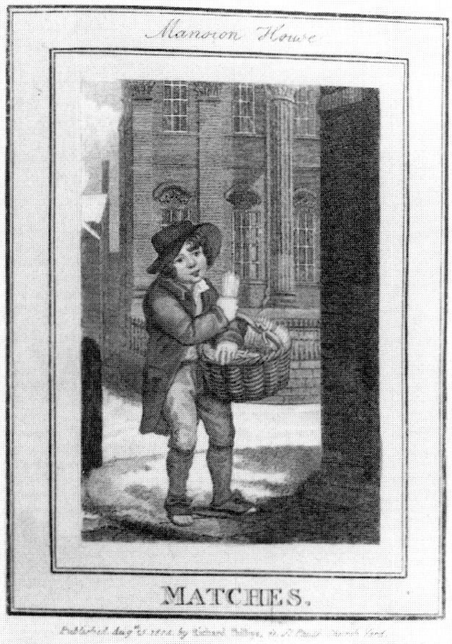

6.11 William Marshall Craig, 'Mansion House. Matches', 1804

transformed from 'men destined to travel in the obscure walk of laborious life' into a mob 'lost to shame'.[34] Cherry sellers (**6.14**), readers are cautioned, 'undersell the shops by twopence or threepence per pounds but their weights are generally to be questioned, and this is so notorious an objection that they universally add *full weight* to the cry of Cherries' (emphasis in original text).

In different tones, the architectural commentaries school readers on the beauties of London's buildings. These buildings are notable for their picturesque variety: they range all the way up to royal palaces like White Hall (**6.15**), described in architectural history's gush:

This beautiful and memorable structure stands in Parliament-street, facing the Horse-guards. It was begun in 1619, from a design of Inigo Jones, in his purest manner, and cost 17,000*l.* The present building is only a small part of a vast plan left unexecuted by reason of the troubles which succeeded. The ceiling, which cannot be too much admired, was painted by Rubens: the subject is the *Apotheosis* of James the First.

Lessons like this, in which the commentator nudges the reader into identifying with the buildings' owners, reach into the interiors of these 'treasure houses' to imagine the lives of their inhabitants, even their diets. In appreciating the Pantheon (**6.12**), the writer penetrates to its concert room with 'pillars painted in imitation of Scagliola marble, and mirrors in the panels, with a handsome orchestra, several retiring rooms, where tea, coffee, jellies &c. were served'.

DESCRIPTION OF THE PLATES.

HOT SPICED GINGERBREAD.

HOT Spiced Gingerbread, sold in oblong flat cakes of one halfpenny each, very well made, well baked, and kept extremely hot, is a very pleasing regale to the pedestrians of London in cold and gloomy evenings. This cheap luxury is only to be obtained in winter; and when that dreary season is displaced by the long light days of summer, the well-known retailer of Hot Spiced Gingerbread, pourtrayed in the Plate, takes his usual stand near the portico of the Pantheon, with a basket of Banbury and other cakes.

THE PANTHEON stands about the middle and on the south side of Oxford-street. It has a fine portico, and the building is of simple and beautiful architecture, but is liable to be overlooked by strangers, as the effect is nearly destroyed by its being erected in a busy and crowded street, and not detached from the surrounding houses. The Pantheon was originally designed for concerts. It contains one large room, finely ornamented with pillars painted in imitation of Scagliola marble, and mirrors in the pannels, with a handsome orchestra, and several retiring rooms, where tea, coffee, jellies, &c. &c. were served. It is at present only used for occasional masquerades in the winter season.

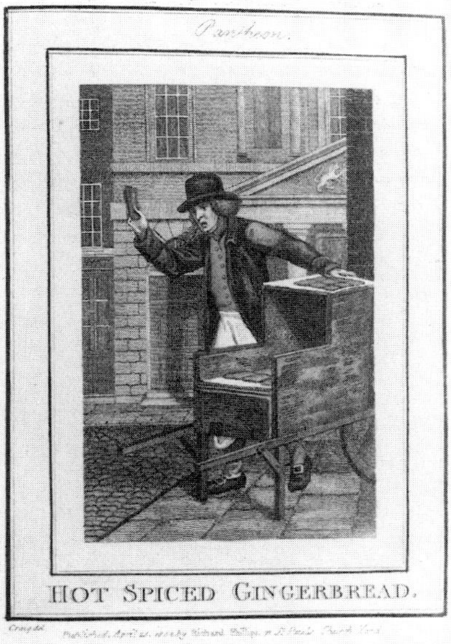

6.12 William Marshall Craig, 'Pantheon. Hot Spiced Gingerbread', 1804

What lies behind these 'preservationist' texts and their neat designs boosting the capital's architecture as a national heritage? When the fortunes of the country rose in the mid 1700s, those of the city fell, a seesaw effect observed by J. D. Passavant in the early nineteenth century, when the preference for the natural over the man-made was peaking. He tells how, on approaching London,

> the smiling, fruitful country, with its enchanting villas, gradually disappears; the atmosphere becomes dense and heavy of respiration – a procession-like crowd of vehicles and pedestrians bespeak the never-ending business of the city and London itself seems a vast desert of men and houses, where a foreigner may feel himself most truly alone.[35]

As early as Thomson's *Seasons* (1740), London was viewed as a place of frivolous pleasure, by the end of the century, a site of iniquity. Denouncing its corruption, pioneered by Hogarth, became a trope in poetry and fiction too.[36] William Cowper argues that London is 'by taste and wealth proclaim'd / The fairest capital of all the world, / By riot and incontinence, the worst'.[37] Mr. Villars, in *Evelina* (1771), condemns the capital as 'the general harbour of fraud and of folly, of duplicity and of impertinence . . .'.[38]

But the sharpest attacks were reserved for the city's physical state, injured by the Industrial Revolution. Such attacks portrayed London as dangerous, ugly, dirty, toxic, and plaguey. 'The capital is become an overgrown monster', according to *Humphry Clinker*'s

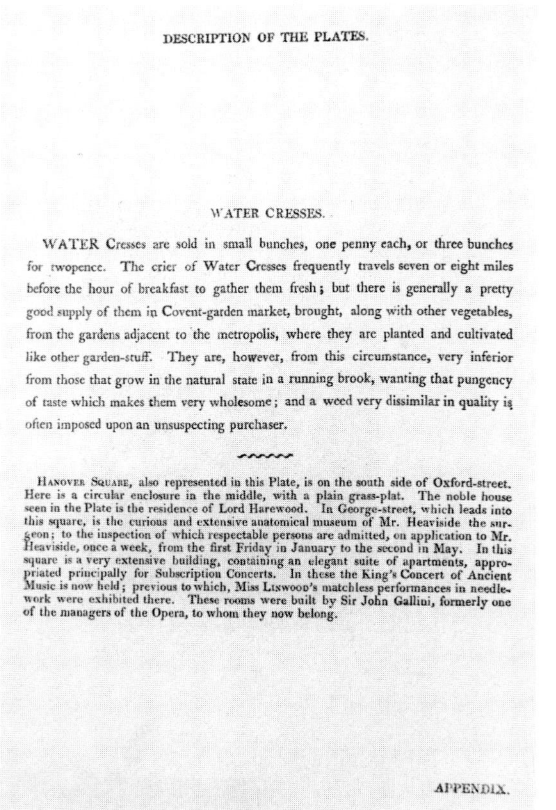
DESCRIPTION OF THE PLATES.

WATER CRESSES.

WATER Cresses are sold in small bunches, one penny each, or three bunches for twopence. The crier of Water Cresses frequently travels seven or eight miles before the hour of breakfast to gather them fresh; but there is generally a pretty good supply of them in Covent-garden market, brought, along with other vegetables, from the gardens adjacent to the metropolis, where they are planted and cultivated like other garden-stuff. They are, however, from this circumstance, very inferior from those that grow in the natural state in a running brook, wanting that pungency of taste which makes them very wholesome; and a weed very dissimilar in quality is often imposed upon an unsuspecting purchaser.

HANOVER SQUARE, also represented in this Plate, is on the south side of Oxford-street. Here is a circular enclosure in the middle, with a plain grass-plat. The noble house seen in the Plate is the residence of Lord Harewood. In George-street, which leads into this square, is the curious and extensive anatomical museum of Mr. Heaviside the surgeon; to the inspection of which respectable persons are admitted, on application to Mr. Heaviside, once a week, from the first Friday in January to the second in May. In this square is a very extensive building, containing an elegant suite of apartments, appropriated principally for Subscription Concerts. In these the King's Concert of Ancient Music is now held; previous to which, Miss LINWOOD's matchless performances in needle-work were exhibited there. These rooms were built by Sir John Gallini, formerly one of the managers of the Opera, to whom they now belong.

APPENDIX.

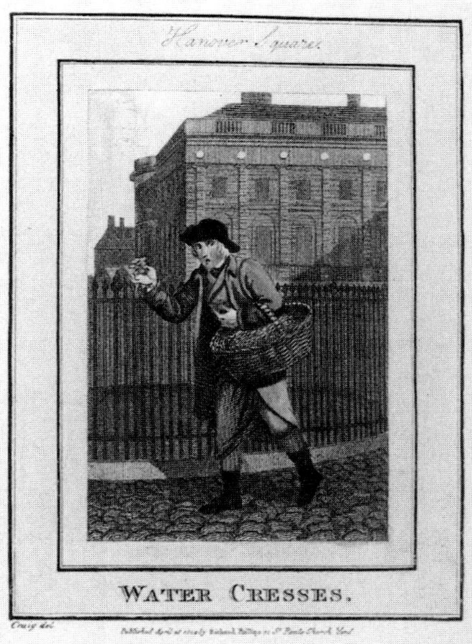

6.13 William Marshall Craig, 'Hanover Square. Water Cresses', 1804

Matt Bramble, who, visiting London in 1771, finds himself breathing

> the steams of endless putrefaction; and these would, undoubtedly produce a pestilence, if they were not qualified by the gross acid of sea-coal, which is itself a pernicious nuisance to lungs of any delicacy of texture . . . If I would drink water, I must quaff the mawkish contents of an open aqueduct, exposed to all manner of defilement or swallow that which comes from the river Thames, impregnated with all the filth of London and Westminster – Human excrement is the least offensive part of the concrete, which is composed of all the drugs, minerals, poisons used in mechanics and manufacture, enriched with the putrefying carcass of beasts and men, and mixed with the scouring of all the wash-tubs, kennels, and common sewers, within the bills of mortality.[39]

To Boswell, writing in 1762, London is a heaven that fills him with 'life and joy'. But to Shelley, writing in 1819, when revulsion is still building, 'Hell is a city much like London'.[40]

Artists following careers linked to the city sought to exonerate it of such charges by topographical volumes celebrating its architectural elegance.[41] Such redemptive work was the special duty of illustrators like Craig. Richard Phillips (who later boasted England 'the most improved country that ever existed in the world'[42]) published Craig's images and texts in *Modern London; Being the History and Present State of the British Metropolis* (1804), where he described the artist's designs as exhibiting 'the very soul of the Metropolis in a way which has never

DESCRIPTION OF THE PLATES.

CHERRIES

APPEAR in the London markets early in June, and shortly afterward become sufficiently abundant to be cried by the barrow-women in the streets at sixpence, four-pence, and sometimes as low as threepence per pound. The May Duke, and the White and Black Heart, are succeeded by the Kentish Cherry, which is more plentiful and cheaper than the former kinds, and consequently most offered to sale in the streets. Next follows the small black Cherry called the Blackaroon, which is also a profitable commodity for the barrows. Other kinds of Cherries, bearing a higher price, are only to be bought in the markets, or at the shops of fruiterers. These barrow-women undersell the shops by twopence or threepence per pound, but their weights are generally to be questioned; and this is so notorious an objection that they universally add *full weight* to the cry of Cherries.

The entrance to St. James's Palace, which stands at the west end of Pall-mall, and fronting to St. James's street, is seen in the Plate. The gate opens to the principal court, on one side of which a covered passage leads to the grand staircase belonging to the guard-rooms, drawing-room, and other state apartments. This entrance and the whole palace is of brick; nor does its external appearance convey any idea of magnificence.

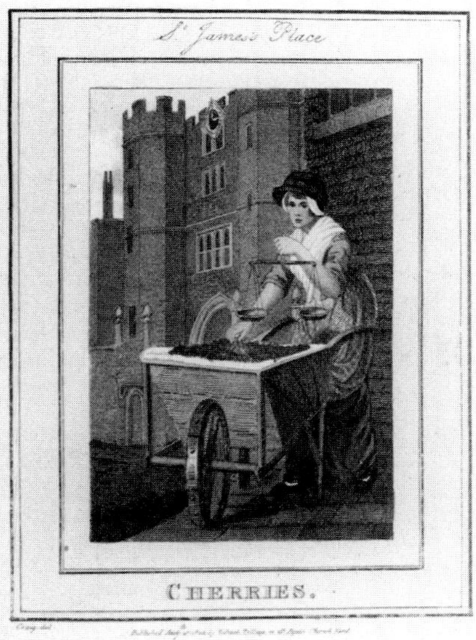

6.14 William Marshall Craig, 'St James Place. Cherries', 1804

before been attempted'.[43] Aimed at 'travelling Virtuosi, whether natives or foreigners', London guidebooks like Phillips's had, as their agenda, boosterism, the subtext of Craig's *Traders*. Addressing the city's moral corruption, the text of *Itinerant Traders*, in an adroit rhetorical ploy, grants the truth of indictments of London. But it reduces the charge to a little pettifoggery carried on by the likes of the glamorous chair mender (**6.16**) – no armed robber or murderess here – with whom 'it is necessary to bargain for a price previous to the delivery of the Chairs, or the Chair-mender, like other itinerant artists, will not fail to demand an exorbitant compensation for his [*sic*] time and labour'. Furthermore, the images promise the imminent reformation of the lower orders by setting them to labour before so many churches. Backgrounds featuring St Martin's Church, New Church Strand, St Paul's Cathedral, St Giles, Shore Ditch Church and Whitfield's Tabernacle make sanctuaries the most common setting in the thirty-one images of *Traders*; such hallowed edifices cast London as the Augustinian City of God, not the biblical Sodom of its detractors. For itinerant 'artists' who resist the reforming church, Craig's city pledges immurement in 'lofty and massy' Newgate prison (**6.17**), a forbidding brick icon of 'picturesque London'.

To rebut charges of physical corruption, *Itinerant Traders* belabours the city's salubriousness. After churches, hospitals are the book's most popular settings; Middlesex, Bethlehem, and the Foundling Hospitals (**6.18**) record London's medical sufficiency as well as its humanity, especially in the

DESCRIPTION OF THE PLATES.

KNIVES TO GRIND.

THE apparatus of the Knife-grinder is accurately delineated in the annexed Plate. The same wheel turns his grinding and his whetting stone. On a smaller wheel, projecting beyond the other, he trundles his commodious shop from street to street, and generally finds some employment in each. He charges for grinding and setting scissars one penny or two pence per pair; for pen-knives one penny each; and table-knives one shilling and sixpence or two shillings per dozen, according to the polish that is required.

WHITEHALL. This beautiful and memorable structure stands in Parliament-street, facing the Horse-guards. It was begun in 1619, from a design of Inigo Jones, in his purest manner, and cost 17,000l. The present building is only a small part of a vast plan left unexecuted by reason of the troubles which succeeded. The ceiling, which cannot be too much admired, was painted by Rubens: the subject is the *Apotheosis* of James the First. The front of the Banquetting-house is seen in the Plate. The northern end of the palace, to the left of the Plate, is that through which King Charles passed to the scaffold. The breach in the wall made for that purpose is now covered on the outside by the adjoining building; but within the palace the same passage is the entrance into that building. The Banquetting-house has for many years past been converted into a chapel.

In the square behind Whitehall palace is an uncommonly fine statue in brass of James the Second, executed by Gibbons the year before that monarch abdicated his throne. At the north end of the Banquetting-house still remains a very high gilt vane, erected by order of James. When the reports were current of the Prince of Orange's intentions to come over and claim the crown, James lodged at Whitehall, and had his bed-room in a part of the palace from which he could see this vane; and by it his hopes and his fears were daily decided. The west wind was the popish, and the east the protestant; if the latter blew, it had a visible effect upon his spirits the whole of the day.

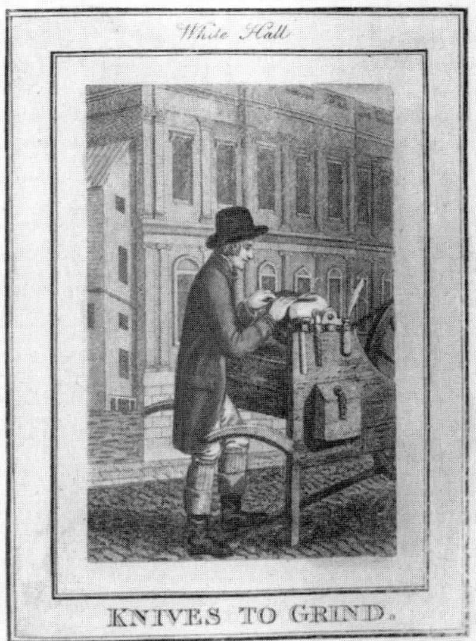

6.15 William Marshall Craig, 'White Hall. Knives to Grind', 1804

treatment of children; the last of the three institutions 'rescued' orphans, like the sweep, who appears before its doors to acknowledge the city's efficacy.[44] London's street vendors seem particularly devoted to cleanliness in *Itinerant Traders*, as if to counter the widespread charge of squalor made by characters like *Humphry Clinker*'s Bramble, whose favourite target was hawkers: the 'dirty barrow bunter in the street cleaning her dusty fruit with her own spittle' and the milkmaid exposing her beverage to 'snot, and tobacco-quids from foot passengers, overflowings from mud carts, spattering from coach-wheels, dirt and trash chucked into it by roguish boys for the joke's sake, the spewing of infants, who have slabbered in the tin measure . . . and finally vermin that drops from the rags of [this] nasty drab'.[45] Contradicting these kinds of polluting actions, Craig's street sweeper, chimney cleaner, and dust collector engage in energetic public sanitation while the brick-dust seller, mat man and sand peddler serve the cause of private hygiene.[46]

If Craig's *Itinerant Traders* responds to the fall of London's physical and moral repute in the late 1700s, John T. Smith's *Vagabondiana* (1817) reacts to the rise of the city's legal and fiscal woes that began in the last quarter of the eighteenth century, but worsened dramatically in the early 1800s.[47] After the Napoleonic Wars, rapid demobilization, an end to wartime spending, and the linked rise in urban joblessness created poverty in London and the countryside that was deeper and more visible than in memory.[48] In

DESCRIPTION OF THE PLATES.

CHAIRS TO MEND.

THE business of mending Chairs is generally conducted by a family or a partnership; one carries the bundle of rush, and collects old Chairs, while the workman, seating himself in some convenient corner on the pavement, exercises his trade. For small repairs they charge from fourpence to one shilling; and for new covering a chair from eighteen pence to half a crown, according to the fineness of the rush required, and the neatness of the workmanship. It is necessary to bargain for price previous to the delivery of the Chairs, or the Chair-mender, like other itinerant artists, will not fail to demand an exorbitant compensation for his time and labour.

SOHO SQUARE stands on the south side and near the eastern extremity of Oxford-street. It has a square enclosure, with a shrubbery in the centre. This square was begun in the time of Charles the Second. The Duke of Monmouth lived in the centre house facing the statue, from which circumstance it was originally called *Monmouth Square*; and, after the execution of that unfortunate nobleman, received the name of *King's Square*. The admirers of the Duke however had the art to get it changed to *Soho*, which was the word of the day at the fatal field of Sedgemoore. In this square is the residence of Sir Joseph Banks, the President of the Royal Society, whose library and collection of natural curiosities are well known. On the south side of the Square, in the right-hand corner leading from Greek-street, stands a house in which Fashion once revelled in all its splendour and dissipation. It was the residence of the once celebrated Mrs. Cornelys, who for taste, wit, vivacity, and elegance of manners, was unrivalled in her day. In this house she established her *coteries*, which were supported by the subscriptions of all the first persons in the country. The entertainments consisted of concerts, dancing, cards, &c. which were followed by *Pic Nic* suppers. Mrs. Cornelys' taste for magnificence and variety of decoration was unbounded; and the magistrates discovered that her entertainments required a license. Her expenses exceeded her subscriptions, and Fashion led to some more novel scene of amusement. Hence this unfortunate lady was doomed to a prison, where, after a confinement of several years, she, who had been the life of the fashionable world, and "the soul of pleasure," ended her days in poverty and distress. This house was also the residence of Field Marshal Conway, but is now divided into two dwellings. A Roman catholic chapel, much frequented, stands in Sutton-street, on the east side of the Square.

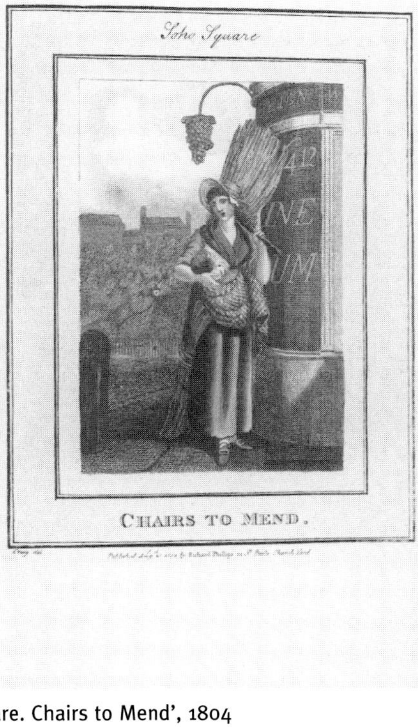

6.16 William Marshall Craig, 'Soho Square. Chairs to Mend', 1804

response, Parliament appointed, between 1816 and 1820, four select committees to investigate the poor laws' workings; other agencies studied immigration and vagrancy. A year after the Select Committee on Vagrancy disbanded (1815–16), Smith published *Vagabondiana, or Anecdotes of Mendicant Wanderers through the Streets of London; with Portraits of the Most Remarkable, drawn from Life by the Author* (1817). It was inspired, Celina Fox shows, by the subsequent policing of the capital's underclasses, which the Select Committee engineered.[49] The committee's work and the reaction of London authorities, especially the constabulary, shrank the number of London's vagabonds so noticeably that Smith expected them to vanish.[50]

Though its title refers only to beggars, Smith's *Vagabondiana* is a Cries in all but name. It hosts the same cast of characters as Cries: the rag-and-bone picker, seller, match vendor, street musician and a new Victorian addition, the crossing sweeper who cleared a path through London's thoroughfares, which 'cannot be crossed without being up to the middle of the leg in dirt'.[51] It even reproduces Müller's blind fiddler (**4.4**) bearing this caption: 'Copied from an Etching by Müller after a Drawing by Gravelot'. For good reason, Smith's editor, J. B. Nichols, called the writer's later *Cries of London* (1839) a continuation and 'an appropriate companion' to *Vagabondiana*.[52] With Mayhew's *London Labour and the London Poor*, Smith's two 'text-centred' books record and provoke an historic shift in attitude toward street hawkers that heralds the death of Cries as a genre.

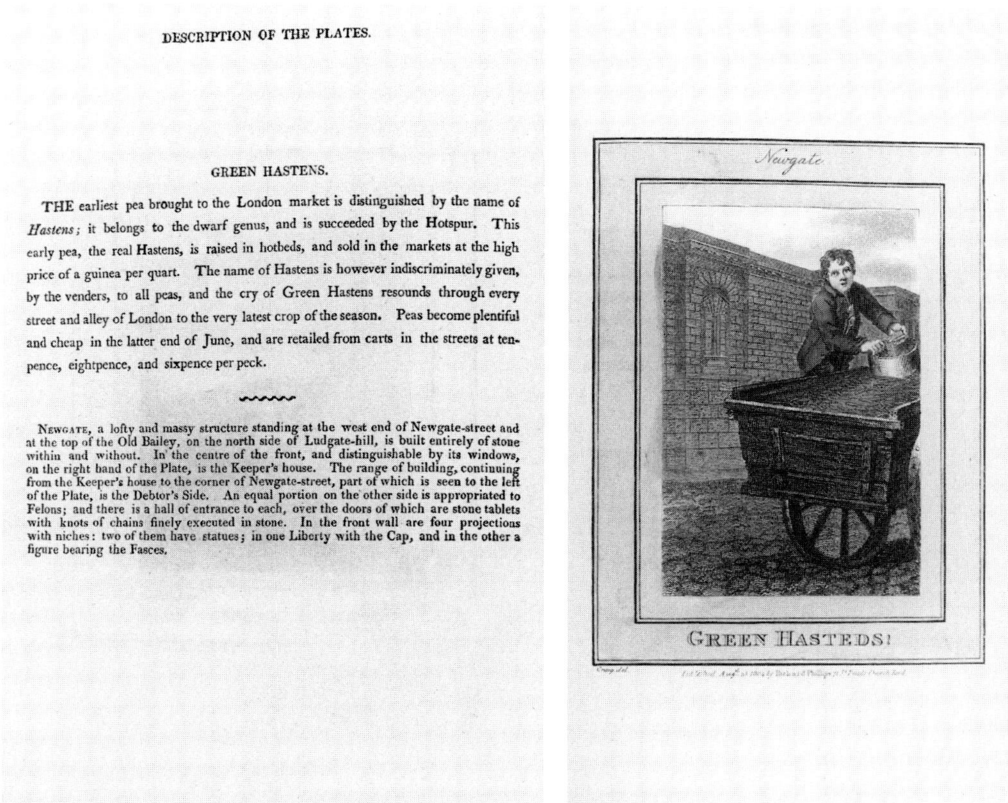

DESCRIPTION OF THE PLATES.

GREEN HASTENS.

THE earliest pea brought to the London market is distinguished by the name of *Hastens*; it belongs to the dwarf genus, and is succeeded by the Hotspur. This early pea, the real Hastens, is raised in hotbeds, and sold in the markets at the high price of a guinea per quart. The name of Hastens is however indiscriminately given, by the venders, to all peas, and the cry of Green Hastens resounds through every street and alley of London to the very latest crop of the season. Peas become plentiful and cheap in the latter end of June, and are retailed from carts in the streets at tenpence, eightpence, and sixpence per peck.

NEWGATE, a lofty and massy structure standing at the west end of Newgate-street and at the top of the Old Bailey, on the north side of Ludgate-hill, is built entirely of stone within and without. In the centre of the front, and distinguishable by its windows, on the right hand of the Plate, is the Keeper's house. The range of building, continuing from the Keeper's house to the corner of Newgate-street, part of which is seen to the left of the Plate, is the Debtor's Side. An equal portion on the other side is appropriated to Felons; and there is a hall of entrance to each, over the doors of which are stone tablets with knots of chains finely executed in stone. In the front wall are four projections with niches: two of them have statues; in one Liberty with the Cap, and in the other a figure bearing the Fasces.

6.17 William Marshall Craig, 'Newgate. Green Hasteds!', 1804

Smith's *Vagabondiana* offers thirty-one plates of cripples, beggars and street sellers. The book's specialties are the blind (who number thirteen) and the mutilated, like the one-eyed, stooped Charles M'Gee (**6.19**), who replace the graceful hawkers of Laroon, but especially Craig and Wheatley.[53] A street cleaner like Craig's sweep, M'Gee and his ilk were living men and women known to the author by personal circumstances as well as by name. The plates are explicated by biographies that 'exhibit some curious customs of the London beggars which have fallen within the author's observation'. One such 'curious custom' is the calling of a woman named Smith, who 'regularly went over London early in the morning to strike out the teeth of dead dogs that had been stolen and killed for the sake of their skins. These teeth she sold to bookbinders, carvers, and gilders, as burnishing tools'.[54] Such narratives move beyond taxonomy and ethnology into public history. They also read like personal reports, for they are tinged with a subjectivity previously suppressed in archetypal depictions of hawkers, but now foregrounded in 'travellers' tales' telling of primitives leading incongruously archaic lives side-by-side with their up-to-date contemporaries. A genre unto themselves, these narratives of poverty and decay were perfected in *London: A Pilgrimage* (1872), which Doré and Jerrold called 'a quest of the picturesque and the typical' and a tale of 'savage London'.[55]

DESCRIPTION OF THE PLATES.

SOOT O!

THE occupation of sweeping Chimneys begins with the break of day. A master Chimney-sweeper patroles the street for custom, attended by two or three boys, the taller ones carrying the bag of soot, and directing the little diminutive creature who, stript perfectly naked, ascends and sweeps the Chimney. The common price is six-pence per Chimney ; but for those of large kitchens, where much scraping is required, they usually demand a shilling. The greatest profit arises from the sale of the soot, which is used for manure.

Formerly it was the custom to cry " Sweep for the Soot O!" the sale of the soot then being the only compensation of the sweeper. The hard condition of Chimney-sweeping devolves upon the smallest and feeblest of the children apprenticed from parish workhouses. The employment in itself stints their growth, and it is unhappily too much the interest of the master so to feed his apprentices as they shall not be liable to outgrow their occupation. It is very common to see Chimney-sweepers of twelve and fourteen years of age who do not exceed the ordinary stature of boys of seven and eight. Many hardships to which these defenceless beings were subjected, have been alleviated by the exertions of the celebrated and benevolent Mr. Jonas Hanway, who obtained an act of parliament, enacting that every Chimney-sweeper's apprentice shall wear a brass plate in front of his cap, with the name and abode of his master engraved on it, thus enabling any humane person to take immediate cognizance of their treatment. Happily, however, for the cause of humanity, a society has been lately established to alleviate the misery of these unfortunate beings, by the adoption of a mode of sweeping Chimnies by a machine, which, upon the examination of several intelligent persons, has been highly approved.

FOUNDLING HOSPITAL, a handsome, plain, and commodious building in Guilford-street, to the north of Holborn, has a centre and wings, and stands at the upper end of a large piece of ground, in which the children of the foundation are allowed to play in fine weather. The whole is enclosed by a wall with gates. At the western gate is a neat porter's lodge. Divine service is performed in the chapel of the Foundling-hospital twice every Sunday, at eleven in the morning and seven in the evening, and is constantly attended by a crowded and elegant audience. Several of Hogarth's pictures, presented by himself, are in the Foundling-hospital, and claim the attention of strangers, particularly his celebrated *March of the Guards to Finchley*. The apartments of the Hospital may be seen Tuesdays, Thursdays, and Fridays. For particulars of this admirable institution see page 204.

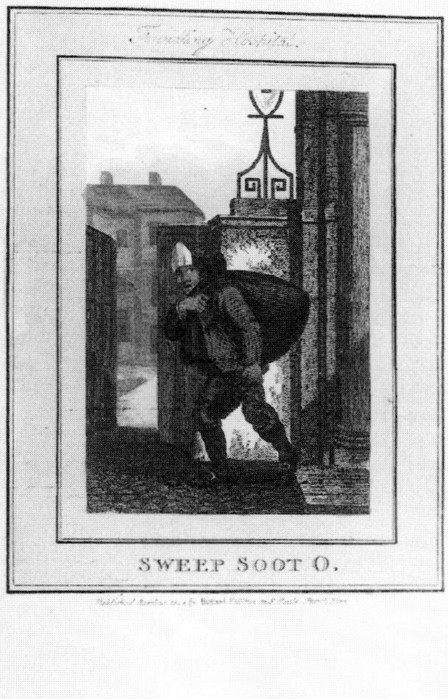

6.18 William Marshall Craig, 'Foundling Hospital. Sweep Soot O', 1804

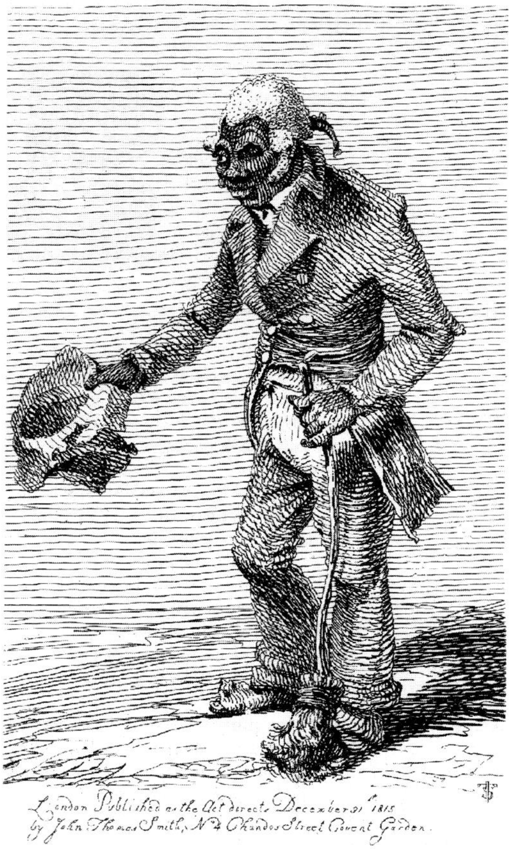

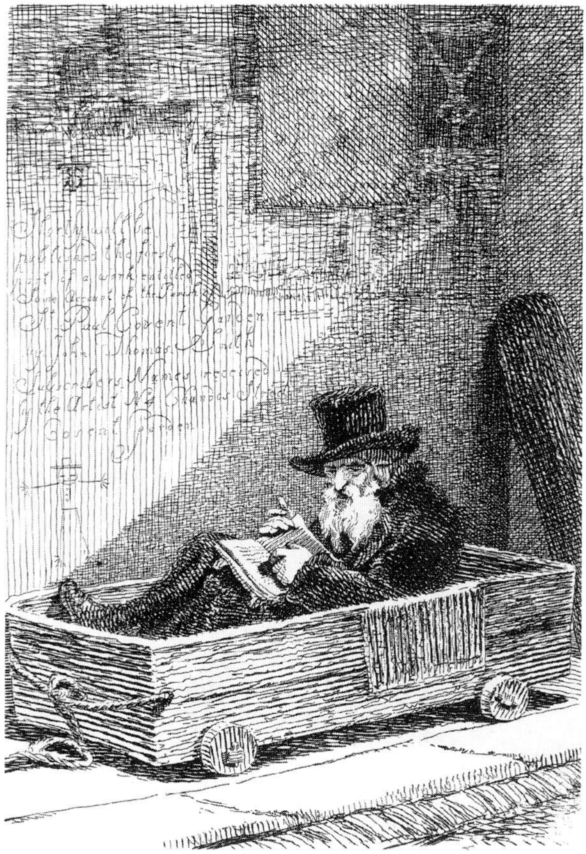

6.19, 20 John T. Smith, 'Charles M'Gee' and 'A Jewish Go-cart Man', from *Vagabondiana* (1817)

In Smith even more than in Ryland, plates are the handmaids of commentary, transformed into a continuous narrative. We read the proto-anthropological and biographic text; we glance at the plates when the unbroken account tells us to. Throughout, we follow the chronicle's themes and didactic interests, ranging narrowly from mutilated black men to 'go-cart, Billies in bowls' and 'sledge-beggars' (**6.20**), who are praised for their industry or blamed for their idleness.[56] But *Vagabondiana*'s most distinctive feature is a set of preliminary remarks twenty-eight pages long, which add up to a short monograph on hawkers and hawking. A preface by Smith justifies the book's 'vulgar' subject by identifying the 'first-rate artists' who have pictured beggars; these range from Michelangelo to Annibale Carracci, whose Cries of Bologna 'are evidently from real characters'.[57] An antiquarian introduction, by the bibliophile Francis Douce, offers a 'sketch of the state and progress of mendacity in former ages'.[58] Smith's preface is not illustrated; Douce's introduction has four small vignettes of beggars copied from drawings of the time of Henry VIII.[59]

Through its preface and introduction, *Vagabondiana* foretells and shapes a new class of book about hawkers. The first characteristic of this class is its reduced dependence on images, restricted in frequency and importance. Illustrations surface in these books, but their role is peripheral – to add force to texts, decorate printed pages or relieve typographic boredom. Sometimes they are etchings, stipple engravings or lithographs; after 1840, they are often photographs. The defining characteristic of these volumes, however, is not so much the kind or subsidiary status of their illustrations or even the primacy of their texts, but the newly biographical, social, and historical character of those texts. They name hawkers' names ('Charles M'Gee a native of Ribon, in Jamaica, born in 1744') and recount their occupations, economies, neighbourhoods and status. Smith is fascinated by their ways of making a living, when sensational, bizarre or taboo, the Polynesian word for uncleanness and contagion.[60] 'Few persons', he assures us, 'particularly those in elevated life, can witness or even entertain a true idea of the various modes by which the lowest classes gain a livelihood'. He illustrates his point with women who scavenge the kennels for discarded lemons to sell to 'the Jew distillers, who extract a further portion of liquor, and thus afford them the means of selling, at a considerably reduced price, lemon drops to the lower order of confections'. But he is even more intrigued by a sewer 'grubber' with the ironic name of 'Flowers' who endured a stench so noxious 'as to deprive him of two of his senses – smelling and tasting, yet Ned Flowers followed this calling for forty years. But there is still a more wretched class of being than the grubbers', he promises, warming to the next wretches, those who wallow in mud to pick up coals fallen into the Thames from barges.[61]

In bias, these texts are descriptive, with a dash of the analytic or a pinch of the critical. Some are reformational and crusading. Most combine these strategies, as does Henry Mayhew's *London Labour and the London Poor*, written to urge 'those who are in "high places", and those of whom much is expected, to bestir themselves to improve the condition of a class of people whose misery, ignorance, and vice' are a disgrace to England.[62] Mayhew's *London Labour*, based on interviews begun just after the publication of *Vagabondiana*, appeared in four volumes between 1851 and 1862; it is still in print. Compiled from newspaper articles he wrote for the philanthropic and evangelical *London Morning Chronicle* of 1849–50, the 2,062 pages of text are embellished by 88 drawings.[63] Accessories after the fact, these drawings help fix the book's message; some are portraits; others are narratives of specific events, as when a fat vermin snaps at the ratcatcher of the sewers. They are based on daguerreotypes by James Beard (1801–85), who drove around London in a cab picking up vendors and posing them in the alien surroundings of a photography studio for thirty-second sittings. His shots, despite their elaborate photographic pedigree, are modelled upon Cries; they use pictorial conventions to mold their subjects into archetypes, abstractions and emblems for the amusement of elite viewers, as two examples show.[64] 'The Mud-Lark' (**6.21**) carries forward the mood and substance of Amigoni's quartet, with its vulnerable, wide-eyed children, easy pathos and insistent linking of the viewer to the viewed by a direct appeal to sensibility, a technique Dr Bernardo perfected in posed photographs of orphans that he hawked in the 1860s.[65] A more striking example of indebtedness, 'The Jew Old-Clothes Man' (**6.22b**) borrows its arrangement and subject from Craig's 'Old Clothes' (**6.22a**), down to the iron fence that defines the peddler as an unwelcome outsider, a threat, a suspect, perhaps a malefactor.

Taking up where Smith's text leaves off, Mayhew (1812–87) writes about the diversity of street trades by which London's poor subsist.[66] He combines piquant observation with social analysis and something new, statistics. Like Smith, he is at his most vivacious when he fleshes out his narrative by real-life portraits of London's 'untouchables': bone grubbers, dust men, pauper street sweepers, scavengers, rubbish carters and London nightmen who practice 'the most offensive, and perhaps the least honourable, of all trades'.[67] Mayhew's obsession with those outcast shunned even by other outcasts is reflected in the fact that he, like Smith, draws them, not just from the streets of London, but from beneath the streets – from its conduits, ditches, rivers, and subterranean drains. His book carries narratives and portraits of sewer hunters, mud larks, sewer flushers, cesspool cleansers and ratcatchers of the sewers (**6.23**). Though street types of all complexions added up to only one-fortieth of the city's working population, they take up three volumes, the most vivid by far of Mayhew's four. Rendered as archetypes, hawkers and their kind become synecdochical figures for the entire underclasses of mid-Victorian London,

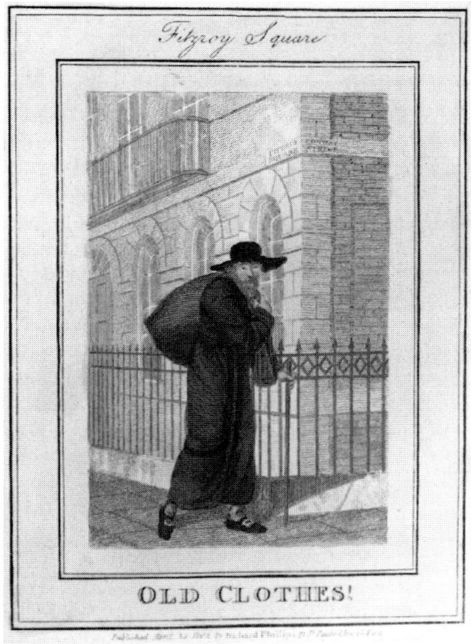

6.22a William Marshall Craig, 'Fitzroy Square. Old Clothes!', 1804

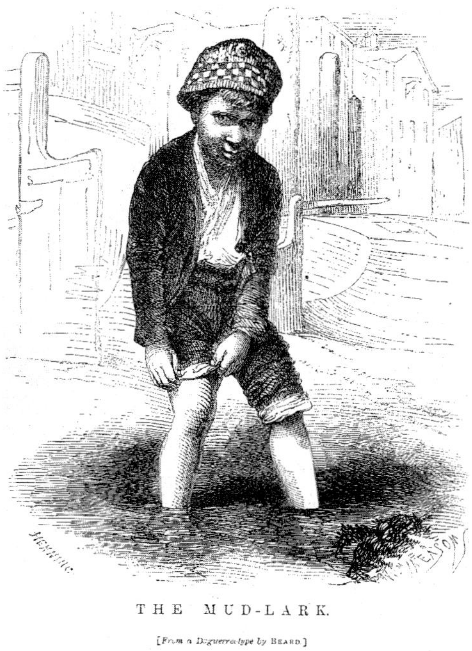

6.21 Richard Beard, 'The Mud-Lark', from *London Labour and the London Poor* (1851–62)

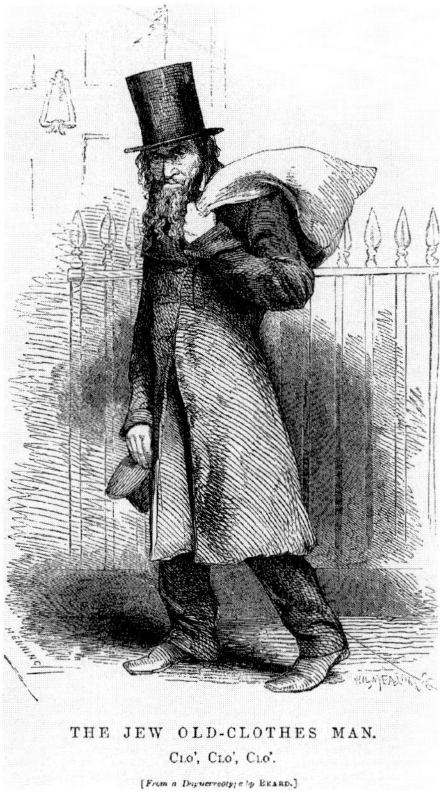

6.22b Richard Beard, 'The Jew Old-Clothes Man', from *London Labour and the London Poor* (1851–62)

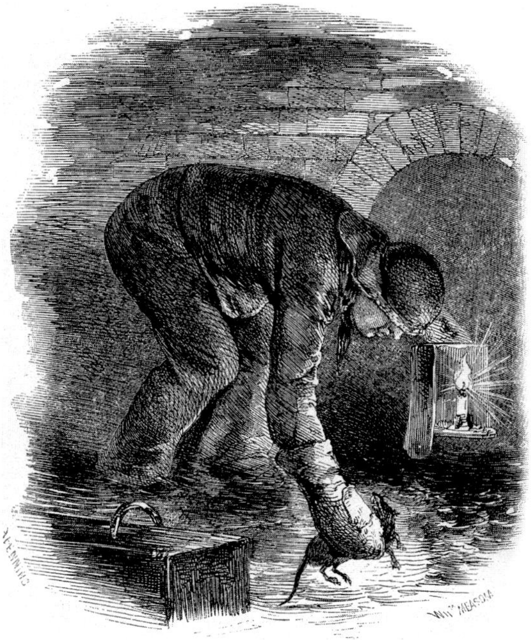

THE RAT-CATCHERS OF THE SEWERS.

[From a Daguerreotype by BEARD.]

6.23 Richard Beard, 'The Rat-Catchers of the Sewers', from *London Labour and the London Poor* (1851–62)

from the benign to the sinister and from the faultless to the fraudulent.[68]

Unlike Smith, who uses straightforward commemoration and old-fashioned moralizing, Mayhew stiffens his narrative with the fashionable methodologies of the ethnologist J. C. Prichard, whose *The Natural History of Man* he read to prepare for his own study.[69] True, the journalist often approaches London's street sellers in didactic terms. But, at a deeper level, his analysis is anthropological and ethnographic, infused with the notion that, lacking conventional evidence and historical testimony, earlier phases of civilization could be understood by observing people still languishing in primal stages of development.[70] He proposes that London's itinerant traders are a 'vagabond race' whose psychologies and physiognomies distinguish them from 'respectable' society. Among their innate tendencies, their 'restless and volatile disposition' expresses the erratic, wandering propensities natural to nomadic peoples and allies them to criminals.[71] Their moral failings include 'their general improvidence – their repugnance to continuous labour – their disregard of female honour – their love of cruelty – their pugnacity – and their utter want of religion'.[72] All are more or less distinguished by prognathous faces: 'high cheekbones and protruding jaws', according to Mayhew.[73] He thinks them as exotic as Iroquois or Tahitians, but less pleasant.[74]

In the second half of the Victorian age, books like *Vagabondiana* and especially *London Labour* thrived. Following the lead of Smith and Mayhew, who blurred the distinction between hawkers and beggars, such volumes catered to Victorians' revulsion at the lower orders of London.[75] From the middle of the nineteenth century into the twentieth, Mayhew's *London Labour*, a sequel called *London's Underworld* (1863) and *Criminal Prisons of London* (1862), written from a deliberately ethnological slant by Mayhew's collaborator, John Binny, established themselves as a genre that had, as its agenda, 'botanizing on the asphalt'.[76] Supplemented by novelistic treatments like Jack London's *People of the Abyss* (1902), this genre of books by flaneurs promoting social observation in city streets as an intellectually respectable avocation fuelled and satisfied the curiosity about marginal people previously addressed by Cries.[77]

Though Cries vanished, the inquisitiveness behind them grew. It was indulged first by words instead of pictures, then by numbers instead of words. The authors of these words and compilers of these numbers were professionals working in nascent disciplines; they laboured not for curious individuals, but for corporate and government bodies anxious about the unwieldy masses confronting the authorities in England's modern industrial society.[78] Part of a bureaucratic and professional expansion, these new 'social' scientists were the economists, epidemiologists, criminologists, statisticians, photographers, colonial district officers, detectives and police who tracked the underclasses.[79] But they also included doctors, lawyers, forensic psychiatrists, architects and sociologists who, eager to use public service as a way to promote professional legitimacy, shaped the agenda of the National Association for the Promotion of Social Science, founded in 1857.[80] Wielding subdivision, measurement, quantification and surveillance, they claimed for their writings the authority and disinterestedness of the scientific method. Whether their approach was statistical or anecdotal, demographic or legal, these writers took over from artists the task of classifying, labelling, stereotyping and representing the urban underclasses. From Mayhew's four pioneering volumes down to the annual library of books and articles addressing the 'culture of poverty', their analyses established the sociological perspective as the one we employ when we 'see' the underclasses today.

The second prophetic book published by John T. Smith was *The Cries of London: Exhibiting Several of the Itinerant Traders of Antient and Modern Times* (London, 1839). Smith was a professional engraver as well as Keeper of Prints and Drawings at the British Museum; he aimed this book at 'the collector of English Costume, as well as the biographer', according to the 'Introduction'.[81] Designated volume two of *Vagabondiana*, Smith's *Cries* is a book about books. Thirteen of its thirty illustrations reproduce not hawkers, but old prints of hawkers; they offer 'Itinerant Traders of former times, collected from engravings executed in the reigns of James I, Charles I and during the Usurpation of Oliver Cromwell, and which, on account of their extreme rarity, are seldom to be seen but in the most curious and expensive Collections'.[82]

Smith's 'curious and expensive' designs, copied from engravings in the British Museum, owe their rebirth to a wave of mass-produced Cries printed by mechanized presses on cheap paper. Flimsy pamphlets like T. Good's *Cries of London*, published by the thousand at the aptly named 'Lion Steam Printing Office', threatened to devour handmade images of earlier times, increasing people's interest in them and producing a self-conscious revival, especially among those perceived as 'artless' and 'primitive'.[83] Smith's 'rarities' come from *The Manner of Crying Things in London*, though he 'improved' and modernized them, the same way L. P. Boitard 'improved' and modernized Laroon's designs eighty years before. To please Victorian tastes, he turned the tankard bearer (**6.24**) into a full-length portrait of a deeply introspective gentleman (**6.24**) who looks down and inward rather than out and forward in search of trade. Indeed, he psychologized such hawkers, softened them and made them melancholics. In portraits that have a photographic tone and were available in coloured versions, he recast some of the least sentimental figures in popular English art into some of the most, transforming them from archetypes to individuals.

Smith's *Cries of London*, which comes with a scholarly commentary identifying the images' dates, publishers, and draftsmen, was the first history of the London Cries. It anticipated and, if echoing titles are guides, it inspired Charles Hindley's *History of the London Cries Ancient and Modern* (1881) and Andrew Tuer's *London Cries* (1883), 'containing an account of London cries from the earliest period'. Tuer sold three different versions of his book: a regular edition, with

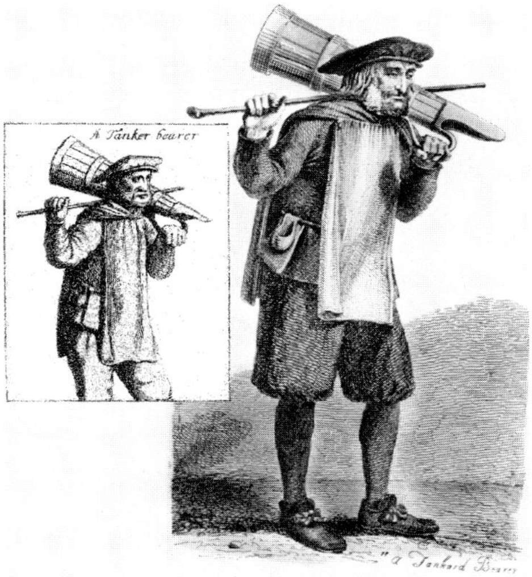

6.24 *left, inset*] 'A Tanker bearer', from *The Manner of Crying Things in London*, *c.* 1644

right] 'A Tankard Bearer', from John T. Smith, *The Cries of London* (1839)

its centrepiece – 'Six Charming Children' – printed in red and brown, selling for a guinea; a large paper edition limited to two hundred and fifty copies with signed proofs, selling for two guineas; and a second large edition of signed proofs printed on satin limited to fifty copies, selling for four guineas.[84] These three books inaugurate and codify the formal study of the London Cries, a tradition of antiquarianism and recovery leading to and shaping, by imitation as well as reaction, this book I am now writing. Of this recovery, the early development tends to censure and the later to espousal, but both consciously distance hawkers from writers and readers, the first by class, the second by time.

Between the 1590s and the 1860s, Cries change their orientation from picture to word; during the same period, they also change the uses they make of visual and verbal traditions. In early broadsides, where pictures dominate, texts are retrospective; they look back to language's oral traditions. Inspired by hawkers' shouts or street ballads, they align themselves with the spoken word and memory. Later commentaries, appearing in ensembles and books where words dominate, are prospective; they look forward to the printed word. Composed especially for the images they accompany, they connect to the written language and to type; they have a rhetorical character and a 'high' literary quality. Müller's long stanzas, with their abstract poetic diction using inkhorn words like 'disconsolate' or 'imbrued', and the heroic couplets framing that diction, derive from the verse heritage of John Dryden and Alexander Pope; Child's rhymes derive from the satires of John Gay and Jonathan Swift. The texts of Cries published after 1750 are even more deeply implicated in the culture of the written word; Kirk's and Ryland's commentaries are formulated to teach reading, writing, book collecting and behaving. As pedagogical tools, they illustrate the power of Cries to shape their culture. For Cries like Kirk's and Ryland's are not mere passive reflections of their world; they are also agents of production. They are dynamic and transformative forces contributing, however modestly, to the rise of literacy and the triumph of the written word.

Texts, as they move from speech to print, shift from public statement to social morality to individual morality and finally to individual knowledge. And they grow increasingly partisan in tone. The first broadside texts, like 'The Bellman of London' (**2.1**) and 'The Common Cryes' (**2.3**) name and label; as they expand in ensembles, they grow polemical. They shift from open, value-free glosses (like 'Cockels', 'Harttichaks', and 'Mackrill' in the bottom line of 'The Common Cryes') to pedantic texts with closed meanings. In this change, Müller's commentaries are pivotal. Preaching toil and forbearance, they offer propaganda inspired by the political contingencies of Georgian England. They usher in a variety of didactic narratives and sententious rhymes ('none to Grief should e'er give way') that serve the genre till it vanishes about 1861, when Walker and Sons published the *New London Cries*, the last recorded book to feature the words 'London Cries' in its title.

As commentaries invent new forms of sententiousness, they purify themselves of vulgarity and bad taste, inherited from oral sources linked to the Middle Ages and the Renaissance. The carnality of early broadsheets, which speak 'Of a Maidenhead lost on Saturday last, / Twixt blanket and featherbed, in great hast', do not die a quick death; humorous mentions of sex and body dirt linger for a hundred and fifty years. They resurface in Müller's 'Baby, Cloaths & All for Three Pence' (**4.3**), where the little boy offers his female playmate a sexual taunt; they are still more explicit in the long text to Child's 'Chimney-Sweeper's Boy' (**4.6**) and 'M'st ye ha' some Golden Pippins' (**4.5**) where the girl is a whore, according to the caption. But Child's lewd commentaries from about 1740 are the last of their kind. In early sheet Cries, such coarseness is displaced from the 'decent' images to 'indecent' texts. But in late ensembles, the same coarseness is displaced from texts to ribald images, illustrated in Rowlandson's ensembles of fast women and lecherous men.

The iconography of Cries – their figures and backgrounds rather than their texts – go through an analogous evolution during the same epoch, moving from symbolic and abstract styles to expressive ones. Broadside Cries simplify the tradition of popular English emblems from the Renaissance. Following the conventions of that genre, which are mannerist and formulary, these Cries centre on objects and figures realized schematically to offer an emblematic portrait of London. Emblematic imagery looks archaic just before 1700, when it is used to address audiences with low status, particularly children and dissenters.[85] About that time, Cries moves to styles that are more expressive and current, though they never abandon diagrammatic imagery and texts; the homiletic structure of Ryland's volumes matching simple pictures with moral commonplaces is fundamentally emblematic. The new styles of the Cries include Müller's portrait narratives, Craig's views and Mayhew's sensationalistic designs based upon photographs. These Cries depict hawkers in historical costumes and pose them against naturalistic or, in the case of Craig's scenes, topographical settings. Such backdrops, impersonating familiar urban quarters, authenticate criers as social types in how they complement or contrast with their subjects.

Against actualized urban panoramas, hawkers shift from static to dynamic figures, from symbols to performers in one-act dramas. But these figures do not depict social types or represent street labour; rather, they mask these realities, at least partially. They enact picturesque rites or, in the case of Mayhew's illustrations, they depict sensational practices. These scenes transform Cries into 'observations' offering folkloric accounts of the colourful and bizarre customs practiced by the lower orders. Such characters promote an image of the nation's lower orders as naïve and tribal, but also peaceful, diligent and unmenacing. Their primitivism takes a new turn in the images of the black beggars, the Jew in the go-cart, and the old clothes man, also a Jew. Here Cries replace the language of class with the language of race, as the opposition between city and country or rich and poor shifts to an antithesis between England and empire.

7

Pastoral and anti-pastoral in the London Cries

WHAT OVERARCHING themes and movements unite the Cries of London across its long, varied history? While the Cries oscillates between the aestheticism of Laroon and the naturalism of Hogarth, its drift is away from the actualized depiction of the daily life of peddlers toward greater sentimentality and prettification, but also toward debates about technique, style and form in art. Dedicated by title to history's forgotten and first inspired by real vendors, this inventive genre shifts inexorably from life to art. Even before Laroon's *Cryes*, it aestheticizes the lower orders. Turning away from the imperfect men and damaged women peopling London's streets, it seeks the ideal forms of these, portraying hawkers under a rubric long operative but only first made explicit in Jerrod and Doré's *London*, where street Arabs are esteemed for possessing 'the rich picturesqueness of rags'.[1] In search of greater formal variety and increasingly complex effects, it romanticizes hawkers but, reacting against the resulting idealization, it also satirizes them, creating an iconography of the city as a dystopia plagued by hawkers' miseries or crimes. Despite this counter-tradition with its sharp satire, Cries more often conceal the lower orders with neat arrangements or amusing distractions, legitimizing them as topics of conventional artistic inspiration.[2]

The genre's audiences and traditions – its styles of imagery and its language – confirm the view that it is an artful construction, a text of the city and its people drawn increasingly from other texts.[3] Beginning with Laroon, the London Cries is the fabrication of artists and publishers cultivating rich buyers biased against real hawkers and the urban underclasses for which they came to stand. This bias, missing from the first broadsheet Cries, surfaced in the seventeenth century, when, as part of the 'great withdrawal', wealthy people abandoned popular culture.[4] Henry Peacham, in the 1606 edition of his *Gentleman's Exercise*, wrote that it is 'no more disgrace to a Lord to draw a fair picture, than to cut his Hawks meat, or play football with his men'; in the 1612 edition, he replaced the last phrase by the words 'play Tennis with his Page'.[5]

To urban elites such as Peacham's gentleman, who avoided drudges not in his employ, vendors were both attractive and repugnant, familiar and unfamiliar. The superior orders loathed those they called 'common wretches that crawl on the earth'; the haughty among them thought it 'monstrous to be told you have a heart as sinful' as theirs.[6] But rich Londoners also feared the servile, whose identities could shift in a flash, from a hawker to a robber dangerous for a single person unarmed to meet alone in a dark alley. Such types were feared, especially during the popular turmoil of the late seventeenth century (when the derogatory word 'mob' first came into the English language), but more intensely still after the French Revolution when Burke's

Reflections turned them into the 'swinish multitude'.[7] Well-bred Londoners, even though they lived cheek by jowl with the lower orders, knew less and less about them. Their rookeries were, by definition, *terra incognita*, and their invisibility made them frightening.[8] By the middle of the Victorian age, according to Henry Mayhew, hawkers had become

> a large body of persons, of whom the public had less knowledge than of the most distant tribes of the earth – the government population returns not even numbering them among the inhabitants of the kingdom, and as adducing facts so extraordinary, that the traveller in an undiscovered country of the poor must, like Bruce, until his stories are corroborated by after investigators, be content to lie under the imputation of telling such tales as travellers are generally supposed to delight in.[9]

The impulse of 'the Quality' to view the lower orders as loathsome or menacing is accompanied by a conflicting impulse to embrace them in a different realm. Repugnance followed by fascination are the conflicting effects of a political edict to spurn the debased, who, to win favor on another level, must be cleaned up, softened, sentimentalized or rendered comic, in accord with the ordering imperative of a higher aesthetic.[10] So, in the course of 'the great withdrawal', elites turned participation into observation. They became polite spectators while commoners became spectacles, in life and art.[11]

The London Cries used art to sanctify as well as mask the character of the mannerless. Hawkers were widely believed to threaten not only civil quiet but also political stability: the Middlesex Sessions Books, noting that they travelled everywhere but disclosed their identities to nobody, abound with references to them as spies, agents of subversion and tools of the two Pretenders, roles that John Kirk's uniquely candid hurdy-gurdy man confesses to: 'To live by hurdy-gurdy I pretend, But to spy your way is all my end.'[12] Serving to reassure the upper class about the real and imaginary threats of the dangerous classes, the genre reintroduced them in a new guise. It rendered them morally satisfying and aesthetically pleasing by giving them the virtues of rural people, who, unlike the swarming classes of the city, seemed docile to elites, especially after romanticism.

The practice of 'perfecting' nature, which, of all artistic imperatives, is the best-known and most widely followed, can convert even the most idle, angry or bestial peddler into a virtuous, simple artisan, either a harmless domestic savage from rural England or a childlike native from the colonies.[13] In Cries, this trope expresses itself in a pastoralism defined by form, subject, and mood. In form, it means symmetrical compositions, static figures, and stereotyped gestures accentuating adherence to familiar iconographic formulae. Sometimes it involves insistent framing of the kind employed by Craig, whose multiple rectangles emphasize the contained, exclusive view of his images. In subject, it means women who are young, fertile, yielding and affectionate; these figures wear folk costumes to sell milk, lovely fruits, and perfect vegetables in the company of animals and children. In mood, it means harmony, nostalgia, sentimentality and sometimes light comedy or persiflage, a common feature of pastoralism.

Before Laroon, the earliest manifestation of this Virgilian decorum is muted and subtle, implied rather than expressed. In the first broadsides published before and after 1600, it surfaces in Cries peopled by hawkers disconnected from the urban economy. The classless, anti-urban figures and the lyric captions of those who sell lettuce, cabbages, cherries, 'ripe damsons' or 'fyne bowpots' of flowers in 'The Bellman of London' (**2.1**) conjure up nature with its gardens and orchards more than London with its burses, manufactories and stock exchanges. As many as a third and sometimes half of the hawkers in these early sheets sell eye-catching fruits and vegetables.[14]

Many more hawkers sell produce with special powers to evoke a fecund English nature. Such bounty appears in the city magically, as if it came into existence in an Age of Gold when the curse of work had not yet been pronounced on the human race.[15] Apples, pears, oranges, and figs, butter, cheese, fresh cream and milk, the most arcadian of all rural largess, cast a simultaneously vernal and autumnal mood over Cries. Their timeless hawkers, sometimes statuesque and immobile, resemble sowers and reapers. These allegories of the seasons and the rural months seem to follow rhythms dictated by God and nature, increasingly called upon to justify the social order.[16] Spring and fall echo in vendors' shouts rich in lyric language like 'ripe', 'sweet' and 'young'.[17]

Casting London's hawkers as milkmaids, flower growers, fruiterers and vegetable gardeners was plausible in the historical period when the first broadside Cries appeared. At the death of Elizabeth in 1603, London was a big town, or rather a small city, populated by 140,000 souls within the walls and without.[18] Distinctions between rustic and urbanite were blurry. The capital of a nation 95 per cent rural, London was settled by migrants from the provinces and visited by rural folk selling their harvests. It was encircled by a countryside that, by comparison to its own land mass, seemed boundless. More important, London was not widely separated from that countryside; it lay open to the heaths, meadows, and hamlets about it, like Deptford and Islington; these represented the dominant rural order to which the capital was subordinate.[19] Despite its walls, England's chief city thronged with peasants whose invasions, temporary and permanent, threatened to drown it.

Furthermore, London's citizens and freemen behaved in ways that made them look as much like rustics as town dwellers. They kept ducks and hens; they built piggeries and bred hogs until the late seventeenth century, when small animal farming moved to Bethnal Green, Stepney, and Tothill Fields. Some cultivated patches of ground, planting flowers or growing fruits and vegetables; in Shakespeare's day, the Bishop of Ely kept a sunny garden in Holborn, not a sparrow's flight from the City: 'My lord of Ely', the Duke of Gloucester addresses the Bishop in *Richard III*, 'when I was last in Holborn, / I saw good strawberries in your garden there'.[20] Other Londoners were horticulturists and herbalists. John Gerard (1545–1612) also kept a garden at Holborn and supervised another plot of savories on the grounds of Lord Burleigh's house.[21] Some freemen, joining the ranks of peasants, even carried on subsistence farming, tending gardens in the city proper or the adjacent countryside; Stow griped of Londoners who built 'garden plots' at Tower Hill.[22]

So early seventeenth-century London, surrounded on all sides by nature, was a rural city, though perhaps the modern historian John Richardson exaggerates in calling it 'a large country town'.[23] Its character as 'city-in-a-garden' is shown by 'Londinum' (**7.1**), a map of the city and the surrounding countryside (there are no suburbs) that Frans Hogenberg cut in 1572 for *Cities of the World*.[24] Hogenberg's workshop produced the first broadside Cries, to which the map is linked thematically; both are matching representations of England's capital, the map exemplifying physical and the Cries illustrating sociological cartography. Within its walls, Hogenberg's London is peppered by spots of greenery and open space, coloured in some maps; these are especially dense to the

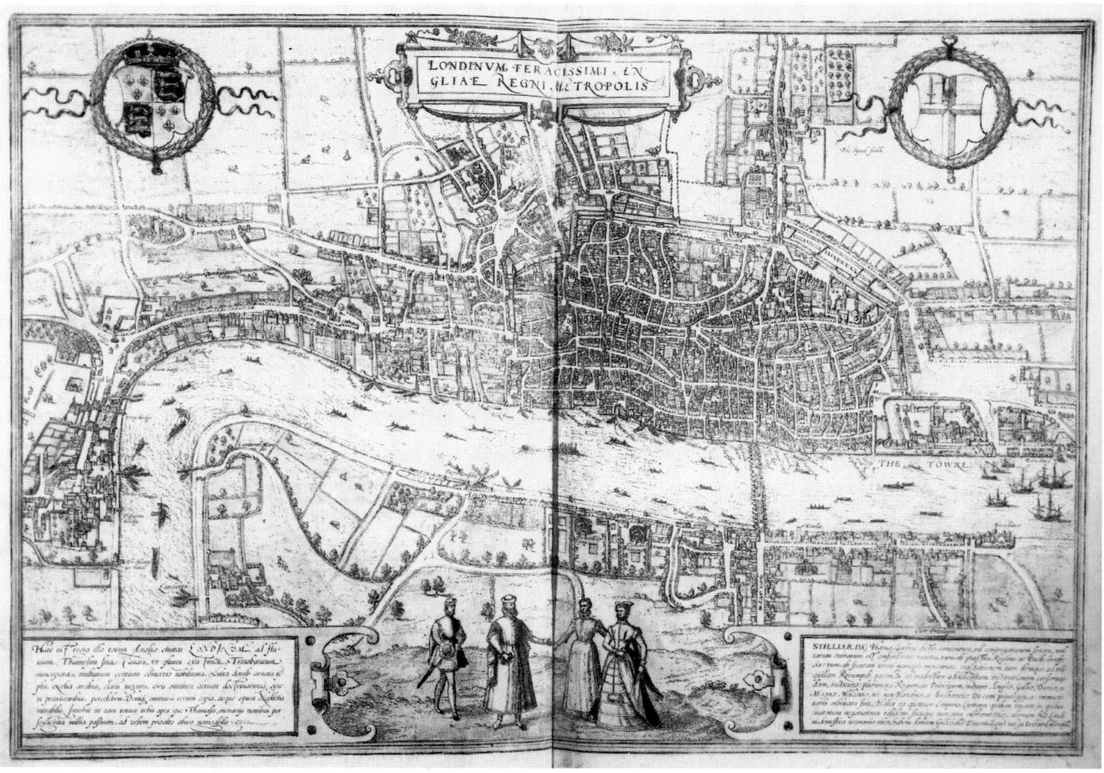

7.1 Franz Hogenberg, 'Londinum', 1573

north and east, where ornamental as well as useful gardens, big and small, abound.[25] Without, it is dominated by meadows, pasture land, streams and open fields that carry images of horses, cows and deer, a form of cartographic symbolism Swift ridiculed when he described 'Afric' geographers who 'o'er unhabitable Downs / Place elephants for want of Towns'.[26] It pictures the city as an aspect of England's larger agricultural order; here is the pastoral spot that Stow evokes when he tells how, in his youth, he 'fetched many a halfe pennie worth of Milke . . . always hote from the Kine'.[27]

By the 1700s, the rural capital of Stow's boyhood had vanished. Writing in 1708, Edward Hatton declared that 'what was in Mr. Stow's time is now like another city', in part because of the changes wrought by the Great Fire.[28] New modes of transport, production and living had increased the difference and distance between city and country. In 1600, Middlesex dominated the capital. A century later, the capital dominated Middlesex, in partial fulfilment of James I's operatic warning: 'Soon London will be all England.' Recovering from the Great Fire of 1666, London in 1700 was the leading metropolis of Europe and 'a kind of Emporium for the whole Earth', as Addison calls it.[29] Fifteen times bigger than it was in 1600 and inhabited by 575,000 men and women, London seemed a monster with no superior in Christendom.[30] It had harvested a critical mass of people sufficient to sequester it from the countryside and render it distinct, except around its remote peripheries.[31] A metropolis with parishes as big as cities, this world unto itself created a distinction having powerful new meaning: the distinction between city and country, the latter inspiring abhorrence, even terror, for the first time during the Restoration, when comedy was relentless in its condemnation all things rural and provincial. Already London had become 'a nation, not a city'.[32]

This London, with its fresh urbanity, inspired joy and excitement, but also crisis and loss: loss of nature, the countryside, innocence, simplicity, intimacy, but especially a familiar way of life based on kinship. This loss, the most unsettling change in the history of modern experience, took the form of melancholy, nostalgia and, ultimately, the Romantic movement. But it also surfaced in the insistent pastoralism of ensembles of Cries published in the late seventeenth century and after. Pioneered by Laroon, this mood denies the city's urbanity by means of an arcadianism of name and content. This arcadianism radiates from images that conjure up a Golden Age of city life when social intercourse was free of class stress, trade was performed in an urban landscape without parasites, and hawkers devoted themselves to simple, vital tasks coloured with rural hues.[33]

Apart from the fact that they sell cherries, cheese and butter, hawkers in early broadsides do not evoke rural life. They do not dress or act in country ways: the apple sellers do not sport flowers in their hair, as Kentish youths like Laroon's vinegar seller do; the women do not wear the short red cloaks favoured by young girls from Norfolk like his vendor of hot baked wardens.[34] The maid crying 'By ani milke' in 'The Common Cryes of London' (**2.3**) is virtually identical to the urban basket women on either side of her; she signals by the same gesture, moves with the same sway, and wears the same clothing as the 'herrings' seller to the left and the 'pippins pys' seller to the right.

If the pastoralism of broadsides is nominal and implicit, that of ensembles is substantive and explicit. It first surfaces in Laroon's *Cryes*, which ennobles hawkers physically and turns numbers of them into personifications that absorb or reflect rustic values: naturalness, mildness, simplicity, industriousness, submissiveness and innocence.[35] It finds its supreme expression in Wheatley's *Itinerant Traders*. The first Cries to be mass marketed, Wheatley's sanitized ensemble exploits the blooming commerce in the picturesque as a discourse enjoying boundless popularity in the 1780s, when its practice of transmuting the social and political into the decorative was made possible by an aesthetic based on poverty, neglect and decay.[36] 'The dirty and tattered garments, the dishevelled hair, and general wild appearances of gypsies and beggar girls are often picturesque', Richard Payne Knight declared in his *Analytical Inquiry into the Principles of Taste* (1805).[37] Having not only tamed wild mountains but also elevated banditti, beggars, 'and all such rough tattered figures' (because these 'picturesque appendages' bear a close analogy 'to old hovels and mills, to the wild forest horse, and other objects of the same kind'), that movement was an ideal means by which to render hawkers and other outcasts – the urban counterparts of banditti, gypsies, and beggars – acceptable to 'the eye of taste'.[38]

Idealizing Cries like Laroon's and Wheatley's prefer peasants to city types, women to men, children to adults, and labouring youngsters to dependent infants. In the nineteenth century, when industrialization produced uniformity and conformity, they prefer eccentrics to types and foreigners to natives. An advertisement promoting Wheatley's *Itinerant Traders of London* explains the theoretical basis that lies beneath these preferences: 'In the civilized Countries of Europe, the prevalence of polite manners softens down the rough originality of feature, and produces a similarity very unfavourable to the picturesque', the notice declared in defence of the *Traders'* focus on people from 'the lower ranks of life': Jews, women, and good (that is, working) children.[39] Among such humble folk, differences in trade, neighbourhood and education produced variety in personality and temperament, creating the diverse, colourful London street life then becoming a tourist attraction unto itself. An anonymous reviewer of Dickens's *Hard Times*, writing in 1854, put the belief this way:

> Differences [among the lower orders] are made more apparent by the absence of those equalizing influences which long continued and uniform education, and social intercourse subject to invariable rules of etiquette, produce upon the cultivated classes. Original and picturesque characters are therefore much more common among the poorer orders; their actions are simpler, proceeding from simpler motives, and they are principally to be studied from without.[40]

In its preference for women, the picturesque favours those whose appearances mark them as 'studio' good-looking. Its bias, expressed in female costume, figure and face, is clear in three milkmaids from Laroon, Boitard, and especially Wheatley; all these men's portraits trade in a fanciful link between London dairy women and English nature. Laroon's merry milkmaid from his sketch (**7.2**) is dressed festively in shoulder knots, an eye-catching bodice neatly laced, and shoes with immense bows and fashionable half-moon toes. Her figure, unbroken by the demands of labour, possesses the ideal shape and carriage of an artist's model.

Boitard's milkmaid (**7.3**), from the 1750s, illustrates a more refined, intricate presentation of this arcadianism, articulated again in costume, but also in body and face.

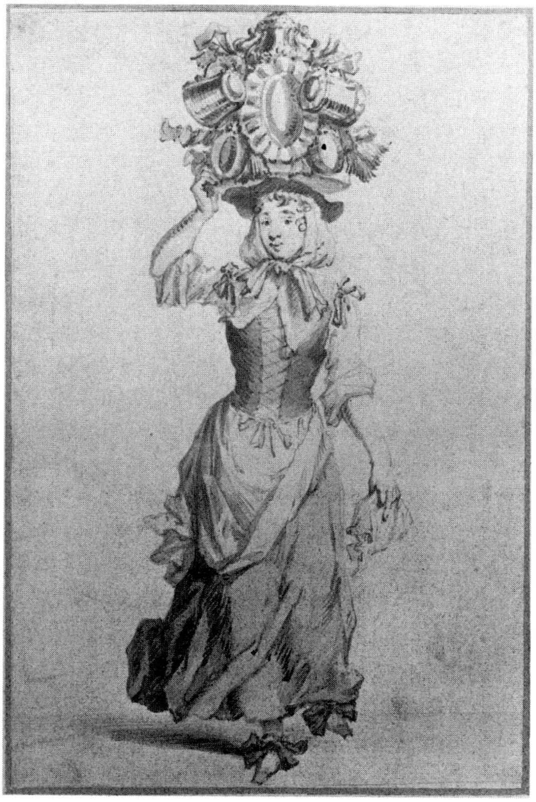

7.2 Marcellus Laroon, *The merry Milk Maid*, *c.* 1687

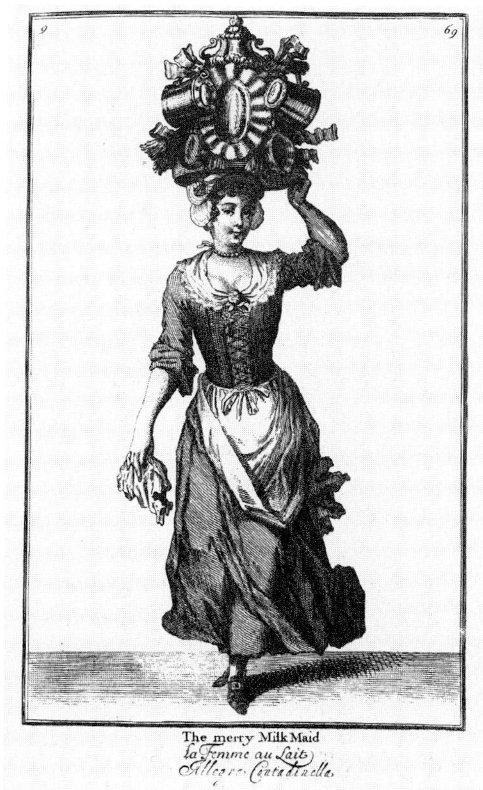

7.3 P. Boitard after Marcellus Laroon, 'The merry Milk Maid', 1759

This coy maid, wearing silver shoe buckles, a lace collar, a stylish little hat and a necklace, is quintessential picturesque, in William Gilpin's sense of the terms as 'expressive of that peculiar kind of beauty which is agreeable in a picture', a definition that accents the concept's reference to art rather than life and supports the view that its power is in proportion to its generality and imprecision.[41] Her ample bosoms project a lacteal fertility that echoes her identity as a milkmaid. The rose between her breasts, evoking nature, ties her to the countryside even more decisively; the equation of village virgin and rose is a popular trope in eighteenth-century England. The pyre of silver vessels, the dancing, and the gala costumes of Laroon's and Boitard's maids link both characters to play rather than work, pleasure rather than pain, and country freedoms rather than city constraints.

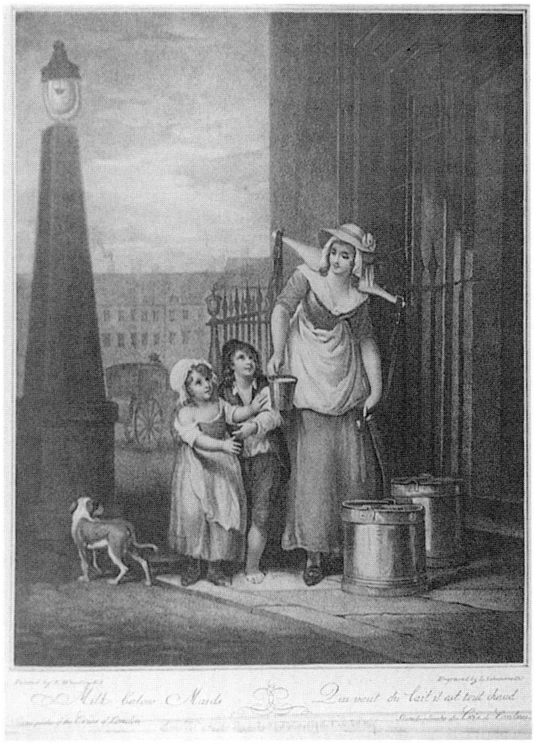

7.4 Francis Wheatley, 'Milk below Maids', 1793

Of all females in all Cries, Francis Wheatley's are the most pastoral, and the most pastoral of all Wheatley's hawkers is the milkmaid (**7.4**), who blends active innocence and passive eroticism. Despite her cry of 'Milk below Maids', she does not sell milk to servants but donates it to the deserving poor. She expresses, in nurturing cherubic orphans with a giant cup of milk (in lieu of the lactations of her own breasts), a sympathy that is explicitly maternal. As well as milk and sympathy, she also offers, in her altruistic conduct, instruction by an example so compelling that it inspires the boy to the same altruism: he puts the girl's hunger ahead of his own. Exercising charity as a part of her daily routine, this London Madonna expresses a serenity in her face that reveals how fully her task absorbs her and how automatically she subordinates making money to doing good.[42] In this role, she reflects as well as promotes a new ideology of British femininity: she is both an early illustration of the cult of motherhood and an example of the evolving ideal of women as ornamental, useful, and especially, philanthropic, just when philanthropy was becoming – as it still remains – the fashionable avocation of ladies from 'the Quality'.[43]

The appearance of Wheatley's milkmaid at the end of the eighteenth century coincided with the rise of landscape as a major genre of English art; Cries and rustic scenes express the same social impulse.[44] Wheatley's milkmaid, indeed all his female hawkers, personify an idealized rural sensibility characterized by love of children, animals, the meek and the deserving poor. Despite the fact that they appear in a London street, they are not city characters. In a spirit of energy and cheer, they hawk peas, oranges, cherries, primroses, and strawberries, rendered as plentiful, ripe, varied and colourful. Their fruits and vegetables link them to the seasons and labours of the field, turning them into peasants preserving ancestral traditions and performing unchanging rites, as if, in the centre of industrial London, they still belonged to an untroubled, pre-industrial age.[45] The figures' appearance and behaviour – their cleanliness, smart gowns, youth, beauty, and manners – render them as paragons of rural virtues: naturalness, spontaneity and other-unworldliness.[46]

Contemporaries alive to the elision of the actual by the ideal noticed the gulf between Wheatley's pictures and city life. The pseudonymous art journalist 'Anthony Pasquin', taking aim at how the painter conflates city with country and idealizes women, protested that 'whenever Mr. Wheatley presents us with a rural Nymph whom he wishes to be peculiarly impressive, he decorates her head with a profusion of party coloured ribbands, like a maniac in Coventry, which play in the breeze, offensive to thought and propriety. As this is not the character of our village Daphnes, why make them so prodigiously fine at the expense of truth'?[47] The painter Edward Edwards (1738–1806) grumbled even more bitterly about the rural character of Wheatley's urban figures, especially the women, in his Cries: 'Wheatley's chief excellence was in rural subjects with figures which, when they represented females, generally bore a meretricious and theatrical air, as is very distinguishable in a set of prints representing the Cries of London, in which the women are dressed with great smartness, but little propriety, better suited to the fantastic taste of an Italian opera stage than the streets of London.'[48]

In its defense, Wheatley's Cries is only the most orthodox purveyor of the 'rustic picturesque'. When the town grows more urban, industrialized and distinct from the country in history, and peddling becomes an increasingly outmoded occupation, its practitioners wax more rustic in art, until country actually comes to stand for city. This paradox is illustrated most explicitly in *The Cries of London, for Every Month in the Year*, a title linking hawkers not just to all four seasons but also to the twelve months of the year. This book, published by J. Davenport for C. Sheppard in 1801 and now – alas – lost, is '*Decorated with Two Cuts for Each Month suitable to the Season*', according to its subtitle.[49] The same paradox takes surprising new forms later, when artists vie with one another to give the arcadianisms of their London Cries unorthodox expressions. Linda Nochlin describes the picturesque in nineteenth-century art as a 'peculiarly elusive wildlife, requiring increasingly skilled tracking as the delicate prey – an endangered species – disappears further and further into the hinterlands, in France as in the Far East'.[50]

Among Cries, Craig's *Traders* (1804), moving from the native within England's national borders to the native without, pioneers the 'far eastern' picturesque that Nochlin identifies as justifying European colonialism. As domestic primitives and native savages were assimilated into national commerce, foreign primitives took their place in London – and in plates like Craig's. A comparative ethnography of selected peoples from near and far, his hawkers from England and its colonies or far-off trade posts are as exotic as the imported luxuries they vend. The Turk hawking medicinal rhubarb from China or Tibet (**7.5**) and the Moroccan selling colourful native slippers from Tangier (**7.6**) both pose in attitudes free of laboriousness, articulating the exotic picturesque in the language of naturalism. Notice the careful delineation and neat colouring of the peddlers' beards, mustachios, turbans, mauve gowns and scarlet pantaloons, by which 'picturesque information' masquerades as documentation.[51] A vital function of the picturesque, Nochlin shows, is

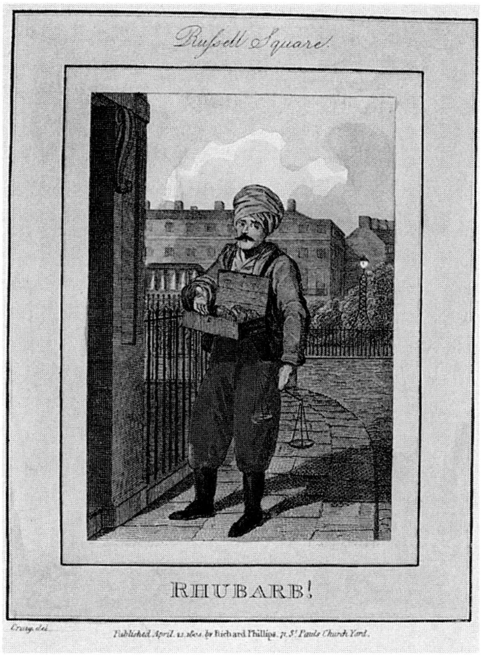

7.5 William Marshall Craig, 'Rhubarb!', 1804

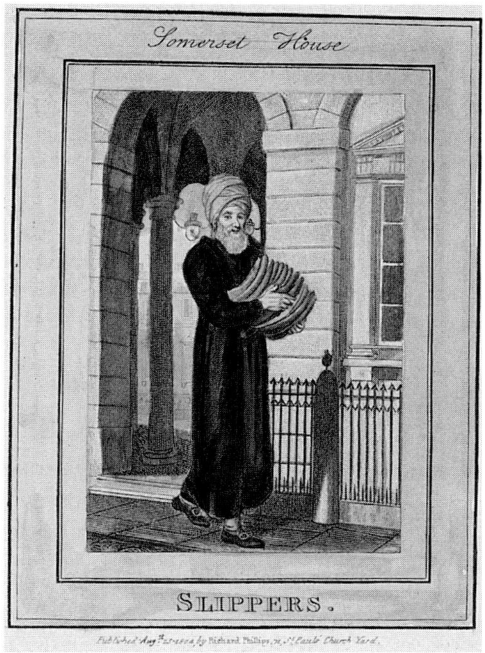

7.6 William Marshall Craig, 'Slippers', 1804

to certify that the people it encapsulates, by how they keep to traditional costumes or native practices, are irredeemably different from – and, in their childlike character, culturally inferior to – the audience buying and appreciating them.

Craig's Turk and Moroccan orientalize the Cries, seeking the picturesque in immigrants not yet assimilated into English society. But Busby's Americans give it folkloric, pathomorphic and philosophical twists. These foreigners never can be assimilated because, instead of trading in this or that exotic commodity, they specialize in exoticism itself. And they embody and perform it. The most striking example, taken from Busby's *Costume of the Lower Orders* (*c.* 1819), is 'Billy Waters' (**7.7**), who also appears in the artist's *Cries of London drawn from life* (1823). A black American violinist and street singer, he wears ostrich feathers on a mariner's hat to evoke a West Indian from the Caribbean. Is he a connoisseurial trophy imported by colonial explorers like the botanist Sir Joseph Banks (1743–1820), who wanted to bring an islander back with him as a souvenir of his trip to the South Pacific 'as some of my neighbors do lions and tygers at a larger expense than he will ever put me to'?[52]

These figures are also emblems of impaired virility, odd male counters to the milkmaids with their exaggerated femininity. As well as fiddling and singing, Billy Waters dances, despite the fact that he has a wooden leg. And Busby's 'Mechanical Fiddler' (**7.8**), a nameless American from Providence, Rhode Island, also scraps on the violin, though he has neither arm nor hand.[53] A figure of ideal deformity, his imperfection expresses his true identity as one of the lower orders.[54] His cultured performance on the fiddle denies the boundary between high and low, but his race and bizarre appearance, which test the limits of normalcy, affirm it. Waters and

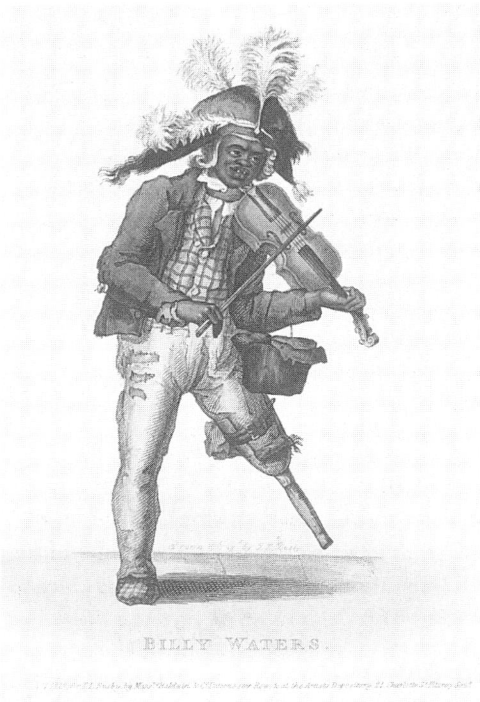

7.7 Thomas Busby, 'Billy Waters, the Dancing Fiddler', from *Costume of the Lower Orders*, *c.* 1819

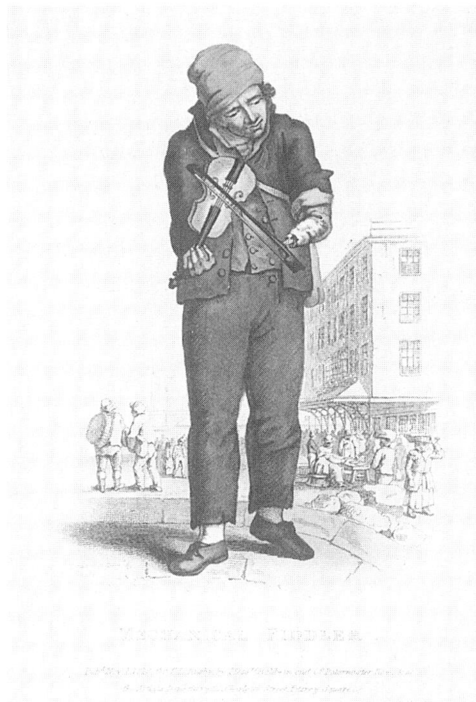

7.8 Thomas Busby, 'Mechanical Fiddler', from *Costume of the Lower Orders*, *c.* 1819

the 'Mechanical Fiddler' both illuminate the way art rescues, denatures, feminizes and civilizes the savage.

The appeal of grotesques and exotics like Billy Waters, 'Mechanic Fiddler', and the other lively types, aimed at 'individuals of taste and fortune' is spelled out self-consciously by Busby in the Introduction to his *Costume of the Lower Orders*, where he labels these characters as studies in 'rustic picturesque character'. Such examples of 'rustic picturesque character' offered middle-class philosophers subjects to examine and ponder: 'Those blessed abundantly by Fortune's favours, are little acquainted with the hardships which men of this description daily endure; the scanty pittance on which they exist, fully exemplifies the words of an excellent Poet, that "Man wants but little here below, / Nor wants that little long".' Published when drawing as a polite accomplishment was trickling down to the middle sort, they also offered amateur artists 'proper subjects for copying . . . to effect which the pen or pencil must be substituted for the etching point'.

The 'rustic picturesque' transforming hawkers from city characters into country types is not the only mode of depiction operating in the Cries of London, though it is the dominant one, formed when Cries quickly codified into a tradition depending upon motifs from continental art. A counter-tradition exists, created out of the naturalism that clings to the 'lower' genres but also forms in reaction to the romanticism of the dominant style. This alternate tradition of picturing hawkers, represented by the prints of Hogarth, Sandby and Rowlandson, is naturalistic rather than sentimental, comic rather than serious, and satiric rather than congratulatory.[55] It is also British and Lockean rather than continental in that it stems from England's empiricist heritage with its emphasis on the primacy, immediacy and reliability of sensation.[56] For good reason, Henry Fuseli complained of his English audience's preference for naturalism, observing that, in matters of art, 'Their taste and feelings all go to realities'.[57]

Casting London as the old Babylon rather than the New Jerusalem, it proposes a view of 'the people' not as noble savages nor as primitives needing to be saved but as the 'insolent rabble' and 'swinish multitude'. It trades in an encyclopedia of evils: crime, sex, drink, rage and fear, which are linked to the city as a place of iniquity true to its origins in the Bible where it is thrown up in defiance of God's order by Cain, who intended to exclude him from its boundaries.[58] The aims of the anti-picturesque tradition are to parody mainstream Cries, put their authenticity in doubt, question their intentionality, and offer more inclusive, historical views of hawkers, views less complimentary and more acrid than those of 'the rustic picturesque'. To the extent that this tradition highlights, as Sandby's images do, the violence of the outcast and the threat that they pose to their 'betters', it trades on that frisson distinguishing the masculine sublime (founded on awe and dread) from the feminine picturesque (established on variety).[59]

But this tradition also serves as a realm of artistic experiment and playful mockery not just of Cries but of social representation itself.[60] To that end, it employs fragmenting strategies in picturing setting and figure. Instead of static, well-defined spaces, expressing order and harmony, it employs busy locales in order to represent strife or crisis. Instead of passive, tame figures, it favours active, brazen subjects placed in off-centre positions and realized in sketchy styles rather than in centred arrangements done in finished manners. Instead of boxing in these figures and scenes with heavy lines, it uses unframed or lightly framed arrangements. All of the pictorial devices suggest social ambiguity, upheaval, political confrontation or instability; they are opposed by motifs suggesting social equilibrium, harmony, balance and placidness, such as elegant houses, noble monuments and classical arcades contained within elaborate, repetitive borders.[61]

Two catalysts operate to create this counter-tradition, with its astringency and anti-urbanism; one is external and social, the other internal and aesthetic. Beginning in the mid-eighteenth century, London underwent a crisis of poverty, the consequence of changes in birth and death rates, growth in population, industrialization in the city and enclosure in the country.[62] Samuel Johnson, speaking of that poverty in 1777, observed that 'The want of Food and Raiment is so common in London . . . that one who lives there has no Compassion to spare for the Wounds given only to Vanity or Softness'.[63] This pauperization lasted into the nineteenth century and spread to every shire. In 1801, when the population of England was nine million, one million people were vagrants.[64] William Cobbett, writing in 1829, contrasted England's past with England's present: previously the nation was famed 'for its good living; that is to say for the plenty in which the whole of the people lived, for the abundance of good clothing and good food which they had'. Not any more. 'Good God! How changed! Now, the very worst fed and worst clad people upon the face of the earth, those of Ireland excepted.' The nation was composed, he wrote, of poor souls 'who are detected in robbing the pig-troughs in Yorkshire; who are eating horse-flesh and grains (draff) in Lancashire and Cheshire;

who are harnessed like horses and drawing gravel in Hampshire and Sussex; who have 3d. a day allowed them by the Magistrates in Norfolk; who, all over England, are worse fed than the felon in the gaols'.[65] In the years between Johnson's reflection and Cobbett's outburst, the plight of England's indigent was so marked, widespread and acknowledged that it prescribed limits on the ways the 'lower orders' could be credibly represented in art, making saccharine interpretations of the lives of street people not simply improbable but preposterous.[66]

Wheatley's violation of the edict requiring some correspondence between social reality and its depiction is the most egregious of any artist of the Cries; it lies at the heart of art critic Anthony Pasquin's complaint that the painter fabricates his characters 'at the expense of truth'. However, even Wheatley responded to the pressure to exhibit a degree of historical accuracy, reflected in a class of mystery men and women, discordant figures who populate his pastoral print's 'dark side', to borrow a phrase made famous by John Barrell. The principal character in 'Two bunches a penny primroses' (**5.16**), an unconscious inversion of Sandby's whore from 'Sweet Nosegay' (**5.6**), is an allegory of springtime and youth. But behind this industrious flower seller and her angelic children sits a shadowy personification of indolence and melancholy who, instead of hawking, squats on a doorstep and cradles her sleepy face in her hand. The basket next to her shows she is a hawker, though she displays none of the prosperity, charm, or energy of the refined flower seller. Similar spectres haunt the backgrounds of other Wheatley Cries. Though difficult to see and still more difficult to read, these faceless apparitions seem to be sturdy beggars, indigents or idlers who follow their trade lackadaisically. In 'Knives, Scissars, and Razors to Grind' (**7.9**), the female who turns – or is turned – away from the scene of philanthropy enacted in the foreground is a mendicant or a vagrant; she carries a baby on her back just as Laroon's false pauper does in 'The London Begger' (**3.17**). The most obscure of these obscure is the stooped, anonymous figure in 'Sweet China Oranges' (**7.10**). Decipherable with great difficulty behind the Jewish orange seller, she also follows no clear calling; she looks like a beggar and a solitary one at that. Not all such figures are phantoms or females. The two unemployed chairmen who rest behind the costermonger in 'Strawberrys, scarlet Strawberrys' (**7.11**) are easier to spot but more difficult to read. Are they lazy or exhausted? Most likely, they are slackers. The vital contrast in the print is between these idle 'beasts-of-burden' and the noble Amazon whose toil, underlined by the

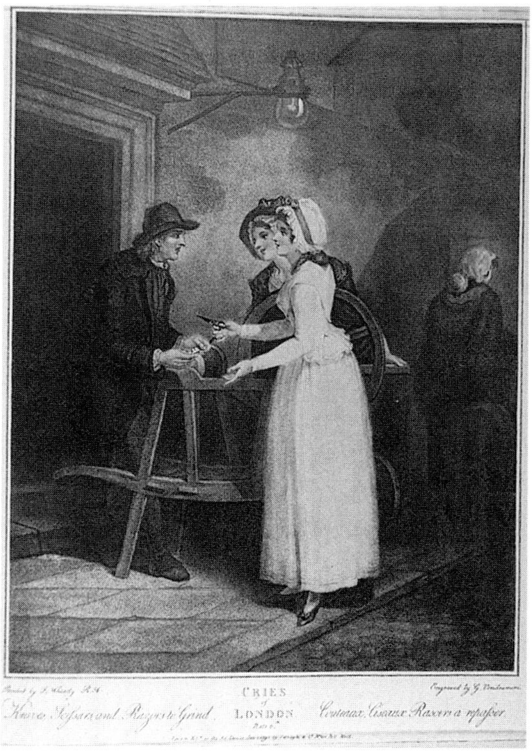

7.9 Francis Wheatley, 'Knives, Scissars, and Razors to Grind', 1795

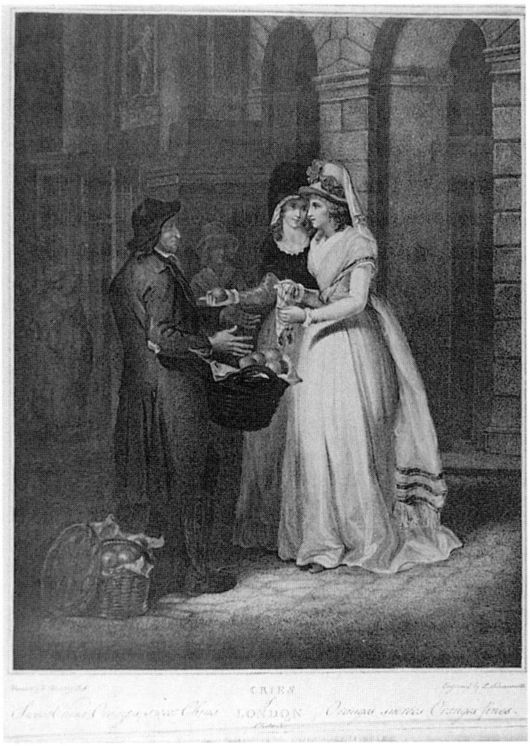

7.10 Francis Wheatley, 'Sweet China Oranges', 1794

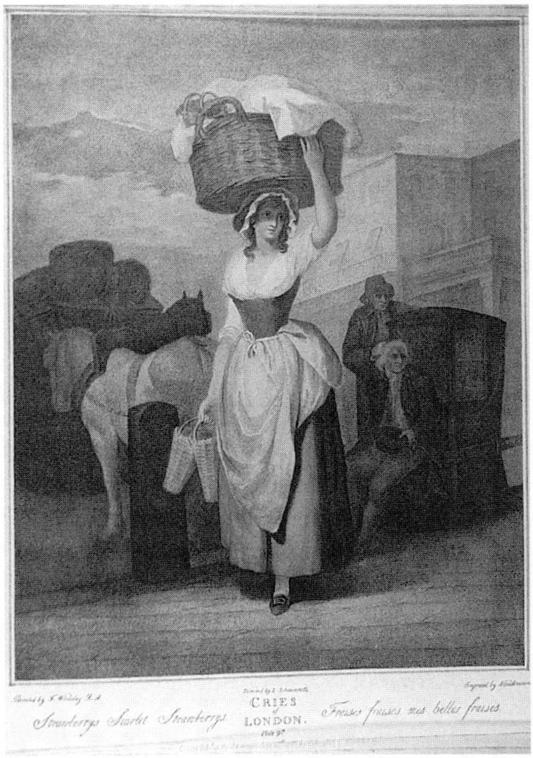

7.11 Francis Wheatley, 'Strawberrys, scarlet Strawberrys', 1795

gigantic basket resting easily on her coiffeured head, offers a charged, didactic corrective to their insouciance.

Gloomy, unsocial apparitions like the chairmen and beggar women, whom all connoisseurs would notice but none would identify with, play two roles in Wheatley's prints. They mirror the sombre realities of hawking in the 1790s more faithfully than Wheatley's vendors of love songs or strawberries. Such spectres argue that even he could not rid his *Cries* of the historical actualities of hawking. Though repressed, these melancholy actualities exerted a creative pressure on his mind that inserted the poor into the margins and backgrounds of his images where they bear witness to a history that their *alter egos*, the sellers of primroses and cherries, are at pains to deny: peddlers were destitute figures whose occupations, in the 1790s, were dying or dead.

As well as unconsciously mirroring the realities of late eighteenth-century social history, these shabby wretches deliberately provide the viewer guidance in differentiating between the two best-known classes of needy Londoners, the idle and industrious poor. Offering likenesses of the idle poor who are destitute by preference and inclination, these lonely figures stand apart from the plates' titular characters, refined beings brimming with social and economic energy who supply semblances of the industrious poor. The dissolute poor, Wheatley's *Traders* show, are recognizable by their dependent infants, lazy habits, lack of complaisance, mean dress and, in other, franker artists' Cries, their beastly natures. By contrast, the industrious are distinguishable by their labouring children, pleasant manner, domesticity, breeding, sartorial neatness, condescension and, ironically, their material sufficiency.

Generalizing from Wheatley's prints to the two traditions under discussion, the pastoral and anti-pastoral currents have the task of distinguishing between the willfully destitute who are penniless by choice or temperament and the good poor who are paupers by divine or social order. Only the poor by lot deserve sympathy and patronage. Unless this distinction is grasped, the labouring needy, who deserve the most help, will attract the least because of their tidy, prosperous appearance; worse still, the willfully sluggish, like Laroon's roguish 'London Begger' (**3.17**), will attract the most by reason of their bleak appearance, often faked, as her rags are.[67]

Among the aesthetic factors generating the London Cries' anti-pastoral tradition, the popularity and overexposure of Laroon's designs dwarf all others. Begun by unceasing republication, the proliferation of his *Cryes* continued with pirated 'Laroons' so numerous and so variously formatted – facsimile ensembles, children's books, broadsides, figurines – that they turned into clichés. Such stock motifs from the past, recycled endlessly, provoked rival native artists who created oppositional images to break with tradition and liberate the Cries by changing its conventions and directions.

Although social and aesthetic forces operating simultaneously are so intertwined that it is difficult to untangle their roles in the creation of a counter-tradition, internal catalysts surface before external. Internal stimuli appear in the drawings of Paul Sandby and the prints of Thomas Rowlandson; they also lurk in Hogarth's 'The Enraged Musician' and 'Distrest Poet', both of which depict milkmaids who are strikingly anti-arcadian.

In *Pagan Mysteries in the Renaissance*, Edgar Wind argues that, of the uncounted historical calamities to which art falls victim, one of the most disfiguring is that pictures conceived in a cyclical spirit have been handed down to us as solitary images.[68] Just such a critical misadventure has befallen 'The Distrest Poet' (**7.12**) and 'The Enraged Musician' (**4.8**), divorced not just from the Cries of London but from each other. Published a few years apart (the first in 1737 and the second in 1741), they were separated in contemporary commentaries, which track the artist's graphic works chronologically, despite the fact that, in advertising the two prints, Hogarth called them a 'Set' and identified the 'Musician' as 'a Companion to a Print, representing a Distress'd Poet'.

That the plates are a twosome appears in their espousal of the same narrow theme: hawkers' noisy intrusions upon artists. But if they share a common subject, they divide in how they realize it, using witty contrasts that grow out of the fact that the 'Musician' takes place prior to any bargain, while the 'Poet' takes place subsequent to many. The first shows a mob of vendors outside crying the street; the second a single hawker inside the house; the first occurs outside an elegant parlour on the ground floor, the second inside a squalid garret high up. The first victim is a single foreigner, the second an Englishman with a menage of wife and child, cat and kittens; the first quarry is a wealthy musician in great demand; the second a poor, neglected poet. The first customer is averse to buying, the second to paying.

Of course the pertinent contrast here is between the milkmaid from 'The Distrest Poet' and her inspiration from the *Cryes* (**7.2**). Laroon's pastoral and Hogarth's antipastoral figures are united by their May Day accessories – a big tower of silver on the head of the first, a small chain of daisies on

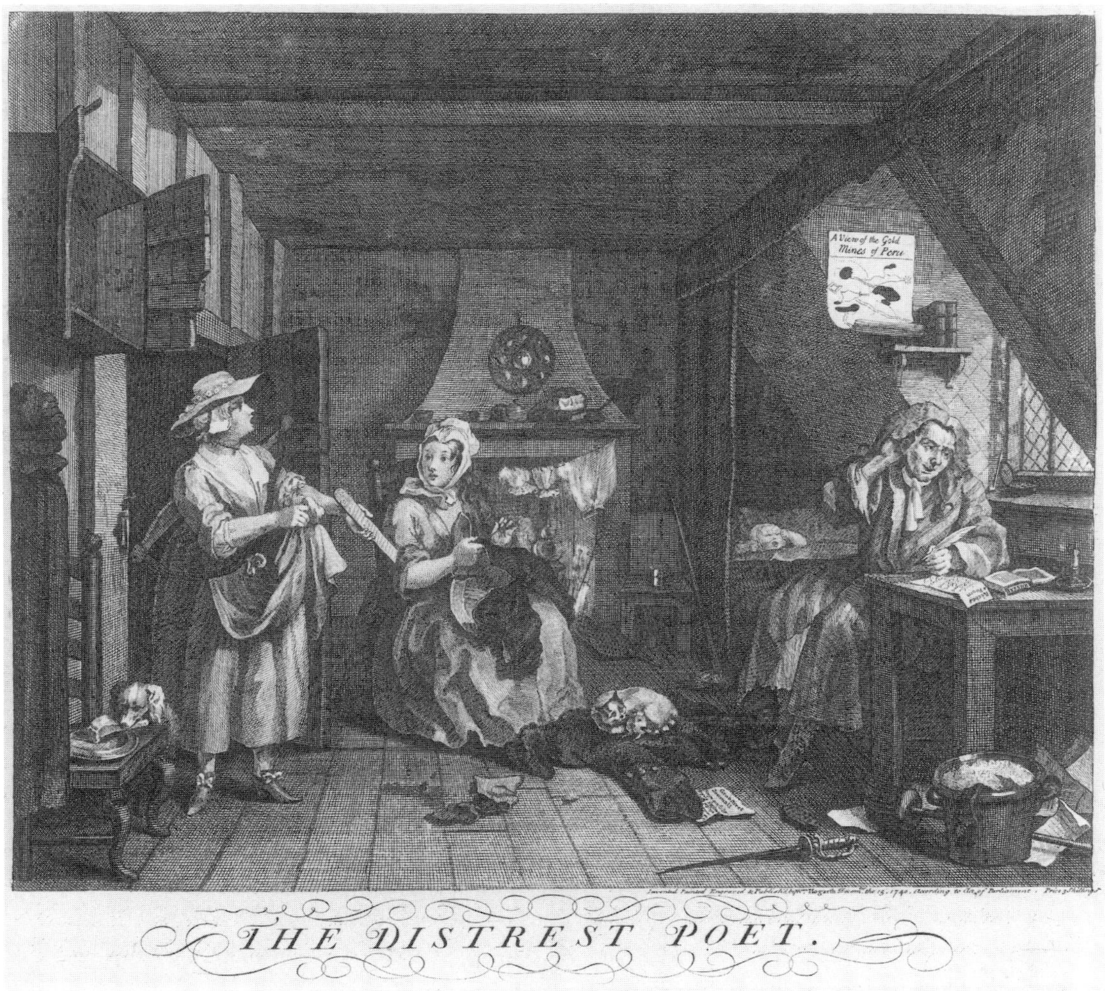

7.12 William Hogarth, 'The Distrest Poet', 1737

the hat of the second, following the older custom of milkmaids who, before 1680, garlanded themselves with flowers that they picked to declare their rural origins.[69] But they are separated by the realities that they evoke. Laroon's figure represents milk selling as dancing; her trade is play, not work. Hogarth's character shows the same business as doubly labourious; her arduous physical exertion (especially her countless climbs up countless stairs to garrets like the starving poet's) is compounded by her economic woes, requiring her to collect money from customers who possess neither present means nor future prospects. Laroon calls his elegant maid 'merry'; Hogarth's milkwife, a burly shape with a formidable voice and a termagant's disposition, is a humourless virago.

Sandby's 'Milkmaid' (**plate 10**), another dunning scene but one that is wholly original, ignores the physical exertions of milk selling to concentrate exclusively on the psychological. Hogarth's scene is panoramic and static; his milkmaid, vying with a wailing baby, broadcasts her complaint across a spacious room that distances her from the poet and his Pollyanna wife, both ignoring her. By contrast, Sandby's scene is claustrophobic, edgy and dynamic; it involves a give-and-take between a milkmaid and an agitated crone who confront each other face to face. The milkmaid presents her tally; the hag grimaces in reaction; anticipating the vendor's response to her refusal to pay, she hugs her pail pre-emptively, defending it against repossession.

Rowlandson's 'Milk' (**7.13**), one of fifty-four small designs from his *Characteristic Sketches of the Lower Orders* (1820), is a threshold scene rich in the same liminal drama and urban satire as Sandby's 'Milkmaid'. But eroticized as a private 'back door' flirtation inappropriately enacted in a public front-door setting, this London tryst is a comic English riposte to the French pastoral genre celebrating gallantry in its most ethereal forms, the *fête galante* that Boucher and Watteau popularized across Europe in the eighteenth century. As a Cries of London, it belongs with anti-pastoral designs contrasting a 'good' milkwife with a 'bad' one. The good one, a faceless drone, follows her trade undeviatingly. But her wanton sister neglects her duty, spilling her beverage and allowing a dog to guzzle from her pail, two blunders that equate gratified desire with milk.

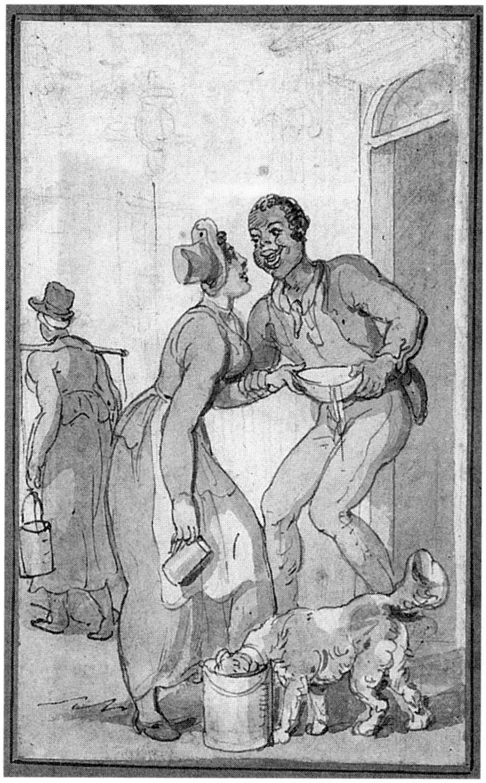

7.13 Thomas Rowlandson, 'Milk', 1820

But what is most remarkable about this disarmingly simple image, which monumentalizes the milkmaid and affirms her naughtiness by her beauty, is that it spurns the cliché of vendors as 'proverbs for endless industry' in favour of a brazen hussy.[70] The propaganda picturing hawkers who labour with superhuman intensity pleased the middling sort of print buyers who had their eye on shaping public attitudes toward work; Rowlandson embodies this conventional view in his 'good' milkmaid, an allegory of drudgery devalued formally by her remoteness and perfunctory realization. His 'bad' milkmaid mocks it – and the 'good' hawkers of Hogarth and Sandby, two apostles of irreverence here exposed as preachers of middle-class orthodoxy.

Rowlandson's *Characteristic Sketches*, the last of three Cries showing London as a theatre of human exuberance, variety and cheerful life, appeared in 1820.[71] It was answered in 1821, when Theodore Gericault's twelve lithographs, *Various Subjects Drawn from Life and on Stone: The English Set*, introduced a higher order of pessimism into

British art. Far from representing what one scholar calls a 'strange choice of subject matter', Gericault's *Various Subjects* treats urban street life in a way that makes three of its designs a London Cries in theme but not in name.[72] The set's other nine prints, extolling magnificent horses, illustrate the disintegration of Cries and the power of topical or voguish subjects to reshape or swallow up the dying genre.

Two of these lithographs by Gericault are instructive reformulations of specific hawking scenes by earlier artists. 'Pity the sorrows of a poor old Man Whose trembling limbs have borne him to your door' (**7.14**), which Richard Godfrey calls 'a grim corrective to the playful English prints of *London Cries*', challenges two previous threshold dramas.[73] It answers the effervescent optimism of Rowlandson's 'Milk' (**7.13**) and intensifies the gloomy contrast between housed and homeless in Sandby's 'Rare Mackerel' (**plate 4**). But its closest parallel is with his 'Wine Seller'

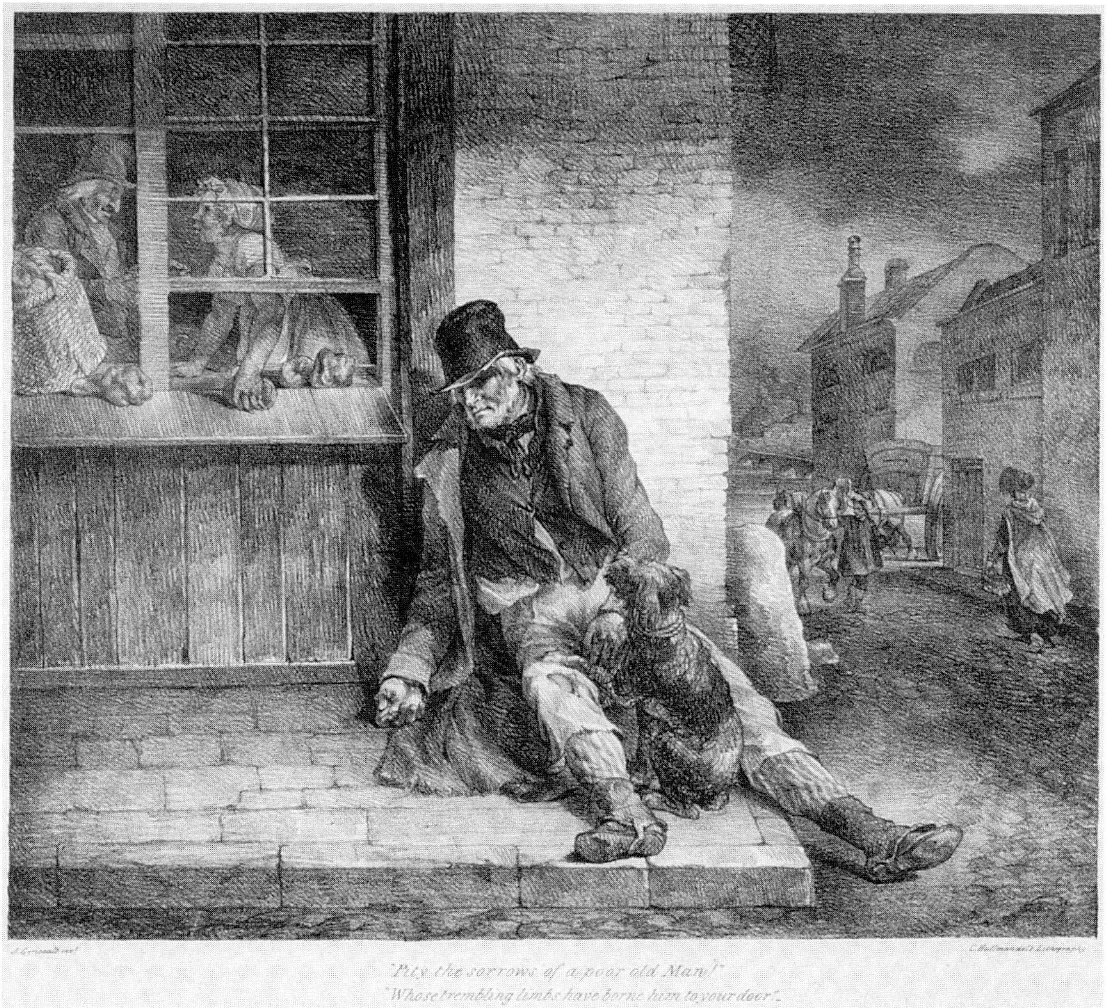

7.14 Theodore Gericault, 'Pity the sorrows of a poor old Man', 1821

(**plate 9**), which also treats the theme of bibulous hawkers. Replacing Sandby's fetching, tipsy girl with a falling-down drunk, 'Pity the sorrows' records with cold naturalism the ritual self-humiliation of a sot who rolls in the gutter.[74] Juxtaposing a foreground with people against a background with horses, it also offers a Swiftian perspective hinting at the superiority of noble, hardworking dray-animals over idle, degenerate humans.[75]

Gericault's 'Piper' (**7.15**), showing a blind musician who plays unheard amidst a foggy wasteland of crumbling masonry, is tied to

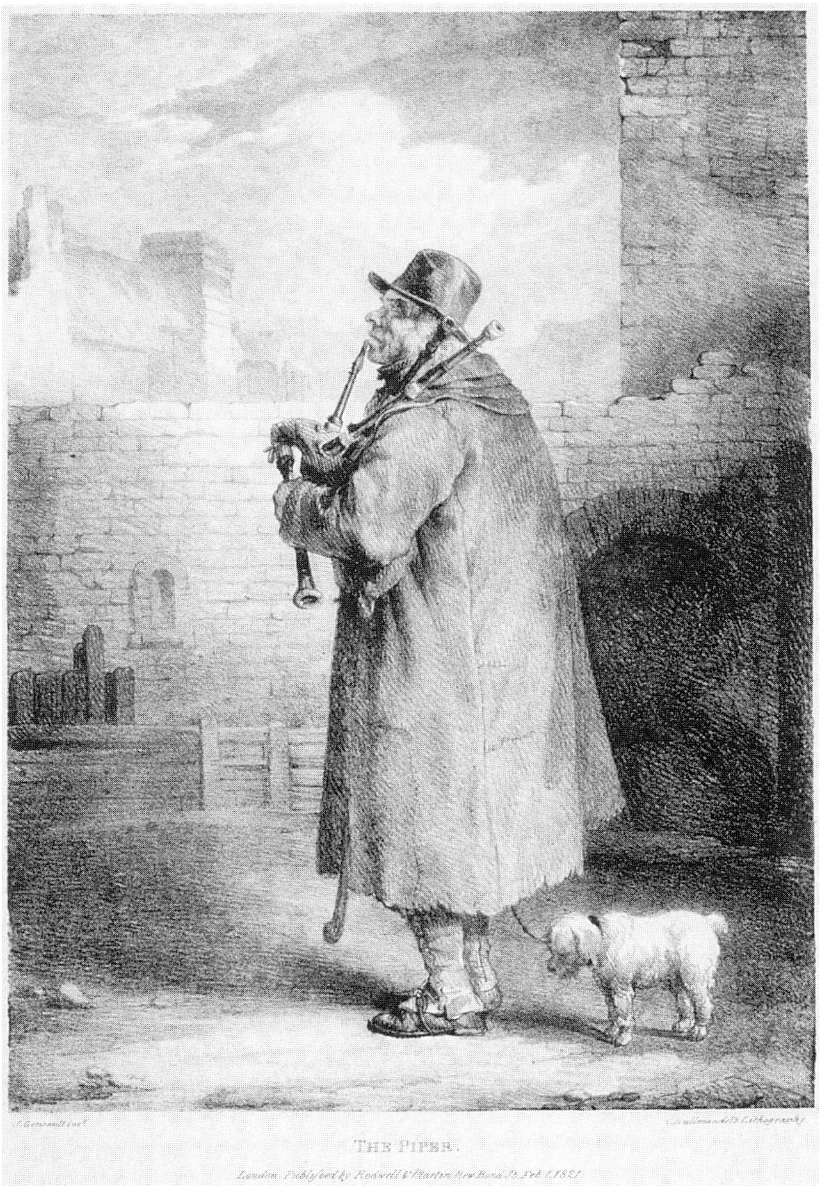

7.15 Theodore Gericault, 'The Piper', 1821

'Pity the sorrows' in its oddly statuesque, even heroic portrayal of an aged man whose only link in life is to his tiny dog, though this poodle's indifference to its master ridicules other artist's depiction of such pets as the faithful companions of peddlers.[76] But this portrait of a wretched musician playing a wind instrument is tied even closer to another independent print with the same subject, 'The Enraged Musician' (**4.8**). Despite its similar anti-pastoral mood centred on a similar piper, however, it reduces Hogarth's identifiable London background to rubble, pares his energetic mob down to one motionless figure and replaces his sympathetic comedy with indifference and despair.

Gericault's two lithographs embody a consciousness that is decisively modern, linked to defeat, failure of purpose, loss of meaning and oblivion – the drunk man is also on death's doorstep.[77] Expressing their creator's astonishment at the misery of London's poor and 'the black horror' of its slums in 1821, they take the depiction of back streets and back-street characters as far in the direction of anti-nostalgia as any artist does, perhaps as far as it can go and still pretend to aesthetic purpose or hope to win buyers among the respectable classes of the nineteenth century.[78] The apocalyptic tone expressed in both lithographs' backgrounds, which reek of industrial ruin, is intensified by their technical monotony, boredom and incoherence. Even form itself seems threatened in these antipicturesque designs in which pictorial structure exposes fundamental assumptions about society and its urban outcasts. In these willfully vapid designs, the city and the human condition are in ruins, devoid of order and without purpose.

By how they combine technical arbitrariness, sensational themes and what Celina Fox calls 'unprecedented objectivity', they illuminate the path that Cries blaze for a new, international class of images: documentary photographs of criminals, the physically abnormal, the retarded, lunatics, prostitutes, tramps and the most bizarrely ironic of all modern street figures, bag ladies. These women carry all their worldly goods in brand-name sacks that make them look like they are prototypical consumers out on a shopping spree. Beginning with Laroon, all these outcasts are housed in Cries, which stereotype them.[79] In the 1840s, they are relocated to European and American documentary photographs enjoying the fresh authority of the empirical.[80] It is a short step from likenesses of prostitutes wearing clothes and walking the street to images of prostitutes naked in brothels. Such 'soft-core' photographs might, for want of a better name, be called forensic pornography. They are exemplified by the work of the Frenchman Eugéne Atget, whose photographs of streetwalkers and brothel women were used to 'extra' illustrate Cesare Lombroso's *Criminal Woman and the Prostitute* (1896).[81] Atget is associated with pictures of empty Parisian streets, said to evoke crime scenes.[82] But about 1900, he also shot eighty street traders in likenesses that he composed, edited and organized in a style self-consciously shaped by the pictorial tradition of Cries.[83] In a circuitous but logical regression, his basket seller, who bears a family likeness to other basket sellers from other Cries (the band box man in Craig's *Trades*, for example), migrated from a photograph back to a line drawing; it was republished, with a number of other designs, in Roger Marx and Tristan Klingsor's *Petits métiers de rues de Paris* (1904).[84]

It is an equally short step from likenesses of living criminals to 'mug shots' of dead criminals – and their corpse-strewn crime scenes, recorded in banal police photographs taken in America and England.[85] Many of these 'scientific' images of nameless bandits and outcasts were shot by equally nameless photographers working for the law, medicine and social institutions demanding evidence, documentation and surveillance. Such functions, expressing a drive to impose a close-meshed net of control on society, are latent in the earliest broadside Cries and manifest in the images and texts of Mayhew.[86] Other photographs in this class were snapped by artists who are household names. Among the best known are the American documentarians Richard Avedon and Diane Arbus. Avedon's *In the American West 1979–1984*, like Laroon's *Cryes*, eliminates all evidence of location by shooting its subjects before a studio backdrop in order to monumentalize, render as archetypes and ultimately elegize the 'men and women who work at hard uncelebrated jobs, the people who are often ignored and overlooked'.[87] Arbus's *Untitled*, published in 1995 after her suicide, describes how she found her 'most transcendent and consistently romantic vision' in photographing 'freaks', whom she described as 'born with their trauma. They've already passed it. They're aristocrats'.[88] Arbus was interested in people 'nobody else would see unless she photographed them', according to her daughter Doon; but she was also concerned about the experience of seeing and the power of images to affect by making the hidden visible.[89] All such images, whether by Gericault, the 'naïve' Atget, the fashionable Avendon, Arbus, or the nameless forensic photographers making 'dead gangster' shots, are a heritage of Cries, a postmodern branch, in which artists represent the poor and powerless to the rich and powerful. Licensed by the first ensembles hawkers, these photographs too engage in titillation, voyeurism, tourism, exoticism, psychologism, anthropology and careerism, offering a forlorn, grisly picture of life, which they present both as bizarre and as familiar, like nightmares.[90]

No doubt the prints of Gericault, Rowlandson, Sandby, and Hogarth picture London and its lower orders more faithfully than those of Laroon, Wheatley and Craig. But the designs of the more extreme pessimists, especially Sandby and Gericault, repulsed the middling sort of collector seeking delight or reassurance in art intended for drawing rooms and parlour walls. That problem is registered self-consciously by Gericault in his 'Paraleytic Woman' (**7.16**), in which a mother, her face reflecting disgust mingled with morbid fascination, gapes involuntarily at a cripple in a wheelchair pushed by a bestial attendant. Depictions of Londoners as diseased and degraded, together with those of the city as a place of physical horrors, especially crime and death – the 'Paraleytic Woman' is sandwiched between a prison and a hearse – are the least popular images in the history of the Cries. Such images show that traditional Cries were not longer viable in the nineteenth century and pinpoint a fatal crisis in the history of a genre offering images of the urban poor that repelled newly assertive bourgeois audiences. Artists seldom flourish in any mode but the celebratory, a law of aesthetic commerce Laroon and Wheatley followed but Sandby and Gericault scorned, to their cost.[91]

Among Cries, the failed appeal of naturalistic designs may also result from their unfamiliar and experimental imagery. By contrast, the enduring popularity of idealized compositions may result from their ahistorical iconography, with its power to comfort and reassure. English Cries, like their continental ancestors, quickly solidify into a tradition

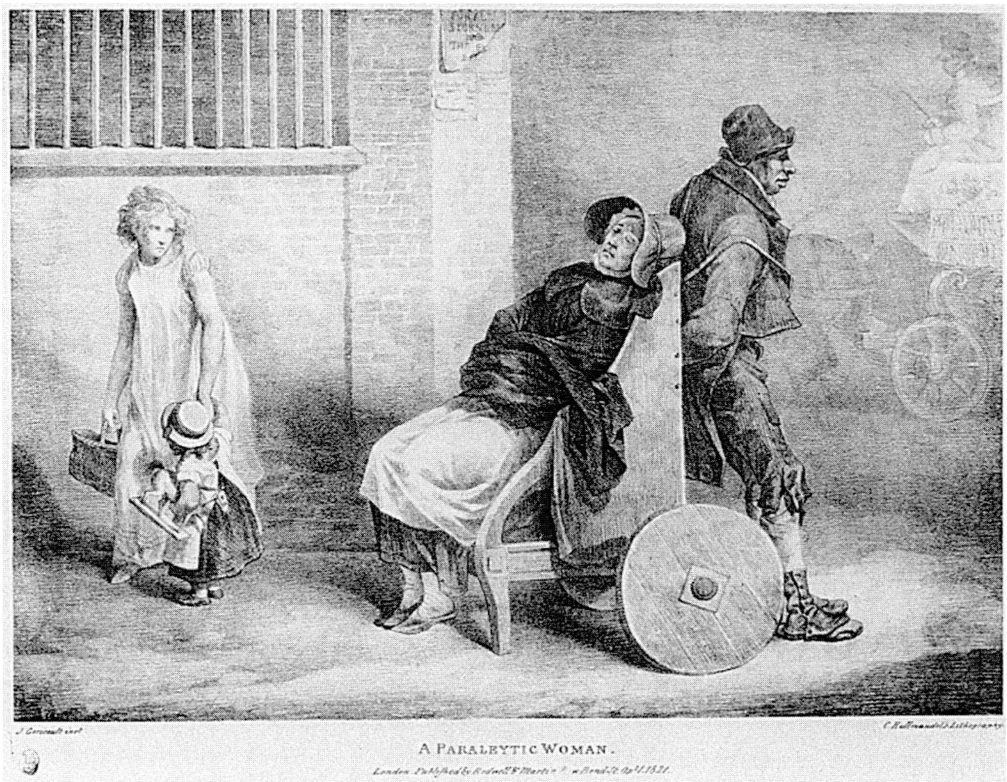

7.16 Theodore Gericault, 'A Paraleytic Woman', 1821

dominated by Laroon leading to Wheatley. Its canon is full of quasi-mythic figures with distant ties to hawking but close links to each other and to the mental life of print buyers eager to see the chaos and noise of street commerce transformed into processions of pacified, isolated figures wearing lovely costumes, selling needful or exotic wares and crying poetic shouts. The most successful of such compositions offer images of cyclical rituals and nostalgic drills in which history is absent and time stands still, as in Busby's 'Milk Girl' (**7.17**). This design's retrospective mood and family resemblance to other milkmaids offer the reassurance called for in a time of change, when hawking was in fast decay. Picturing the milk vendor as an archaic, charming and docile throwback to feudalism, this rural figure, whose passive attitude belies her strenuous calling, is an ideal antidote to the restless urban proletariat created in growing numbers by the Industrial Revolution when Busby's *Costume* (*c.* 1819) appeared.

Described by its creator as 'painted and engraved from nature', the image is shaped by an awareness of earlier milkmaids and represents an improvement of Boitard's improvement of Laroon's 'merry Milk Maid' (**4.11**). Busby's design keeps Boitard's front pose, big eyes, coy face, and big breasts bursting out of the same laced bodice, but it improves on its prototype by updating the milkmaid's costume to 1820s styles, especially the smart hat and elegant boots. Busby's portrait recuperates Laroon's preindustrial

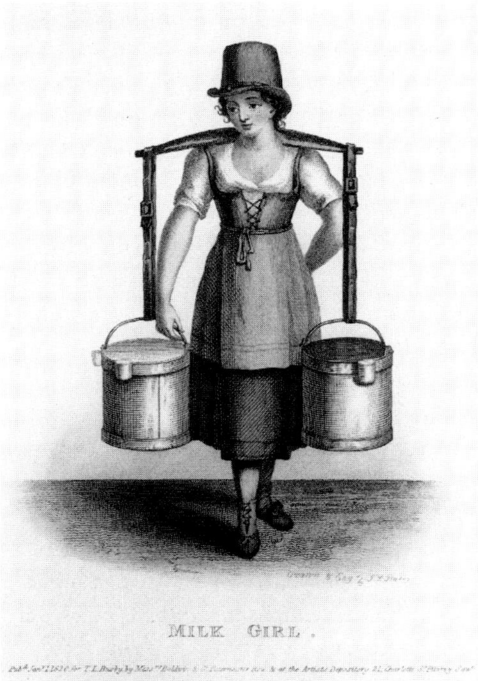

7.17 Thomas Busby, 'Milk Girl' from *Costume of the Lower Orders*, *c.* 1819

original – the mother of all merry milkmaids – in how its figure forgoes idle play to labour sweetly beneath her yoke, an atavistic device that casts her as 'sister to the ox' and justifies calling the image 'feudal'.

This view of hawkers as serf-like, industrious, rural and picturesque, together with the linked conception of the capital as a 'town-in-the-garden', is not unique to Cries. It surfaces in Addison's *Spectator*, whose Will Honeycomb prefers hawkers' voices 'to the sound of larks, and nightingales, with all the music of the fields and woods'.[92] The same view receives more elaborate expression in John Gay's *Trivia or the Art of Walking the Streets of London* (1716), arguably English literature's prototypical urban poem and its half-ironical, half-celebrative contribution to that genre called 'in praise of cities'.[93] Gay escorts the reader in a witty progress that moves through the four seasons of the year, harmonizing the rhythms of nature with the cycles of the liturgical calendar with the shouts of London's hawkers. Posing as a connoisseur of city life, the poet links these shouts, described in colourful Theocritan imagery, with health, plenty, gain and festivity. The following lines are cited from an advertisement that quoted the poem to promote Wheatley's London Cries:

Successive Crys the Season's Change declare,
And mark the Monthly Progressive of the Year.
Hark how the Streets with treble Voices ring,
To sell the bounteous Product of the Spring!
Sweet smelling Flow'rs and Elder's early Bud
With Nettle's tender Shoots, to cleanse the Blood:
And when June's Thunder cools the sultry Skies
Ev'n *Sundays* are prophan'd by Mackrell Cries
Wallnuts the Fruit'rer's Hand in Autumn, stain
Blue Plumbs, and juicy Pears augment his Gain;
Next Oranges the longing Boys entice,
To trust their Copper-Fortunes to the Dice.
When Rosemary and Bays, the Poet's Crown
Are bawl'd, in frequent Cries, through all the Town,
Then judge the festival of *Christmas* near,
Christmas, the joyous Period of the Year.[94]

Perhaps Gay and his readers, together with Laroon, his disciples such as Busby and Wheatley and their viewers, relished the city best when it was least urban. Riveted to the streets of London amidst what Dickens calls 'the rising clash and roar of the day's struggle', print makers and poets reinvented the capital so their publisher's urban audiences might see in it a perfect rural past rather than an increasingly gloomy, brutal present.[95] What publishers, engravers or versifiers sold and audiences bought in the city of the Cries was not the metropolis they knew, but a more perfect reflection – holier, purer, softer, more Elysian.[96]

In this mythical spot, opposites reconcile. Labour goes in *mufti* as leisure; the marginal mix with the middle; and the rich, who are not cruel or corrupt, succour the poor, who are not lazy or bitter. Here the whirling, populous city shades into the Edenic, ennobled countryside; and nature, in a mood of prelapsarian bounty, heaps walnuts, blue plums and juicy pears on figures who are indistinguishably rural fruiterers and urban hawkers. Inevitably, this conceit leads from the artful to the imaginary and the surreal; it metamorphoses London hawkers into fantasies like the Jewish 'Old Clothesman' (**7.18**), 'The Fruiterer' (**7.19**), the shocking 'Orange Merchant' (**7.20**), and the other droll types who populate Charles Tilt's *Figures of Fun* (1833). Powered by a retreat from the social, such exuberant caprices demonstrate that, in the nineteenth century, when other nations turned commercial, urban, industrial or revolutionary, England remained a green and pleasant land.

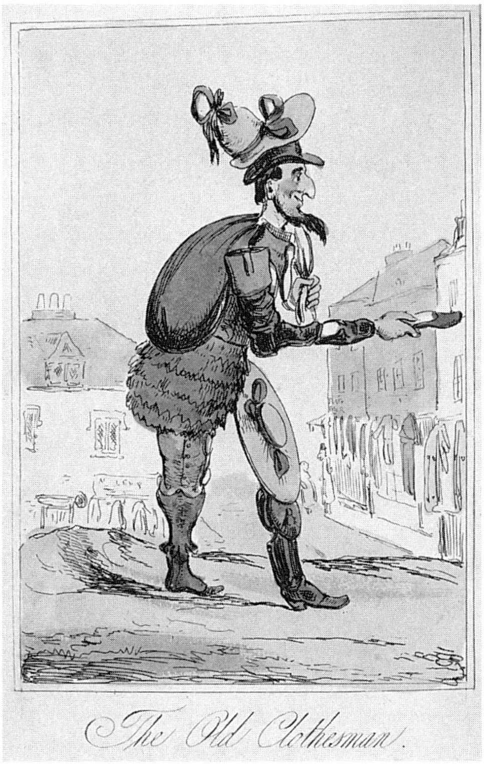

7.18 Charles Tilt, 'The Old Clothesman', 1833

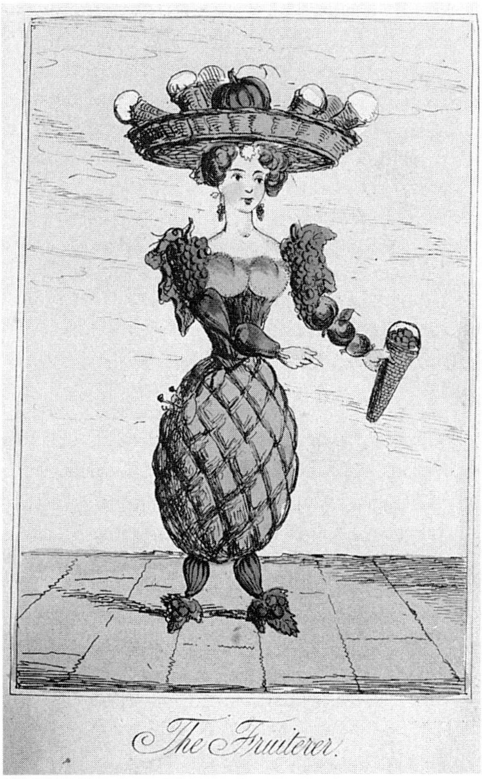

7.19 Charles Tilt, 'The Fruiterer', 1833

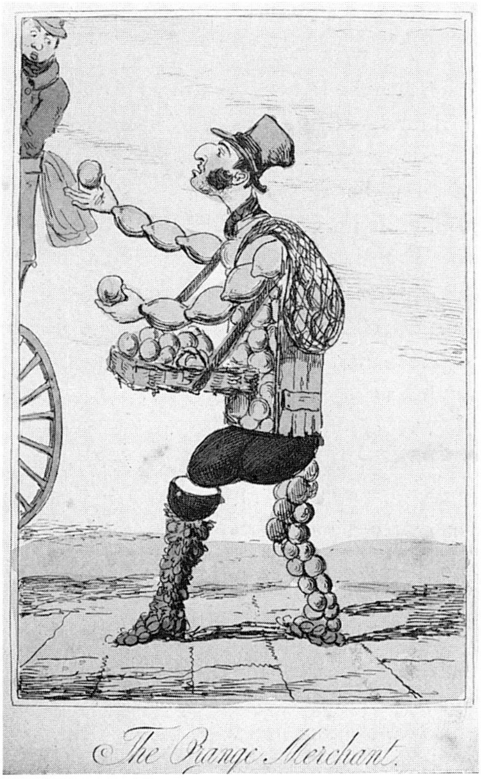

7.20 Charles Tilt, 'The Orange Merchant', 1833

Notes

Chapter 1

1 See, for example, the advertisement for Yardley toiletries 'as timeless as a woman's beauty', in 'Purveyors of the practical & hard-to-find', *The Vermont Country Store* (Christmas 2000), p. 80. See also the text that accompanies jams and teas from Blake House Farm, Blake End, Gt Saling, Essex, UK.

2 For clarity, I use 'Cries' as the plural and 'the Cries' as the singular form of this noun.

3 Karen Jones, 'Street cries in pictures', *The Quarterly Journal of the Library of Congress*, 25 (1968), 10; the latest example of hawkers in art I know of is Bob Pullen's *London Street People Past and Present*; issued in London by Lennard Publishing in 1989, it contrasts nineteenth-century with twentieth-century photos of the same kinds of traders.

4 For American Cries, see d'Alte Welch, *Bibliography of American Children's Books* (Worcester: American Antiquarian Society, 1972), pp. 76–80.

5 Vincent Milliot, *Les Cris de Paris out le peuple travesti* (Paris: Publications de la Sorbonne, 1985), pp. 98–112.

6 Hellmut Lehmann-haupt, *The Book of Trades in the Iconography of Social Typology* (Boston: Boston Public Library, 1976), p. 8; 'the humblest classes' is used by John Phillips in his *Itinerant Characters: Drawn and Etched from Life*, published by William Darton in 1829.

7 These classes of buyers and sellers are drawn from the print catalogues of Rudolph Ackermann (*A Catalogue of Various Prints* [1805]) and Robert Sayer (*New and Enlarged Catalogue for the Year 1766*).

8 For a different way of classifying Cries, see Milliot, *Cris de Paris*, p. 84.

9 Laroon's *Cryes* has two title pages, one featuring a woman and the other a man, as if to emphasize the gendered nature of its portraits.

10 Walter Besant, *London in the Time of the Stuarts* (London: Black, 1903), p. 122. The antiquarian Andrew Tuer mentions such a collection, especially splendid, which I seek to trace. It belonged to a Mr J. E. Gardner who possessed prints and drawings illustrating London that numbered 'considerably over 120,000', many illustrating Cries (Andrew Tuer, *Old London Street Cries* [London, 1885], p. 7).

11 Sheila O'Connell, *The Popular Print in England* (London: British Museum Press, 1999), p. 210. O'Connell asks if such differences are due to variations in national print production or intellectual interests. For a useful survey of the scholarship on popular French, German, Netherlandish and Italian prints, see O'Connell, pp. 218–22.

12 Tessa Watt, *Cheap Print and Popular Piety 1550–1640* (Cambridge: Cambridge University Press, 1991); Keith Moxey, *Peasants, Warriors and Wives Popular Imagery in the Reformation* (Chicago: University of Chicago Press, 1989); Dwight Miller, *Street Criers and Itinerant Tradesmen in European Prints* (Stanford: Department of Art, 1970); Celina Fox, *Londoners* (London: Thames and Hudson, 1987), p. 156 and following; Karen Beall, *Cries and Itinerant Trades Kaufrufe und Strassenhändler* (Hamburg: Hauswedell, 1975). In contrast to English Cries, continental prints showing hawkers and street types, especially the Cries of Paris, have never fallen out of sight or favour. The labours of French writers like Robert Massin and especially Vincent Milliot, whose useful book has a detailed bibliography of that scholarship, have done much to prevent Cries from being ignored by popular and scholarly audiences.

13 On defining the broadside, see David Landau and Peter Parshall, *The Renaissance Print 1470–1550* (New Haven: Yale University Press, 1994), p. 169.

14 Pepys's collection of London Cries has been elegantly republished as *The Cryes of London* (Old Hall Press, 1994) with a helpful introduction by Richard Luckett.

15 Landau and Parshall, *Renaissance Print*, p. 2.

16 For the link boy's ties to the erotic, see Richard Wendorf, *Sir Joshua Reynolds: The Painter in Society* (Cambridge, MA: Harvard University Press, 1996), p. 157. These images are preserved uncut in the Lewis Walpole Library, Farmington, Connecticut.

17 The book is dated from a notice in *The Public Advertiser* (London) on 21 December 1754; this advertisement also records the fact that the book's images were sold in several different formats.

18 Thomas Busby, 'Owen Clancey', in *Costume of the Lower Orders* (London, 1820).

19 For Cries formatted as jigsaws and panoramas, see Richard Balzer, *Peepshows: A Visual History* (New York: Abrams, 1998), figure 116; and Linda Hannas, *The English Jigsaw Puzzle 1760–1890* (London: Wayland, 1972), figure 24. Hannas records Cries in jigsaw form by Thomas H. Jones, William Parson, N. Carpenter and an unknown publisher.

20 Karl Marx, *Marx–Engels: Selected Works* (London: Lawrence and Wishart, 1951), 1:267.

21 For example, rat catchers would seem to be people of low social status; but James I had an official rat catcher in 1623 whom he paid 8d a day. Robert Smith, the self-styled 'rat-catcher to Princess Amelia', was an author as well as the publisher of *The Universal Directory for Taking Alive and Destroying Rats, and all other kinds of four-footed and winged vermin, in a manner hitherto unattempted: calculated for the use of the gentleman, the farmer, and the warrener* (London: the Author, 1768).

22 Joseph Townsend, *A Dissertation on the Poor Laws by a Well-Wisher to Mankind* [1786] (Berkeley: University of California Press, 1971), p. 35.

23 A. L. Beier, *Masterless Men: The Vagrancy Problem in England 1560–1640* (London: Methuen, 1985), p. 96.

24 The distinction between God's poor and the devil's is Richard Younge's in *The Poores Advocate* (London, 1654), chapters 14, 9.

25 *Statutes of the Realm*, 11 vols, London, 1810–28, 14 Eliz. c. 5; 39 Eliz. c. 4.

26 Kenneth Rogers, *Old London: Cornhill, Threadneedle Street and Lombard Street* (London: Whitefriars Press, 1935), p. 43.

27 For a historical study of the dishonest trades in central European tradition, see Werner Danckert's *Unehrliche Leute: Die verfemten Berue* (Bern: Francke Verlag, 1963).

28 Beier, *Masterless Men*, p. xxi.

29 Robert Cleaver, *A Plaine and Familiar Exposition of the Ten Commandments* (London, 1628), p. 238.

30 In *The Compleat Tradesman or the Exact Dealers Companion* (London, 1864), the pseudononymous author N. H. terms hawking a trade few sober men meddle with (p. 46). It was never far from begging or stealing (Robin Myers and Michael Harris, *Spreading the Word: The Distribution Networks of Print 1550–1850* (Winchester: St Paul, 1990), p. 89).

31 George Cruikshank, *The Cries of London* (London, n.d.), p. vi.

32 The hierarchies of the outcast are recorded by Thomas Wright in *The Great Unwashed* (London, 1868) and by other early sociologists before him.

33 William King, *A Journey to London in the Year 1698* (London, 1698), p. 2 (emphasis in original text).

34 Laurence Fontaine notes that in the Victorian period, if peddlers stopped at a middle-class home, they did so to sell to the maid or manservant (*History of Pedlars in Europe* (Durham: Duke University Press, 1996), p. 89). Tuer calls a costermonger named Bill Sykes, 'A benefactor to the poorer portion of humanity' (p. 46).

35 Joseph Lancaster, *Improvements in Education, as it Respects the Industrious Classes of the Community* (London, 1805), pp. 5–6. Patricia Crane brought this important quote to my attention.

36 'Lord' George Sanger, *Seventy Years a Showman* (London: Dent, 1926), pp. 190–1.

37 Henry Mayhew, *London Labour and the London Poor* (London, 1851–62), 4:17–27 (emphasis in original text).

38 Holme's print illustrates his *Academy of Armory*, a cosmography translating the creatures of the world into the forms of heraldry.

39 Harold Perkin, *Origins of Modern English Society* (New York: Routledge, 1991), p. 26; for another Cruikshank image depicting England's social classes in a similar vein, see his 'Corinthian Capital', engraved as a frontispiece to Pierce Egan's *Life in London*.

40 The exception is the milkmaid, who ranked two grades above other street vendors.

41 For a reading of this print, see Guilland Sutherland, 'Cruikshank and London', in Ira B. Nadel and F. S. Schwarzbach, *Victorian Artists and the City* (Oxford: Pergamon Press, 1980), p. 109.

42 I am indebted to Jeff Rosen ('Posed as rogues: The crisis of photographic realism in John Thomson's *Street Life in London*', *Image*, 36 (1993), 9–10) for showing me the Cruikshank print. Cruikshank's tiers employ the same niches as the first London Cries.

43 O'Connell, *Popular Print in England*, p. 62.

44 For a discussion of this topic, see Janet Malcolm, 'The real thing', *NYRB*, 44 (9 January 1997), 12–16.

45 Roy Strong, *Recreating the Past: British History and the Victorian Painter* (New York: Pierpont Morgan Library, 1978), p. 36.

46 Henry Angelo, *Reminiscences of Henry Angelo* (London, 1830), 2:224.

47 For a discussion of this theme, see Carole Fabricant, 'Response of Carole Fabricant to Warren Montag's comment', *Eighteenth-Century Fiction*, 9 (1997), 337–41.

48 Dror Wahrman, *Imagining the Middle Class: The Political Representation of Class in Britain c. 1780–1840* (New York: Cambridge University Press, 1995), p. 6.

49 The phrase 'sexually possessable' is Griselda Pollock's, 'Van Gogh and the poor slaves: Images of rural labour as modern art', *Art History*, 11 (1988), 412.

50 For a full discussion of these issues, see Marilyn Brown's book (to which I am indebted), *Gypsies and Other Bohemians* (Ann Arbor: UMI, 1985), pp. 24–32.

51 Cruikshank, *Cries of London*, p. iv.

52 Edmund Burke, *Reflections on the Revolution in France* (London, 1789), 3:296.

53 Sheila McTighe, 'Perfect deformity, ideal beauty, and the *Imaginaire* of work: The reception of Annibale Carracci's *Arte di Bologna* in 1646', *Oxford Art Journal*, 16 (1993), 75.

54 When Sir Henry Wotton, in Venice, had to be found in a hurry, the messenger sought him first – and found him – in a print and book stall, where he had gone to chat and buy (Leona Rostenberg, *English Publishers in the Graphic Arts 1599–1700* (New York: Burt Franklin, 1963), p. ix).

55 In this survey, I locate Cries in the history of the print written by Timothy Clayton. I am especially indebted to Clayton's *The English Print* (New Haven: Yale University Press, 1997) at the start of chapters 3, 4 and 5, where I closely follow his account of the development and evolution of popular art. I am also indebted to Anthony Griffiths's *The Print in Stuart Britain 1603–1689* (London: British Museum Press, 1998) and Landau and Parshall's *Renaissance Print*, mines of information on my topic.

56 Milliot, *Cris de Paris*, p. 127.

57 Griffiths, 'Preface' in O'Connell, *Popular Print*, p. 6.

58 This definition of 'ecphrasis' is drawn from the *OED*.

59 Mark Hallett, *The Spectacle of Difference: Graphic Satire in the Age of Hogarth* (New Haven and London: Yale University Press, 1999), p. 82.

Chapter 2

1 A. M. Hind, *Engraving in England in the Sixteenth and Seventeenth Centuries: Part 1 The Tudor Period; Part 2 The Reign of James I; Part 3 The Reign of Charles I*, ed. Margery Corbett and M. Norton (Cambridge: Cambridge University Press, 1952–62), pp. 64–7.

2 In assuming that engraved Cries (E2 and E3) by foreign craftsmen appeared before woodcut Cries (E7 and E8) by native English artists, I follow Beall, *Cries and Itinerant Trades*, pp. 116–22.

3 The term 'copper scratcher' is quoted by Diana Donald in *The Age of Caricature* (New Haven: Yale University Press for the Paul Mellon Centre for Studies in British Art, 1996), p. 2, and goes back to one of Gillray's commentators.

4 Robert Walton, 'An advertisement of several things that are made and sold by Rob. Walton at the Globe and Compasses' (London, n.d.). Oxford, Bodleian Library, Gough Maps 46, fo. 169 (emphasis in original text).

5 Mary Webster contrasts Carracci's 'more imaginative and pictorial' designs with 'the simple woodcuts issued in England' (*Francis Wheatley* (London: Routledge and Kegan Paul, 1970), p. 82).

6 Quoted in Griffiths, *Print in Stuart Britain*, p. 72.

7 F. P. Wilson, 'Illustrations of social life II: Street cries', *Shakespeare Survey*, 13 (1960), 108.

8 On the print trade at this time, see Griffiths, *Print in Stuart Britain*, pp. 13–14.

9 For the development of print selling, see Landau and Parshall, *Renaissance Print*, p. 298.

10 Milliot, *Cris de Paris*, p. 118.

11 For the bellman as an allegorical figure in popular ballads, see Watt, *Cheap Print*, pp. 113–14. The account of the bellman's job comes from 'Reading Records', in *Diary of the Corporation*, ed. J. M. Guilding (London, 1896), 3:308. I follow Beall in designating this print the earliest Cries of London (*Cries and Itinerant Trades*, p. 118).

12 As a rule of thumb by which to date, I propose that the more self-referential information they contain and the bigger their peddlers, the later they were published. By 'self-referential information', I mean facts about the sheets' creation, production and sale: artists' names, booksellers' addresses and sheets' prices or dates. When these factors are in conflict, as they are with respect to 'The Common Cryes of London', I rank self-referential information as more important than size.

13 Fox, *Londoners*, p. 156; she rightly argues that this sheet 'would seem to be the earliest extant London series of *Cries*' (156). Corbett and Norton (Hind, *Engraving in England Part III*, p. 5) think it is based on a woodcut from the reign of James I;

C. P. Maurenbrecher (*Europaische Kaufrufe* (Dortmund: Harenberg Kommunikation, 1980), 1:152) dates it to 1630; Beall, (*Cries and Itinerant Trades*, E4) locates it in the early seventeenth century.

14 I base the earlier date on the idea that the Hogenberg influence could hardly have lingered thirteen years before finding expression.

15 Back on the continent after his English excursion, Franz Hogenberg etched and scraped the Cries of Cologne (1589) with figures that, in volume, statuesque pose and expressive gesture, resemble the hawkers in the first English Cries.

16 Watt, *Cheap Print*, 353; Frederic Antal's *Hogarth and His Place in European Art* (New York: Basic Books, 1962), p. 230, dates this woodcut to the reign of James I (1566–1625). Watt's date for Pepys's impression of this woodcut is 1610, which means that it was printed before its owner was born. On the English style of these prints, see Roy Strong, *English Icon: Elizabethan and Jacobean Portraiture* (London: Paul Mellon Centre for the Study of British Art, 1969), 3ff.

17 Alexander Globe records an advertisement for it with the title 'Parte of the Criers of London' (6.1) in 1653 (*Peter Stent London Printseller circa 1642–1665* (Vancouver: University of British Columbia Press), p. 122). This design too is a plagiary; its 'chmiennie sweper', dressed in distinctive English rags, derives from the same hawker in Pepys's 'Cryer'. Pirating to exploit demand for a popular design must be carried out before that design's fame evaporates; so this engraving may have originated as early as *c.* 1610–20, a decade or so after its prototype.

18 Milliot, *Cris de Paris*, pp. 96, 112.

19 The earliest English collector of Cries was the second Earl of Ellesmere, whose *Manner of Crying Things in London* (the Earl's own made-up title inscribed in his hand *c.* 1640) is preserved in the Huntington, San Marino.

20 Two happy exceptions are Fox's *Londoners*, which devotes a full chapter to Cries, and Watt's *Cheap Print*, which does treat broadsides but not Cries in particular.

21 Charles Hindley has written *A History of the Cries of London*, 2nd edn (London, 1884), but this antiquarian book, published in 1884 in a revised, expanded second edition, is rambling and digressive, though it has useful illustrations (which, unfortunately, are not dated, attributed or documented). The book's important social information is its chief strength. In her *Londoners*, Celina Fox offers a fine account of why Cries were produced at all; I am indebted to chapter 7 of her book, 'Street Traders'.

22 John Brewer and Roy Porter (eds), *Consumption and the World of Goods* (London: Routledge, 1993), carries one image of hawking, which is unattributed and French: 'Selling to the populuxe [*sic*] market: the *colporteur*'.

23 For the price of prints in the seventeenth century, see Globe, *Peter Stent*, pp. 26–33, especially p. 28. For the price of ballads, see Joy Wittenberg, *Disorderly Women and Female Power* (Charlottesville: University of Virginia Press, 1992), pp. 28–41, and Watt, *Cheap Print*, pp. 11–12.

24 See Peter Stent's 'Catalogue of books, pictures, and maps' of 1662, Appendix A, aV. Bodleian Library, Oxford.

25 Phelps Brown and Shelia V. Hopkins, 'Seven centuries of building wages', in Eleanor M. Carus-Wilson (ed.), *Essays in Economic History* (1954–62), 2:177.

26 Henry Peacham, *The Worth of a Penny* (London, 1641), sig. D1.

27 William W. Robinson, '"This passion for prints": Collecting and connoisseurship in northern Europe during the seventeenth century', in Clifford S. Ackley (ed)., *Printmaking in the Age of Rembrandt* (Boston: Museum of Fine Arts, 1981), pp. xxvii–xxxv.

28 Watt, *Cheap Print*, p. 3; Hallett, *Spectacle of Difference*, p. 25. It is worth noting that print sellers regularly advertise their wares as available 'in Oxon' and 'in Cambridge' or even delivered to 'Subscribers in Both Universities at their severall Colledges' (Sarah Tyacke, *London Map-Sellers 1660–1710* (Tring: Map Collector Publications, 1987), pp. 20, 23, 28).

29 C. G. A. Clay, *Economic Expansion and Social Change: England 1500–1700* (Cambridge: Cambridge University Press, 1984), 1:197; Lorna Weatherill, *Consumer Behaviour and Material Culture in Britain 1660–1760* (London: Routledge, 1988), p. 74.

30 Clark and Slack, *English Towns*, p. 68.

31 Weatherill gives fascinating information on the percentages of farmers owning pictures in *Consumer Behaviour*, pp. 79–85.

32 Walton, 'An advertisement'; John Overton, 'A catalogue of books (London, *c.* 1672).

33 Globe, *Peter Stent*, p. 2.

34 Rostenberg, *English Publishers*, pp. 25, 44, 55.

35 Globe, *Peter Stent*, p. vii.

36 Globe, *Peter Stent*, p. 7; Watt, *Cheap Print*, p. 143.

37 For a list of shops selling prints in the early seventeenth century, see Globe, *Peter Stent*, pp. 212–16.

38 Rostenberg, *English Publishers*, p. 76.
39 Landau and Parshall, *Renaissance Print*, p. 231.
40 Richard Altick, *Paintings from Books* (Columbus: Ohio State University Press, 1985), p. 80.
41 Griffiths, *Print in Stuart Britain*, p. 105.
42 John Gay, *Trivia; or, the Art of Walking the Streets of London* (London, 1714), Book II, line 28.
43 Shakespeare, *Henry IV, Part Two*, II.i. 147–51.
44 See Tyacke, *London Map-Sellers*, pp. 3–105.
45 Rostenberg, *English Publishers*, p. 14; William T. Whitley, *Artists and their Friends in England 1700–1799* (London: Medici Society, 1928), 1:7, 156–8; 2:241.
46 Rostenberg, *English Publishers*, p. 14.
47 Peter Burke, *Popular Culture in Early Modern Language* (Aldershot: Wildwood House, 1988), p. 110; Peter Clark, *English Alehouse: A Social History* (London: Longman, 1983), pp. 70, 72, 129. Robert Walton sold 'England's Glory' (1676), a map of London rebuilt after the fire, for eight pence plain and two shillings and eight pence 'coloured on cloth' (Rostenberg, *English Publishers in the Graphic Arts*, p. 49).
48 On how inns were replacing churches as centres of popular culture in the century before the Revolution, see Clark, *English Alehouse*, pp. 157–8. The stationer-print seller Cade had his shop in the entrance to the Globe tavern, where Pepys records making visits and buying engravings on 27 June 1666, and again on 21 November 1666.
49 Fontaine, *Pedlars in Europe*, p. 192.
50 The image is reproduced and analysed by O'Connell, *Popular Print*, 1.3.
51 Pepys cut up his broadside Cries to paste them into his folios, where they survived. For other examples, see Milliot, *Cris de Paris*, p. 117.
52 Rostenberg, *English Publishers*, p. 10; F. J. Fisher, 'The development of London as a centre of conspicuous consumption in the sixteenth and seventeenth centuries', *Transactions of the Royal Historical Society*, 4th edn, series 30 (London, 1948), 37–50.
53 On the survival of early broadsides, see Watt, *Cheap Print*, p. 141.
54 A. Hyatt Mayor, 'The oldest European woodcuts', in *Prints and People* (New York: New York Graphic Society, 1972), n.p.
55 Ann Bermingham, *Landscape and Ideology: The English Rustic Tradition, 1740–1860* (Berkeley: University of California Press, 1986), pp. 48–9.
56 For example, the Rijksmuseum's 'Radish' (1626), by an unknown hand.
57 Watt, *Cheap Print*, pp. 167–8.
58 John Evelyn, *Sculptura: or, the History and Art of Chalcography and Engraving* (London, 1662), p. 139.
59 Evelyn, *Sculptura*, pp. 138, 141.
60 Robinson, 'This Passion for Prints', pp. xxvii–xxxv.
61 Heylyn, *Cosmographie in Four Bookes*, p. 28.
62 A. W. Aspitol, *Catalogue of the Pepys Library at Magdalene College Cambridge, Volume III: Prints and Drawings* (Woodbridge: D. S. Brewer, 1980), pp. 45, 361–5.
63 Richard Luckett, *The Cryes of London: The Collection in the Pepys Library at Magdalene College, Cambridge* (Burton Salmon: Old Hall Press, 1994), pp. x–xi.
64 Howard C. Levis, *Extracts from the Diaries and Correspondence of John Evelyn and Samuel Pepys Relating to Engraving* (London: Ellis, 1915), p. 96.
65 Peter Heylyn, *Cosmographie in Four Bookes Containing the Chorographie and Historie of the Whole World* (London, 1682), p. 28.
66 In words that parallel Brown's, Stow wrote of making 'a discovery of *London*, my native soyle and Countrey' (John Stow, *The Survey of London Reprinted from the Text of 1603*, C. L. Kingsford (ed.), 1:xcvii); Thomas Brown, *Amusements Serious and Comical, Calculated for the Meridian of London* (London, 1700), p. 18).
67 For a specific act of appreciating a print, see the entry in Pepys's diary for 22 November 1666.
68 Donald Lupton, *London and the Countrey Carbonadoed and Quartered into Several Characters* (London, 1632), p. 4.
69 Beth F. Tobin, *Picturing Imperial Power: Colonial Subjects in Eighteenth-Century British Painting* (Durham, NC: Duke University Press, 1999), p. 178.
70 William M. Ivins, *Prints and Visual Communication* (Cambridge, MA: MIT Press, 1969), p. 75.
71 Milliot, *Cris de Paris*, p. 267.
72 Lewis Mumford, *The City in History* (New York: Harcourt, Brace and World, 1961), p. 435.
73 Joan Thirsk, *Economic Policy and Projects: The Development of a Consumer Society in Early Modern England* (Oxford: Clarendon Press, 1978), p. v; McTighe, 'Perfect Deformity', p. 86.
74 Clay, *Economic Expansion*, 1:33.
75 John Stow, 'The temporal government of London: The haberdashers', in *A Survey of the Cities of London and Westminster* (London, 1755), pp. II, 4A (emphasis in original text).
76 N. H., *Compleat Tradesman*, p. 25.
77 Thomas S. Moore (ed.), *The Goods and Chattels of Our Forefathers* (Chichester: Phillimore, 1976), p. 53. In *Consumer Behaviour*, Weatherill points out (pp. 3–8) that only four per cent of the

probate inventories (filed between 1675 and 1725) she examined recorded knives and forks; labourers generally did not make inventories.

78 Weatherill, *Consumer Behaviour*, p. 153.

79 Thirsk, *Economic Policy*, p. 8.

80 On aping behaviour, see E. A. Wrigley, 'A simple model of London's importance in changing English society and economy 1650–1750', *Past and Present*, 37 (1967), 51, 67; the description of 'trickle down' is Pryse Gordon's, quoted in Whitley, *Artists and their Friends*, 2:27.

81 Moore, *Goods and Chattels*, p. 53.

82 Thirsk calls the caterpillar image a commonplace of English economic thinking at this time (*Economic Policy*, p. 8).

83 In the early eighteenth century, Swift's M. B. Draper, recommending a practice long out of vogue but not yet forgotten, told of trucking 'with my Neighbours the Butchers, and Bakers, and Brewers, and the rest, Goods for Goods, and the little Gold and Silver I have, I will keep by me like my Hearts Blood till better Times, or until I am just ready to starve' (Jonathan Swift, *The Draper's Letters*, ed. Herbert Davis (Oxford: Blackwell, 1941), p. 7).

84 Dorothy Davis, *Fairs, Shops and Supermarkets: A History of English Shopping* (Toronto: University of Toronto Press, 1966), pp. 3–5; Clay, *Economic Expansion*, 1:4.

85 Margaret Spufford, *The Great Reclothing of Rural England* (London: Hambeldon Press, 1984), p. 99.

86 On Raleigh, see Lupold von Wedel, 'Journey through England and Scotland made by Lupold von Wedel in the years 1584 and 1585', in *Transactions of the Royal Historical Society*, trans. Gottfried Von Bülow, n.s., 9 (1895), 265.

87 Phillip Stubbes wrote 'bellicheer' as one word (*Anatomie of Abuses* (London, 1583)); Clay, *Economic Expansion*, 2:5–6; 2:25.

88 Von Wedel, 'Journey', 268.

89 Weatherill, *Consumer Behaviour*, pp. 128–34. Fell's figure is close to Gregory King's estimate of 46 percent of expenditures for food bought.

90 Fresh-water fish was owned and enjoyed privately; often poached, it seldom came to public market.

91 Henri Misson, *Memoirs and Observations of M. Misson in his Travels over England*, trans. J. Ozell (London, 1719), p. 35.

92 Davis, *Fairs, Shops and Supermarkets*, p. 91.

93 Fynes Moryson, *An Itinerary Written by Fynes Moryson Gent. First in the Latine Tongue, and then Translated By Him into English containing his Ten Yeeres Travell Through the Twelve Dominions of Germany, Bohmerland, Sweitzerland, Netherland, Denmarke, Poland, Italy, Turky, France, England, Scotland & Ireland* (London, 1617), p. 152.

94 The phrase comes from 'The Peddlar Opening his Pack', which is earlier than 1620 (Hyder Edward Rollins, *A Pepysian Garland* (Cambridge: Harvard University Press, 1971), p. 117).

95 Lupton, *London and the Countrey*, p. 2.

96 Peter Stallybras and Allon White, *The Politics and Poetics of Transgression* (London: Methuen, 1986), p. 39.

97 The quotation is from John Denham's 'Cooper's Hill' (1642); see Sir John Denham, *The Poetical Works of Sir John Denham*, ed. T. H. Banks (New Haven: Yale University Press, 1928), p. 62. About this time, London constituted 'an almost insatiable market for luxury commodities', according to Clay, *Economic Expansion*, 1:209.

98 For a discussion of luxury and necessity, see Weatherill, *Consumer Behaviour*, pp. 14–16. No doubt those social shifts ratcheting up constraints on behaviour, which Norbert Elias has described as 'the civilizing process', also affected these classifications (*The History of Manners: The Civilizing Process*, trans. Edmund Jephcott (New York: Pantheon, 1978), 1:51–84).

99 Who bought these goods, we may reasonably ask? They appealed, among others, to the 1,500 royal householders living in St James's (later in Whitehall Palace), who represented only a fragment of those employed by a court thriving on fancy wares imported by foreign merchants or made by domestic craftsmen.

100 For the market for flowers among gentlemen and better-off members of the middle class, see Thirsk, *Economic Policy*, p. 46.

101 *Cyvile and Uncyvile: A Discourse Very Profitable* (London, 1579), p. 39. On lemons, see Thomas Jenner's *A Book of Fruits and Flowers*, *c.* 1652 (quoted in Rostenberg, *English Publishers*, p. 32).

102 Moryson, *Itinerary*, p. 152.

103 N. H., *Compleat Tradesman*, p. 1.

104 Roy Porter, *London: A Social History* (Cambridge, MA: Harvard University Press, 1994), p. 41.

105 E. S. Godfrey, *Development of English Glass-making 1560–1640* (Oxford: Clarendon Press, 1975), especially chapters 2, 9, and 10. The term 'conveniency' is Bernard Mandeville's, from his *The Fable of the Bees*, ed. Irwin Primer (New York: Capricon, 1962), p. 77. The Falstaff quotation comes from *Henry IV Part Two*, II.i.154.

106 Marmaduke Rawdon, *The Life of Marmaduke Rawdon* (London, 1863), p. 25.
107 Thirsk, *Economic Policy*, pp. 83–92; Clay, *Economic Expansion*, 1:41; Stubbes, *Anatomie of Abuses*, n.p.
108 Fontaine, *Pedlars in Europe*, p. 2.
109 The words 'The Weekly. inteligenc.' appear below the panel carrying the sheet's title; they may refer to another Overton publication.
110 Walter Benjamin, *Illuminations* (London: Fontana, 1973), p. 228.
111 As well as luxuries, prints were scarce commodities; in the case of images like these, runs amounted to a few hundred (Watt, *Cheap Print*, p. 141).
112 Watt, *Cheap Print*, p. 143.
113 Burke, *Popular Culture*, pp. 245–8.
114 Reading Records, *Diary*, p. 308.
115 Christopher Herbert, 'Rat worship and taboo in Mayhew's London', *Representations*, 23 (1988), 1–24, but especially 14.
116 See Beall's E2, first state, and E3 in *Cries and Itinerant Trades*, p. 118; Sean Shesgreen, 'The cries of London in the seventeenth century', *Publications of the Bibliographical Society of America*, 86 (1992), 288.
117 A popular English broadsheet with texts and images entitled 'Copy of a Letter, Written by Our Blessed Lord & Saviour Jesus Christ' promised that 'whosoever shall have a copy of this letter, and keep it in their houses, nothing shall hurt them'. It was published in Plymouth about 1840.
118 Samuel Pepys, *Diary*, ed. Robert Latham and William Matthews, 11 vols, (Berkeley: University of California Press, 1970–83), 26 March 1665.
119 David Freedberg, *The Power of Images* (Chicago: University of Chicago Press, 1989), pp. 32, 76; I am indebted to Freedberg throughout this discussion.
120 Robert Herrick, *Poetical Works*, ed. L. C. Martin (Oxford: Oxford University Press, 1965), p. 121.
121 Stubbes' description of the underclasses in his *Anatomie of Abuses*, n.p.
122 Spufford, *Great Reclothing*, pp. 6–22.
123 Stow identifies John Lydate as the poem's author, an attribution now rejected (Derek Pearsall, *John Lydgate* (Charlottesville: University of Virginia, 1970), p. 218).
124 E. P. Hammond, *English Verse between Chaucer and Surrey* (Durham: Duke University Press, 1927), pp. 237–9. I have edited Hammond's texts for readability (emphasis in original text).
125 Daniel Defoe, *A Review of the State of the British Nation* (London, 1704–13), 25 June 1709, p. 142.
126 The terms are Thomas Harmann's from *A Caveat for Common Cursitors Vulgarly Called Vagabonds* (London, 1566).
127 This description of people making and selling starch appears in a proclamation of James I issued in 1610 (J. F. Larkin and P. L. Hughes, *Stuart Royal Proclamations* (Oxford: Clarendon Press, 1973–83), 1:189).
128 William Sewel, 'Visions of labor', in Steven Kaplan and Cynthia Koepp (eds), *Work in France* (Ithaca: Cornell University Press, 1986), p. 266.
129 Jan Bremmer, 'Walking, standing and sitting', in Jan Bremmer and Herman Roodenburg, *A Cultural History of Gesture* (Ithaca: Cornell University Press, 1991), p. 20.
130 For analogies or parallels between columns and human figures, see Peacock, 'Inigo Jones as a figurative artist', in Lucy Gent and Nigel Llewellyn, *Renaissance Bodies* (London: Reaktion Books, 1995), p. 161.
131 Robert Jütte, *Poverty and Deviance in Early Modern Europe* (Cambridge: Cambridge University Press, 1994), pp. 8–9.
132 David Katz, *The Jews in the History of England* (New York: Oxford University Press, 1994), p. 109.
133 For a list of these sheets and an analysis of them, see my 'Cries of London in the seventeenth century'.
134 Griffiths, *Print in Stuart Britain*, p. 90.
135 Richard Godfrey, *Printmaking in Britain* (New York: New York University Press, 1978), p. 19.
136 George Vertue, *A Description of the Works of the Ingenious Delineator and Engraver Wenceslaus Hollar* (London, 1759), p. 146; *The Eighteenth Volume of the Walpole Society 1929–1930: Vertue Note Books* (Oxford: Oxford University Press, 1930), 18:34.
137 Walton, 'An advertisement'.
138 Walton was active between 1654 and 1687, according to Rostenberg, *English Publishers*, pp. 44–50. Walton's advertisement appears in Thomas Porter's *A New Booke of Mapps* (London, 1655).
139 Griffiths, *Print in Stuart Britain*, p. 105.
140 The full title of Hollar's work is *Ornatus Muliebris Anglicanus – or – the Severall Habits of English Women from the Nobilitie to the Contry Woman, as they are in these times.*
141 She is so identified in an early copy of this book in the Folger Library, Washington, DC.
142 Richard Godfrey, *Wenceslaus Hollar: A Bohemian Artist in England* (New Haven: Yale University Press, 1994), p. 75.

143 Mayor, *Prints and People*, p. 37.

144 Davis, *Fairs, Shops, and Supermarkets*, p. 122.

145 Burke, *Popular Culture*, p. 248. On prints as urban entertainment, see Hallett, *Spectacle of Difference*, pp. 20–1.

146 J. W. Smeed, *The Theophrastan Character: The History of a Literary Genre* (Oxford: Clarendon Press, 1985), pp. 383–5.

147 Smeed, *Theophrastan Character*, p. 24; the fiddler is Samuel Butler's character and the milkmaid is John Overbury's (emphasis in original text).

148 On the imitations of Laroon's ensemble, see Sean Shesgreen, 'The editions, imitations, and the influence of Marcellus Laroon's *Cryes of the City of London*', *Studies in Bibliography*, 35 (1982), 258–71.

149 Fox, *Londoners*, p. 157.

150 Sean Shesgreen, '*The Manner of Crying Things in London*: Style, authorship, chalcography, and history', *Huntington Library Quarterly*, 159 (1995), 414–16.

151 Helen Farquhar, 'Additional notes on silver counters of the seventeenth century', *The Numismatic Chroncle and the Journal of the Royal Numismatic Society*, 5th series, 5 (1925), 78–120.

152 For an account of the plagiaries of this sheet, see Shesgreen, 'Cries of London in the seventeenth century'.

153 Robert Greene's Hee Conny-catcher identifies the Royal Exchange, Westminster Hall and St Paul's as the 'common-haunted places' of petty crooks in *A Disputation Betweene a Hee Conny-Catcher, and a Shee Conny-Catcher, whether a Theefe or a Whoore, is most hurtfull in Cousonage, to the Common-Wealth* (1592). Reprinted in *Cony-Catchers and Bawdy Baskets*, ed. Gamini Salgado (Harmondsworth: Penguin, 1977).

154 Garrett's advertisment is quoted in Rostenberg, *English Publishers*, p. 76; Clayton, *English Print*, p. 25; Godfrey, *Printmaking in Britain*, pp. 9, 18. Even McTighe refers to 'this crude broadsheet imagery of market workers' in her essay on the Cries of Carracci ('Perfect deformity', 76).

155 Clayton, *English Print*, p. xi.

156 Henry Peacham, *The Compleat Gentleman* (1634; reprint with an introduction by G. S. Gordon, Oxford: Clarendon Press, 1956), p. 129; the first English academy for working from the life was organized in 1711.

Chapter 3

1 Griffiths, *Print in Stuart Britain*, p. 244.

2 Like the first broadside sheets, these two ensembles have been neglected and disparaged. On Amigoni's ensemble, there is no literature. On Laroon's there is quite a bit (see the bibliography in my *Criers and Hawkers of London* (Stanford: Stanford University Press, 1990)); however his *Cryes* continues to be disparaged. An anonymous reviewer in *TLS* (13 July 1967, 609–10) thinks the chief merit of the images lies in their legends. On the shifting status of art in this epoch, see David Solkin, *Painting for Money: The Visual Arts and the Public Sphere in Eighteenth-Century England* (New Haven: Yale University Press, 1993), especially the 'Introduction'.

3 Whitley, *Artists and their Friends*, 1:3.

4 Vertue, 'Note Books,' *Walpole Society*, 22:7.

5 Laroon actually moved to London with his father who emigrated there shortly after 1660.

6 Writing in his *Autobiographical Notes*, Hogarth claims that the Engravers Act, sometimes called the Hogarth Act, 'has so effectually done my business but has made prints a considerable [commodity] of this country, there being more business of that kind done in this Town than in Paris or any where else as well' (William Hogarth, *The Analysis of Beauty with the Rejected Passages from the Manuscript Drafts and Autobiographical Notes*, ed. Joseph Burke (Oxford: Clarendon Press, 1955), p. 216).

7 Horace Walpole, *Anecdotes of Painting in England* (London, 1826), 4:114.

8 Amigoni's designs are now extremely rare, surviving only in a few odd copies scattered here and there; the only set I know of is preserved in the Metropolitan Museum of Art in New York, which has a portfolio of Cries (Miller, *Street Criers*, p. 22).

9 Ivins, *Prints*, p. 47.

10 On Carracci, see especially McTighe, 'Perfect deformity', 75–91; A. Marabottini, 'Sui Disegni di Anniable Carracci per le "Arti di Bologna" ', in Giovanni Incisa della Rocchetta, *Studi Offerti a Giovanni Incisa della Rocchetta* (Rome: Societa Romana di storia patria, 1973), pp. 273–82; A. Hyatt Mayor, 'Alive, alive o', *Metropolitan Museum Bulletin*, 11 (1953), 164–7. A. Marabottini published a modern edition of the *Arti di Bologna* (Rome) in 1996. Overton's classification of prints appears in an advertisement in the *London Gazette* of 10–13 December 1715.

11 Miller, *Street Criers*, p. 5.

12 Landau and Parshall, *Renaissance Print*, p. 49.

13 Robert Raines, *Marcellus Laroon* (London: Routledge and Kegan Paul, 1966), pp. 5–6.

14 R. Campbell, *The London Tradesman* (London, 1747), p. 101.

15 Henry Fielding, *Joseph Andrews*, ed. Martin Battestin (Middletown, CT: Wesleyan University Press, 1967), Book III, chapter 6. For the disputed meaning of Joseph's allusion, see William B. Coley, 'Fielding, Hogarth and three Italian masters', *Modern Language Quarterly*, 24 (1963), 386–91, and John Shipley, 'Ralph, Ellys, Hogarth and Fielding: The cabal against Jacopo Amigoni', *Eighteenth-Century Studies*, 1 (1967–68), 313–31.

16 On Italians as artists with good noses for broad markets, see West, 'Xenophobia and Xenomania', in Shearer West (ed.), *Italian Culture in Northern Europe in the Eighteenth Century* (Cambridge: Cambridge University Press, 1999), p. 127.

17 Leslie G. Hennessey, 'Jacopo Amigoni: An artistic biography with a catalogue of his Venetian paintings' (Ph.D. dissertation, University of Kansas, 1983), pp. 46, 56.

18 Forty-nine of Laroon's images are preserved in the collection of the Duke of Marlborough at Blenheim Palace, Woodstock; four more are in a private collection in London. The Laroon drawings at Marlborough were discovered in 1981, when the Library there was under a periodic evaluation. No record specifies when the Laroon drawings came to Blenheim. However, Whitley records that Laroon's son, Captain Marcellus Laroon, who inherited his father's art, fought under Marlborough at Oudenarde (*Artists and their Friends*, 1:10). On the strength of this connection, it seems likely that the first Duke of Marlborough acquired the sketches directly from Captain Laroon.

19 Wolfgang Holler, 'Amigoni', in Jane Turner (ed.), *The Dictionary of Art* (London: Macmillan, 1996), 1:784–5. Wagner appears to have etched Amigoni's oils himself; Tempest probably had Laroon's sketches engraved by Richard Savage and other craftsmen in his atelier. On Tempest's apprenticeship under Hollar, see James Granger, *Biographical History of England*, 5th edn (London, 1824), 4:147.

20 Amigoni's prints carry no price; I base my estimate on G. Child's plagiarized copies of Amigoni's images (4.2 and 4.3), which went for 6d. each.

21 On Wagner's print shop, see Leslie Hennessey, 'Friends serving itinerant muses', in Shearer West, *Italian Culture in Northern Europe in the Eighteenth Century* (Cambridge: Cambridge University Press, 1999), p. 33.

22 On the cost of inserting advertisements in London papers, see Tyacke, *London Map-Sellers*, p. xvi, and David Kunzle, 'Plagiaries of the *Rake's Progress*', *Journal of the Warburg and Courtald Institute*, 29 (1966), 318, n. 17.

23 *The London Gazette*, 28–31 May 1688.

24 McTighe, 'Perfect deformity', 78.

25 Horace Walpole also owned Laroon's *Cryes*, but he bought it at a later date when it had become a rare book, as did the connoisseur and collector, Joseph Gulston. The Gulston copy is now in the Lewis Walpole Library, Farmington, Connecticut; the Gulston collection was formed between 1745 and 1786.

26 Pepys's *Cryes* is in the Pepysian Library, Magdalene College, Cambridge; Narcissus Luttrell's copy is in the British Museum. Joseph Addison may have also owned a copy; he was intensely interested in hawkers, as appears in his essays on the subject in the *Spectator* and *Tatler*, specifically No. 251 in the *Spectator*, which carried an ad for the book on 8 November 1709; von Uffenbach records buying a copy in his *Travels* (see next note).

27 Zacharias Conrad von Uffenbach, *London in 1710 from the Travels of Zacharias Conrad von Uffenbach*, trans. and ed. W. H. Quarrels and Margaret Mare (London: Faber & Faber, 1934), pp. 154–5.

28 Von Uffenbach, *Travels*, p. 154.

29 Sir John Mill's copy is in the University of London; the Duke of Devonshire's is in the Pierpont Morgan Library, New York.

30 The most interesting of the Blenheim sketches are reproduced in my *Criers and Hawkers*.

31 Edward Arber (ed.), *The Term Catalogues 1668–1709* (London: privately printed, 1903–6), 2:207, 218, 231, 240, 281, 647.

32 Of the forty-nine Laroon sketches preserved at Blenheim, Tempest rejected seven.

33 Landau and Parshall, *Renaissance Print*, p. 38.

34 Whitley, *Artists and their Friends*, 1:374.

35 On frames as signifiers of value, see West, 'Framing hegemony', pp. 63–96; and Duro, 'Containment and transgression', p. 46, both in Paul Duro, *The Rhetoric of the Frame: Essays on the Boundaries of the Artwork* (Cambridge: Cambridge University Press, 1996).

36 For the practice of adorning closets with prints, see the entry in Pepys's *Diary* for 24 August 1666. In a letter to Algarotti of December 1736, Lady

Mary Wortley Montague speaks of her 'closet meditations'.

37 Clayton, *English Print*, p. xii.

38 A contemporary source quoted in Whitley, *Artists and their Friends*, 1:4.

39 Bainbrigge Buckeridge, 'An essay toward an English school of painters', in Roger de Piles, *The Art of Painting*, 3rd edn (London, 1754), p. 444.

40 Shesgreen, *Criers and Hawkers*, p. 225.

41 This judgment of Le Blanc is quoted in Whitley, *Artists and their Friends*, 1:54.

42 Anne Hollander, *Seeing Through Clothes* (Berkeley: University of California Press, 1993), p. 389; Diana Donald, 'Characters and caricatures: The satirical view', in Nicholas Penny (ed.), *Reynolds* (New York: Abrams, 1986), pp. 363–4.

43 Laroon's *Cryes* is published just when the feeling for adornment in dress was becoming so widespread that even labourers and the poor began to follow the fashion in a silent revolution as important in its way as the rise of literacy. See Elizabeth Wilson, *Adorned in Dress* (London: Virago Press, 1985), p. 23; Daniel Roche, *The Culture of Clothing*, trans. Jean Birrell (Cambridge: Cambridge University Press, 1989), p. 110.

44 *The London Gazette*, 31 May to 4 June 1688.

45 Valerie Traub, 'Mapping the global body', in Clark Hulse and Peter Erickson, *The Visual Culture of Renaissance England* (forthcoming), p. 6.

46 Milliot, *Cris de Paris*, p. 174.

47 Milliot, *Cris de Paris*, p. 168.

48 Fowl came to London chiefly from Norfolk in the seventeenth century (Rostenberg, *English Publishers*, p. 61).

49 Charles P. Moritz, *Journeys of a German in England in 1782*, trans. and ed. Reginald Netter (New York: Rinehart and Winston, 1965), p. 24.

50 Moryson, *Itinerary*, p. 179.

51 The London neighbourhood called Alsatia was a hotbed of crime in the seventeenth century; plate 9 of Hogarth's *Industry and Idleness*, set in an Alsatian tavern, gives the flavour of the place. The identity of the Squire of Alsatia is revealed in Granger, *Biographical History of England*, 4:168–9.

52 Robert Greene, *A Notable Discovery of Cozenage* (1591); reprinted in Arthur F. Kinney (ed.), *Rogues, Vagabonds, and Sturdy Beggars* (Amherst: University of Massachusetts Press, 1990), pp. 165–8.

53 This cry was often raised by thieves to discover where victims hid their purses (Greene, *Disputation Betweene a Hee Conny-Catcher*, p. 274).

54 This information on Creswell appears in Granger, *Biographical History of England*, 6:20, but Granger got it from Pepys: 'I have described as many of them [Laroon's vendors] as Mr. Secretary Pepys has taken into his collection. We are beholden to that gentleman for the names of several persons, which are written under the portraits' (Granger, *Biographical History of England*, 6:10, n. 10).

55 Crawley, 'Sexual background of dress', 73.

56 Jean-Christophe Agnew, *Worlds Apart: The Market and the Theatre in Anglo-American Thought 1550–1750* (Cambridge: Cambridge University Press, 1986), p. 66.

57 Granger, *Biographical History of England*, 6:178.

58 Johann W. Archenholz, *A Picture of England* (London, 1789), 1:73.

59 Peter Stallybrass, 'Worn worlds: Clothes and identity on the Renaissance stage', in Margreta DeGrazia, Maureen Quilligan, and Peter Stallybrass (eds), *Subject and Object in Renaissance Culture* (Cambridge: Cambridge University Press, 1996), pp. 289–320.

60 Hollander, *Seeing Through Clothes*, pp. 133, 263.

61 William King, *The Art of Dress* (London, 1717), p. 16.

62 For an account of artists as peddlers of their own prints, see Landau and Pershall, *Renaissance Print*, p. 347.

63 Tempest, in a letter to Francis Place, identifies Laroon as the provider of this kind of art: 'Mr Place Yors I recd though the ladys have solely left painting *Mezzotintos*, yet they doe sell a little especially fancy's Heads & bawdy soe I am provideing 3 or four new ones Against the Terme 2 Queens, a new confession 2 fancys after Laroone . . .' (A. J. Finberg (ed.), *The Walpole Society 1921–1922* (Oxford: Oxford University Press, 1922), 10:65).

64 Pieter van Laer's *Self-Portrait as a Conjurer* is an example of this genre (Barry Wind, *A Foul and Pestilent Congregation: Images of 'Freaks' in Baroque Art* (Aldershot: Ashgate, 1998), p. 117).

65 Wind, *Foul and Pestilent Congregation*, p. 6.

66 Wind, *Foul and Pestilent Congregation*, p. 123.

67 The diarist describes Clark as a man 'who tho' gross enough of Body, was of so flexible and subtle a Texture, as to contort his Members into several disfigurations, and to put out of joynt almost any Bone or *Vertebra* in his Body and re-place it again' (John Evelyn, *Numismata: A discourse of medals, antient and modern* (London, 1697), p. 277).

68 Landau and Parshall, *Renaissance Print*, p. 257.

69 Pritchard Mayor. 'Martis Vicesimo primo die Novembr', 1682. Ann.que Regini Regis CAROLI Secundi, Angl', &*c*. xxxiv.

70 Granger, *Biographical History of England*, 6:10.

71 McTighe, 'Perfect deformity', 75.

72 The full title of this treatise is *Essay sur les maladies des artisans, traduit du latin de Ramazzini, avec des notes et des additions, par M. de Foucray* (Paris, 1777).

73 Griselda Pollock, 'Stark encounters: Modern life and urban work in Van Gogh's drawings of the Hague 1881–3', *Art History*, 6 (1983), 35.

74 On these games, see Thomas F. Crane, *Italian Social Customs* (New Haven: Yale University Press, 1920), pp. 263–70; on the prints, see McTighe, 'Perfect deformity', n. 39.

75 See the advertisement for Laroon's *Cryes* in *The London Gazette* for 28–31 May 1688.

76 Geoffrey Chaucer, 'General prologue', lines 95–6.

77 Quoted in Rostenberg, *English Publishers*, p. 5; for Norgate's life, see the entry in the *DNB* under his name.

78 *L'Art de dessiner proprement les plan, porfils, elevations geometrales, & perspective, soit d'architecture militaire out civile . . . et la manière de s'en servir dans les veuës des siègnes, campemens, & autres morceaux de paysage* (Paris, 1697), preface. I am indebted to MacGregor for this quotation which I quote in his translation.

79 McTighe, 'Perfect deformity', 75–91.

80 For more on this edition of Ripa, see Griffiths, *Print in Stuart Britain*, p. 173.

81 The Carracci used this ensemble of hawkers as an accoutrement for their teaching, according to Miller, *Street Criers*, p. 11.

82 The designs making up *The Manner of Crying Things in London* were cut on silver counters or coins during the Commonwealth. See L. A. Lawrence, 'On a portion of a set of silver counters exhibiting London criers and their Cries', *British Numismatic Journal*, 2nd series, 14 (1918), 49–55.

83 Taylor's manuscript is preserved in the Rare Book Room of Northwestern University, Evanston, Illinois.

84 Peacham, *Compleat Gentleman*, pp. 127, 129.

85 The phrase 'a spurious, Pyratical Copy' belongs to Jonathan Pincheck, a fanmaker, complaining of a pirate who stole one of his designs (quoted in Clayton, *English Print*, p. 81).

86 One set of these prints, not recorded in Beall, is preserved in the Print Room of the British Museum. Another larger set of Laroon copies, Beall's E13, titled 'Ancient Cries of London', measuring 6 × 11 cm is also preserved in the British Museum, London. This suite of twenty-one etchings is bound with a title embossed on its outside cover. The etchings are reverse copies of Laroon with English captions below the images. The Guildhall Library, London, has a another set of these etchings containing nineteen prints with 'Colly Molly Puffe' in two states.

87 For the publishing history of Laroon's *Cryes*, see Shesgreen, *Criers and Hawkers*, pp. 88–98.

88 William King, in his *Art of Cookery* (London, 1708), gives a humorous history of street vending 'machines' in which he points out that the wheelbarrow, a late development, displaces the horse and cart used by farmer-hawkers:

> *Tom Bold* did first begin the Strolling Mart,
> And drove about his Turnips in a Cart:
> Sometimes his Wife the Citizens wou'd please,
> And from the same machine sell Pecks of Pease.
> Then Pippins did in Wheel-barrows abound
> And Oranges in Whimsey-boards abound.
> (King, *Art of Cookery*, p. 99)

89 For a romantic rearrangement of this prints' props of dog, wheelbarrow and vegetation, see Reynolds's fancy picture, *Master Henry Hoare* (1788).

90 Victor Hugo, *Les Miserables* (Paris: Garnier Freres, 1963), p. 515. Quoted from Pollock, 'Stark encounters', 340.

91 William Cadogan, *An Essay upon Nursing and the Management of Children from their Birth to Three Years of Age* (London, 1748), p. 6. For children under the age of one, death rates ranged from 13 per cent to 15 per cent, peaking in the years between 1700 to 1750; for children between one and nine years of age, rates ranged between 22 per cent and 28 per cent, according to modern estimates (Linda Pollock, *A Lasting Relationship: Parent–Child Relations from 1500 to 1990* (London: Fourth Estate, 1983), p. 94).

92 David Porter, *Considerations on the Present State of Chimney Sweepers* (London, 1792), pp. 10–18; Jonas Hanway, *The State of Master Chimney-Sweepers and their Journeymen, Particularly of the Distressed Boys* (London, 1779), pp. 9–31.

93 Patricia Crown, 'Portraits and fancy pictures by Gainsborough and Reynolds: Contrasting images of childhood', *British Journal for Eighteenth-Century Studies*, 7 (Autumn 1984), 164. For a discussion of children in English art during this time, see James Christen Steward, *The New Child: British Art and the Origins of Modern Childhood*

1730–1830 (Berkeley: University Art Museum, 1995), to which I am indebted in what follows.

94 Martin Postle, *Angels and Urchins: The Fancy Picture in Eighteenth-Century British Art* (Nottingham: Djanogly Art Gallery, 1998), p. 6.

95 Postle's account of the origins of the fancy picture (*Angels and Urchins*, pp. 9–12) differs from my speculative suggestion.

96 These designs appear in Postle's *Angels and Urchins* as plates 38 (print), 39 (oil) and 40.

97 For an extensive treatment of this theme, see Martin Postle, *Sir Joshua Reynolds: The Subject Paintings* (Cambridge: Cambridge University Press, 1995), chapter 2: 'The infant academy'.

98 Robert Rosenblum, *The Romantic Child: From Runge to Sendak* (London: Thames and Hudson, 1988), p. 24.

99 For the vicious city and innocent country, see Raymond Williams, *The City and the Country* (New York: Oxford University Press, 1973), pp. 148–9.

100 On this general topic, see David Kunzle, 'The ravaged child in Hogarth', in Virginia Tufte and Barbara Myerhoff (eds), *Changing Images of the Family* (New Haven: Yale University Press, 1979), p. 100. An emblem of industry rather than woe or 'at-your-service' obsequiousness, the coster is something of a hoyden, lacking the physical and psychological refinement of the males.

101 Miller, *Street Criers*, p. 9.

102 Quoted in Solkin, *Painting for Money*, p. 169.

103 Francesca Boris and Giampiero Cammarota, 'La collezione de Carlo Broschi detto Farinelli', *Accademia Clementina Atti E Memorie*, new series, 27 (190), 210.

104 Granger, *Biographical History of England*, 1:x.

105 Granger, *Biographical History of England*, 6:179.

106 For a full discussion of this topic, see Sean Shesgreen, 'The new urbanity of Marcellus Laroon's *Cryes of the City of London*', *Harvard Library Bulletin*, 35 (Autumn 1987), 255–79.

107 James Caulfield, *Portraits, Memoirs, and Characters of Remarkable Persons from the Reign of Edward the Third to the Revolution* (London, 1813), 3:259.

108 On Hogarth's portrait of his servants, see Kunzle, 'Ravaged child', pp. 139–40.

109 Christopher Hill, 'Pottage for freeborn Englishmen: Attitudes to wage-labour', in Christopher Hill, *Change and Continuity in Seventeenth-Century England* (Cambridge, MA: Harvard University Press, 1975), pp. 219–38.

110 In *Much Ado about Nothing*, Leonato asks if Don Pedro lost many gentlemen at war, to which a messenger replies, 'But few of any sort, and none of name' (I.i.); McTighe, 'Perfect deformity', 85.

111 On this subject see, Anita Schorsch, *Images of Childhood: An Illustrated Social History* (New York: Mayflower Books, 1979).

112 Samuel Curwen, *The Journal of Samuel Curwen*, ed. Andrew Oliver (Cambridge: Harvard University Press, 1972), 2:672; Stewart, *New Child*, p. 163.

113 For a discussion of the link between Cries and fancy pictures, see Postle, *Angels and Urchins*, p. 8.

114 John Kirk mined Abraham Bosse's *Cries of Paris* and Amigoni's London Cries to illustrate his pack of fifty-two playing cards, which carries 'Boot Black' as 'Black your Shoes your HONOUR' (see 6.8).

Chapter 4

1 Clayton, *English Print*, p. 10.

2 This catalogue is reproduced by O'Connell, *Popular Print*, p. 177.

3 *Walpole Society*, 18:122, 146.

4 John Nichols and George Steevens, *The Genuine Works of William Hogarth* (London, 1808–10), 1:97–102; Hogarth, *Autobiographical Notes*, pp. 216, 225.

5 Abbé Jean Bernard Le Blanc, *Letters on the English and French Nations* (London, 1747), 1:162.

6 Jean Andre Rouquet, *The Present State of the Arts in England* (London, 1755), p. 27.

7 Clayton, *English Print*, p. 204; Joshua Reynolds, *Discourses on Art*, ed. Robert Wark (New Haven: Yale University Press, 1975), p. 16.

8 These are the words of a critic reviewing three paintings by E. Nicol in *Art, Politics and Proceedings* (August 1866), p. 1.

9 *Walpole Society*, 41:85.

10 Campbell, *London Tradesman*, p. 96.

11 My attribution is based upon the fact that in the 'The Blind Musician' the words 'J. S. Müller fecit' appear in the design's lower right hand corner, naming Johann Sebastien Müller, a German artist who came to London in 1744 and worked there until his death in 1785. While 'Sculps' in 'Baby, Cloaths' indicates that the Nurenberg engraver merely cut the image, 'fecit' in the 'Musician' implies that he also created it and the three other pictures that make up the ensemble. 'Fecit et sculp' and 'invent et sculp' are commonly equated and taken to mean that the signatory was responsible for creating the design and engraving it. See Alexander Globe's statement in *Peter Stent*,

p. 5; and the examples in Richard Godfrey, *English Caricature 1620 to the Present* (London: Victoria and Albert Museum, 1984), p. 16.

12 On blindness and ballad making, see Burke, *Popular Culture*, pp. 100 and 255.

13 Here, and in subsequent discussions of this ensemble, I borrow heavily from Sarah Jordan's 'The anxieties of idleness: Idleness in eighteenth-century literature and culture' (Ann Arbor: University Microfilms, 1994); this Brandeis University dissertation (1993) has an invaluable and extensive account of attitudes toward the idleness of the poor between 1700 and 1800.

14 Daniel Defoe champions this wisdom for the middle and upper classes in *Giving Alms No Charity* (London, 1704): 'There is a general Taint of Slothfulness upon our Poor, [so that] there's nothing more frequent, than for an *Englishman* to Work till he has got his Pocket full of Money, and then go and be idle, *or perhaps drunk*, till 'tis all gone, and perhaps himself in Debt'. Ten years after the appearance of *The Blind Musician*, when John Clayton rephrases the assumption in *Friendly Advice to the Poor*, it has hardened into gospel: 'But it is a melancholy Truth, which cannot be concealed, and must not be dissembled, that much of the Poor's Misery is owing to themselves; and may with great Justice be imputed to that Idleness, Extravagance, and Mismanagement, which are as notorious, as the Poverty that proceeds from them' (John Clayton, *Friendly Advice to the Poor* (Manchester, 1755), p. 5, emphasis in original text).

15 John T. Smith, *Lives of Famous London Beggars with Forty Portraits of the Most Remarkable* (London, n.d.), p. 25.

16 Deborah Nord, *Walking the Streets of Victorian London* (Ithaca: Cornell University Press, 1995), p. 2.

17 Nord, *Victorian London*, p. 11.

18 Jean-Christophe Agnew, *Worlds Apart: The Market and the Theater in Anglo-American Thought 1550–1750* (Cambridge: Cambridge University Press, 1986), p. 14.

19 *Allgemeines Künstlerlexicon* (München: Saur, 2000) has an entry for Child claiming he produced six such London street-scenes; I know of only these two.

20 The most recent edition of Bénézit's *Dictionnaire* has a perfunctory and unconvincing entry describing Child as English engraver active in London in the eighteenth century (E. Bénézit, *Dictionnaire critique et documentaire des penitres, sculptures, dessinateurs, et graveurs*, ed. Jacques Busse (Paris: Gründ, 1999)). No details of the kind that might establish his identity are offered.

21 I am indebted to Sheila O'Connell for information on these prints, which are headed 'History of England', plates 2 and 15; they show the kings of England from William I to Richard II and from Henry IV to James I.

22 I have discovered only two surviving copies of Child's prints; it is possible that more than two designs were engraved, given the low survival rate of copies.

23 Postle, *Angels and Urchins*, pp. 16, 17–19.

24 For another example, see 'Which you will for a halfpenny' is one of a set of three Cries preserved in the Lewis Walpole Library, Farmington; the other two prints, notably sentimental in tone, are titled 'The cherry girl', and 'Paddy O' Blarney'. 'Which you will', carries a publication line: 'Published 26th. Sept. 1791 Robt. Sayer & Co. Fleet Street London'.

25 Throughout this discussion, I am indebted to Gladys Wilson's 'One God! One Farinelli!', *Apollo*, 140 (1994), 45–51.

26 Hennessey, 'Jacopo Amigoni', p. 34; Walpole, *Anecdotes*, 4:112; Vertue, 'Note books', *Walpole Society*, 3:75.

27 I am indebted here to Shipley, 'Ralph, Ellys, Hogarth and Fielding', 313–31.

28 Farinelli is satirized in a popular print pictured in the *Rake's Progress*, Plate II; in that print, he sits on a pedestal above an altar on which hearts burn for him. At the bottom, Hogarth added a cartoon of the singer standing on a pedestal surrounded by women offering the singer their burning hearts and shouting, 'One God! One Farinelli'. For more ties between Farinelli, Amigoni and Hogarth, especially the *Rake*, see J. Howard, 'Hogarth, Amigoni, and "The rake's levee": New light on *A Rake's Progress*', *Apollo*, 146 (1997), 31–7.

29 John Hawkins, *A General History of the Science and Practice of Music* (London, 1776), 4:321.

30 Adrian Baird, 'Jacopo Amigoni in England', *Burlington Magazine*, 115 (1973), 735.

31 On Amigoni's friendship with Farinelli, see Hennessey, 'Friends serving itinerant muses', in West, *Italian Culture in Northern Europe*, pp. 20–45.

32 For the contents of Farinelli's collection of 330 pictures, see Francesca Boris and Giampiero Cammarota, 'La collezione di Carlo Broschi detto Farinelli', *Academia Clementina: Atti e Memorie*, new series 27 (1990), 187–237.

33 *Grub-Street Journal*, no. 289 of 10 July 1735. On this portrait, engraved by Wagner, see Hennessey, 'Jacopo Amigoni', 40.

34 Baird, 'Jacopo Amigoni in England', 735.

35 Boris and Cammarota, 'La collezione de Carlo Broschi', 210, items 34, 35.

36 *Grub-street Journal*, no. 289, 10 July 1735.

37 David Bindman, *Hogarth and His Times* (Berkeley: University of California Press, 1997), p. 128.

38 Ronald Paulson, *Hogarth's Graphic Works*, 3rd rev. edn (London: The Print Room, 1989), pp. 110–11.

39 Antal, *Hogarth*, p. 230; Bindman, *Hogarth*, p. 128.

40 For a discussion of these issues, see Mark Hallett's 'Hogarthomania and print culture', *Art History* (1998), 449–53.

41 'The Enraged Musician' belongs with Hogarth's *Shrimp Girl* (1740–50) thematically but also formally. Antal believes that the oil sketch of the shrimp seller was done to be included in the design of the print, but for some reason, the milk wife replaced the fish wife in the final version (Antal, *Hogarth*, pp. 116–17). Hogarth's *Shrimp Girl* is usually dated *c.* 1740–45.

42 Hogarth originally planned an ensemble of three prints, *The Enraged Musician* and *The Distressed Poet*, 'To which will be added, a Third on Painting, which will compleat the Set', an advertisement in the *London Daily Post and General Advertiser* promised for 24 November 1740. The third print with painting as its subject reveals that the theme of representation was rolling around in the artist's mind when he issued the *Musician*.

43 These names and those of the aristocrats mentioned in the next sentence (except for Lord Biron) all appear on subscription tickets reproduced in Bindman's *Hogarth* and Paulson's *Hogarth's Graphic Works*.

44 For Walpole's critical remarks, see *Anecdotes*, 4:134.

45 Respecting the success of Overton's edition of Laroon's *Cryes*, I interpret the heavily reworked date on that ensemble's title page to mean that the publisher reissued it four times between 1711 and 1733: in 1711, 1713, 1731, and 1733. I assume that re-engraving the dates for reissue caused the distortion I point to.

46 The connection between Laroon's *Cryes of the City of London* and Hogarth's *Enraged Musician* was first made by Frederick Antal. In *Hogarth and his Place in European Art*, he pointed out that Laroon's ensemble 'was still being republished with variations (e.g., by Boitard, one of Hogarth's pirates) during Hogarth's working years. Though it is seldom possible to recognize the literal origins of figures from the Laroon set in Hogarth's engravings, yet in some of them, such as *The Enraged Musician* and *The Execution of the Idle Apprentice at Tyburn*, both teeming with street traders, the continuation of the tradition is clearly apparent' (230).

47 See Coley, 'Fielding, Hogarth, and three Italian masters', 389 and n. 14. The nickname was given Hogarth by Orator Henley, according to Vertue. At this point in his career, Amigoni was thriving; he had recently received a cash bonus – £200 more than he asked – to paint Lord Tankerville's staircase (Walpole, *Anecdotes*, 4:113).

48 Vertue, 'Note books', *Walpole Society*, 6:192, 193.

49 This calculation does not take into account ink, paper and the labour of lettering engravers (texts were often scraped by specialists in cutting texts who charged so much per letter) and expert printers (who pressed the plates).

50 Globe, *Peter Stent*, pp. 30–1; Griffiths, *Print in Stuart Britain*, pp. 29–30.

51 John Ruch, 'A French engraver in early Georgian England: Bernard Baron his early life, his metier', *Nouvelles de l'estampe*, 12 (1973), 21.

52 I estimate the cost of Amigoni's prints on the basis of G. Child's travesties of them discussed above. In addition, Bickham's *Rake's Rendez-vous*, comparable in size and issued in 1735, sold for sixpence.

53 Hogarth, *Autobiographical Notes*, pp. 201–3.

54 *Walpole Society 1966–1968: Hogarth's Apology for Painters*, ed. Michael Kitson (Glasgow: Glasgow University Press, 1968), 41:67.

55 Hogarth, *Autobiographical Notes*, p. 216.

56 Hogarth, *Autobiographical Notes*, p. 201.

57 Kagan, '*Urbs* and *Civitas*', in David Buisseret (ed.), *Envisioning the City: Six Studies in Urban Cartography* (Chicago: University of Chicago Press, 1998), p. 80.

58 John Nichols and George Steevens, *Biographical Anecdotes of William Hogarth* (London, 1781), 2:213–14.

59 F. G. Stephens, *Catalogue of Prints and Drawings in the British Museum. Division I. Political and Personal Satires* (London, 1873–83), 3 (Part I), 410–13.

60 John Richardson, *London and its People* (London: Barrie and Jenkins, 1995), p. 74.

61 That this is the house of the musician and not the dwelling of his noble patron is argued by the presence of ink and quill in the picture. These objects suggest he is at home, composing a musical score.

62 Nichols and Steevens, *Biographical Anecdotes*, p. 102. On Hogarth's Act, see David Hunter's important essay, 'Copyright protection for engravings and maps in eighteenth century Britain', *The Library*, 9 (1987), 128–47.

63 Commonly called Hogarth's Act, this law elevated English printmakers from factotums in a chain of servile cultural production to independent entrepreneurs and liberal artists enjoying a professional standing comparable to poets, playrights and novelists.

64 Le Blanc, *Letters*, 1:110; Le Blanc lived in England from 1737 to 1744.

65 *A Descriptive Catalogue of Thirty-six Pictures Painted by George Morland* (London, nd), p. 2.

66 Jean Andre Rouquet, *Lettres de Monseiu ** á un de ses Amis á Paris* (London, 1746), p. 13.

67 For his identity, see John Ireland, *Hogarth Illustrated*, 2nd edn (London, 1793–1812), 2:119.

68 Daniel Defoe, *The True-Born Englishman: A Satyr* ([London], 1701), p. 20.

69 Stephens, *Catalogue of Prints and Drawings*, 3 (Part I), 411.

70 Peter Chamberlen, *The Poor Man' s Advocate* (London, 1649), p. 44.

71 *A General View of the Agriculture of the Country of Middlesex* (London, 1794), p. 13.

72 Janet K. Page, 'The hautboy in London's music life', *Early Music* (1988), 359–71; David Lasocki, 'The French hautboy in England 1673–1730', *Early Music* (1988), 339–57. I am indebted to Alison Deadman for the references to Page's and Lasocki's work.

73 In wearing a beard when all others go clean-shaven, he resembles the Jew in the second plate of *A Harlot' s Progress*.

74 Frank Felsenstein, *Anti-Semitic Stereotypes: A Paradigm of Otherness in English Popular Culture* (Baltimore: Johns Hopkins University Press, 1995), especially chapters 2 and 3.

75 Ireland, *Hogarth Illustrated*, 1:120.

76 For Hogarth's familiarity with Laroon, see Ronald Paulson's *Hogarth* (New Brunswick: Rutgers University Press, 1991–93), 1:257; Bindman, *Hogarth*, p. 128.

77 Antal, *Hogarth*, p. 230, note 88.

78 Marjorie Bowen, *William Hogarth: The Cockney' s Mirror* (New York: Appleton Century, 1936), p. 196.

79 John Barrell, *The Dark Side of the Landscape* (Cambridge: Cambridge University Press, 1980), p. 49; for an instructive account of the conventions of georgic poetry, to which I am indebted, see Barrell's long discussion of Gainsborough.

80 Ireland, *Hogarth Illustrated*, 1:21.

81 Craig, *Description of the Plates*, 'Cats and dogs' meat', n.p.

82 Curwen, *Journal*, 2:586.

83 Francis Place, *The Autobiography of Francis Place*, ed. Mary Thale (Cambridge: University Press, 1972), p. 229.

84 Ireland, *Hogarth Illustrated*, 2:122.

85 Bindman, *Hogarth*, p. 128.

86 Stephens, *Catalogue of Prints and Drawings*, 3 (Part 1), 410–13.

87 William Ellis, *The Modern Husbandman* (London, 1750), 5 (Part 2), 92.

88 Hugh Cunningham, *Children of the Poor: Representations of Childhood since the Seventeenth Century* (Oxford: Blackwell, 1992), p. 52.

89 *Spectator*, No. 365, 29 April 1712.

90 Misson, *Memoirs and Observations*, p. 307.

91 Peter Earle, in *The Making of the English Middle Class* (Berkeley: University of California Press, 1989), also documents pawnbrokers lending money to hawkers and 'such as persons who cry fish, fruit or other wares . . . to purchase the several commodities they deal in' (p. 50).

92 Charles Phythian-Adams, 'Milk and soot', in Derek Fraser and Anthony Sutcliffe (eds), *The Pursuit of Urban History* (London: Arnold, 1983), p. 100.

93 William Hone, *The Every-Day Book* (London, 1833), 1:571; John T. Smith, *A Book for a Rainy Day: or, Recollections of the Events of the Last Sixty-six Years*, 2nd edn (London, 1845), p. 15. Smith also records that the milkmaid's plate was hired, not loaned.

94 *Whitehall Evening Post* (26 May 1763); Roger Young, 'George Walker's *Costume of Yorkshire* (1814): The representation and negotiation of class difference and social unrest', *Art History*, 19 (1996), 401–6.

95 Ireland, *Hogarth Illustrated*, 1:123.

96 Only three prints from Laroon's seventy-four show multiple hawkers.

97 Brown, *Amusements*, p. 20.

98 Brown, *Amusements*, pp. 20–1 (emphasis in original text).

99 Ned Ward, *The London Spy* (London: Folio Society, 1955), pp. 195–6.

100 Paulson, *Hogarth's Graphic Works*, pp. 110–11. On the fish seller, see Ireland, *Hogarth Illustrated*, 1:122.

101 Stephens, *Catalogue of Prints and Drawings*, 3 (Part I), 410–13.

102 Addison, speaking in the voice of Ralph Crotchet, actually called vocal cries 'barbarisms' (*Spectator*, No. 251).

103 Grose, *The Olin*, 2nd edn (London, 1796), pp. 210–11.

104 Ireland, *Hogarth Illustrated*, 1:120–1.

105 Ireland, *Hogarth Illustrated*, 2:123.

106 Ben Jonson's Morose left London every Saturday at ten o'clock or on holiday eves to avoid hearing the bells of the city; later he constructed a room with double walls, triple ceilings, and caulked windows, in which he lived by candlelight. In a section of his book entitled, 'Of the Manners of the English', the German visitor Paul Hentzner takes special notice of the perverse love that British people have for public kinds of dins: they 'are vastly fond of great noises that fill the ear, such as the firing of cannon, drums, and the ringing of bells', he writes in *Travels in England* (composed in 1598 and published in London in 1797), 'so that it is common for a number of them, that have got a glass in their heads, to go up into some belfry, and ring the bells for hours together for the sake of exercise' (p. 64).

107 E. S. de Beer, 'Places of worship in London about 1738', in A. E. J. Hollaender and William Kellaway (eds), *Studies in London History Presented to Philip Edmund Jones* (London: Hodder and Stoughton, 1969), p. 594.

108 Hogarth was not alone in holding these views. Walpole wrote that 'Amigoni's women are mere chalk, as if he had only painted from ladies who paint themselves' (*Anecdotes*, 4:112). The Hogarth quotations are from the *Walpole Society: Apology for Painters*, 41:104; and from Britophil's essay in the *London Magazine* of 23 July 1737.

109 This quotation comes from the Britophil essay in the *London Magazine* of 23 July 1737.

110 Jonathan Swift, *Journal to Stella*, ed. Harold Williams (Oxford: Oxford University Press 1963), 2:581.

111 Peter Earle, *A City Full of People* (London: Methuen, 1994), p. 49.

112 Hogarth was fond of evoking biblical themes and subjects, especially those having to do with apocalyptic cleansing; for his evocation of this topos in *Strolling Actresses* and *Night*, see my *Hogarth and the Times-of-the-Day Tradition* (Ithaca: Cornell University Press, 1983), p. 154.

113 Henry Fielding, *The Journal of a Voyage to Lisbon*, ed. Austin Dobson (London, 1892), p. 48.

114 See, for example, his treatment of Churchill in late satiric prints.

115 Nichols and Steevens, *Biographical Anecdotes*, 2:155.

116 Kunzle, 'Ravaged child', p. 101; I differ from Kunzle in my emphasis on the comedy in Hogarth's depictions as well as in the natural viciousness of children, which he underemphasizes.

117 The *OED* records Swift using 'blackguard' in this sense: 'The little blackguard who gets very hard His halfpence for cleaning your shoes'.

118 Nichols and Steevens, *Genuine Works*, 2:121.

119 Nichols and Steevens, *Genuine Works*, 2:121.

120 William Hazlitt, *Conversations of James Northcote* (London: Dent, 1949), p. 52.

121 Daniel Defoe, *Everybody's Business is Nobody's Business* (London, 1725), p. 20.

122 Daniel Defoe, *Some Considerations upon Street-Walkers* (London, 1726), p. 44.

123 William Blake, *William Blake's Writings*, ed. G. E. Bentley (Oxford: Oxford University Press, 1978), 2:1038.

124 Antal, *Hogarth*, p. 240.

125 For a discussion of this issue, to which I am indebted, see Simon Shaw-Miller, '"Concerts of everyday living": Cage, Fluxus and Barthes, interdisciplinarity and inter-media events', *Art History*, 19 (1996), 1–25.

126 *Spectator*, 18 December 1711.

127 For an exploration of this theme, see Edith Wyss, *The Myth of Apollo and Marsyas in the Art of the Italian Renaissance* (Newark: University of Delaware Press, 1996).

Chapter 5

1 Nichols, *Biographical Anecdotes*, p. 38.

2 Rouquet, *Present State of the Arts in England*, p. 28.

3 William Blake, *Poetry and Prose* (New York: Doubleday, 1965), p. 679.

4 *London Magazine*, Appendix, 30 (1761), p. 701.

5 Solkin, *Painting for Money*, pp. 247, 266; Clayton, *English Print*, p. xii.

6 Quoted in Whitley, *Artists and Their Friends*, where the journal is not identified. I have punctuated the quotation for clarity.

7 David Macpherson, *Annals of Commerce, Manufactures, Fisheries, and Navigation* (London, 1805), 4:183–4.

8 Laurence Binyon, *English Water-Colours*, 2nd edn (London: Black, 1944), p. 22.

9 For formal links between Laroon and Wheatley, see Postle, *Angels and Urchins*, p. 82.

10 Hogarth also operatically declared 'the impossibility to there ever being a market in this Kingdom or in any part of the world that can maintain more than twelve artists in a way that may be thought an adequate recompense for so tedious a study' (*Walpole Society: Apology for Painters*, 79; Paulson, *Hogarth*, 3:313).

11 Milliot, *Cris de Paris*, pp. 111, 132.

12 About 1709, Pierce Tempest sold the coppers of his *Cryes* to Henry Overton; in 1733, the plates passed from Henry Overton to his brother Philip Overton, a partner since about 1709. Philip Overton died in February 1745 but his widow Mary carried on his business. Robert Sayer secured Tempest's copperplates when he bought Mary's shop and stock sometime between 23 March 1748 and 28 January 1749 (Donald Hodson, *County Atlases of the British Isles* (Tewin (Hertfordshire): Tewin Press, 1989), 2:186–9).

13 Robert Sayer, *New and Enlarged Catalogue for the Year 1766* (London, 1766), item 28; Clayton, *English Print*, p. 119. Sayer's catalogue describes this edition of Laroon as 'The Cries of London, for the present year 1766. Being a Collection of humorous *Characters*, in eighty-six Prints, done under the Direction of Mr. *Boitard* and neatly engraved' (emphasis in original text). I have not seen an edition with eighty-six prints.

14 Paulson, *Hogarth's Graphic Works*, p. 89.

15 Boitard updates men's hats and shoes but ignores their faces. In his treatment of women, however, he updates faces and dress, including accessories.

16 'Nosegays' is signed 'P Angier Sculp'. Of Paul Angier, little more is known than that he lived in London about 1749 and worked for booksellers. 'Ivy' is signed 'I Fougeron Sculp'. Ignace Fougeron is even more obscure; he was active in London in the eighteenth century (Bénézit, *Dictionnaire*, 1:337; 5:603). Both men worked under Boitard who certainly designed and cut the Sayer title page where he takes full credit for the book's 'additions & Improvements'.

17 I am indebted to Penelope Ruddock, Curator of the Bath Assembly Rooms and Museum of Costume, for help with these two figures' costumes.

18 James Laver, *Taste and Fashion from the French Revolution until Today* (New York: Dodd, Mead and Co., 1938), p. 183.

19 Pollock, 'Van Gogh and the poor slaves', 417.

20 Quoted in Davis, *Fairs, Shops and Supermarkets*, p. 89. These two Boucher images are unrelated to the French artist's *Les Cris de Paris*, twelve designs published in 1737.

21 Beth F. Tobin, *Picturing Imperial Power: Colonial Subjects in Eighteenth-Century British Painting*. (Durham: Duke University Press, 1999), p. 121.

22 Boitard's *Cries of London in Six Parts* flourished for sixty-one years before passing from Sayer's hands into R. H. Laurie's; he published the last edition in 1821.

23 On Francis Vivares, see Clayton, *English Print*, p. 115.

24 Jessica Christian, 'Paul Sandby and the military survey of Scotland', in Nicholas Alfrey and Stephen Daniels (eds), *Mapping the Landscape: Essays on Art and Cartography* (Nottingham: Castle Museum, 1990), pp. 18–22.

25 Luke Herrmann, *Paul and Thomas Sandby* (London: Batesford, 1986), p. 13; Whitley, *Artists and their Friends*, 2:363.

26 A decade later, Sandby returned to the business of art as a tool of surveillance and 'pacification' when he became Chief Drawing Master of the Royal Military Academy in Woolwich (1768–97), where he trained army officers to draw for tactical ends, as he did in Scotland.

27 *London Review and Literary Journal*, 8 November 1809. For current estimates of Sandby, see Bruce Robertson, *The Art of Paul Sandby* (New Haven: Yale Center for British Art, 1985), p. 11; Andrew Wilton, *British Watercolours 1750 to 1850* (Oxford: Phaidon, 1977), p. 196.

28 Michael Charlesworth treats Paul and Thomas Sandby in his 'Thomas Sandby climbs the Hoober stand: The politics of panoramic drawing in eighteenth-century Britain', *Art History*, 19 (1996), 247–66.

29 Paulson, *Hogarth*, 3:134–40.

30 E. H. Ramsden, 'The Sandby brothers in London', *Burlington Magazine*, 89 (1947), 16–18.

31 Johnson Ball says, 'It was probably Laroon who stimulated Paul Sandby's interest in "The Cryes of London" drawn by Laroon's father in the previous century and published by Pierce Tempest' (*Paul and Thomas Sandby Royal Academicians* (Cheddar, Somerset: Charles Skilton, 1985), p. 128). Sandby's *Rustic Scenes, Figures, Landscapes* is preserved in the Huntington (pressmark 32330HEH).

32 Wilton, *British Watercolours*, p. 11.

33 Herrmann, *Paul and Thomas Sandby*, p. 22.

34 Robertson, *Art of Paul Sandby*, p. 10.

35 Bainbrigge Buckeridge, 'An essay toward an English school', in Roger de Piles, *The Art of Painting*, 3rd edn (London, 1754), p. 444.

36 Walpole's set is preserved in the Lewis Walpole Library, Farmington, Connecticut; for Banks and Sandby, see *The Gentleman's Magazine*, December 1809, p. 1177, which carries the artist's obituary. For Maria Walpole, see Ball, *Paul and Thomas Sandby*, p. 128.

37 See Bruce Robertson, 'Paul Sandby and the early development of English watercolor' (Ph.D. dissertation, Yale University, 1986), 1:178–201.

38 Donald, *Age of Caricature*, p. 1; Paulson, *Hogarth's Graphic Works*, p. 90. On Boitard's role as a pirate of English prints, which may have sharpened Sandby's animus, see Kunzle, 'Plagiaries of the *Rake's Progress*', 311–48.

39 Though most of Sandby's sketches were unpublished in his own day, one (or more?) was exhibited; *A Catalogue Of a Capital Collection of Drawings Now Exhibiting at the Great Room, No. 28, Haymarket* (n.p., n.d.) lists under Sandby, 'One of the cries of London'; it was offered for ten shillings and sixpence.

40 The drab in the 'Musician' croons and sells 'The Ladies Fall'.

41 Spicer, 'Renaissance Elbow', in Bremmer and Roodenburg (eds), *Cultural History of Gesture*, p. 97.

42 Hallett, *Spectacle of Difference*, p. 106.

43 This title is mine, not Sandby's; for convenience of reference, I have given generic titles to Sandby's untitled images.

44 Barrell, *Dark Side of the Landscape*, p. 52.

45 Roodenburg, 'The "hand of friendship"', in Bremmer and Roodenburg (eds), *Cultural History of Gesture*, p. 154.

46 Brown, *Gypsies and Other Bohemians*, pp. 74–100.

47 Sotheby and Co., *Catalogue of Fine Old Master Engravings and Etchings* (1961), Lot 202.

48 Richardson, *London*, p. 155.

49 The parallel between Sandby's failure and the failure of Gustave Dore's *London: A Pilgrimage* (1872) is instructive, for it surely has the same cause – the disapproval of English audiences growing out of a distaste for the macabre side of life in London, the other side of the taste for the picturesque.

50 A. P. Oppe, *Drawings of Paul and Thomas Sandby* (Oxford: Phaidon, 1947), p. 10.

51 Godfrey, *Printmaking in Britain*, p. 40.

52 Stephen Calloway, *English Prints for the Collector* (London: Lutterworth Press, n.d.), p. 60. As sought after today as when the suite first appeared, Wheatley's series now decorates bars of soap from Yardley and tea canisters from Fortnum and Mason.

53 Obituary, *Gentleman's Magazine* (1801), 857; James Gandon and Thomas Mulvany, *The Life of James Gandon Esq.* (Dublin, 1846), p. 208; Kenneth Garlick and Angus Macintyre, *Diary of Joseph Farington* (New Haven: Yale University Press, 1978–98), 3:849–54.

54 Webster, *Francis Wheatley*, p. 85.

55 Quoted in W. Roberts, *The Cries of London* (London: Connoisseur, 1924), p. 12.

56 A fourteenth was engraved in 1921.

57 For details of ownership, see W. Roberts, *F. Wheatley, R.A.* (London: Otto, 1910), p. 30.

58 The Wheatley Cries are advertised in *The Morning Herald* of June 1795; that notice is reprinted by Roberts in *Cries of London*, p. 13.

59 Mary Webster, 'Francis Wheatley's *Cries of London*', *Auction*, 3 (1970), 46.

60 Colnaghi's venues of sale points also to rich urban buyer; *The Itinerant Trades of London* was marketed in Bath, Bristol, York, Margate, Oxford and Pall Mall.

61 Solkin, *Painting for Money*, p. 187; Tobin, *Picturing Imperial Power*, p. 23.

62 Barrell, *Dark Side of the Landscape*, p. 77.

63 The Landseer judgement of stipple as 'effeminate', from his 1806 lectures to the Royal Institution, comes from Sarah Hyde's 'Angelica Kauffman', *Print Quarterly*, 10 (1993), 186. The Landseer view of stipple as 'peculiarly expressive of softness' appears in John Landseer, *Lectures on the Art of Engraving* (London, 1807), p. 125.

64 Cruikshank, *Cries of London*, p. iv.

65 Clayton, *English Print*, p. 246.

66 Thomas Bernard, *Reports of the Society for Bettering the Condition and Increasing the Comforts of the Poor* (London, 1898–1914), 1:262.

67 Malcolm Salaman, 'Wheatley's "Cries of London"', *Apollo*, 10 (1929), 252.

68 John Barrell, *The Birth of Pandora* (Philadelphia: University of Pennsylvania Press, 1992), p. 18.

69 The Huntington has two additional drawings not issued as part of this series: 'Crumpets and Muffins, all hot!' and 'Eels, all Alive'.

70 These prices come from Ackermann's *Catalogue of Various Prints, Adapted for Furniture, Ornaments, etc.* (1802).

71 Buckeridge, 'Essay toward an English school', p. 383.

72 G. Brown, *A New Treatise on Flower Painting* (London, 1799), p. 1.

73 British Museum, *Catalogue of Prints and Drawings in the British Museum* (London, 1870–1954), 7: 595.

74 The Museum of London owns the original sketches to 'Last Dying Speech and Confession' (entitled also '12 Months in London November' and measuring 28 × 20 cm), 'Buy a Rat or a Mouse Trap' (bearing the words '13 Month' in the artist's hand and measuring 26 × 19.2 cm); and 'Do you want any brickdust' (27.7 × 21 cm). The Museum of London also owns 'Nightwatch' (36 × 25 cm), not engraved but similar in style and format to the eight prints.

75 The sketch reproduced here comes from an album of uncertain authority now in the Yale Center for British Art. This album contains a full complement of Sandby designs copied, in all likelihood, by a student who, like others before him, was using a suite of Cries to perfect his drawing technique.

76 Peter Linebaugh, *The London Hanged* (Cambridge: Cambridge University Press, 1992), p. 95.

77 Pritchett was referring to Rowlandson's illustrations of Smollett's characters, but the remark describes a range of the artist's figures (V. S. Pritchett, *The Living Novel* (Vintage Books, 1967), p. 21).

78 In parody of Wheatley's picturesque and rural themes, Rowlandson's subjects swim in blood: the farmer's throttled geese, the bumpkin's trapped rats and a fishwife's eels waiting to be skinned alive for the first buyer (from a sketch in the Huntington that Ackermann did not engrave).

79 Joseph Grego, *Rowlandson the Caricaturist* (New York, 1880), 2:354.

80 John Brewer, *The Common People and Politics 1750–1790s* (Cambridge: Chadwyck-Healey, n.d.), p. 26.

Chapter 6

1 Milliot, *Cris de Paris*, p. 12.

2 Marcia Pointon, *Naked Authority* (Cambridge: Cambridge University Press, 1990), p. 30.

3 Roland Barthes, in *Arcimboldo* (Parma: Ricci, 1978), p. 26, asserts that word and image only blend at 'the slightly mad edges of creation, outside classicism'.

4 Stephen Behrendt, 'Sibling rivalries: Author and artist in the early illustrated book', *Word and Image*, 13 (1997), 35.

5 For this subject, see Hoh-Cheung Mui and Lorna Mui, *Shops and Shopkeeping in Eighteenth-Century England* (London: Routledge, 1989), especially chapters 3 and 4.

6 Mayhew, *London Labour*, 1:iii.

7 Patricia Crain, *The Story of A: A Poetics of Alphabetization in America from the New England Primer to the Scarlet Letter* (Stanford: Stanford University Press, 1999), p. 73.

8 N. H. Keeble, *The Literary Culture of Nonconformity* (Athens: University of Georgia Press, 1987), p. 136.

9 Steward, *New Child*, p. 192.

10 Quoted in William B. MacGregor, 'The authority of prints: An early modern perspective', *Art History*, 22 (1999), 397.

11 John Locke, *Some Thoughts Concerning Education*, ed. John and Jean Yolton (Oxford: Clarendon Press, 1989), p. 212 (emphasis in original text).

12 Francis Boscawen, *Admiral's Wife; Being the Life and Letters of the Hon. Mrs. Edward Boscawen from 1719 to 1761*, ed. Cecil Aspinall-Oglander (New York: Staples Press, 1949), p. 170.

13 Amigoni's quartet of hawkers posing as boys and girls seems a likely candidate for the kind of recycling I am thinking of here. Evidence that Laroon's *Cryes* was given to the very young appears in two volumes marred by childish scribbles; one is preserved in the Huntington and the other in the Lilly.

14 The Lilly Library copy bears the following inscription: 'The Geift [*sic*] of Mr. Manning to his niece Hannah Palmer new years day 1757'.

15 John Marshall, in 1708, advertised a list of popular books available at his shop in Gracechurch Street, according to Harvey Darton (*Children's Books in England: Five Centuries of Social Life*, 3rd edn, rev. Brian Alderson (Cambridge: Cambridge University Press, 1982), p. 69); that list mentions 'Birds, beasts, London crys, etc.'. His Cries, untraced, is probably a broadside adorned with a single cut showing a generic hawker.

16 A 'pottle' is a liquid measure of two quarts and any vessel holding that volume. This panorama is preserved in the Cotsen Library, Princeton, New Jersey.

17 The phrase 'weak accomptants' comes from *An Useful Table for Weak Accomptants* of about 1692.

18 John Harris's *The Butterfly's Ball and the Grasshopper's Feast*, published in 1807, is usually credited with beginning 'the comparatively new ideas that juvenile reading could be purely

pleasurable' (Joyce Whalley and Tessa Chester, *A History of Children's Book Illustration* (London: Victoria and Albert Museum, 1988), p. 42).

19 No record of the offending garter's mottoes survives, though a different London Cries confirms – and extols – the fad of decorating women's under things with 'love's adages':

Sweet posies on them you will find,
All pleasing still to love,
And every one, say what you will,
Such mottos must approve.

This verse is drawn from a set of unidentified Cries of London pasted into an extra illustrated album of that title in the Houghton Library, Harvard University, Cambridge Massachusetts.

20 Leigh Hunt, *The Autobiography of Leigh Hunt* (London, 1860), pp. 49–50. I am indebted to Andrea Immel for these quotations.

21 The phrase 'Awful Warning' is Darton's in *Children's Books in England*, p. 243.

22 Whalley and Chester, *Children's Book Illustration*, pp. 14, 36.

23 Darton, *Children's Books in England*, p. 316.

24 *Public Advertiser*, 21 December 1754.

25 Rostenberg, *English Publishers*, p. 73. Kirk's advertisement appears in *The Public Advertiser*, 17 December 1759.

26 Bouchard's original drawings are preserved in the British Museum under the title *Recueil des Desseins Faits par Edme Bouchardon dont il a Fait Present a Son Amis Mariette* (Miller, *Street Criers*, p. 17). On Bouchardson, see Milliot, *Cris de Paris*, pp. 50–1.

27 This pack of cards was reprinted in 1978 by Harry Margary, Lympne Castle, Kent, in association with the Guildhall Library, London. A private collector in Baltimore owns a set of these cards.

28 A few copies of Smith's *Cries of London* appeared in a large paper edition with thirty hand-coloured plates.

29 On this genre of city scenes, see Hallett, *Spectacle of Difference*, p. 179.

30 It is likely that *Itinerant Traders* was sold at Tabart's Juvenile Library, which forms the background to Craig's 'Band boxes'. On Tabart as a bookseller, see Marjorie Moon, *Benjamin Tabart's Juvenile Library* (Winchester: St Paul's Bibliographies, 1990), p. 4.

31 I estimate the cost of Craig's book based on the fact that W. Bent's *The London Catalogue of Books with Their Prices and Publishers Containing the Books published in London and those altered in Size or Price since the Year 1800 to October 1818* lists *Modern London* as selling for three guineas. Craig's *Description of the Plates*, printed on large paper and luxuriously bound, could not have cost less than a guinea.

32 Shelia Smith, '"Savages and martyrs": Images of the urban poor in Victorian literature and art', in Nadel and Schwarzbach, *Victorian Artists and the City*, p. 20.

33 Doré and Jerrold, *London*, p. 62; Barrell, *Birth of Pandora*, p. 4.

34 Burke, *Reflections on the Revolution*, pp. 53, 102.

35 J. D. Passavant, *Tour of a German Artist in England* (London, 1836), pp. 12–13.

36 Bermingham, 'Elegant females and gentlemen connoisseurs', in Ann Bermingham and John Brewer, *The Consumption of Culture 1600–1800 Image, Object, Text* (London: Routledge, 1995), p. 491; Janet Todd, *Sensibility* (London: Methuen, 1986), p. 14.

37 William Cowper, 'The sofa', in H. S. Milford (ed.), *The Poetical Works of William Cowper*, 4th edn (London: Oxford University Press, 1950), p. 144.

38 Frances Burney, *Evelina, or the History of a Young Lady's Entrance into the World* (Oxford: Clarendon Press, 1930), p. 145.

39 Tobias Smollett, *Humphrey Clinker*, ed. Angus Ross (Harmondsworth: Penguin, 1967), p. 119.

40 James Boswell, *London Journal 1762–1763* (New York: McGraw-Hill, 1950), p. 42; Percy Bysshe Shelley, *Poetry and Prose*, ed. Donald Reiman and Sharon Powers (New York: Norton, 1977), p. 330.

41 John Tagg, *The Grounds of Dispute: Art History, Cultural Politics and the Discursive Field* (Minneapolis: University of Minnesota Press, 1992), p. 136; Griselda Pollock, 'Vicarious excitements: *London: A Pilgrimage* by Gustave Doré and Blanchard Jerrold', *New Formations* (1988), 4:25.

42 Richard Phillips, *A Personal Tour through the United Kingdom* (London, 1828), p. 1.

43 *Modern London*, whose author may have first commissioned Craig's designs, is an offshoot of Robert Dodsley's *London and its Environs Described* (1761), the first guide to the capital and its suburbs designed to 'serve both as a guide and an instructor to the travelling Virtuosi, whether natives or foreigners'.

44 On this theme, see Solkin, *Painting for Money*, pp. 160–74.

45 Smollett, *Humphrey Clinker*, p. 122.

46 The sandman sold his abrasive to clean kitchen utensils and protect floors from dirty feet; see Tuer, *Old London Street Cries*, p. 97.

47 A facsimile edition of *Vagabondiana* was published by Sherwin and Freutel of Los Angeles in 1970.
48 Fox, *Londoners*, p. 188.
49 Fox, *Londoners*, p. 188.
50 Fox, *Londoners*, p. 188.
51 Craig, 'Blackfriars Bridge, Poor Sweep'.
52 J. B. Nicholas, who edited Smith's *Cries of London*, refers to it as 'an appropriate companion to Mr. Smith's "Vagabondiana" in his prefatory "Advertisement" '.
53 McTighe, 'Perfect deformity', 87.
54 John T. Smith, *Vagabondiana; or, Anecdotes of Mendicant Wanderers through the Streets of London; with Portraits of the Most Remarkable, Drawn from the Life* (London, 1817), p. 41.
55 Pollock, 'Vicarious excitements', 4:25–50. The phrases 'quest for the picturesque and the typical' and '*savage* London' appear on pages 2 and 44 of *London: A Pilgrimage*.
56 Fox, *Londoners*, p. 166.
57 Smith, *Vagabondiana*, p. 3.
58 Smith, *Vagabondiana*, pp. 1, 9.
59 This count does not include two printers' ornaments – decorative capital letters with beggars entwined. The engravings of the drawings, one of which Douce owned, appear opposite p. 20 and on p. 24.
60 Christopher Herbert, 'Rat worship and taboo in Mayhew's London', *Representations*, 23 (1988), 1.
61 Smith, *Vagabondiana*, p. 44.
62 Mayhew, *London Labour*, 1:xvi.
63 Eileen Yeo and E. P. Thompson, *The Unknown Mayhew* (New York: Schocken, 1972), p. 20.
64 Fox, *Londoners*, p. 166.
65 Cunningham, *Children of the Poor*, pp. 136–42.
66 Fox, *Londoners*, p. 160.
67 Mayhew, *London Labour*, 2:174.
68 Fox, *Londoners*, p. 166.
69 Mary Cowling, *The Artist as Anthropologist: The Representation of Type and Character in Victorian Art* (Cambridge: Cambridge University Press, 1989), pp. 125–6; Sandra Phillips, Mark Haworth-Booth and Carol Squiers, *Police Pictures: The Photograph as Evidence* (San Francisco: Chronicle Books, 1998), p. 14.
70 George Stocking, *Victorian Anthropology* (New York: Oxford, 1987), p. 15; Herbert, 'Rat worship', 1–24.
71 Mayhew, *London Labour*, 3:373.
72 Mayhew, *London Labour*, 1:3.
73 Mayhew, *London Labour*, 1:3; Cowling, *Artist as Anthropologist*, pp. 184–90.
74 Burke, *Popular Culture*, p. 14.
75 Fox, *Londoners*, p. 160; Cunningham, *Children of the Poor*, pp. 110–11.
76 Walter Benjamin, *Charles Baudelaire*, trans. Harry Zohn (London: New Left Books, 1997), p. 36.
77 A litany of books devoted to 'unknown' or 'unexplored' London, bearing titles that vie in their sensationalism, include John Hollingshead's *Ragged London in 1861* (1861), James Greenwood's *A Night in a Workhouse* (1866) and *The Wilds of London* (1866), Andrew Means, *Bitter Cry of Outcast London* (1883), Robert Mudie's *Babylon the Great; A Dissection of Men and Things in the British Capital* (1825) and R. G. Smith's *Horrible London* (1889). The last of this genre devoted to what A. J. Munby called 'rude picturesqueness', published when the phrase 'Darkest London' had become a conventional epithet to describe the East End, turn less readable but more systematic and empirical. The founder of the Salvation Army, William Booth, in his *Life and Labour of the People* (1889–91) and *In Darkest England* (1890), uses statistics to anatomize the sources and structure of poverty. But Jack London's *People of the Abyss* (1902) is penned in a personal style, bolstered with drawings by Gustave Doré and photos by London himself.
78 Cowling, *Artist as Anthropologist*, p. 183.
79 For a discussion of recent literature about this movement, see A. James Hammerton's 'Old wine in new bottles? Changing London histories', *Journal of British Studies*, 37 (1998), 98–104.
80 Yeo and Thompson, *Unknown Mayhew*, p. 88.
81 Smith was appointed Keeper in 1816 and held the post until his death in 1833.
82 John T. Smith, *The Cries of London Exhibiting Several of the Itinerant Traders of Antient and Modern Times* (London, 1839), p. 1.
83 *Cries of London* (London: T. Goode, 'Lion Steam Printing Office', Clerkenwell Green). Copies of this book are preserved in the Huntington, San Marino, and the British Library, which dates it '1853'(?). T. Goode worked at 30 Aylesbury from 1847 to 1859.
84 O'Connell, *Popular Print*, p. 205.
85 Eirwen E. C. Nicholson, 'Emblem v. caricature', in Alison Adams (ed.), *Emblems and Art History* (Glasgow: Glasgow Emblems Studies, 1996), p. 150.

Chapter 7

1 Jerrold and Doré, *London*, p. 62.
2 Milliot, *Cris de Paris*, p. 351.

3 Stallybrass and White, *Politics and Poetics*, p. 193.
4 Burke, *Popular Culture*, p. 29.
5 Henry Peacham, *The Gentleman's Exercise* (London, 1606), p. 3.
6 These are the words of the Duchess of Buckingham writing to Lady Huntington in 1741 (quoted by M. D. George, *England in Johnson's Day* (London, 1928), p. 37).
7 Burke, *Reflections on the Revolution*, p. 117; Burke, *Popular Culture*, p. 264.
8 Fox, *Londoners*, p. 190.
9 Mayhew, *London Labour*, 1:iii.
10 Solkin, *Painting for Money*, p. 139. See also Stallybrass and White, *Politics and Poetics*, pp. 4–5.
11 Stallybrass and White, *Politics and Poetics*, p. 42.
12 See the five of clubs in Kirk's Cries formatted as a pack of playing cards; a facimile of these with a useful head note by Ralph Hyde has been published by Harry Margary.
13 Williams, *Country and City*, 128.
14 See, for example, 'The Common Cryes of London' (2.3) and 'The Cryer' (1.1) in which, respectively, a third and a half of the hawkers sell produce from the land.
15 Linda Nochlin, 'The imaginary Orient', *Art in America*, 71 (1983), 123.
16 Bermingham, *Landscape and Ideology*, p. 1.
17 See, for example, shouts such as 'cherriripe', 'bye my sweet strawing Yearbs', 'Ripe, yeoung Beanes', 'I have ripe straw buryes', and 'I ha ripe Couccumber' from 'Parte of the Cryers', 'The Cryes of London', and *The Manner of Crying Things*.
18 Jan de Vries, *European Urbanization 1500–1800* (Cambridge: Harvard University Press, 1984), p. 42.
19 Williams, *Country and City*, 48.
20 *Richard the Third*, III. iv; mentioned in Hindley, *Cries of London*, p. 12.
21 Richardson, *London*, p. 40.
22 Porter, *London*, p. 43.
23 Richardson, *London*, p. 62.
24 James Howgego, *Printed Maps of London* (London: Dawson, 1978), No 2; Ruthardt Oehme, *Old European Cities* (London: Thames and Hudson, 1965), pp. 65–8.
25 Hogenberg's 'Londinum' is based on an earlier map of London, the so-called Copperplate map of *c.* 1553–59; though incomplete, the Copperplate map is a useful tool by which to interpret and clarify 'Londinum'.
26 Jonathan Swift, *On Poetry* (London, 1733), p. 12.
27 Stow, *Survey of London*, 1:126.
28 Edward Hatton, *A New View of London or, An Ample Account of that City* (London, 1708).
29 *The Country Spy; or, A Ramble thro' London* (London, n.d.), p. 1.
30 De Vries, *European Urbanization*, p. 152; Porter, *London*, p. 66.
31 Porter, *London*, p. 67.
32 Benjamin Disraeli, *Lothair* (London, 1870), p. 115.
33 Roland Barthes, 'The plates of the *Encyclopedia*', in Susan Sontag, *A Barthes Reader* (New York: Hill and Wang, 1982), p. 221.
34 Shesgreen, *Criers and Hawkers*, pp. 104, 124.
35 Bermingham, *Landscape and Ideology*, pp. 52–4.
36 Stephen Copley and Peter Garside, *Politics of the Pictuesque: Literature, Landscape and Aesthetics Since 1770* (Cambridge: Cambridge University Press, 1994), p. 6.
37 Richard Payne Knight, *An Analytical Inquiry into the Principles of Taste* (London, 1805), p. 194.
38 Barrell, *Dark Side of the Landscape*, pp. 105–6. The quotations on the picturesque come from Uvedale Price, *Essay on the Picturesque* (London, 1794), pp. 69–70, and William Gilpin, *Observations Relative Chiefly to Picturesque Beauty, Made in the Year 1772 on Several Parts of England* (London 1789), 2:45–7. For Gilpin, 'the eye of taste' was the same as 'the picturesque eye'; both describe the subject of his discourse, an inhabitant of the polite world (Barrell, *Birth of Pandora*, p. 97).
39 *Morning Herald*, June 1795.
40 *Westminster Review*, new series (October 1854), pp. 604–8.
41 William Gilpin, *Essay on Prints* (London, 1768), p. xii. On the conceptual imprecision of the term, see Stephen Copley and Peter Garside, *Politics of the Picturesque* (Cambridge: Cambridge University Press, 1994), p. 1.
42 Solkin, *Painting for Money*, pp. 157–213; Barrell, *Birth of Pandora*, p. 18.
43 Tobin, *Picturing Imperial Power*, p. 115.
44 Bermingham, *Landscape and Ideology*, p. 1.
45 Bermingham, *Landscape and Ideology*, p. 81.
46 I am indebted to Bermingham (*Landscape and Ideology*, pp. 53–4) throughout this discussion.
47 Anthony Pasquin (pseudonym), *A Liberal Critique of the Exhibition of the Royal Academy* (London, 1794), pp. 31–2.
48 Edward Edwards, *Anecdotes of Painters* (London, 1808), p. 269.
49 This book, which I have not seen, is not recorded in Beall or in any of the standard juvenile bibliographies or catalogues. It was

offered for sale by Torgrim-Harris (29a Caron Street, Winchester, Hampshire, England) in *An Alphabet of Old Books 1985/6* where it is described as '16mo. 30 pp. plus advertisement/colophon leaf'.

50 Nochlin, 'Imaginary Orient', pp. 126–7.

51 Tobin, *Picturing Imperial Power*, p. 5.

52 Quoted in Harriet Guest, 'Curiously marked: Tattooing, masculinity, and nationality in eighteenth-century British perceptions of the South Pacific', in John Barrell, *Painting and the Politics of Culture* (Oxford: Oxford University Press, 1992), pp. 102–4.

53 'Mechanical Fiddler' also appears in Busby's *Costume of the Lower Orders* (*c.* 1819).

54 McTighe, 'Perfect deformity', 78.

55 Frederic Antal, 'Reflections on classicism and romanticism', *Burlington Magazine*, 78 (1941), 19.

56 Linda Dowling, *The Vulgarization of Art: The Victorians and Aesthetic Democracy* (Charlottesville: University Press of Virginia, 1996), especially chapter 1.

57 Joseph Farington, *The Diary of Joseph Farington*, ed. Kenneth Garlick and Angus Macintyre (New Haven and London: Yale University Press, 1978–98), 3:91.

58 Max Byrd, *London Transformed: Images of the City in the Eighteenth Century* (New Haven: Yale University Press, 1992), p. 36.

59 Malcolm Andrews, 'The metropolitan picturesque', in Copley and Garside, *Politics of the Picturesque*, p. 287.

60 Milliot, *Cris de Paris*, p. 279.

61 Rosen, 'Atget's populism', 53–4.

62 Williams, *Country and City*, p. 98.

63 Hester Thrale, *Thraliana: The Diary of Mrs. Hester Lynch Thrale*, ed. Katharine Balderston (Oxford: Clarendon Press, 1942), p. 184.

64 William Clarkson, 'Inquiry on pauperism and poor rates', *Pamphleteer*, 8 (1816), 390.

65 William Cobbett, *The Poor Man's Friend* (London, 1829), paragraphs 92 and 93.

66 Williams, *Country and City*, p. 183; Porter, *London*, p. 247.

67 Barrell, *Dark Side of the Landscape*, p. 76.

68 Edgar Wind, *Pagan Mysteries in the Renaissance*, 1958 (New York: Norton, 1968), p. 129.

69 Cunningham, *Children of the Poor*, p. 52.

70 The phrase is adapted from Wordsworth's 'Michael'.

71 Gray, *Victorian Artists and the City*, p. 45.

72 Celina Fox, 'Gericault's lithographs of the London poor', *Print Quarterly*, 1 (1988), 63. Despite this judgment, Fox ties Gericault's images to John T. Smith's *Etchings of Remarkable Beggars* (London, 1815), a continuation of Cries, and sees both as expressions of the economic crisis of the period. For scholars linking *Several Subjects* to Cries, see Antal, 'Reflections on classicism', 20; Lynn Matteson, 'Gericault and English "Street Cries"', *Apollo*, 106 (1977), 304–6.

73 Godfrey, *Printmaking in Britain*, p. 91.

74 But perhaps the man is insane or even starving to death? See Fox, 'Gericault's lithographs', 62.

75 Lorenz Eitner, *Gericault: His Life and Work* (London: Orbis Publishing, 1982), p. 229.

76 Edgar Munhill, 'Savoyards in French eighteenth-century art', *Apollo*, 87 (1968), 92.

77 Williams, *Country and City*, p. 239.

78 Eitner, *Gericault*, p. 222. Gericault's lithographs were unpopular, creating trouble between the artist and his publisher, Rodwell & Martin. Weak sales stopped the planned multiplication of *Various Subjects*, just as they had that of Sandby's *Twelve London Cries*; worse still, the French artist was compelled to pay Rodwell & Martin money from his pocket to cover printing costs (Eitner, *Gericault*, p. 229).

79 Fox, 'Gericault's lithographs', 63.

80 The first instance of police photography took place in New York in 1846 (Phillips *et al.*, *Police Pictures*, p. 18).

81 The influential novelist and scriptwriter, Pierre Mac Orlan, used Atget's photographs (*c.* 1925) to illustrate his personal copy of Cesare Lombroso's *Le Femme criminelle et la prostitutée* (1896).

82 Walter Benjamin, 'The work of art in the age of mechanical reproduction', in *Illuminations*, trans. Harry Zohn (New York: Harcourt Brace, 1969), p. 226.

83 Rosen, 'Atget's populism', 51.

84 On Atget, see Molly Nesbit, *Atget's Seven Albums* (New Haven: Yale University Press, 1992), pp. 33–5, and Rosen, 'Atget's populism', 50–63, especially 51.

85 Phillips, *Police Pictures*, p. 20.

86 For a collection of such pictures, see Phillips, *Police Pictures*. These functions are not present in cheap images of criminals and malefactors popular in England from the middle of the eighteenth century. I am thinking here of Hogarth's 'Sarah Malcolm', 'Simon Lord Lovat', and the like.

87 Richard Avedon, *In the American West 1979–1984* (New York: Abrams, 1985).

88 Diane Arbus, *Untitled* (New York: Aperture, 1995).

89 Arbus, *Untitled*.

90 Patricia Bosworth, 'Things nobody else would see', *Sunday New York Times Book Review*, 22 October 1995, p. 36.
91 Nochlin, 'Imaginary Orient', 189.
92 *Spectator* No. 251.
93 On Gay's *Trivia* and other forms of verbal and visual satire, see Hallett, *Spectacle of Difference*, p. 184.
94 Gay, *Trivia*, Book II, pp. 40–1 (emphasis in original text).
95 Charles Dickens, *Dombey and Son*, ed. Alan Horsman (Oxford: Clarendon Press, 1974), p. 639.
96 For a treatment of this theme in the Victorian period, see Elizabeth Helsinger's *Rural Scenes and National Representation: Britain 1815–1850* (Princeton: Princeton University Press, 1997).

Index